D1266855

DEBRETT'S
Correct Form

HER MAJESTY THE QUEEN

Portrait study by Karsh of Ottawa   *Camera Press, London*

DEBRETT'S
Correct Form

AN INCLUSIVE GUIDE TO
EVERYTHING FROM DRAFTING WEDDING
INVITATIONS TO ADDRESSING
AN ARCHBISHOP

Compiled and edited by Patrick Montague-Smith
Editor of Debrett

DEBRETT'S PEERAGE LTD.
THE VIKING PRESS • NEW YORK

Copyright © Debrett's Peerage Ltd.

All rights reserved

First published in 1970

Second printing 1976

Third printing 1977

Fourth printing 1978

Printed in Great Britain

Library of Congress catalog card number: 78-62662

ISBN 0-670-26233-1

CONTENTS

NOTE

As many varied subjects are covered, and several border upon others, the index should be consulted for the appropriate reference.

A few remarks upon certain Offices are included, such as the various departments which comprise the Royal Household and their functions; but where information is readily available from other sources it has been omitted.

In many instances forms of address are in a transitional state from elaborate formality to considerable informality. Some have been simplified, such as for clergy of the Church of England, resulting from a diocesan conference held in 1968 under the guidance of the Archbishop of Canterbury. Others, such as those which concern the peerage, have remained virtually unchanged from last century, apart from the simplification of elaborate endings to letters. New forms have either been laid down or adopted when women have been appointed to certain offices for the first time, such as a High Court Judge and Diocesan Chancellor.

In the main I have given two styles for the written form, and sometimes also for the spoken form, which I have labelled 'formal' and 'social'. The latter is usually adopted when the writer knows his correspondent. Most of the examples given are of fictitious titles and names, but actual instances are shown where they are considered to be appropriate.

In Part V, detailed information will be found concerning invitations and functions, both official and private, including table plans, guests lists, precedence, admission cards, place cards, and speeches.

This edition has been thoroughly revised, and certain Sections completely re-written. Part IV takes into account the extensive changes in Local Government in England and Wales, Northern Ireland and Scotland; also those in the Legal system and consequent on the establishment of the United Reformed Church. A new feature concerns Usage in America, which now forms Part VI, and in other Foreign Countries which forms Part VII.

ACKNOWLEDGEMENTS

I am deeply grateful to the following who have given me much help and advice:

Captain Geoffrey Bennett, D.S.C., F.R.Hist.S., R.N., lately Hon. Secretary, The London Mayors Association

Sir Anthony R. Wagner, K.C.V.O., D.Litt., Garter Principal King of Arms

Walter J. Verco Esq., C.V.O., Norroy and Ulster King of Arms

Sir Iain Moncreiffe of that Ilk, Bt., Ph.D., F.S.A., D.L., Albany Herald of Arms

Major Francis Jones, C.V.O., T.D., F.S.A., Wales Herald of Arms Extraordinary

The Reverend Stanley B-R. Poole, M.A.

E. Grey-Turner Esq., M.C., T.D., M.A., M.R.C.S., L.R.C.P., Secretary, British Medical Association

Church Information Office, The Church of England

The Editors of the Commonwealth Universities Yearbook (published by The Association of Commonwealth Universities)

and many others, including Embassies and Government Departments, who were kind enough to answer my questions.

I also thank the Managing Director of Debrett's Peerage Ltd., Mr. H. B. Brooks-Baker, for assistance on American Usage (Part VI), and Mrs. J. M. Burge for typing my manuscript.

INTRODUCTION

By Sir Iain Moncreiffe of that Ilk
Bt., Ph.D., F.S.A., D.L.

In this invaluable guide to usage Mr. Patrick Montague-Smith combines a sense of historic names and styles with a helpful understanding of the practical need of courteous people to find a guide to present-day usage through our fascinating Hampton Court maze of precedence, lettering, and modes of address. The world would be a duller place if we lost the Knight of Glin, the Master of Lovat or The O'Donoghue of the Glens.

I was in Salt Lake City when I was interviewed by successive telephone calls on the American wireless. Questioner after questioner asked, 'What does *Sir* Moncreiffe think about . . .?' until the studio bell rang and a voice said 'Mr. Moncreiffe; I do call you Mr., don't I?' I thought 'less of that' and caught him out with the reply: 'Well, you could call me *Mr.* as I'm a Master of Arts, but you can call me *Dr.* if you prefer.' The other side of the coin turned up at a press conference in Denmark. An intelligent journalist said 'I see you are a Doctor of Philosophy. Why do you prefer to be called *Sir* Iain?' The reply then was: 'Because as a baronet I am a living memorial to a greater man than myself, while having earned the doctorate myself I would only be swanking if I pretended it bettered his life-work.' How sad it would be if we had no such living memorials as the Duke of Wellington or the Earl Attlee, to cite far more historic examples.

New titles are more fun than they would be in an entirely non-hereditary system like that of the American senators, because they equate the new to the old in a continuous flow of history. A new snobbery is being encouraged whereby some peers' eldest sons think themselves so grand that they won't use their courtesy titles (this is a friendly dig at Lord Silchester). It's different when a real function is involved, like the peerages of Sir Max Aitken or Mr. Victor Montagu (an M.P. as Viscount Hinchingbrooke, but disclaimed the Earldom of Sandwich when he succeeded his father), where they choose to remain free of the Upper House. My late cousin, who shared this house with me, used to call himself normally Lord James Stewart Murray and only be Duke of Atholl when functioning as such, for he said to be Duke of Atholl and live at Easter Moncreiffe would be like being King of Bulgaria and living at Nice.

The custom of putting letters after people's names has only arisen in comparatively modern times, but has proliferated as our enormous increase of population—and the rewarding of service to the economy and not just to the State—has led to a great expansion of our Orders of Chivalry and higher honours, together with the multiplication of degrees and appointments. Since these letters are but abbreviations, we can write them as we please. However, custom has evolved certain standard abbreviations, and most people seek guidance about present conventions. Officially and in business it's polite to get all that lettering right; for what's the use of earning all those gongs if the poor fellow can't use them?

Unconventional abbreviations can be misleading. For instance, whenever Henry Douglas Home writes to me he puts the letters B.F. after my name. I always take it that they stand for Brave Fellow.

We have only two hereditary knights, the Knight of Kerry who is the Green Knight, and the Knight of Glin who is the Black Knight; for the White Knight has gone amissing these many years. It may therefore seem rather unnecessary to need to know the correct way of addressing them. However, I was asked this very question by the barman of one of my clubs which one of the two hereditary knights had just joined. The correct answer, which is given in this book, is just 'Knight.' So, if staying at Glin Castle, you will know to say 'Good-night, Knight.'

I myself also have to put up with being laughed at for having such a quaint name as Moncreiffe of that Ilk, which simply means 'Moncreiffe of that same,' and which we have used since the Middle Ages because it gives other people such fun.

Like most of you, I'm a keen reader of gossip columns. The only thing is, it's hard really to believe the latest rumour about one's friends' private lives when the gossip writer evidently knows them so little as to be unable to get their names right. Anybody who refers to Lady Mary de Vere as 'Lady de Vere' or to Lady Montmorency as 'Lady Mary Montmorency' can't know much about them really. So all columnists *must* get their bosses to buy this book for them, so that they can add verisimilitude to otherwise bald and unconvincing stories.

EASTER MONCREIFFE, PERTHSHIRE

IAIN MONCREIFFE OF THAT ILK

GENERAL INSTRUCTIONS

HEADED LETTERS

It is of considerable assistance to correspondents when all letters, except those which are purely social, include the sender's name and appropriate letters at the top, e.g.:

'From Air Marshal Sir John Donne, K.C.B., O.B.E., M.C.'[1]

A reply is often wrongly addressed because the writer has no knowledge of the correct letters, or sometimes the rank. Even when this information can be obtained (such as by access to a reference book), this usually takes time and trouble.

When the writer is a woman, this practice gives the recipient the advantage of knowing whether she should be styled with a title (e.g. Lady Blank) or, much more often, Mrs. or Miss Blank. One also knows that the correct form of address is Mrs. Henry Johnson, instead of, according to her signature, Mrs. Lillian Johnson or Mrs. L. J. Johnson.

The inclusion of this information on correspondence does not infringe the bounds of modesty; in fact it is thoughtful. As an exception, because it sounds pretentious, 'Esq.' or 'Mr.' is usually omitted, e.g. 'From John Brown M.V.O.' The addition of Esq. presents no difficulty to those who reply.

This system has many advantages over typing the name under the signature, which only facilitates the deciphering of hand-writing, because it is not customary to include the letters after the name here, and seldom a title.

BEGINNING A LETTER

The writer has to decide whether to adopt the formal or social form of address. A letter to a complete stranger should be written in the

---

[1] Throughout this book (with the special exception of pp. 180–3, and where indicated) full stops have been inserted between the letters of honours, decorations, etc., after persons' names. They may, however, be omitted provided that the various groups of letters are separated by commas, e.g. KBE, CB, MC. The practice of separating them by no more than a space, e.g. KBE CB MC, is *not* recommended.

formal style. When a reply is received in the social style, this should normally be followed in further correspondence. The individual beginning is to be found in each section throughout this book.

If a very formal style is adopted, 'Sir' or 'Madam' takes the place of 'Dear Sir' or 'Dear Madam'. The very formal styles adopted in ending a letter are given on p. 3.

SOCIAL STYLE

The more friendly style of inserting 'My' before 'Dear ——', may be adopted when warranted, but this is not generally included in the examples to keep them as simple as possible.

The style 'Dear Jones' is often adopted when male correspondents know each other and they are either both equal in age and importance, or when writing to a younger man in a more junior position.

The American system of including both the christian and surname is growing in Britain. This is frequently adopted as half-way between the use of the surname or the christian name, e.g. 'Dear John Robinson'. Many do not like this form, but others, especially the younger generation, consider it to be useful in the business world, where informality is on the increase.

ENDING A LETTER

The various stereotyped very formal styles of ending letters have now become almost obsolete, except for the following:

1. Letters to The Queen and members of the Royal Family.
2. Official and formal letters to Ambassadors, High Commissioners, Governors, and similar senior officials.
3. Official or formal letters within the Armed Forces.

The following endings of letters are now generally used, but the very formal styles which are given in the next section may occasionally be preferred.

FORMAL

(a) I remain (*or* I am),

Your Grace, Most Reverend Sir, Right Reverend Sir, Your Excellency, My Lord, My Lord Mayor, Mr. Mayor, Mr. President, Mr. Chairman, Sir, Madam, etc.
Yours faithfully (*or* Yours truly)

(b) or more simply, Yours faithfully (*or* Yours truly).

It is generally considered that there is a distinction between *faithfully* and *truly* (sometimes *very truly*), but usually *faithfully* is used in business, and *truly* (or *very truly*) when one does not know the recipient but the subject is not a matter of business, this being slightly less distant than *yours faithfully*.

SOCIAL

Yours sincerely (*or* Yours very sincerely),

VERY FORMAL STYLES FOR ENDING A LETTER

Although the following styles are now seldom used, they are included for those who may prefer them.

Even so, they are a simplified version of what was once in vogue, when there was an elaborate scale of '*Most devoted and most obedient*', '*Most obedient*', '*Most humble and devoted*', '*Most humble and obedient*' etc., and other styles with '*Most*' omitted.

When the conclusion '*I have the honour to be*' or '*remain*' is used, the second line of '*My Lord Duke*', '*My Lord*', '*Sir*', or '*Madam*' is sometimes omitted.

Dukes and Duchesses

    I have the honour to be (*or* to remain),
        My Lord Duke (Madam),
            Your Grace's obedient servant,

Other Peers, and those with the style of Lord

    I have the honour to be (*or* to remain),
        My Lord,
            Your Lordship's obedient servant,

Other Peeresses, and those with the style of Lady

    I have the honour to be (*or* to remain),
        Madam,
            Your Ladyship's obedient servant,

Baronets, Knights and Esquires (including Privy Counsellors and Ministers of the Crown)

    I have the honour to be (*or* to remain),
        Sir,
            Your obedient servant,

Untitled Ladies

    I have the honour to be (*or* to remain),
        Madam,
            Your obedient servant,

Archbishops

As for a *Duke,* with the substitution of *Your Grace* or *My Lord Archbishop* in the second line. For further details, see Churches Section, p. 112.

Bishops

As for *Other Peers* (above), with the alternative styles of *My Lord Bishop* or *Right Reverend Sir* in the second line. For further details, see Churches Section, pp. 114–115.

Other Appointments

As for *Baronets, Knights* and *Esquires* or *Untitled Ladies* (above), with the appropriate appointment in the second line, i.e. Mr. President, Madam President, Mr. Chairman, Madam Chairman, Very Reverend Sir (or Mr. Dean), Reverend Sir, etc.

JOINT FORMS OF ADDRESS
See Part V.

CHRISTMAS CARDS
See Part V.

FORM OF ADDRESS OF MEMBERS OF THE FAMILY BETWEEN THE DEATH
AND FUNERAL OF A PEER OR BARONET

When a peer, peeress in her own right or baronet dies, it is customary for letters written to members of his (or her) family to be addressed by the titles or styles by which they were previously known until after the funeral has taken place.

Consequently a letter of sympathy to the eldest son of the late Lord Rugeley, written before his father's funeral, should be addressed to The Hon. John Rugeley, even though he has succeeded his father as Lord Rugeley.

For this reason, members of the family are described at the funeral as they were previously known, whereas at a memorial service some days later they are referred to by their new titles and styles.

This custom is followed by courtesy even when the successor to the title is only remotely related to the deceased, and the two families may have had little or no contact with each other.

OFFICIAL LISTS

As a general rule the form used on an official or similar list should be as for addressing an envelope, except that if the list is in alphabetical order, the name should come first, e.g.

Baxter, Admiral Sir George, K.C.B., D.S.O.
Baxter, Lady
Beecher, Edward J., M.P.
Beecher, Mrs. Edward
Bilston, The Very Reverend John, K.C.V.O., D.D.
Bilston, Mrs. John
Bosham, The Right Hon. the Earl of, P.C.
Bosham, The Right Hon. the Countess of
Brook, The Right Hon. Richard, M.P.
Bullion, Colonel P.R., M.C., J.P., D.L.
Bullion, Mrs. P. R.
Burton, the Worshipful the Mayor of

CORRESPONDENCE WITH FIRMS

Whenever possible, correspondence is addressed to an individual member of a firm, either by his, or her name or appointment, such as The Chairman, The Managing Director, The Secretary, or The Manager.

When a firm writes to another firm, 'Gentlemen' sometimes takes the place of the usual 'Dear Sirs'. This form is also occasionally adopted by a private individual when writing to an organization or group.

The term 'Mesdames', the feminine equivalent of 'Sirs', is not normally used in business circles, either at the commencement of the letter or on the envelope. It may be avoided by writing to an individual: 'Dear Madam' or 'Dear Mrs. Jones'.

Use of Messrs

The use of the prefix 'Messrs.' (a contraction of the French Messieurs), as the plural of 'Mr.', is becoming archaic for commercial firms in Britain, Australia and New Zealand, but is still generally used by the professions, especially the law. It is not generally used in Canada or in the United States.

For those who prefer to use the term 'Messrs.', this is restricted to firms with personal names, e.g.

Messrs. Berkeley, Stratton & Co.
Messrs. Ethelred Smith & Sons
Messrs. John & Henry Whitegate

It is never used in the following instances:

(a) Limited Companies
(b) Firms which do not trade under a surname, or the surname does not form the complete name, e.g.

> The Devon Mechanical Toy Co.
> Anglo-Icelandic Travel Services
> John Baker's School of Motoring
> The Maurice Wainwright Scholastic Agency.

(c) Firms whose name includes a title, e.g. Sir John Jones & Partners.
(d) Firms which bear a lady's name, e.g. Josephine Taylor & Associates. (See use of 'Mesdames' above.)

MULTIPLE SURNAMES

Usually, but not invariably, those with double-barrelled names use both names for everyday purposes, and those with triple-barrelled names the final name only, e.g. the Douglas-Homes use both names, whereas the Twisleton-Wykeham-Fiennes are often generally known as Fiennes, and the Montagu Douglas Scotts as Scott.

There are exceptions, for some with two names often use only the second. One remembers that Sir Winston Churchill did not use 'Spencer', though his surname was Spencer-Churchill, and some Fitzalan Howards are generally known as Howard. The Earl of Minto's surname is Elliot-Murray-Kynynmound (but not his collaterals); his family is usually known by the first name of Elliot. Others prefer to use all three names, such as some of the Cave-Browne-Caves.

A few families have four or more surnames. Sometimes the final two are used for everyday purposes, e.g. the Hovell-Thurlow-Cumming-Bruce family as 'Cumming-Bruce', and the Stirling Home Drummond Morays as the 'Drummond Morays'.

Practice varies according to the individual's wishes. Sometimes all the surnames are restricted to formal occasions such as in wedding announcements and legal documents: it is more usual for all surnames to be placed on the envelope. *If the practice is not known, it is not wrong to use all the surnames.*

A multiple surname was often acquired by Royal Licence from the eighteenth century onwards. When a member of a family marries an heiress who bears arms, and he (or a descendant) desires to commemorate her surname in addition to his own, the Sovereign's permission for such a change is necessary. By common law a change of name in itself is not regulated in the United Kingdom, in which respect we differ from many other countries and states. One's surname is that by which one is commonly known; but a deed poll is usually required as legal proof of identity and this officially records the change of name. A deed poll may be registered in the College of Arms in any appropriate case. In Scotland a change of name and arms is recognized by Lyon Court, and in other cases the Lord Lyon King of Arms issues a certificate of a change of name.

In recent years it has become fashionable in England to dispense with hyphens, a practice which probably originated in Scotland in order to place the emphasis on the final name, though a few families never adopted them.[1] Without a hyphen it is sometimes difficult to know whether an individual has one surname or two, especially if the signature includes an initial, e.g. J. Leslie Thomas. Is he Mr. John Leslie Thomas, or Mr. Leslie Thomas who prefers to use his second christian name? Accordingly, should one start a letter 'Dear Mr. Leslie Thomas', or 'Dear Mr. Thomas'?

There is a distinction between a surname and a family name. In England the latter is often added to the surname to show the identity of a particular family or a branch. For example, should the surname be Smith, and in one branch most or all children are christened Abel, they are known collectively as the 'Abel Smiths'. Due to the fluid system of names in England it often happens that some members of this family adopt the family name as an additional surname, with the result that their children no longer have this name included as their final christian name.

In Wales, as surnames usually evolved from male line christian names, there are a great number of people with such surnames as Jones, Powell, Evans, Davies, Morgan and Price. This has resulted in the frequent use of an additional name for identification purposes. Sometimes this becomes a surname, and sometimes not.

Also, for the same reason, in England and elsewhere those with a common surname, such as Smith or Brown, often acquire an additional name. This sometimes arises by tacking on a second christian name, especially if derived from a surname, accelerated by the practice of using this second christian name in the signature, e.g. John Berkeley Brown is known by the christian name of Berkeley, and he signs 'J. Berkeley Brown'.

[1] In Scotland the majority of those with multiple names do not use hyphens.

People therefore call him and his wife Mr. and Mrs. Berkeley Brown, instead of Mr. and Mrs. Brown as they do for his brother Mr. George Brown. In course of time his children become known by the double name of Berkeley-Brown.

LEGAL DOCUMENTS

Peers and Peeresses (in their own right, and wives and widows of Peers) are accorded their full formal styles with their christian names, *but with no surname*, viz.:

> The Most Noble Charles John Duke of Blank
> The Most Noble Anne Frances Duchess of Blank
> The Most Honourable Charles John Marquess (of) Blank
> The Most Honourable Anne Frances Marchioness (of) Blank
> The Right Honourable Charles John Earl (of), Viscount, *or* Baron Blank
> The Right Honourable Anne Frances Countess (of), Viscountess *or* Baroness Blank.[1]

Those territorial designations of Viscounts and Barons which do not form an integral part of the title, and which are not ordinarily used, may be added if desired (see p. 26).

'Lord' before Marquess and Viscount is now considered to be archaic.

Peers by courtesy and their wives are not accorded the prefix 'Most Honourable' or 'Right Honourable' (unless they are members of the Privy Council). The full description is as under:

> John Mulgrave Esquire commonly called Lord John Mulgrave.
> Sir John Brandon Knight Bachelor commonly called Lord Brandon.
> Emily Addison Spinster commonly called the Honourable Emily Addison,

but the use of the courtesy title only, such as John George Viscount Hammersmith, is generally considered to be sufficient.

The heir apparent of a peer of Scotland is designated John George Master of . . . commonly called Lord . . . (or appropriate rank). Similarly, the heir presumptive of a peer of Scotland is so designated with the appropriate courtesy style in the peerage, if applicable. (See *Scottish Title of Master,* p. 58.)

---

[1] Though the term Baroness is sometimes restricted to a peeress in her own right, and wives of Barons are described as 'Lady' in lieu, there is no good reason for this distinction.

Baronets are accorded 'Baronet' after the name. Knights Bachelor are accorded 'Knight Bachelor' or 'Knight' after the name.

Membership, etc., of Orders of Chivalry are either spelt in full (with or without the honorific prefix of the Order, e.g. Knight Commander of the *Most Excellent* Order of the British Empire), or by the recognized abbreviations, e.g. K.B.E.

Wives and widows of Baronets and Knights are formally described as 'Dame Frances Elizabeth Smith' or as 'Mary Elizabeth Lady Smith'. It is incorrect to place 'Lady' *before* the christian name, as this signifies that she is the daughter of a Duke, Marquess, or Earl.

For further information and styles for others in legal documents see *Encyclopaedia of Forms and Precedents*, Butterworth & Co., 4th edition, 1970, Vol. XV, pp. 802, 803, 810–821.

SHARE CERTIFICATES

As above, with the recognized abbreviations, but it is not usual to include territorial designations for Viscounts and Barons which are not ordinarily used. Dukes and Duchesses may be described by the slightly less formal 'His (Her) Grace'. Surnames are *never* used.

As many firms prepare certificates and plates for addresses by the same process, it is recommended that wives of Baronets and Knights should be described as 'Mary Elizabeth Lady Blank', *not* 'Lady Mary Elizabeth Blank', which is incorrect.

PASSPORTS

Every passport includes a person's christian names as a means of identification.

Passports for peers have the appropriate abbreviated prefix before the title, which is followed by any letters which signify orders, decorations etc. The christian names appear underneath, e.g.

> The Rt. Hon. the Earl of Sonning, M.C.
> John Henry George.

Otherwise as for Share Certificates.

MEMORIALS, INSCRIPTIONS AND PLAQUES

These usually contain all the christian names of a peer or peeress, with or without the appropriate prefix (The Most Hon., The Rt.

Hon. etc.) which, if included, is usually given in full. A peer's surname and the territorial part of a peerage style (see p. 26) may be used if desired. A peer or baronet is sometimes numbered, particularly when a father and son received identical christian names. It is a matter for the family to decide whether orders, decorations and degrees are to be included, and if so, which. It is also a matter of choice whether coats of arms are to be displayed, if applicable. If there is any doubt about their accuracy, reference should be made to the College of Arms or, for Scottish families, to the Lord Lyon King of Arms.

Part I

THE ROYAL FAMILY

The Sovereign

The Queen Mother and other Members of the Royal Family

Mistress of the Robes and Ladies in Waiting

Her Majesty's and other Royal Households

THE ROYAL FAMILY

The Sovereign

Except from personal friends, all communications should be addressed to 'The Private Secretary to Her Majesty The Queen'.

These letters should ask him to 'submit for Her Majesty's consideration (or approval) . . .'; ask 'if Her Majesty's attention may be directed to . . .'; or suggest that 'it may interest Her Majesty to know that . . .', etc.

Such a letter should be addressed to the holder of the Office and not by name, but subsequent correspondence should be sent to the actual writer of the reply.

The letter is a straightforward one, commencing 'Dear Sir', but the first reference to The Queen should be written 'Her Majesty', and thereafter 'The Queen'. The phrase 'Her Majesty' should be substituted for 'She' and 'Her Majesty's' for 'Her'.

For those who wish to communicate direct with The Queen, the following is the style used. Letters in the third person are now obsolete.

BEGINNING OF LETTER

 Madam,
 With my humble duty,

(In the body of the letter 'Your Majesty' should be substituted for 'You' and 'Your Majesty's' for 'Your'.)

ENDING OF LETTER

 I have the honour to remain (*or* to be),
  Madam,
   Your Majesty's most humble and obedient servant,

ENVELOPE

Her Majesty The Queen.

VERBAL ADDRESS

'Your Majesty' for the first time. Subsequently 'Ma'am'. This should always rhyme with Pam. Pronunciation to rhyme with Palm has not been correct for some generations. See also *Introduction to The Queen* (below).

DESCRIPTION IN CONVERSATION

Her Majesty, *or* The Queen, as applicable.

INTRODUCTION TO THE QUEEN

On introduction, and on leaving, a bow[1] or curtsey is made.

In conversation with The Queen, the rules mentioned under *Verbal Address* apply. 'Your Majesty' should be substituted for 'You'. References to other members of The Royal Family are made to 'His/Her Royal Highness' or the appropriate title (e.g. The Duke of Edinburgh, The Prince of Wales). When introducing another person to The Queen it is only necessary to state the name of the person to be introduced, i.e. 'May I present . . . , Your Majesty?'

OFFICIAL SPEECHES

At official functions a speech should start 'May it please Your Majesty'. Either 'Your Majesty' or 'Ma'am' may be used during the speech.

LOYAL MESSAGE

The following is the usual style for a loyal message from an organisation on some special occasion:

'On the occasion of the (centenary dinner) of the Society of Manufacturers to be held at . . . . . . on . . . . . . the President with humble duty has the honour to submit loyal greetings to Her Majesty The Queen from all who will be present.'

The message should be addressed to the Private Secretary to The Queen, and should be sent in sufficient time before the occasion to allow for a gracious reply.

[1] The head only, *not* from the waist.

Queen Elizabeth The Queen Mother

The same instructions as for The Sovereign apply, with 'Queen Elizabeth The Queen Mother' substituted for 'The Queen'.

Other Members of The Royal Family

Unless the writer is personally known to the Prince, Princess, Duke, etc., concerned, it is the usual practice to write to the Equerry, Private Secretary, or Lady in Waiting of the particular member of the Royal Family.

These letters should be addressed to the holder of the Office and not by name, but subsequent correspondence should be sent to the actual writer of the reply.

The letter is a straightforward one, commencing '(Dear) Sir' or '(Dear) Madam' but reference for the first time to the particular member of the Royal Family should be written 'His (Her) Royal Highness', and subsequently to 'The Duke of . . .' 'Prince . . .' or 'Princess . . .' as applicable. The phrase 'His (Her) Royal Highness' should be substituted for 'He (She)', as far as possible, without peppering the letter with these formal descriptions as was done in the past. Likewise 'His (Her) Royal Highness's' for 'His (Her)'.

For those who wish to communicate directly with a member of the Royal Family with the prefix His (or Her) Royal Highness, the style given below is used. Orders of Chivalry are now accorded to members of the Royal Family, with the exception of The Queen and Queen Elizabeth The Queen Mother.

BEGINNING OF LETTER

    Sir, (Madam,)

In the body of the letter 'Your Royal Highness' should be substituted for 'you' and 'Your Royal Highness's' for 'your'.

ENDING OF LETTER

    I have the honour to remain (or 'to be'),
        Sir (Madam),
            Your Royal Highness's most humble and obedient
                servant,

ENVELOPE

'His (Her) Royal Highness', followed on the next line by the name, e.g.:

The Princess Anne, Mrs. Mark Phillips
The Princess Margaret, Countess of Snowdon
The Duke of Gloucester
Princess Alice, Duchess of Gloucester
Princess Alexandra, The Hon. Mrs. Angus Ogilvy
Princess Alice, Countess of Athlone

Children of a Sovereign are given 'The' before Prince or Princess.[1]

Members of the Royal Family, apart from the Sovereign's children, who are not peers are addressed according to their particular branch of the Royal Family, e.g.:

'His Royal Highness
Prince Michael of Kent.'

The 'of Kent' is included in all written forms, viz. envelopes, invitations, etc.

Wives of Princes have a style similar to their husbands, e.g.

'Her Royal Highness The Duchess of Gloucester.'

Before his succession to the Dukedom, the Duchess was styled Her Royal Highness Princess Richard of Gloucester. Should Prince Michael of Kent marry, his wife will have a similar style.

VERBAL ADDRESS

'Your Royal Highness' for the first time. Subsequently 'Sir' (or 'Ma'am'). Pronunciation should be an ordinary 'Sir', or 'Ma'am' to rhyme with 'Pam'. Sire, or Ma'am to rhyme with Palm are archaic and not now used.

INTRODUCTION TO A MEMBER OF THE ROYAL FAMILY

On introduction, and on leaving, a bow[2] or curtsey is made.

The method ranges from the formal to the more informal. The formal system was the invariable practice in the past, and should follow that described in *Introduction to The Queen*, with, of course, the substitution of 'Your Royal Highness' for 'Your Majesty' and subsequently 'Sir' or 'Ma'am' (to rhyme with Pam).

The more informal method is preferred by some members of the Royal Family, particularly those of the younger generation.

If there is any doubt concerning which degree of formality is preferred by a particular Prince or Princess etc. reference should be made to the respective Private Secretary, Equerry,[3] or Lady in Waiting.

[1] See p. 62, note 1.
[2] The head only, *not* from the waist.
[3] Pronounced Eq-*uerry*.

Even when the more informal method is adopted, a member of the Royal Family should always be addressed in conversation as 'Your Royal Highness' for the first time, and subsequently as 'Sir' or 'Ma'am', and references to other members of the Royal Family, as Her Majesty, or His/Her Royal Highness, or more informally by their title, e.g. The Duke of Kent, or Prince Michael.

When introducing another person to a member of the Royal Family, it is only necessary to state the name of the person to be introduced, e.g. 'May I present . . ., Your Royal Highness?'

OFFICIAL SPEECHES

At official functions a speech should start, 'Your Royal Highness(es)'. 'Sir' or 'Ma'am' may be used during the speech.

Her Majesty's Household

The Queen Regnant and The Queen Dowager each appoint a Mistress of the Robes, Ladies of the Bedchamber, and Women of the Bedchamber. The last named take consecutive turns of duty, and are generally known as 'Ladies in Waiting'. This duty is usually of a fortnight's duration. On commencing a tour of duty it is notified in the Court Circular in 'The Times' and 'Daily Telegraph' that . . . has succeeded . . . as Lady in Waiting.

By custom, the Mistress of the Robes is a peeress, usually a Duchess. The present Mistress of the Robes to The Queen is the Duchess of Grafton, and to the Queen Mother, the Duchess of Abercorn.

The Mistress of the Robes and Ladies of the Bedchamber normally accompany The Queen or The Queen Mother only on State or other important occasions.

Ladies in Waiting are appointed to Lady members of the Royal Family who are Royal Highnesses.

All these Ladies are members of Her Majesty's or other Royal Households.

Forms of address are according to the rank of the lady concerned.

The Queen's Household is headed by three Great Officers, the Lord Chamberlain, the Lord Steward, and the Master of the Horse, and is organized into separate departments, which are briefly mentioned below.

The Lord Chamberlain is Head of The Queen's Household, and supervises all royal ceremonial, except such State functions as a Coronation, Opening of Parliament, or a State Funeral, which are arranged by the Earl Marshal, and a State Banquet, which is arranged by the Lord Steward. The Lord Chamberlain supervises all The Queen's functions except those of a domestic category. Consequently, on Her Majesty's behalf he organizes and sends out invitations to such functions as a Garden Party. He also administers the Ecclesiastical and Medical Households, and makes such appointments as The Librarian of Windsor Castle, Keeper of the Jewel House or the Tower of London, The Master of the Queen's Music (formerly spelt 'Musick') and the Poet Laureate.

The Lord Steward is in technical control of all The Queen's domestic arrangements, and personally is in charge of State Banquets, for which he sends out invitations on Her Majesty's behalf, supervises the function and presents the guests. Day to day arrangements are exercised by the Master of the Household. He sends other invitations on Her Majesty's behalf, apart from those issued by the Lord Chamberlain.

The Master of the Horse is responsible for The Queen's safety. At ceremonial occasions, such as The Queen's Birthday Parade, often known as 'Trooping the Colour', he rides immediately behind the Sovereign. In a procession such as the State Opening of Parliament, his carriage immediately follows The Queen's. His day to day functions are exercised by the Crown Equerry.

The Departments of the Royal Household are as follows:

1. The Private Secretary's Office, which includes the Press Secretary's Office and the Royal Archives (kept at Windsor Castle).

2. The Privy Purse and Treasurer's Office, which includes the Royal Almony.

3. The Lord Chamberlain's Office (at St. James's Palace) which includes:

(a) The Surveyor of Pictures and Works of Art;
(b) The Marshal of the Diplomatic Corps;[1]
(c) The Central Chancery of the Orders of Knighthood.

4. The Master of the Household's Office.
5. The Royal Mews.

Her Majesty has a separate Household in Scotland.

---

[1] Not to be confused with the Vice-Marshal of the Diplomatic Corps who is an official of the Foreign and Commonwealth Office.

The Keeper of the Privy Purse and Treasurer to The Queen deals with all financial matters.

The Master of the Household supervises The Queen's domestic household not only at Buckingham Palace but wherever Her Majesty is resident at the time.

The Crown Equerry is the senior member of the Royal Household in the Royal Mews Department (after the Master of the Horse), and is responsible for all The Queen's travelling arrangements.

The Vice-Chamberlain is a political appointment, and is appointed on the advice of the Prime Minister. He is a Member of Parliament and serves as a Government Whip. He submits to The Queen a daily summary of the proceedings in Parliament.

The Treasurer and *The Comptroller of the Household* are also political appointments in the Household. In the House of Commons they act as Whips, and assist Her Majesty at the State Opening of Parliament.

The Captain of the Corps of Gentlemen of Arms and the *Captain of the Yeomen of the Guard* are also political appointments and are Government Whips in the House of Lords.

The Lords in Waiting are members of the House of Lords. Their female counterparts are known as Baronesses-in-Waiting. By custom, two Lords in Waiting are non-political. The remaining five or six, who take their turn for duty for a month at a time, are appointed by the Government, being junior Government ministers in the House of Lords. Lords in Waiting perform duties for the Sovereign, such as to represent Her at the arrival and departure of visiting Heads of State, at memorial services, and on special occasions.

———————

The forms of address to members of Her Majesty's Household are according to the rank of the member concerned.

Other Royal Households

Queen Elizabeth The Queen Mother has her own Household at Clarence House, with her Lord Chamberlain, Comptroller, Treasurer, Private Secretary, and Equerry.

The Duke of Edinburgh's Household at Buckingham Palace includes his Treasurer and Private Secretary, and Equerry.

The Prince of Wales, The Princess Anne, The Princess Margaret, Princess Alice, Duchess of Gloucester, The Dukes of Gloucester and Kent, and Princess Alexandra all maintain small Households. Correspondence with these members of the Royal Family is dealt with by the Private Secretary concerned or, in the case of Princess Alexandra, by her Lady in Waiting.

The forms of address to a member of these Households are according to the rank of the person concerned.

Invitations

For invitations from and to Her Majesty The Queen and other members of the Royal Family see *Part V*.

Part II

THE PEERAGE

Younger son of a Duke or Marquess, his wife, widow and former wife

Younger son of an Earl, his wife, widow and former wife

Son of a Viscount or Baron, his wife, widow and former wife

Daughter of a Duke, Marquess or Earl

Daughter of a Viscount or Baron

Brothers and sisters of a Peer whose father did not live to succeed to a peerage

Disclaimed Peer, his wife and children

Scottish title of Master

Summary of titles

THE PEERAGE

TITLES AND STYLES OF THE PEERAGE

The most complicated series of titles and styles concern the Peerage. They are summarized on p. 62 and consist of the following groups:

1. *Peer* (of five grades, viz. Duke, Marquess, Earl, Viscount, and Baron).
2. *Peeress* (Duchess, Marchioness, Countess, Viscountess, and Baroness; either in her own right,[1] or the wife, widow, or former wife[2] of a peer).
3. *Courtesy Lord* (Son and heir apparent of a Duke, Marquess and Earl and eldest son of the heir apparent).
4. *Wife, Widow and Former wife[2] of a Courtesy Lord.*
5. *The other sons of a Peer*—with the courtesy style of 'Lord' or 'The Honourable' before the christian name, i.e.,

    (a) Younger sons of a Duke and Marquess (Lord John Brown);
    (b) Younger sons of an Earl, and *all* sons of a Viscount and Baron (The Honourable John Brown, abbreviated to The Hon. John Brown or the more old-fashioned style of 'The Honble John Brown').

6. *Sons of a Courtesy Lord.* They have courtesy styles which follow the same system mentioned in group 5.
7. *Wives of sons of a Peer or Courtesy Lord*—mentioned in group 5 (Lady John Brown, or The Hon. Mrs. John Brown).

[1] At the present time all peeresses in their own right are Countesses or Baronesses.
[2] Strictly speaking the former wife of a peer is not a peeress, but details are placed here for convenience.

8. *Daughters of a Peer—*

   (a) Daughter of a Duke, Marquess and Earl (Lady Mary Brown);
   (b) Daughter of a Viscount and Baron (The Hon. Mary Brown, if unmarried, or, The Hon. Mrs. Brown if married).

9. *Daughters of a Courtesy Lord.* They follow the same system mentioned in group 8.

PEER

There are five grades of the Peerage:

DUKE
MARQUESS
EARL
VISCOUNT
BARON (or *Lord of Parliament* in the Peerage of Scotland, see below)

The son and heir apparent of a Duke, Marquess, or Earl, may by courtesy use and be known by the title of one of his father's peerage dignities of lower grade than that by which his father is known. See *Children of a Peer* (p. 43).

Similarly, the eldest son of a courtesy lord of the grade of Marquess or Earl may by courtesy also use and be known by the title of one of his grandfather's peerage dignities, provided that it is of a lower grade than that used by the father. See *Bearers of Peerage Titles by Courtesy* (p. 44).

The Peerage, so far as oral and written forms of address are concerned, falls into two sections, each with different rules:

1. DUKE—see *Duke* (p. 27).
2. OTHER PEERS—see *Peer Other Than a Duke* (p. 33).

Though popularly known collectively as 'the Peerage', it is technically divided into five separate Peerages, viz. the Peerage of England, of Scotland, of Ireland, of Great Britain, and of the United Kingdom.

The separate Peerages of *England* and *Scotland* continued until 1707, when the two Kingdoms combined under the Act of Union. The Peerages were then united and styled the Peerage of *Great Britain*. From that year the Peerage of Great Britain and the separate Peerage of *Ireland* existed until 1801, when Great Britain and Ireland were combined under a second Act of Union. Since 1801 the Peerage has been styled the Peerage of the *United Kingdom*.

The *Peerage of Ireland* was not entirely discontinued at the Union of 1801. Creations after that date were made occasionally as a form of reward but they do not carry the right to sit in the House of Lords (e.g. Lord Curzon of Kedleston in 1898).

It is important that the description, Peerages of Scotland and Ireland, are used only in the technical sense of creation and do not imply that a peer is a Scotsman or Irishman, e.g. Lord Fairfax of Cameron in the Peerage of Scotland, and Viscount Gage in the Peerage of Ireland, both belong to English families.

THE PEERAGE OF SCOTLAND

The term MASTER is used by the heir apparent, the heir presumptive and, as a courtesy title, by the heir of a courtesy lord, see *Scottish Title of Master* (p. 58).

In the Peerage of Scotland there is no rank of Baron, since in Scotland this term concerns a Barony of land. The equivalent rank of Baron in the Peerage of Scotland is Lord of Parliament, abbreviated to 'Lord'.

THE PEERAGE OF IRELAND

If an Irish peer holds a peerage dignity of a lower grade which enables him to sit in the House of Lords, he is introduced there by the peerage which enables him to sit, e.g. the *Earl of Arran* sits in the House as *Baron Sudley*. For all other purposes he is known by his higher title, i.e. as *Earl of Arran*.

With but few exceptions, peers are known by the senior peerage which they possess; such exceptions include the Earl Brooke and of Warwick who is known as the Earl of Warwick, Lord Leconfield and Egremont as Lord Egremont, Lord Sheffield and Stanley of Alderley as Lord Stanley of Alderley, and Lord Trevethin and Oaksey as Lord Oaksey. For those who have several peerages of the same grade, the choice of style rests with the peer himself, e.g. the Duke of Richmond, Lennox and Gordon is generally known as the *Duke of Richmond and Gordon*. Some peers use both or all their peerages of the same grade, such as Lord Oranmore and Browne, while others only use one, e.g. Lord Henley and Lord Northington who only uses the former, an Irish peerage, except within the House of Lords.

TITLE OF A PEER

Every Viscount and Baron is described in his Letters Patent of creation as being of a place in the United Kingdom, followed by the appropriate county, e.g. BARON REDMAYNE, of Rushcliffe in the county of Nottingham. The place may be his residence, domicile, former constituency, or some location with which he has a connection. Such description is called the territorial designation and is *not* used except in very formal documents.

A few peers have two territorial designations of which one at least must be of a place in the United Kingdom (e.g. Viscount Allenby, of Megiddo and of Felixstowe in the county of Suffolk; Baron Keyes, of Zeebrugge and of Dover in the county of Kent; Baron Wilson, of Libya and of Stowlangtoft in the county of Suffolk).

Some peers have a territorial or place name which actually forms part of their title, such as Baron Ritchie of Dundee, Baron Russell of Liverpool, and Baron Brassey of Apethorpe. Such titles must always be used in full. They are so printed in the heading of the article concerned in DEBRETT, and are so given in the Roll of the House of Lords.

This territorial part of the peerage title may be granted for two main reasons:

(a) *as a special honour,*

Earl Mountbatten of Burma

(b) *as a method of differentiation from the title of another peer*,

Baron Erroll of Hale, to distinguish him from the holder of the Earldom of Erroll.

This is particularly prevalent now that surnames are so often adopted as peerage titles.

Differentiation may also be necessary if the first part of the title chosen sounds like another existing peerage, even though the spelling may vary, e.g. Baron Hylton and Baron Hilton of Upton, Baron Layton and Baron Leighton of St. Mellons.

A territorial or place name which forms part of a peerage title has not always been that of a place in the United Kingdom (e.g. Earl of Ypres). War leaders frequently embody the name of their battles or campaigns in their titles.

Some Peerages of England and Scotland before the Union of 1707, and of Ireland before the Union of 1801, are duplicated, such as:

> The Earldom of Arran (Scotland), held by the Duke of Hamilton
>
> The Earldom of Arran (Ireland)
>
> The Earldom of Carrick (Scotland), held by the Prince of Wales
>
> The Earldom of Carrick (Ireland)
>
> The Earldom of March (England), held by the Duke of Richmond and Gordon
>
> The Earldom of March (Scotland), held by the Earl of Wemyss and March

Duke

(*For summary see p. 62.*)

BEGINNING OF LETTER

Formal	My Lord Duke
Social	Dear Duke
	Dear Duke of Hamilton may be used if the acquaintanceship is slight

ENDING OF LETTER

Formal	Yours faithfully (see also p. 2)
Social	Yours sincerely

ENVELOPE

Formal	His Grace the Duke of Hamilton[1]
Social	The Duke of Hamilton

Note: A few Dukes prefer to be styled 'His Grace', even in social correspondence.

VERBAL ADDRESS

Formal	Your Grace
Social	Duke
Employee Status	Your Grace

[1] When preceded by other word(s), 'The' or 'the' may be used as preferred, though the Royal Family use the former.

DESCRIPTION IN CONVERSATION

A Duke is always so described (unlike the four lower grades of the peerage, viz. Marquess, Earl, Viscount, and Baron, who in speech are all called 'Lord—', e.g. Lord Bath).

If reference is only made to one Duke, he may be called 'the Duke'. If distinction is necessary, or on introduction, he should be referred to as 'the Duke of Ramsgate'. Employee status, 'His Grace'.

LIST OF DIRECTORS AND PATRONS

It is optional whether the formal style (His Grace the Duke of Ramsgate) or the social style (The Duke of Ramsgate) is adopted, so long as the same style is followed for all other patrons, etc., in a list. It is *recommended* that the social style should be used.

FORMAL STYLE

The formal style of 'The Most Noble' has given place to the more informal 'His Grace', but the former is still used occasionally in official announcements, documents and on monuments. For *Legal Documents* see p. 8, and for *Share Certificates,* for *Passports,* and for *Memorials, Inscriptions and Plaques,* see p. 9.

MEMBERSHIP OF THE PRIVY COUNCIL

If a Duke be a Privy Counsellor, the letters P.C. should be included after his title, since it would not be otherwise apparent that he holds that office. The letters P.C. follow any orders and decorations he may hold, e.g. '(His Grace) the Duke of Dover. K.C.V.O., C.B.E., P.C.'. See *Privy Counsellor* (p. 80).

ECCLESIASTICAL, AMBASSADORIAL, OR ARMED FORCES RANK

These precede ducal rank, i.e.

> The Very Reverend the Duke of Ramsgate
> His Excellency the Duke of Ramsgate
> Major the Duke of Ramsgate

SIGNATURE

By title only, e.g. Ramsgate.

STYLE FROM SOURCES OTHER THAN THE CROWN

See p. 35.

Wife of a Duke

(*For summary see p.* 62.)

BEGINNING OF LETTER

Formal	Madam *or* Dear Madam[1]
Social	Dear Duchess
	Dear Duchess of Somerset may be used if the acquaintanceship is slight.

ENDING OF LETTER

Formal	Yours faithfully (see also p. 2)
Social	Yours sincerely

ENVELOPE

Formal	Her Grace the Duchess of Norfolk
Social	The Duchess of Norfolk

VERBAL ADDRESS

Formal	Your Grace
Social	Duchess
Employee Status	Your Grace

DESCRIPTION IN CONVERSATION

A Duchess is *always* so described, unlike the four lower grades of the peerage, who in speech are called Lady Blank.

If reference be only made to one Duchess, she may be called 'the Duchess'. If distinction is necessary, or on introduction she should be referred to as 'the Duchess of Norfolk'. *Employee status*, 'Her Grace'.

LIST OF DIRECTORS AND PATRONS

It is optional whether the formal style (Her Grace the Duchess of Ramsgate) or the social style (The Duchess of Ramsgate) is adopted, so long as the same style is followed for all other patrons, etc. in a list. It is *recommended* that the social style should be used.

---

[1] Strictly speaking, the commencement of 'Madam' is the very formal style, for which the corresponding conclusion is given on p. 3. This form of conclusion is now seldom used, and 'Madam', instead of the more usual 'Dear Madam', is sometimes adopted at the beginning of a very formal or official letter.

FORMAL STYLE

The formal style of 'The Most Noble' has given place to the more informal 'Her Grace' but the former is still used occasionally in official announcements, documents and on monuments. For *Legal Documents* (see p. 8) and for *Share Certificates,* for *Passports* and for *Memorials, Inscriptions and Plaques* (see p. 9).

SIGNATURE

Christian name and title, e.g. Helen Middlesex.

Widow of a Duke

Officially the widow of a Duke is known as 'The Dowager Duchess of Southampton', unless there is already a Dowager Duchess in that family still living. In the latter event, the widow of the senior Duke retains this title for life, and the widow of the junior Duke is known by her christian name, e.g. 'Mary, Duchess of Southampton'.

Socially many prefer to use their christian name in preference to 'The Dowager Duchess of Southampton'. An announcement is often made in the Press. Otherwise it will be necessary to discover her wishes. If in doubt I *recommend* the use of the christian name.

If the present holder of the Dukedom is unmarried, *socially* the widow of the previous Duke does not use the term of either 'The Dowager Duchess of Southampton' or 'Mary, Duchess of Southampton' but continues to be known as 'The Duchess of Southampton'.

Should the present Duke marry, it is usual for the widowed Duchess then to announce the style she wishes to adopt.

BEGINNING OF LETTER

Formal	(Dear) Madam[1]
Social	Dear Duchess
	Dear Duchess of Middlesex may be used if the acquaintanceship is slight

ENDING OF LETTER

Formal	Yours faithfully (see also p. 2)
Social	Yours sincerely

[1] See p. 29, note [1].

ENVELOPE

Formal	Her Grace the Dowager Duchess of Middlesex *or*
	Her Grace Mary, Duchess of Middlesex (as applicable)
Social	The Dowager Duchess of Middlesex *or*
	Mary, Duchess of Middlesex (as applicable)

VERBAL ADDRESS

As for the wife of a Duke.

DESCRIPTION IN CONVERSATION

As for a Duchess. If distinction from the wife of the present Duke is necessary, or on introduction, she should be described as 'The Dowager Duchess of Middlesex' or 'Mary, Duchess of Middlesex' as applicable. *Employee status,* 'Her Grace'.

LIST OF DIRECTORS AND PATRONS

Formal	Her Grace the Dowager Duchess of Southampton *or*
	Her Grace Mary, Duchess of Southampton
Social	The Dowager Duchess of Southampton *or* Mary, Duchess of Southampton

For the choice of formal or social style, see wife of a Duke.

FORMAL STYLE

As for wife of a Duke.

SIGNATURE

As for wife of a Duke.

Former Wife of a Duke

If a marriage to a Duke has been dissolved, his former wife continues to use her title as a Duke's wife, preceded by her christian name.

The continuance of her title henceforward is regarded as a name rather than the retention of the attributes and status of the wife of a peer. Accordingly she is not entitled to the prefix of 'Her Grace'.

In Scotland, due to the difference in laws for divorce, a former wife is legally equivalent to a widow in England. On marriage, as well as adopting her husband's surname, she also retains her maiden name as an alias. Should her marriage to a Duke be dissolved and she marries again, she also retains her first husband's title as an alias. Socially, former wives of Dukes in Scotland are usually treated as former wives of Dukes in general, unless any specific ruling is announced by Lyon King of Arms.

BEGINNING OF LETTER

As for the wife of a Duke.

ENDING OF LETTER

As for the wife of a Duke.

ENVELOPE

Formal and Social   Mary, Duchess of Wiltshire

VERBAL ADDRESS

Formal   Madam
Social   Duchess
Employee Status   Your Grace[1]

DESCRIPTION IN CONVERSATION

Duchess of Blankshire. If some distinction from the wife of the present Duke is necessary, she should be described as Mary, Duchess of Blankshire. *Employee status,* 'Her Grace'.

LIST OF DIRECTORS AND PATRONS

Mary, Duchess of Wiltshire.

REMARRIAGE

She adopts her style from her present husband: e.g. Mary, Duchess of Blankshire marries Mr. Cuthbert Jones and becomes Mrs. Cuthbert Jones.

---

[1] Although officially she is no longer entitled to the prefix of 'Her Grace' since she is no longer a peeress, by custom this rank continues to be given to her verbally. As former wives of other peers are referred to as 'My Lady' or 'Your Ladyship' (Employee status p. 36), there is no other alternative by which she could be known. It is *recommended* therefore that she should be referred to as 'Her Grace'.

If she has a courtesy style from her father, she will revert to this on remarriage, e.g. Lady Mary Brown marries first the Duke of Blankshire and secondly Mr. John Green. Upon her second marriage she is known as Lady Mary Green.

Similarly, if the Hon. Mary Brown marries first the Duke of Blankshire and secondly Mr. John Green, she becomes the Hon. Mrs. Green.

Peer, Other than a Duke—
Viz. Marquess, Earl, Viscount, and Baron
(*For summary of titles see p.* 62.)

Peers of the grades of Marquess,[1] Earl, Viscount, and Baron are all referred to in conversation as Lord Washington. The use of their exact rank is socially incorrect, unless for some reason it has to be specifically mentioned. It is, however, used on envelopes, visiting cards and invitations.

The only exception to the above general rule is at a formal function. The exact peerage title may then be given at the first mention of a peer, but he is usually subsequently referred to, or invited to speak, as 'Lord Washington'.

The fifth grade of the peerage, a Baron, is never referred to by this title, except in legal or formal documents (see p. 8), but always as Lord Gretton, both verbally and in correspondence. In the Peerage of Scotland, the term 'Lord' (Lord of Parliament) is the legal term of the fifth grade in the peerage, because the term 'Baron' is used in a feudal sense relating to land tenure.

The use of 'Baron' is restricted to a foreign title which is never translated as '*Lord* Braun'. See *Non-Royal Titles* (p. 376).

BEGINNING OF LETTER

Formal	My Lord
Social	Dear Lord Tweeddale

ENDING OF LETTER

Formal	Yours faithfully (see also p. 2)
Social	Yours sincerely

---

[1] The official spelling of this title is 'Marquess', and this is adopted in the Roll of the House of Lords. Some newspapers, not 'The Times', spell the word 'Marquis', as for the title in France. In the past, when spelling was not standardized, both forms were adopted in Britain. Some Scottish Marquesses, in memory of the 'Auld Alliance' with France, prefer to use the French spelling.

ENVELOPE

Formal	The Most Hon. the Marquess of Tweed-dale[1]
(see p. 38, note [2])	The Rt. Hon. the Earl of Gainsborough[1]
	The Rt. Hon. the Viscount Falkland[2]
	The Rt. Hon. the Lord Gretton[3]

Social	The Marquess of Tweeddale
	The Earl of Gainsborough
	The Viscount Falkland
	The Lord Gretton

DESCRIPTION OF A PEER WITHIN A LETTER, ARTICLE, CAPTION, ETC.

The first formal reference to a peer is usually made to his exact rank. Subsequent references to a peer of all these four grades may be made to Lord Tweeddale, Lord Falkland, etc.

References to these peers in social letters usually do not quote the exact rank but give the style of Lord, viz. Lord Tweeddale, not The Marquess of Tweeddale.

VERBAL ADDRESS

Formal	My Lord
Social	Lord Tweeddale
Employee Status	My Lord *or* Your Lordship[4]

DESCRIPTION IN CONVERSATION

Lord Gainsborough—this style applies to all four grades of the Peerage.

Employee Status	His Lordship

LIST OF DIRECTORS AND PATRONS

It is optional whether one adopts the formal style, viz.:

The Most Hon. the Marquess of Findon
The Rt. Hon. the Earl of Storrington
The Rt. Hon. the Viscount Washington
The Rt. Hon. the Lord Ashington

[1] There are some Marquessates and Earldoms whose titles do not include the word 'of', e.g. The Marquess Conyngham, The Earl Sondes.
[2] All Viscounts in the Peerage of Scotland were created 'of' somewhere, but only The Viscount of Arbuthnott normally uses it.
[3] The only Baron who sometimes uses 'of' is Baron of Dunsany, but he is usually known as 'Lord Dunsany'.
[4] The difference is purely grammatical, e.g. 'Yes, my Lord'; 'Will your Lordship come this way?'.

or the social style, viz.:

> The Marquess of Findon
> The Earl of Storrington
> The Viscount Washington
> The Lord Ashington

so long as the same style is followed for all other patrons, etc., in the list. It is *recommended* that the social style should be used.

MEMBERSHIP OF THE PRIVY COUNCIL

If a peer be a Privy Counsellor, the letters P.C. should be included after his name, orders, and decorations, since it would not otherwise be apparent that he holds that Office.

A Marquess still has the prefix or formal style of Most Hon., and an Earl, Viscount, and Baron all have the prefix or formal style of Rt. Hon., which is also the attribute of a Privy Counsellor. See *Privy Counsellor* (p. 80).

ECCLESIASTICAL, AMBASSADORIAL OR ARMED FORCES RANK

These precede a peer's rank in correspondence, e.g.:

> His Excellency the Earl of Storrington
> The Rev. Canon the Viscount Washington
> Major the Lord Ashington.

SIGNATURE

By title only, e.g., Washington.

STYLE FROM SOURCES OTHER THAN THE CROWN

It is not customary in *formal* usage to combine the style emanating from other sources with titles conferred by the Sovereign. 'Alderman the Lord Jones' and 'Professor the Lord Smith' are solecisms. In *social* usage this is not uncommon, though deprecated by purists.

Life Peer and Life Peeress

A life peer or peeress and a Law Lord and his wife have exactly the same style and attributes as an hereditary peer.

Children of life peers or peeresses and Law Lords have the same courtesy styles as the children of an hereditary peer. They continue to bear these for life. For the son of a Baron see p. 53 and the daughter of a Baron, p. 55. For Law Lords (Lords of Appeal in Ordinary), see p. 207.

Peeress in Her Own Right

(*For summary see p.* 62.)

At present all peeresses in their own right are either Countesses or Baronesses. In the Peerage of Scotland, the term Lady (Lady of Parliament) is the legal term of the fifth grade of the peerage because the term 'Baroness' is used in a feudal sense relating to land tenure.

All peeresses in their own right, whether their peerage is hereditary or for life, are addressed as for the wife of a peer of the applicable grade, but a Baroness has the option of two alternative styles.

The use of the continental style of 'Baroness' for social purposes is of fairly recent origin. It is believed that the first to term themselves 'Baroness' were Baroness Zouche (who styled herself Baroness de la Zouche) and Baroness Burdett-Coutts. As several Life Baronesses have been created since the Peerage Act 1963, its use has now become widespread. It is *recommended* that the personal wishes of the lady concerned should be ascertained as to which form of address should be used, 'Baroness' or 'Lady'.

A husband derives no title or style from his wife.

BEGINNING OF LETTER

As for the wife of a peer, other than a Duke, though a Baroness may prefer the style of 'Baroness' instead of 'Lady'. In this case, socially, she should be addressed:

Dear Baroness Green

Most Baronesses in their own right prefer the style Dear Lady Green.

Note : 'Baroness' should not be used on its own, as is sometimes done. One would not address a peeress just as 'Lady'. The style is, however, correct for a continental Baroness, see *Non-Royal Titles* (p. 376).

ENDING OF LETTER

Formal	Yours faithfully (see also p. 2)
Social	Yours sincerely.

ENVELOPE

As for the wife of a peer, other than a Duke (p. 38), but if a Baroness prefers the style of 'Baroness' she should be addressed:

Formal	The Rt. Hon. the Baroness Green
Social	The Baroness Green.

WRITTEN DESCRIPTION

See wife of a peer, other than a Duke (p. 38).

VERBAL ADDRESS

As for the wife of a peer, other than a Duke, with the option, for Baronesses, of the style 'Baroness Green' instead of 'Lady Green' if preferred. 'Lady Green' is the style usually adopted.

Note : 'Baroness' should not be used on its own. See *Beginning of Letter* above.

DESCRIPTION IN CONVERSATION

Formal and Social	Lady Teddington *or* Baroness Teddington
Employee Status	Her Ladyship.

LIST OF DIRECTORS AND PATRONS

It is optional whether one adopts the formal or the social method so long as the same style is followed for all other patrons, etc., in the list. It is *recommended* that the social style should be used.

SIGNATURE

Teddington (as for a peer).

CHILDREN

The children of a peeress adopt the same courtesy titles and styles as do the children of a peer, e.g. the Countess of Sutherland's son and heir is Lord Strathnaver: Baroness Spencer-Churchill's daughter is the Hon. Lady Soames.

Wife of a Peer, Other than a Duke

(*For summary see p.* 62.)

The wife of a Marquess is a Marchioness
The wife of an Earl is a Countess
The wife of a Viscount is a Viscountess
The wife of a Baron is a Baroness

The last named title is not used, except in formal documents, the usual style being Lady Blank. The exception is that a Baroness in her own right has the option of using it in place of Lady Blank.

'Baroness' in continental titles is never translated as '*Lady Blank*' (see *Non-Royal Titles,* p. 376).

For nearly all purposes a peeress of all these four grades of the peerage is referred to in conversation as 'Lady Blank'. The use of the exact rank in speech (e.g. Viscountess Blank) is socially incorrect, unless for some reason it needs to be specifically mentioned, but it is always used on envelopes and visiting cards. An exception may occasionally be made at a formal function, such as in the introduction of a speaker who is a peeress, when normally her exact rank is mentioned for the first time only, e.g. 'We are very happy to have the Countess of Hallamshire here tonight. Lady Hallamshire, as you know . . .'

BEGINNING OF LETTER

Formal
(Dear) Madam[1]
Dear Lady Angmering (irrespective of which of the four grades of peerage is applicable)

ENDING OF LETTER
Formal
Yours faithfully (see also p. 2)
Social
Yours sincerely

ENVELOPE
Formal[2]
The Most Hon. the Marchioness of Bath
The Rt. Hon. the Countess of Derby
The Rt. Hon. the Viscountess Kemsley
The Rt. Hon. the Lady Poole

Social
The Marchioness of Bath
The Countess of Derby
The Viscountess Kemsley
The Lady Poole

WRITTEN DESCRIPTION

Where a Viscountess or Baroness is referred to in the body of a formal letter, article, caption, etc., she may be described as

[1] See p. 29, note [1]. The term 'My Lady' is not used as the feminine equivalent of 'My Lord' but is restricted to Employee status.
[2] There is no definite rule concerning the use of the word 'The' before these styles. As some consider that the double use of 'The' is superfluous 'Most Hon. the Marchioness of Bath' may, if desired, be used. This practice is not, however, recommended.

Viscountess Molesey or Lady Surbiton without the prefix 'the'. Any subsequent reference to such a peeress can be made to Lady Molesey, without regard to her exact rank in the peerage.

Informal letters again do not usually refer to the exact rank at all, but as Lady Molesey throughout.

The second and subsequent reference to a Marchioness or a Countess can be made to Lady Bath, without regard to her exact rank. Informal letters do not usually refer to her exact rank at all, but as Lady Bath throughout.

VERBAL ADDRESS

Formal	Madam (*not* My Lady[1])
Social	Lady Poole
Employee Status	My Lady *or* Your Ladyship[2]

DESCRIPTION IN CONVERSATION

Formal and Social	Lady Poole
Employee Status	Her Ladyship

LIST OF DIRECTORS AND PATRONS

It is optional whether one adopts the formal or the social method so long as the same style is followed for all other patrons, etc., in the list. It is *recommended* that the social style should be used.

SIGNATURE

By christian name and title, e.g., Helen Middlesex.

Widow of a Peer, Other than a Duke

Officially the widow of a peer of the above-mentioned grades is known as 'The Dowager Marchioness Conyngham', 'The Dowager Countess of Pembroke and Montgomery', etc., unless there is already a dowager peeress of the family still living. In the latter event, the widow of the senior peer of the family retains the title of Dowager for life, and the widow of the junior peer in that family is known by her christian name, e.g. 'Mary, Marchioness of Hammersmith', until she becomes the senior widow.

Many dowager peeresses prefer the use of their christian name in preference to the word 'Dowager'. An announcement is often

[1] See p. 29, note [1]. The term 'My Lady' is not used as the feminine equivalent of 'My Lord' but is restricted to Employee status.
[2] The difference is purely grammatical, e.g. 'Yes, my Lady'; 'Will your Ladyship come this way?'. These forms are now only used by shops, etc., and by those of Employee status.

made in the press. Otherwise it is necessary to discover the wishes of the lady concerned. If in doubt, I recommend the style of 'Mary, Lady Blank' (or appropriate rank), as the majority of peers' widows do not like the style of dowager.

When the present peer is unmarried, *by custom* the widow of the late peer continues to call herself as she did when her husband was living, i.e. without the prefix of (a) dowager, or (b) her christian name. Should the present peer marry, it is usual for the widowed peeress to announce the style by which she wishes to be known in future, i.e. 'The Dowager Lady (or appropriate rank) Lancing' or 'Mary, Lady Lancing'.

BEGINNING OF LETTER

Formal	(Dear) Madam[1]
Social	Dear Lady Lancing

ENDING OF LETTER

Formal	Yours faithfully (see also p. 2)
Social	Yours sincerely

ENVELOPE

Formal (see p. 38, note [2])	The Most Hon. the Dowager Marchioness of Hammersmith The Rt. Hon. the Dowager Countess of Flintshire The Rt. Hon. the Dowager Viscountess Angmering The Rt. Hon. the Dowager Lady Lancing *or* The Most Hon. Mary, Marchioness of Hammersmith (or applicable title)
Social	The Dowager Marchioness of Hammersmith The Dowager Countess of Flintshire The Dowager Viscountess Angmering The Dowager Lady Lancing *or* Mary, Marchioness of Hammersmith (or applicable title)

[1] See p. 29, note [1].

VERBAL ADDRESS

Formal	Madam
Social	Lady Hammersmith
Employee Status	My Lady *or* Your Ladyship[1]

DESCRIPTION IN CONVERSATION

Lady Hammersmith. If distinction is necessary or on introduction she should be described as 'the Dowager Lady Hammersmith' or 'Mary, Lady Hammersmith'. *Employee status,* 'Her Ladyship'.

LIST OF DIRECTORS AND PATRONS

It is optional whether one adopts the formal or the social method so long as the same style is followed for all other patrons, etc., in the list. It is *recommended* that the social style should be used.

SIGNATURE

By christian name and title, e.g. Helen Hammersmith.

REMARRIAGE

If the widow of a peer remarries, she adopts her style from her present husband, e.g. The Dowager Lady Green having married Mr. Edward Brown would be known as Mrs. Edward Brown.

Should a peer's widow who has a courtesy style as a peer's daughter marry again, she reverts to the use of the courtesy style derived from her father, e.g. if Lady Mary White (daughter of the Earl of Ditton) marries first the Marquess of Surbiton and secondly Mr. Thomas Jones, she will be known as Lady Mary Jones. Should the Hon. Mary Smith (daughter of Viscount Twickenham) marry first Lord White and secondly Mr. Robert Green, she is known as the Hon. Mrs. Green.

Former Wife of a Peer, Other than a Duke

If a former wife of a Marquess, Earl, Viscount, or Baron does not marry again, she may continue to use the title as she did when she was married to the peer, with the prefix of her christian name. *She no longer uses the formal style of a peeress,* viz.:

The Most Hon. for a Marchioness
The Rt. Hon. for a Countess, Viscountess and Baroness

[1] See p. 39, note [2].

On remarriage, she takes her style from her present husband.

In Scotland, due to the difference in divorce laws, a former wife is legally equivalent to a widow in England. On marriage, as well as adopting her husband's surname, she also retains her maiden name as an alias. Should her marriage to a peer be dissolved, and she marries again, she also retains her first husband's title as an alias.

Socially, former wives of peers in Scotland are usually treated as are former wives of peers in general, unless any specific ruling is announced by Lyon King or Arms.

BEGINNING OF LETTER

Formal	(Dear) Madam[1]
Social	Dear Lady Surbiton

ENDING OF LETTER

Formal	Yours faithfully (see also p. 2)
Social	Yours sincerely

ENVELOPE

Formal and Social	Mary, Countess of Surbiton

VERBAL ADDRESS

Formal	Madam
Social	Lady Surbiton
Employee Status	My Lady *or* Your Ladyship[2]

DESCRIPTION IN CONVERSATION

Lady Surbiton. If distinction from the wife of the present peer is necessary, or on introduction, she should be described as 'Mary, Lady Surbiton'. *Employee status,* 'Her Ladyship'.

LIST OF DIRECTORS AND PATRONS

Mary, Countess of Surbiton.

SIGNATURE

Christian name and title, e.g. Mary Surbiton.

[1] See p. 29, note [1].
[2] See p. 34, note [4].

REMARRIAGE

On remarriage she adopts her style from her present husband, e.g. the former wife of the Earl of Surbiton marries Mr. John Brown: she is known as Mrs. John Brown. If she has a courtesy style derived from her father she will revert to this on remarriage, e.g. (a) Lady Mary Green marries first the Viscount Ferring and secondly Mr. John Smith: she becomes Lady Mary Smith; (b) The Hon. Mary Smith marries first the Lord White and secondly Mr. John Brown: she becomes the Hon. Mrs. Brown.

Widow of one who would have succeeded to a Peerage had he survived

The Queen may issue a Royal Warrant conferring on the lady concerned the title, rank, place, pre-eminence, and precedence which would have been hers if her late husband had survived and succeeded to the title.

This privilege has been granted in certain instances when the lady's husband died on active service.

Example

The Hon. Roger Mortimer, son and heir of Viscount March, is killed in action. On the Peer's death, Roger's widow may be accorded by Royal Warrant the title of the Viscountess March, as if her husband had survived and succeeded to the peerage.

Children of a Peer

The children of a peer use either:

(a) a peerage title by courtesy, *or*
(b) a courtesy style.

A courtesy title indicates and reflects a legal right of precedence, unless in particular cases they are confirmed or recognized by the Sovereign.

The son and heir apparent[1] of a Duke, Marquess, or Earl

---

[1] The heir apparent to a dignity is either the eldest son, the eldest surviving son (where a deceased elder brother has left no heir apparent) or the only son of the holder of a dignity. When the heir apparent is deceased, *his* heir apparent succeeds him in this respect. A woman can only be an heiress apparent when she is the eldest child (without surviving brothers with issue) or the only child of a deceased heir apparent. Legally the holder of a dignity, so long as he lives, may have a son. Thus Queen Elizabeth II was never heiress apparent to the Crown since she could have been displaced in succession by the birth of a brother.

The heir presumptive to a dignity is the next in line, but who could be displaced in succession by the birth of an heir apparent. Thus a relative of a peer is only his heir presumptive until such time as the peer has a son and heir apparent. Alternatively, when a dignity may pass in the female line, the holder's daughter is heiress presumptive until such time as a son is born. If there be more than one daughter, but no son, they are co-heirs to an English Barony created by writ of summons. This falls into abeyance between them or their representatives.

Although 'heir' is used loosely for the heir apparent or heir presumptive, legally it means the person in occupation of the title, estate, etc.

may use one of his father's peerage titles by courtesy providing it is of a lesser grade than that used by his father. If the Duke, Marquess or Earl is of the Peerage of Scotland, see *Scottish Title of Master*, p. 58.

The younger sons of a Duke or Marquess have the courtesy style of 'Lord' before christian name and surname.

The younger sons of an Earl, and *all* sons of a Viscount or Baron have the courtesy style of 'The Hon.' before christian name and surname.

The daughters of a Duke, Marquess, or Earl have the courtesy style of 'Lady' before christian name and surname.

The daughters of a Viscount or Baron have the courtesy style of 'The Hon.' before christian name and surname.

A peer's sons and daughters who are legitimated under the Legitimacy Act 1926, as amended by the Act of 1959, are now under an Earl Marshal's Warrant accorded the same courtesy styles as the legitimate younger children of peers, though they have no right of succession to the peerage or precedence from it.

Courtesy styles may continue to be borne by the children of peers who have disclaimed their peerages if desired. See *Children of a Disclaimed Peer* (p. 58).

A few children of peers or courtesy lords prefer not to use their courtesy titles or styles, and this fact is noted in their fathers' respective paragraphs in DEBRETT.

The children of the younger sons of a peer have no titles or special styles.

Children who are or have been adopted by a peer do not acquire any titles, styles and precedence as a result of such adoption.

Bearers of Peerage Titles by Courtesy

Though the bearer of a peerage title by courtesy enjoys none of the privileges of a peer, he is addressed as such with the following exceptions:

1. A Marquess by courtesy is not given the formal style of 'The Most Hon.', e.g. Marquess of Tavistock.[1]
2. An Earl, Viscount or Baron by courtesy is not given the formal style of 'The Rt. Hon.' e.g. Earl of Burford,[1] Viscount Sandon and Lord Porchester.

[1] Some Marquessates and Earldoms used as courtesy titles do not contain the word 'of' in their title, e.g. Earl Grosvenor.

3. A peer by courtesy is not addressed as 'The' in correspondence. This is restricted to actual peers.[1]

Normally he is called 'Lord Blank', but if there is a special reason for a Marquess or Earl by courtesy to be referred to by his exact courtesy title, he is called verbally, 'the Marquess of Blandford' or 'the Earl of Burford', this being the usual colloquial form of reference. The definite article is never given to courtesy Viscounts and Barons.

The eldest (or only) son and heir apparent of a Duke, Marquess or Earl may by courtesy use a title in the peerage of a rank junior to his father. This is usually, but not invariably, the second senior peerage borne by the peer (e.g. the son and heir apparent of the Duke of Rutland is known as the Marquess of Granby). The question is discussed in the *Complete Peerage*, Vol. IV, App. E, and by Valentine Heywood in his *British Titles*, 1951.

Second Heir to a Peerage

When a Marquess or Earl by courtesy has an eldest (or only) son (who consequently is his second heir apparent), he, too, may use a courtesy title in the peerage, provided that it is junior in rank to that by which his father is known, e.g. Lord Howland is the son of the Marquess of Tavistock, who is son and heir of the Duke of Bedford.

For the eldest son of an Earl by courtesy in the Peerage of Scotland, see *Scottish Title of Master* (p. 58).

Grandson who is Heir Apparent of a Peer

When the heir apparent of a Duke, Marquess or Earl is deceased, but has left a son (who then becomes the heir apparent to the peer), he is allowed to use the courtesy title borne by his father. In 1955, Viscount Swinton was created Earl of Swinton. His son and heir, the Hon. John Cunliffe-Lister, had died of wounds in 1943, leaving male issue. On the creation of the Earldom, the elder of these sons, the present Earl of Swinton, became heir apparent to his grandfather and known by courtesy as Lord Masham.

If the eldest son of a Viscount or Baron predeceases his father, his children do not use the courtesy style of 'The Honourable'. Thus the present Lord Kingsale, who succeeded his grandfather, did not have the style of 'The Honourable' when his grandfather was the peer.

[1] Some hold that the prefix of 'The' is an abbreviation for The Most Noble, The Most Hon. and The Rt. Hon.

Examples of Peerage Titles borne by Courtesy

There is no hard and fast rule about which title borne by a peer is selected for use by his eldest son as a peer by courtesy, though in most families custom is followed. If the Marquess of Lansdowne has a son, his heir is usually known as Earl of Kerry or Earl of Shelburne in alternate generations. When the 6th Marquess of Ailesbury died, he was succeeded in that dignity by his eldest son, known by courtesy as Earl of Cardigan. The latter's son, however, preferred to retain the use of his courtesy title of Viscount Savernake and was not known as Earl of Cardigan. He since succeeded as the 8th Marquess of Ailesbury. See the *Complete Peerage,* Vol. IV, App. E.

All courtesy titles used are shown in DEBRETT under the heading of the peer concerned.

The following examples of (1) the peer, (2) his son and heir apparent, and (3) the heir's eldest son, are included to show how the system varies according to the particular peerage. Each example given consists of a different sequence of rank in the courtesy titles. Where a rank has been omitted, this is usually because the peer does not possess a peerage dignity of that grade (e.g. the Marquess of Bath is not also an Earl, but he is also the Viscount Weymouth, and by courtesy his eldest son is styled Viscount Weymouth). In two instances the peerage ranks shown in parentheses do not exist at present, but they are normally used as courtesy titles.

The third heir in line of succession has not been included in the examples, but if a courtesy Earl is the second heir, *and he has sons,* the eldest would also use a courtesy title, a Viscountcy or Barony, as applicable.

1. The Duke of Leinster
2. Marquess of Kildare
3. Earl of Offaly

1. The Duke of Abercorn
2. Marquess of Hamilton
3. Viscount Strabane

1. The Duke of Bedford
2. Marquess of Tavistock
3. Lord Howland

1. The Duke of Grafton
2. Earl of Euston
3. (Viscount Ipswich)

1. The Duke of Richmond and Gordon
2. Earl of March and Kinrara
3. Lord Settrington

1. The Duke of Manchester
2. Viscount Mandeville

1. The Duke of Somerset
2. Lord Seymour

1. The Marquess Camden
2. Earl of Brecknock
3. Viscount Bayham

1. The Marquess of Zetland
2. Earl of Ronaldshay
3. Lord Dundas

1. The Marquess of Bath
2. Viscount Weymouth

1. The Marquess of Exeter
2. (Lord Burghley)

1. The Earl of Lindsay
2. Viscount Garnock

1. The Earl of Westmorland
2. Lord Burghersh

Peers by courtesy are eligible to sit in the House of Commons.

Wife of a Peer by courtesy

The wife of a peer by courtesy is addressed as the wife of a peer of the same rank, but with the following exceptions (also mentioned under a peer by courtesy):

1. The wife of a Marquess by courtesy is *not* given the formal style of 'The Most Hon.', e.g. Marchioness of Kildare.
2. The wife of an Earl, Viscount or Baron by courtesy is *not* given the formal style of 'The Rt. Hon', e.g. Countess of Ronaldshay.
3. The wife of a peer by courtesy is *not* given the prefix 'The' in correspondence.

Widow of a Peer by courtesy

The widow of a peer by courtesy is addressed as the widow of a peer of the identical rank, with the following exceptions, also mentioned under the wife of a peer by courtesy:

1. Without the prefix of 'The Most Hon' (Marchionesses) or 'The Rt. Hon' (Peeresses of lower grades).
2. Without the prefix 'The' before the title.

If the courtesy title has passed to her late husband's brother or other relation, she would prefix her title by her christian name. If it has passed to her son or stepson, she would prefix the title by her christian name when he marries.

Former Wife of a Peer by courtesy

She is styled as the former wife of a peer, other than a Duke (see p. 41).

Younger Sons of a Duke or Marquess

The younger sons of a Duke or Marquess are known by the courtesy style of Lord, followed by their christian name and surname, e.g. Lord Edward FitzGerald.

BEGINNING OF LETTER

Formal	My Lord
Social	Dear Lord Edward
	The surname may be added if the acquaintanceship is slight

ENDING OF LETTER

Formal	Yours faithfully (see also p. 2)
Social	Yours sincerely

ENVELOPE

Formal and Social	Lord Edward FitzGerald

VERBAL ADDRESS

Formal	My Lord
Social	Lord Edward
Employee status	My Lord *or* Your Lordship[1]

[1] See p. 34, note [4].

DESCRIPTION IN CONVERSATION

Lord Edward. If distinction is necessary, or on introduction, he is described as Lord Edward FitzGerald. *He should never be described as Lord FitzGerald*, and there is no authority for the prefix of 'The' before his name. *Employee status,* 'His Lordship'.

LIST OF DIRECTORS AND PATRONS

Lord Edward FitzGerald

MEMBERSHIP OF THE PRIVY COUNCIL

Precede his style with 'The Rt. Hon.', e.g.:
The Rt. Hon. Lord Edward FitzGerald (see *Privy Counsellor*, p. 80)

ECCLESIASTICAL, AMBASSADORIAL, OR ARMED FORCES RANK

These should precede his rank, e.g.:
His Excellency Lord Edward FitzGerald
Rear-Admiral Lord Edward FitzGerald

SIGNATURE

Edward FitzGerald

Wife of a Younger Son of a Duke or Marquess

The wife of a younger son of a Duke or Marquess is known as *Lady,* followed by his christian and surname, e.g. the wife of Lord Edward FitzGerald is known as Lady Edward FitzGerald. This style is identical for the wife of a younger son of a courtesy Marquess.

If she derives senior precedence as the daughter of a Duke or Marquess from that which she acquired on marriage, she may continue to use *her* prefix instead of *his*, e.g. Lady Mary Jones, married to Lord Edward Brown, may if she wishes, be known as Lady *Mary* Brown instead of Lady *Edward* Brown, but this is seldom done today. This form should only be used if it is known that it is preferred. It is, however, generally used by such ladies whose marriage has been dissolved.

BEGINNING OF LETTER

Formal	(Dear) Madam[1]
Social	Dear Lady Edward
	The surname may be added if the acquaintanceship is slight e.g. Dear Lady Edward FitzGerald

ENDING OF LETTER

Formal	Yours faithfully (see also p. 2)
Social	Yours sincerely

ENVELOPE

Formal and Social	Lady Edward FitzGerald

VERBAL ADDRESS

Formal	Madam
Social	Lady Edward
Employee Status	My Lady *or* Your Ladyship[2]

DESCRIPTION IN CONVERSATION

Lady Edward. If distinction is necessary, or on introduction, she should be described as Lady Edward FitzGerald.

She should not be described as Lady FitzGerald, and would only be described as Lady Mary FitzGerald if she were senior in precedence to her husband, and she prefers to use her own style. Employee status, 'Her Ladyship'.[2]

LIST OF DIRECTORS AND PATRONS

Lady Edward FitzGerald

Widow of a Younger Son of a Duke or Marquess

Her style in widowhood does not change, except on remarriage, when she adopts her style from her husband. See *Wife of a younger son of a Duke or Marquess* (p. 49).

[1] See p. 29, note [1].
[2] See p. 39, note [2].

Former Wife of a Younger Son of a Duke or Marquess

She continues to be known by the same title she held on marriage, e.g. the former wife of Lord George Jones is still known as Lady George Jones.

If she has a courtesy style derived from her father, it is probable that she will revert to its use on dissolution of her marriage, e.g. Lady Mary Green formerly married to Lord George Black, will probably be known as Lady Mary Black.

Younger Son of an Earl

The style of 'The Honourable' is only used on the envelope in correspondence, in written descriptions or in formal documents. It is never used in conversation or on invitations or visiting cards, when the correct style is 'Mr.' or his ecclesiastical, Armed Forces rank, etc.

The more usual abbreviation is 'The Hon'. but the more old-fashioned form 'The Honble.' is sometimes used.

Sons of Earls by courtesy also have the same style as sons of Earls.

BEGINNING OF LETTER

Formal	(Dear) Sir[1]
Social	Dear Mr. Brown

ENDING OF LETTER

Formal	Yours faithfully (see also p. 2)
Social	Yours sincerely

ENVELOPE

Formal and Social	The Hon. John Brown

VERBAL ADDRESS

Mr. Brown (or appropriate rank, e.g. Major Brown).

DESCRIPTION IN CONVERSATION

Mr. Brown

[1] Strictly speaking, the commencement of 'Sir' is the very formal style, for which the corresponding conclusion is given on p. 3. This form of conclusion is now seldom used, and 'Sir' instead of the more usual 'Dear Sir' is sometimes adopted at the beginning of a very formal or official letter.

ECCLESIASTICAL, AMBASSADORIAL, OR ARMED FORCES RANK

These should precede his rank in correspondence, e.g.:
> The Reverend and Hon. John Brown
> His Excellency the Hon. John Brown
> Major the Hon. John Brown

Wife of a Younger Son of an Earl

The wife of a gentleman with the courtesy style of 'The Honourable' is known by her husband's christian name and surname, with the addition of 'Mrs'. as a prefix. Thus, the wife of 'The Hon. John Brown' is 'The Hon. Mrs. John Brown'.

If she is the daughter of a Duke, Marquess, or Earl, with the style of 'Lady' followed by her christian name, she continues to use this style with her husband's surname, i.e. Lady Mary Brown.

If she is the daughter of a Viscount or Baron, with the style of 'The Hon.', she does not use her husband's christian name, e.g. if The Hon. Jane White marries Mr. John Brown she is known as The Hon. Mrs. Brown. There is no difference in her style if her husband also has the style of 'The Honourable'.

'The Honourable' is *never* used in conversation, invitations, or visiting cards.

BEGINNING OF LETTER

Formal	(Dear) Madam
Social	Dear Mrs. Brown

ENDING OF LETTER

Formal	Yours faithfully (see also p. 2)
Social	Yours sincerely

ENVELOPE

Formal and Social	The Hon. Mrs. John Brown

VERBAL ADDRESS

> Mrs. Brown

DESCRIPTION IN CONVERSATION

> Mrs. Brown

Widow of a Younger Son of an Earl

There is no difference in the form of address in widowhood. Should she remarry, she adopts her style from her new husband. See *Wife of a Younger Son of an Earl* (p. 52).

Former Wife of a Younger Son of an Earl

There is no difference in the form of address on the dissolution of her marriage, but should she remarry, she adopts her style from her new husband. See *Wife of a Younger Son of an Earl* (p. 52).

Son of a Viscount or Baron

All the sons of a Viscount or Baron, and of those who by courtesy enjoy the style and title of Viscount or Baron, have the courtesy style of 'The Honourable'.

In all respects the forms of address are identical with those accorded to a *Younger Son of an Earl* (p. 51).

For the elder son of a Viscount or Baron, in the Peerage of Scotland, see *Scottish Title of Master* (p. 58).

Wife of a Son of a Viscount or Baron

There is no difference in the form of address from that of the wife of a younger son of an Earl. See *Wife of a Younger Son of an Earl* (p. 52).

Widow of a Son of a Viscount or Baron

There is no difference in her form of address as a widow from when her husband was alive, provided that she does not remarry. In this case she adopts her style from her new husband. See *Wife of a Younger Son of an Earl* (p. 52).

Former Wife of a Son of a Viscount or Baron

There is no difference in the form of address on the dissolution of her marriage, provided that she does not remarry. In this case, she adopts her style from her new husband. See *Wife of a Younger Son of an Earl* (p. 52).

Daughter of a Duke, Marquess or Earl

A daughter of a Duke, Marquess or Earl has the style of 'Lady' before her Christian name and surname: e.g. the eldest daughter of the Duke of Norfolk is Lady Tessa Balfour.

A daughter of those who by courtesy enjoy the title of a Marquess or Earl, has the identical style of 'Lady'.

On marriage she continues to use the same style, with her husband's surname, i.e. Lady Mary Brown marries Mr. John Black: she becomes Lady Mary Black. In no case does she drop from 'Lady Mary Brown' to 'The Hon. Mrs. Brown', even though her husband has this prefix.

Should she marry a peer she adopts his title, e.g. if 'Lady Mary Brown' marries the Earl of Flintshire, she becomes 'The Countess of Flintshire', even though his precedence is lower than hers.

If she marries a courtesy lord, and the precedence she derives from this is lower than that she derives from her father, she has the option of:

(a) adopting the usual style of the wife of a courtesy lord, e.g. Viscountess Molesey, *or*

(b) continuing her own style followed by the courtesy title, e.g. Lady Mary Molesey.

In practice very few ladies now adopt course (b) unless the marriage has been dissolved, as it is difficult therefrom to determine the relative degree of precedence. It was generally used a generation ago.

If she marries the younger son of a Duke or Marquess, who has the courtesy style of Lord John Jones, again she has the option of:

(a) adopting the usual style of the wife of a younger son of a Duke or Marquess, e.g. Lady John Jones, *or*

(b) continuing her own style followed by her surname, e.g. Lady Mary Jones.

BEGINNING OF LETTER

Formal	(Dear) Madam[1]
Social	Dear Lady Mary
	The surname may be added if the acquaintanceship is slight, e.g. Dear Lady Mary Jones

ENDING OF LETTER

Formal	Yours faithfully (see also p. 2)
Social	Yours sincerely

ENVELOPE

Formal and Social	Lady Mary Smith

VERBAL ADDRESS

Social	Lady Mary
Employee Status	My Lady *or* Your Ladyship[2]

DESCRIPTION IN CONVERSATION

Lady Mary.

If distinction is necessary, or on introduction, she is described as Lady Mary Smith. *Employee status,* 'Her Ladyship'.

LIST OF DIRECTORS AND PATRONS

Lady Mary Smith.

Daughter of a Viscount or Baron

A daughter of a Viscount or Baron, or of those who by courtesy use the style and title of a Viscount or Baron, bears the courtesy style of 'The Honourable'.

When she is unmarried this style is followed by her christian name (e.g. The Hon. Mary Brown[3]). After marriage she drops the use of her christian name and uses her surname only, following Mrs. (e.g. the Hon. Mrs. Smith). The style of 'The Honourable' is not used before 'Miss'.

[1] See p. 29, note [1].
[2] See p. 39, note [2].
[3] The alternative abbreviation of 'The Honble', now regarded as old-fashioned, may be used if preferred.

The style of 'The Hon.' is only used on an envelope, in written descriptions (usually only on the first mention) and in formal documents. It is never used in conversation, or on invitations or visiting cards where the correct style is 'Miss' or 'Mrs.'

A husband does not derive any style or title from his wife.

BEGINNING OF LETTER

Formal	(Dear) Madam[1]
Social	Dear Miss Brown *or*
	Dear Mrs. Brown (as applicable)

ENDING OF LETTER

Formal	Yours faithfully (see also p. 2)
Social	Yours sincerely

ENVELOPE

Formal and Social	The Hon. Mary Brown
	(unmarried ladies only)
	The Hon. Mrs. Brown

VERBAL ADDRESS

Miss Brown or Mrs. Brown (as applicable)

DESCRIPTION IN CONVERSATION

Miss Brown or Mrs. Brown (as applicable)

LIST OF DIRECTORS AND PATRONS

The Hon. Mary Brown (unmarried ladies only)
The Hon. Mrs. Brown

Brothers and Sisters of a Peer, whose Father did not live to succeed to a Peerage

The Queen may issue a Royal Warrant conferring on the brothers and/or sisters of a peer the style and precedence of the sons or daughters of a peer which would have been theirs had their father lived and succeeded to the peerage in question.

[1] See p. 29, note [1].

Disclaimed Peer

Under the Peerage Act of 1963, it is possible to disclaim an hereditary peerage of England, Scotland, Great Britain or the United Kingdom for life. The disclaimer is irrevocable, and operates from the date by which an instrument of disclaimer is delivered to the Lord Chancellor.

When a peerage has been disclaimed, no other *hereditary* peerage shall be conferred. Two examples of this have occurred. The second Viscount Hailsham disclaimed his hereditary peerages for life in 1963, in order to sit in the House of Commons. As the Rt. Hon. Quintin Hogg, he was elected as Member for St. Marylebone. In 1970 he was appointed Lord Chancellor and received the customary life peerage, becoming Lord Hailsham of St. Marylebone. Sir Alec Douglas Home, previously the 14th Earl of Home, was created Lord Home of the Hirsel (Life Peerage) in 1974. A life peerage cannot be disclaimed.

The principal provisions of the Peerage Act are summarized in DEBRETT.

As soon as a peer has disclaimed his peerage he reverts to the status held before he inherited the peerage, and he is not accorded any courtesy title or style which he previously possessed deriving from that peerage.

Even if he disclaims the peerage within a few days after succession he must first have succeeded as a peer immediately on his predecessor's death, and for that interval he will figure in the numbering in works of reference, e.g. 12th Earl of Flintshire.

Should he also be a baronet or knight, these dignities and appropriate styles are retained, being unaffected by his disclaiming the peerage.

EXAMPLES

> Victor E. P. Montagu, Esq.
> (previously the Earl of Sandwich)

> Sir Max Aitken, Bt., D.S.O., D.F.C.
> (previously the Lord Beaverbrook)

Wife of a Disclaimed Peer

Immediately her husband disclaims his peerage she reverts to the same style as her husband, e.g. if he becomes Mr. John Jones she becomes Mrs. John Jones.

If her husband is also a Baronet or has been knighted, she will use the title of 'Lady Jones'.

If she inherited any courtesy style from her father she may revert to its use, e.g. Lady Mary White marries Lord Blank who disclaims his peerage, and thereby becomes Mr. Blank. His wife may then revert to the style of Lady Mary Blank. The Hon. Mary White who marries Lord Blank similarly reverts to The Hon. Mrs. Blank.

Children of a Disclaimed Peer

The children of a disclaimed peer retain their precedence as the children of a peer, and any courtesy titles and styles borne while their father was a peer. It is open to any child of a disclaiming peer to say that he or she no longer wishes to be known by these styles, e.g. the children of Sir Max Aitken (previously Lord Beaverbrook) and Mr. Victor Montagu (previously the Earl of Sandwich) have retained such styles, but those of Dr. William Collier (previously Lord Monkswell), and Mr. Anthony Wedgwood Benn (previously Viscount Stansgate) have decided not to use them.

Scottish Title of Master

There are three kinds of Master, all of which are connected with the Peerage of Scotland, see p. 24.

They are:

1. The heir apparent (usually the eldest son) of a peer, or peeress in her own right.[1]

2. The heir presumptive of a peer, or a peeress in her own right.[1]

3. The son and heir of an heir apparent (as in 1 above), who bears a peerage by courtesy.

1. *Heir Apparent*

He bears the title of Master, which is a legal dignity in its own right. As such he was ineligible to sit in the old Scottish Parliament, or for a Scottish seat in the House of Commons at Westminster, but only for an English seat, until the law was amended in the late eighteenth century.

[1] For the meanings of heirs apparent and presumptive, see p. 43, note [1].

Generally the Master's designation is the same as the peerage title, having evolved to show whose heir he was, e.g. the son of Lady Sempill is the Master of Sempill. If the peer is known by more than one peerage or designation, e.g. Lord Belhaven and Stenton, his son and heir is known by the first designation, the Master of Belhaven. See also *Titles Borne by Scottish Peers and Masters* (p. 61).

As the eldest sons of the first three grades of peers (Dukes, Marquesses, and Earls) use courtesy titles, heirs apparent fall into two categories.

> (a) *Heir Apparent of a Duke, Marquess, Earl or a Countess in her own right*[1]—Though socially he is generally known by his courtesy title in the peerage, he is referred to by his substantive title of Master in all legal documents, commissions or proceedings in court, e.g. the son and heir of the Marquess of Lothian is referred to as 'Michael, Master of Lothian, commonly called Earl of Ancram'.

> (b) *Heir Apparent of a Viscount,*[2] *Lord or Lady of Parliament*[3] —The title of Master is borne both legally and socially.

2. Heir Presumptive

The heir presumptive of a peer of Scotland may bear the title of Master, which he gives up when he ceases to be heir to the peerage. One historic case was the heir presumptive to Lord Glamis. For two periods Sir Thomas Lyon was designated Master of Glamis, but he first gave up the title on the birth of his nephew. Later he became heir presumptive for eighteen years and was again Master of Glamis until his great-nephew was born.

If the heir presumptive is not a close relation of the peer, it is necessary for the Lord Lyon to approve his use of the title.

See also *Titles Borne by Scottish Peers and Masters* (p. 61).

3. Son and heir of the Heir Apparent who has a Peerage by Courtesy

The grandson of a peer of Scotland bears by courtesy the title of Master. In practice this usage is limited to an Earl's grandson, since a grandson of a Duke or Marquess is generally known by a courtesy title.

The Master's designation is usually the same as his father's courtesy title, since the title evolved to show whose heir he was. Thus when the Earl of Strathmore has a son and a grandson, the

[1] There is no Duchess or Marchioness in her own right in the Peerage of Scotland.
[2] There is no Viscountess in her own right in the Peerage of Scotland.
[3] For Lord of Parliament see pp. 33 and 90.

son and heir is Lord Glamis, and the latter's son and heir is the Master of Glamis. If the designation does not follow the usual practice it is by family arrangement and by the decision of the Lord Lyon. The following are exceptions to the general custom:

The Earl of Crawford (Chief of the Lindsays) is father of Lord Balniel. Prior to the succession in 1975 of Lord Balniel as 29th Earl of Crawford, his son and heir was the Master of Lindsay. In the lifetime of the Countess of Seafield, her son and heir was Viscount Reidhaven, and the latter's son and heir was the Master of Deskford.

See also *Titles Borne by Scottish Peers and Masters* (p. 61).

BEGINNING OF LETTER

If he is a peer by courtesy (see p. 44), otherwise as follows:

Formal	(Dear) Sir[1]
Social	Dear Master of Glamis

ENDING OF LETTER

Formal	Yours faithfully (see also p. 2)
Social	Yours sincerely

ENVELOPE

The Master of Glamis
Major the Master of Glamis

VERBAL ADDRESS

Formal	
Social	} Master
Employee Status	

DESCRIPTION IN CONVERSATION

The Master
If distinction is necessary, or on introduction:
The Master of Glamis

SIGNATURE

Thomas, Master of Glamis

WIFE OF MASTER

The wife of a Master is called by the appropriate peerage style, if applicable. The wife of the Master of Rollo is known as the Hon. Mrs. David Rollo. If a Master, as heir presumptive to a peer, has no alternative peerage style, then as Mrs. John Blank.

[1] See p. 51. note [1].

MISTRESS

When the Mastership is held by a woman the official designation is 'Mistress of Blank' (e.g. Mistress of Mar). For obvious reasons the style is not much in favour among ladies nowadays, and is seldom used.

TITLES BORNE BY SCOTTISH PEERS AND MASTERS

The Scots Parliament ruled that a peer who belonged to a cadet (younger) branch of a family must not use his *surname only* for his peerage, as this is restricted to the chief of the whole name, consequently he must be Lord Blank 'of' somewhere to distinguish him. There are several examples in the peerage, e.g. Lord Hay of Yester, a title of the Marquess of Tweeddale, and Lord Forrester of Corstorphine, a title of the Earl of Verulam. Today this rule still applies for United Kingdom peerages. Even though the chief is not a peer, someone else of his name cannot use the undifferenced name for his title. Thus when Lord Mackintosh of Halifax was created a peer in 1948, he could not be styled Lord Mackintosh alone, as he was not Chief of Clan Mackintosh.

Masters who belong to cadet (younger) branches may not use only that part of their father's titles which is identical to the surname. In this category is Lord Balfour of Burleigh, who is not the Chief of the Balfours. (In fact he is not a Balfour at all, as the peerage passed through the female line.) Consequently when his heir was a male he was the Master of Burleigh and not the Master of Balfour.

During the seventeenth century the Earl of Roxburghe (forebear of the Duke) and then Chief of the Kers, obtained a pronouncement in Parliament that his heir apparent alone was to be known as Lord Ker. The Earl of Lothian's heir, a Ker cadet, was to be known in distinction as Lord Ker of Newbottle. (Subsequently the Marquess of Lothian succeeded as Chief of the Kerrs (and Kers), the Dukes of Roxburghe having become Chiefs of the Innes family.)

These lengthy titles became abbreviated for ordinary purposes, and the peer came only to use the latter part of his title. Thus Lord Ker of Newbottle became known as Lord Newbottle. Today the heir apparent of the Earl of Wemyss (who is also Lord Douglas of Neidpath) is known as Lord Neidpath. An exception is Lord Balfour of Burleigh. He is not known as Lord Burleigh, to save confusion with the English peerage of Lord Burghley, borne by the Marquess of Exeter and usually adopted as the courtesy title for his heir apparent.

Summary of Titles

PEER, BARONET, KNIGHT AND DAME

As the terms of address for a peer, peeress and their children *and* a baronet and knight and their wives are complicated, the titles and styles are summarized below, with a few general notes. For full information, see the appropriate title or style.

	Husband	Wife	Eldest Son	Other Sons	Daughters
Peer	The Duke of Blank	The Duchess of Blank	Courtesy peerage title	Lord John Brown	Lady Mary Brown
	The Marquess of Little-hampton	The March-ioness of Littlehampton	Courtesy peerage title	Lord John Smith	Lady Mary Smith
	The Earl of Worthing	The Countess of Worthing	Courtesy peerage title	The Hon. John Robinson	Lady Mary Robinson
	The Viscount Angmering	The Viscount-ess Angmering	The Hon. John Green	The Hon. John Green	The Hon. Mary Green
	The Lord Ferring	The Lady Ferring	The Hon. John Grey	The Hon. John Grey	The Hon. Mary Grey
Baronet	Sir John Findon, Bt.	Lady Findon	Untitled	Untitled	Untitled
Knight	Sir John Black	Lady Black	Untitled	Untitled	Untitled
Dame	Untitled	Dame Mary	Untitled	Untitled	Untitled

CORRESPONDENCE

In social correspondence a peer or peeress is addressed with the prefix of 'The' before the title, as in the table above.[1]

In formal correspondence the following styles are adopted:

His Grace the Duke of . . .

Her Grace the Duchess of . . .

The Most Hon. the Marquess (of) . . .

The Most Hon. the Marchioness (of) . . .

The Rt. Hon. the Earl (of) . . .

The Rt. Hon. the Countess (of) . . .

The Rt. Hon. the Viscount . . .

The Rt. Hon. the Viscountess. . .

The Rt. Hon. the Lord . . .

The Rt. Hon. the Lady . . .

(A Peeress in her own right may prefer the style of The Rt. Hon. the Baroness . . .)

[1] It is optional whether the initial "T" of 'The' is written with a capital or small letter when preceded by another word, with the exception of The Queen and Queen Elizabeth The Queen Mother when the capital "T" must be used.

Neither series of prefixes ('The Most Hon.' or 'The Rt. Hon.') are accorded to those who by courtesy are known by a peerage title or style.

For Baronets, Knights, their wives and Dames, see these Sections.

VERBAL ADDRESS

A Duke or Duchess is always known by his or her exact title. Other peers, peeresses and those who by courtesy are known by a peerage title are referred to as Lord and Lady Blank. For Baronets, Knights, their wives and Dames, see these Sections.

COURTESY LORD

He assumes by courtesy the title of a peerage usually the second in rank held by the peer, but which must be of a lesser grade than that used by the peer, i.e. the eldest son of a Marquess may be styled Earl, Viscount, or Baron.

The eldest son of a courtesy lord of the rank of Marquess or Earl also assumes a courtesy title. This is usually the third in rank held by the peer, but of necessity of a grade junior to his father's.

They are treated socially as if they were peers, but in correspondence see below.

PEERESS IN HER OWN RIGHT

She is styled as for the wife of a peer, but a Baroness sometimes prefers to use that title instead of 'The Lady . . .'.

Her children have the same style as that accorded to the children of a peer of equivalent rank.

LIFE PEER OR PEERESS

He or she is addressed identically as an hereditary peer or peeress.

The children have the same style as those of an hereditary peer or peeress.

MARRIED DAUGHTERS OF A PEER

They take their husband's surname, e.g. Lady Mary Blank or The Hon. Mrs. Scarlet, unless they marry a peer or courtesy lord. See the appropriate section for a possible exception in the latter case.

WIDOW OF A PEER

She is known either as (a) The Dowager Countess of Worthing or appropriate rank (which is the official style), or (b) Mary, Countess of Worthing, which is usually adopted. She does not have the first option if a Dowager Countess of Worthing is still living. On remarriage she loses any title derived from her late husband.

WIDOW OF A BARONET

She is known either as (a) Dowager Lady Findon, or (b) Mary, Lady Findon, with the same proviso as for the widow of a peer. On remarriage she loses any style derived from her late husband (see p. 70).

WIDOW OF A KNIGHT

She retains the same style as a knight's wife (see pp. 76-77).

FORMER WIFE OF A PEER OR BARONET

She has the style of Mary, Countess of Worthing or Mary, Lady Brown, but on remarriage she loses any title or style derived from her former husband (see pp. 31, 41 and 71).

FORMER WIFE OF A KNIGHT

She retains the same style as a knight's wife, but on remarriage she loses such style derived from her former husband (see p. 78).

Part III

OTHER TITLES AND STYLES

Baronet, Baronetess, Baronet's wife, widow, and former wife

Widows of those who would have succeeded to a Baronetcy had their husbands survived

Knight, his wife, widow, and former wife

Dame

The Privy Council

Members of the Orders of Chivalry below the rank of Knight, and recipients of Decorations and Medals conferred by the Crown

Untitled gentleman, married and unmarried lady

Scottish titles and territorial designations

Irish Chieftainries and other Irish titles

Position of letters after the name

The Aga Khan, and the Maltese and Canadian Nobility

OTHER TITLES AND STYLES

Baronet

A baronetcy is an hereditary dignity the holder of which is accorded the prefix of 'Sir' and the suffix of 'Baronet' to his name. The suffix is invariably abbreviated in correspondence. Usually 'Bt.' but the more old-fashioned 'Bart.' is sometimes preferred.

Scottish baronets sometimes use their territorial titles in conjunction with their surnames. In this case, 'Bt.' should appear at the end, e.g. Sir John Macmillan of Lochmillan, Bt. See *Scottish Titles and Territorial Designations*, p. 90.

For summary of titles, see p. 62.

BEGINNING OF LETTER

Formal	(Dear) Sir[1]
Social	Dear Sir John
	If the acquaintanceship is slight, the surname may be used in addition, e.g. Dear Sir John Brown

ENDING OF LETTER

Formal	Yours faithfully (see also p. 2)
Social	Yours sincerely

ENVELOPE

Formal and Social	Sir John Brown, Bt.

[1] See p. 51, note [1].

VERBAL ADDRESS

Formal and Social   Sir John
Employee Status   Sir John

DESCRIPTION IN CONVERSATION

    Sir John

If distinction is necessary, or on introduction, he is described as Sir John Brown. *Employee Status,* 'Sir John'.

PRIVY COUNSELLOR

    The Rt. Hon. Sir John Brown, Bt.

    It is unnecessary to add the letters P.C. since "The Rt. Hon·" is sufficient indication. See also *Privy Counsellor*, p. 80.

ECCLESIASTICAL, AMBASSADORIAL, OR ARMED FORCES RANK

These should precede 'Sir':

    His Excellency Sir John Brown, Bt.
    The Hon. Sir John Brown, Bt.
    The Rev. Sir John Brown, Bt.[1]
    Major Sir John Brown, Bt.

    All other letters after the name *follow* 'Bt.':

    Lt.-Gen. Sir John Brown, Bt., K.C.B., C.B.E., D.S.O.
    The Reverend Sir John Brown, Bt., D.C.L.

SIGNATURE

    John Brown

STYLE FROM SOURCES OTHER THAN THE CROWN

It is not customary in *formal* usage to combine styles emanating from other sources with titles conferred by the Sovereign. Alderman Sir John Smith and Professor Sir William Brown are solecisms. In *social* usage this is not uncommon, though deprecated by purists.

Baronetess

When a lady inherits a baronetcy she is known as a Baronetess, with the official style of 'Dame Mary Brown, Btss.'.

    Although a few baronetesses were created in the past, there is now only one lady on the Roll of the Baronets. Few baronetcies

---

[1] A Church of England clergyman who is a Baronet is styled 'Sir', whereas if a knighthood is conferred upon him he does not receive the accolade.

still in existence, all of them Scottish, can be inherited in the female line. Succession to a baronetcy follows the remainders specified in the letters patent of creation.

The form of address is the same as for a Baronet's Wife, with the exception of the envelope, which is addressed as follows:

Lady Dunbar of Hempriggs, Btss.

Wife of a Baronet

The wife of a baronet has the style of 'Lady' before her surname. The old-fashioned style of 'Dame', followed by her christian names and surname (e.g. Dame Edith Brown) is no longer in general use, but is retained for legal documents. It is useful for these purposes in that it allows for the identification of a particular Lady Brown by the use of her christian names. An alternative *legal* style is for the christian names to be placed before 'Lady'. See p. 9. For *correspondence,* where confusion with others of the same surname could arise, 'Lady' may be followed by the christian name in brackets, as mentioned below (under *Envelope*). This form is often used in publications.

If a baronet's wife has a courtesy style of Lady Mary, this is used in full, e.g. Lady Mary Brown.

If she has the courtesy style of 'The Honourable' this precedes 'Lady Brown', e.g. The Hon. Lady Brown.

The wife of a Scottish baronet who uses his territorial designation should be so addressed, e.g. Lady Macmillan of Lochmillan.

BEGINNING OF LETTER

Formal	(Dear) Madam[1]
Social	Dear Lady Brown[2]

ENDING OF LETTER

Formal	Yours faithfully (see also p. 2)
Social	Yours sincerely

ENVELOPE

Formal and Social   Lady Brown

If it is necessary to distinguish the wife of a particular baronet from another with the same title and surname, such as at an hotel or conference, the christian name may be added in brackets,

[1] See p. 29, note [1].
[2] This is the feminine equivalent for both Dear Sir John Brown, and Dear Sir John.

e.g. Lady (Edith) Brown. This form should only be used in special circumstances.

VERBAL ADDRESS

Social	Lady Brown
Employee Status	My Lady *or* Your Ladyship[1]

DESCRIPTION IN CONVERSATION

Social	Lady Brown
Employee Status	Her Ladyship

Widow of a Baronet

Officially the widow of a baronet immediately becomes the Dowager Lady Brown on the death of her husband, unless the widow of a senior baronet of the same creation is still alive, when she becomes Mary, Lady Brown.

Many dowager ladies prefer to use their christian name rather than the word 'Dowager', so the wishes of the lady concerned should be ascertained. If in doubt, I recommend the style of 'Mary, Lady Brown', which the majority prefer.

Should she remarry, she takes her style from her present husband.

By custom, when the present baronet is unmarried, the widow of the late baronet continues to call herself Lady Blank, the same style as when her husband was living. Should the present baronet marry, it is usual for the widow of the baronet to announce the style by which she wishes to be known, i.e. 'Dowager Lady Brown' or 'Mary, Lady Brown'.

The widow of a Scottish baronet who uses his territorial title should be so described, e.g. Dowager Lady Macmillan of Lochmillan, or Mary, Lady Macmillan of Lochmillan.

BEGINNING OF LETTER

Formal	(Dear) Madam[2]
Social	Dear Lady Brown

ENDING OF LETTER

Formal	Yours faithfully (see also p. 2)
Social	Yours sincerely

[1] See p. 39, note [2].
[2] See p. 29, note [1].

ENVELOPE

Formal and Social   Dowager Lady Brown *or*
Mary, Lady Brown

The word 'The' should not be included as a prefix as this would imply that the lady was a Peeress.

VERBAL ADDRESS

Social   Lady Brown

Employee Status   My Lady *or* Your Ladyship[1]

DESCRIPTION IN CONVERSATION

Social, Lady Brown. If distinction is necessary, or on introduction, she should be described as Mary, Lady Brown.

Employee Status   Her Ladyship

Former wife of a Baronet

See *Widow of a Baronet* (p. 70).

She is addressed as the widow of a Baronet with the style Mary, Lady Brown, provided that she does not remarry.

Widows of those who would have succeeded to a Baronetcy had their husbands survived

The Queen may issue a Royal Warrant by which the lady concerned may enjoy the same title, rank, place, pre-eminence, and precedence as if her late husband had survived and succeeded to the title.

This privilege is usually only granted when her late husband died on active service.

Children of a Baronet

They do not have any special style, but follow the rules for addressing untitled ladies or gentlemen. Children who are or have been adopted are not in line of succession to a baronetcy by reason of such adoption.

[1] See p. 39, note [2].

Knight

The dignity of knighthood is the one which is most frequently conferred. It carries the prefix of 'Sir', but unlike a baronetcy it is only held for life.

The recipient is allowed to use this prefix and also the appropriate letters for those of Orders of Chivalry (see p. 74) from the date of the announcement in the 'London Gazette': he does not wait for the accolade to be conferred upon him.

There are two kinds of knighthood conferred by the Sovereign: (1) Knights of the various Orders of Chivalry, identified by the appropriate letters after the name, see below, page 74; and (2) Knights Bachelor, which in ordinary correspondence, carry no letters after the name (see page 75).

For summary of titles, see p. 62.

BEGINNING OF LETTER

Formal	(Dear) Sir[1]
Social	Dear Sir John
	If the acquaintanceship is slight, the surname may be used, e.g. Dear Sir John Smith.

ENDING OF LETTER

Formal	Yours faithfully (see also p. 2)
Social	Yours sincerely

ENVELOPE

Formal and Social	Sir John Smith (with the appropriate letters after his name).

VERBAL ADDRESS

Formal and Social	Sir John
Employee Status	Sir John

DESCRIPTION IN CONVERSATION

Sir John. If distinction is necessary, or on introduction, he is described as Sir John Smith. *Employee Status*, 'Sir John'.

MEMBERSHIP OF THE PRIVY COUNCIL

The Rt. Hon. Sir John Smith.

[1] See p. 51, note [1].

It is unnecessary to add the letters P.C., since 'The Rt. Hon' is sufficient indication. See also *Privy Counsellor*, p. 80.

ECCLESIASTICAL, AMBASSADORIAL, OR ARMED FORCES RANK

These precede 'Sir'.

> The Hon. Sir John Brown, K.C.B.
> His Excellency Sir John Brown, K.C.M.G.
> Major Sir John Brown

A clergyman of the Church of England, if appointed a knight of one of the Orders of Chivalry, does not receive the accolade, and is thus not accorded the prefix '*Sir*' before his name but he places the appropriate letters of the Order of Chivalry concerned after his name, e.g.:

> The Rt. Rev. the Lord Bishop of Sevenoaks, K.C.V.O.

Clergy of other Churches may receive the accolade and thus use 'Sir'.

If a Knight of an Order of Chivalry is subsequently ordained a clergyman of the Church of England, he has no need to relinquish the prefix of 'Sir', e.g. The Rev. Sir (George) Herbert Andrew, K.C.M.G., C.B.

SIGNATURE

> John Smith

A PEER WHO RECEIVES A KNIGHTHOOD OF AN ORDER OF CHIVALRY

He adds the appropriate letters of the Order after his name, e.g.:

> The Viscount Angmering, K.C.V.O.

STYLE FROM SOURCES OTHER THAN THE CROWN

It is not customary in *formal* usage to combine the style emanating from other sources with titles conferred by the Sovereign. Alderman Sir William Brown and Professor Sir Edward Hailstorm are solecisms. In social usage this is not uncommon, though deprecated by purists.

HONORARY KNIGHTHOOD

When a foreign national receives an honorary knighthood of an Order of Chivalry, he is not entitled to prefix 'Sir' before his name, but he may place the appropriate letters after his name, e.g. General Omar Vanderbilt, K.C.B. Should he subsequently become a naturalised British subject, he will be entitled to receive the accolade. Having become a full knight of the appropriate Order, he will then use 'Sir' before his name.

1. KNIGHTS OF THE ORDERS OF CHIVALRY

The two senior Orders of Chivalry are very exclusive. Unlike the other Orders (see below), they consist of one class only. They carry the following letters after the name:

Knight of the Garter	K.G.[1]
Knight of the Thistle	K.T.

The remaining Orders of Chivalry consist of several classes of which the first two carry Knighthoods, viz.:

Class 1—Knight Grand Cross or Knight Grand Commander

Class 2—Knight Commander

The appropriate letters for the various Orders of Chivalry are as follows in order of precedence:

	Knight Grand Cross or Knight Grand Commander	*Knight Commander*
Order of the Bath	G.C.B.	K.C.B.
Order of the Star of India[2]	G.C.S.I.	K.C.S.I.
Order of St. Michael & St. George	G.C.M.G.	K.C.M.G.
Order of the Indian Empire[2]	G.C.I.E.	K.C.I.E.
Royal Victorian Order	G.C.V.O.	K.C.V.O.
Order of the British Empire	G.B.E.	K.B.E.

For lower classes of the Orders of Chivalry which do *not* carry Knighthoods, see *Members of the Orders of Chivalry below the rank of Knight* (p. 82).

There is no difference in the form of address of a Knight Grand Cross (or Knight Grand Commander) and a Knight Commander. In both cases the appropriate letters are placed after the names.

Should a knight be promoted within the same Order, he ceases to use the appropriate titles of his lower rank, e.g. if General Sir John Brown, K.C.B. is raised to a G.C.B. he becomes General Sir John Brown G.C.B.

[1] Ladies of this Order do not have any letters after their names. L.G. is incorrect.
[2] No appointments have been made since 1947, but there are several surviving Knights of these Orders.

The same applies to a knight of an Order of Chivalry who previously belonged to the same Order, but of a class which did not carry a knighthood. Thus Colonel John Brown, C.B. on promotion to a K.C.B. becomes Colonel Sir John Brown, K.C.B. and henceforward drops the C.B.

When a knight receives more than one Order of the same class, the letters appear in order of precedence of the Orders concerned, and *not* according to the date he received them, e.g. a Knight Grand Cross of the Bath, the Royal Victorian Order and the British Empire, is addressed as follows:

Field Marshal Sir John Brown, G.C.B., G.C.V.O., G.B.E.

When a knight receives more than one Order of a different class, the higher grade of a junior Order is placed before the lower grade of a senior Order, e.g.:

Lt. Gen. Sir John Brown, G.B.E., K.C.M.G., C.B., C.V.O.

Where a knight has received several Orders of Chivalry, *all* the appropriate letters must be included after his name in correspondence. The style 'etc, etc.' after the first letters mentioned is a slight both to the individual and to the Orders concerned. It is, however, permissible in *social* correspondence with a K.G. or K.T. to omit other letters after the name.

An honorary Knight of an Order of Chivalry uses the appropriate letters after his name, but without the prefix 'Sir' because he is not eligible to receive the accolade.

2. KNIGHT BACHELOR

In legal and official documents 'Knight' may be added after the name of a Knight Bachelor. Otherwise neither 'Knight', nor 'Kt', nor 'K.B.' should be added. (Note. 'K.B.' signified a Knight of the Bath before the Order was reorganized into three classes in 1815, e.g. after the battle of Cape St. Vincent in 1797 Commodore Horatio Nelson became Rear-Admiral Sir Horatio Nelson, K.B.). See *Legal Documents* (pp. 8–9.)

Knighthood does not affect the use of letters already borne, e.g. if a *Mr.* John Brown, C.B., C.V.O., O.B.E. is created a Knight Bachelor, he becomes *Sir* John Brown, C.B., C.V.O., O.B.E.

PRECEDENCE OF LETTERS[1]

Victoria Cross[2]	V.C.
George Cross[2]	G.C.

[1] This is not always identical with the precedence to which the person is entitled, e.g. no precedence has been accorded to holders of the Victoria Cross. For *Precedence* see Part V.
[2] Does not confer a Knighthood upon recipient.

Knight of the Garter	K.G.
Knight of the Thistle	K.T.
Knight Grand Cross of the Order of the Bath	G.C.B.
Order of Merit[1]	O.M.
Knight Grand Commander of the Star of India[2]	G.C.S.I.
Knight Grand Cross of the Order of St. Michael and St. George	G.C.M.G.
Knight Grand Commander of the Indian Empire[2]	G.C.I.E.
Knight Commander of the Royal Victorian Order	K.C.V.O.
Knight Grand Cross of the Royal Victorian Order	G.C.V.O.
Knight Grand Cross of the British Empire	G.B.E.
Companion of Honour[1]	C.H.
Knight Commander of the Bath	K.C.B.
Knight Commander of the Star of India[2]	K.C.S.I.
Knight Commander of St. Michael and St. George	K.C.M.G.
Knight Commander of the Indian Empire[2]	K.C.I.E.
Knight Commander of the Royal Victorian Order	K.C.V.O.
Knight Commander of the British Empire	K.B.E.

(Then follow letters below the rank of knight, commencing with C.B.);[3] see also *Dame*, p. 78, and *Members of the Orders of Chivalry below the rank of Knight* (p. 82).

Wife of a Knight

The wife of a knight is known as 'Lady', followed by her surname, and she is addressed as is the wife of a baronet.

The old-fashioned style of 'Dame' followed by christian name and surname, e.g. Dame Edith Brown is no longer in general use, but is retained for legal documents. It is useful for this purpose because it allows for the identification of the particular Lady Brown by the use of her christian names. An alternative *legal* style is for her christian names to be placed *before* 'Lady'. For *correspondence*, where confusion with others of the same surname could arise, 'Lady' may be followed by the christian

[1] Does not confer a Knighthood upon recipient.
[2] No longer conferred.
[3] Letters which signify membership of The Most Venerable Order of the Hospital of St. John of Jerusalem do not appear after the name. Bailiffs and Knights of Justice and of Grace do not receive the accolade.

name in brackets. This form is often used in publications. See *Envelope*. She should never be styled Lady Barbara Brown, unless the daughter of a Duke, Marquess or Earl.

If a knight's wife has the courtesy style of 'Lady Mary', this is used in full, e.g. Lady Mary Smith.

If a knight or the wife of a knight has the courtesy style of 'The Honourable', this style precedes 'Lady Smith', e.g. The Hon. Lady Smith.

The wife of a Church of England clergyman who receives a knighthood but is not eligible to receive the accolade continues to be addressed as Mrs. John Smith, but she has the precedence of a Knight's wife.

The wife of an honorary knight continues to be addressed as Mrs. John Braun.

BEGINNING OF LETTER

Formal	(Dear) Madam[1]
Social	Dear Lady Brown[2]

ENDING OF LETTER

Formal	Yours faithfully (see also p. 2)
Social	Yours sincerely

ENVELOPE

Formal and Social	Lady Brown

Note: Where there may be more than one lady of the same title and surname, such as at an hotel or conference, the christian name may be added in brackets, e.g. Lady (Edith) Brown. This form should, however, *only* be used in special circumstances.

VERBAL ADDRESS

Formal and Social	Lady Brown
Employee Status	My Lady or Your Ladyship[1]

DESCRIPTION IN CONVERSATION

Social	Lady Brown
Employee Status	Her Ladyship

Widow of a Knight

She is addressed as the wife of a knight, provided that she does not remarry, when she will take her style from her present husband.

[1] See p. 29, note [1].
[2] This is the feminine equivalent for both 'Dear Sir John' and Dear Sir John Brown'.

Former wife of a Knight

She is addressed as the wife of a knight, provided that she does not remarry, when she will take her style from her present husband.

Children of a Knight

They do not have any special style, but follow the rules for addressing untitled ladies and gentlemen.

Dame

A Dame is the feminine equivalent of a knight of an Order of Chivalry. Similarly, the title is always used in conjunction with the christian name. For the legal use of 'Dame' see also p. 9.

The recipient is allowed to use the prefix and appropriate letters from the date of the announcement in the 'London Gazette'.

Dames are appointed to the following Orders of Chivalry, and as for knights, there are two classes:

	Dame Grand Cross	Dame Commander
Order of the Bath	G.C.B.	D.C.B.
Order of St. Michael and St. George	G.C.M.G.	D.C.M.G.
Royal Victorian Order	G.C.V.O.	D.C.V.O.
Order of the British Empire	G.B.E.	D.B.E.

The rule for promotion in the same Order of Chivalry and the precedence of the Orders applies as for a knight.[1]

A peeress (including holders of a peerage title by courtesy) who is appointed a dame adds the appropriate letters after her name, e.g. The Countess of Dorking, D.C.V.O. The daughter of a Duke, Marquess, or Earl, with the style Lady Mary Brown, adds the appropriate letters after her name, e.g. Lady Mary Brown, D.B.E.

As a dame, the wife *or* widow of a baronet or knight is usually known as Dame Irene Smith, D.B.E., but a few ladies prefer to continue their former style of Lady Smith, D.B.E. (as did Baroness Spencer-Churchill when Lady Churchill). She should be addressed as Dame Irene Smith, D.B.E., unless her preference for the latter style is known.

---

[1] Letters which signify membership of The Most Venerable Order of the Hospital of St. John of Jerusalem are not included after the name. Dames Grand Cross and Dames of Justice and of Grace do not bear the title of 'Dame' before the name.

A lady styled 'The Hon.' is addressed 'The Hon. Dame Mary Jones, D.B.E.'. As a dame is the feminine equivalent of a knight, the style of 'Mrs.' is incorrect. An exception is The Princess Anne who, though a G.C.V.O., is addressed as 'H.R.H. the Princess Anne, *Mrs*. Mark Phillips'.

A husband does not derive any style or title from his wife.

When a dame of an Order of Chivalry is gazetted by her professional, rather than her legal, name she usually prefers to be so addressed, e.g. Dame Margot Fonteyn, D.B.E.

When a dame is the wife or widow of a knight, she generally prefers to separate the honour acquired in her own right from that derived from her husband; e.g., when Miss Daphne du Maurier (widow of Sir Frederick Browning) was raised to the rank of a Dame of the British Empire, she chose to be addressed either as Lady Browning, D.B.E., or Dame Daphne du Maurier, D.B.E.

For summary of titles, see p. 62.

BEGINNING OF LETTER

Formal	(Dear) Madam
Social	Dear Dame Mary
	When the acquaintanceship is slight, the surname may be used, e.g. Dear Dame Mary Smith

ENDING OF LETTER

Formal	Yours faithfully (see also p. 2)
Social	Yours sincerely

ENVELOPE

Formal and Social	Dame Mary Smith, D.B.E. (or applicable Order)

VERBAL ADDRESS

Social	Dame Mary
Employee Status	Dame Mary

DESCRIPTION IN CONVERSATION

Dame Mary. When distinction is necessary, or on introduction, she is described as Dame Mary Smith.

Children of a Dame

They do not have any special style, but follow the rule for addressing untitled ladies and gentlemen.

The Privy Council

The Privy Council is the ancient executive governing body of the United Kingdom presided over by the Sovereign and exercises many functions, some of which have been entrusted to it by Acts of Parliament, which may be legislative, administrative or judicial. Its decisions are usually embodied in Orders in Council or Proclamations.

Membership is for life, with the style of 'Right Honourable'. Privy Counsellors are appointed by the Crown from persons distinguished in various walks of public life, at home and in the Commonwealth, including some members of the Royal Family, the Archbishops of Canterbury and York, the Bishop of London, the Lord Chancellor, many members of the Judiciary such as Lords of Appeal, all Cabinet Ministers, and some overseas Prime Ministers. The Lord President of the Council is usually a senior member of the Cabinet.

A full Council is now only assembled for the Accession of a new Sovereign, and a member does not attend any Council unless specially summoned. Those summoned are generally, though not invariably, members of the Government. A routine Council meeting is usually held at Buckingham Palace by the Sovereign (or, in Her absence abroad, by Counsellors of State), and must be attended by at least three Privy Counsellors and the Clerk of the Council.

The Cabinet owes its origin to the Privy Council, of which it was 'an inner Council' or committee.

Much of the work of the Privy Council is done in committee, of which the most important is the Judicial Committee, the final Court of Appeal outside the United Kingdom (where the House of Lords is the Supreme Court of Appeal), though certain Commonwealth countries have abolished appeals to the Privy Council (e.g. Canada and India) and established instead their own Supreme Courts of Appeal. The Queen does not preside at meetings of committees of the Privy Council.

PRIVY COUNSELLOR

The spelling *Privy Councillor* is also used, but as the Privy Council Office prefer the above spelling it has been adopted throughout this book.

The letters P.C. follow *all* honours and decorations awarded by the Crown. This is because membership of the Privy Council is an appointment or office held rather than an honour conferred.[1]

By precedence a Privy Counsellor immediately follows a Knight of the Garter or the Thistle (in Scotland), and the letters P.C. are often *incorrectly* given next position after K.G. or K.T. The position of letters after the name is not always identical with precedence, e.g. V.C. is given first place by Royal Warrant, though such precedence has not been accorded.

BEGINNING OF LETTER

Formal and Social	There is no special form used when writing to a member of the Privy Council e.g.
Formal	My Lord, (Dear) Sir,[2] (Dear) Madam[3]
Social	Dear Lord Blank, Dear Lady Blank, Dear Mr. Blank, Dear Mrs. Blank, Dear Miss Blank.

ENDING OF LETTER

Formal	Yours faithfully (see also p. 2)
Social	Yours sincerely.

ENVELOPE

Peer or Peeress

He (or she) is addressed according to his (or her) peerage rank, with the letters P.C. after the title and Orders conferred.

Formal	The Rt. Hon. the Earl of Dorking, K.C.V.O., P.C.
Social	The Earl of Dorking, P.C.
Social	The Baroness Jones, P.C.

Others

'The Rt. Hon.' is always placed before the name both in formal and social usage. There is no need to add the letters P.C. after the

[1] Valentine Heywood, in his *British Titles*, 1951, points out that there are many offices which give precedence. 'You may put a man's offices before, or after, his name and style, but you cannot put them in the middle of it. You cannot say "The Right Hon. Winston Spencer-Churchill, Prime Minister, C.H." You must say either "Prime Minister—The Right Hon. Winston Spencer-Churchill, C.H." or "The Right Honourable Winston Spencer-Churchill, C.H., Prime Minister" . . . although the office of Prime Minister gives precedence above C.H. Nor does it in any way alter this, if, on the analogy of the P.C., you abbreviate Prime Minister into P.M.' When Garter King of Arms proclaimed the styles of the Duke of Connaught at his funeral, after reciting fully his styles, he ended 'One of His Majesty's Most Honourable Privy Council, Field-Marshal in the Army.'
[2] See p. 51, note [1].
[3] See p. 29, note [1].

name, since 'The Rt. Hon.' is sufficient indication of membership of the Privy Council.

Other ranks such as ecclesiastical, ambassadorial, Armed Forces, etc., precede 'The Rt. Hon.'. (See below.)

Ladies who are Privy Counsellors drop the use of 'Miss' or 'Mrs.'.

Examples

The Rt. Hon. Sir John Smith, M.P.

Lt. Col. the Rt. Hon. John Jones

The Rt. Hon. Barbara Castle, M.P.

The Rt. Rev. and Rt. Hon. the Lord Bishop of London

His Excellency the Rt. Hon. Sir Christopher Smith.

VERBAL ADDRESS

Membership of the Privy Council does not affect verbal address in any way. A peer, peeress, baronet, knight, or an untitled lady or gentleman is addressed as any other person of the same rank who is not a Privy Counsellor, i.e. Lord Blank, Lady Blank, Admiral Blank, Mr. Blank, Mrs. Blank, or Miss Blank.

DESCRIPTION IN CONVERSATION

Membership of the Privy Council does not affect description in any way. The Rt. Hon. Sir John Smith is known as 'Sir John Smith', Lt. Col. the Rt. Hon. John Jones as 'Colonel Jones' and the Rt. Hon. Barbara Castle, M.P. as 'Mrs. Castle'.

WIFE (OR HUSBAND) OF PRIVY COUNSELLOR

They acquire no style or title.

Members of the Orders of Chivalry below the rank of Knight, and recipients of Decorations and Medals conferred by the Crown

They are addressed according to their rank, with the appropriate letters after their name in order of precedence. The use of all these letters is obligatory, e.g. John Brown, Esq., C.B.E., M.V.O., T.D.

The recipient is allowed to use the appropriate letters for the Order from the date of announcement in the 'London Gazette'.

Those promoted within the same Order of Chivalry do not continue to show the letters of the lower class of that Order, e.g. if Brigadier John Smith, O.B.E., is promoted to C.B.E. he is addressed as Brigadier John Smith, C.B.E., the O.B.E. being dropped.

Precedence of letters

The full list of honours and awards in order of precedence *of letters* is given below. A baronet has the letters Bt. or Bart. immediately after the name, and before any letters which signify honours. See *Baronet* p. 67.

It should be noted that V.C. and G.C. have precedence over *all* letters signifying Orders (including knightly grades therein), Decorations and Medals.

The Order of Merit (O.M.) and Companion of Honour (C.H.) are important honours which bestow no title on the holder. The letters O.M. follow G.C.B., and C.H. follow G.B.E.

For membership of The Most Venerable Order of the Hospital of St. John of Jerusalem, see p. 76, note [3] and p. 78, note [1].

Precedence of letters signifying Orders, Decorations and Medals

The following is the list of Orders, etc., conferred by the Crown below the rank of knight, in order of precedence of letters. See p. 86 for The Order of Canada, The Order of Australia, and the Queen's Service Order of New Zealand.

The placing of the letters M.V.O. depends upon whether of fourth or fifth class, both of which have identical letters, see below.

Victoria Cross	V.C.	(precedes all letters including knights)
George Cross[1]	G.C.	(after V.C., but precedes all other letters, including knights)
Order of Merit	O.M.	(follows G.C.B. see *Knightage*, p. 76)
Order of Victoria and Albert[2,3]	V.A.	(follows G.C.I.E. see *Knightage*, p. 76)
Order of the Crown of India[2,3]	C.I.	(before G.C.V.O. see *Knightage*, p. 76)
Companion of Honour	C.H.	(follows G.B.E. see *Knightage*, p. 76)
Companion of the Order of the Bath	C.B.	

[1] In October 1971 The Queen approved the exchange by which holders of the Albert Medal (A.M.) and the Edward Medal (E.M.) receive the George Cross. These medals were only awarded posthumously after 1948.
[2] No longer bestowed.
[3] Conferred exclusively upon ladies.

Companion of the Order of the Star of India[2]	C.S.I.
Companion of the Order of St. Michael and St. George	C.M.G.
Companion of the Order of the Indian Empire[2]	C.I.E.
Commander of the Royal Victorian Order	C.V.O.
Commander of the Order of the British Empire	C.B.E.
Distinguished Service Order	D.S.O.
Member of the Royal Victorian Order (if Class IV)	M.V.O.
Officer of the Order of the British Empire	O.B.E.
Imperial Service Order	I.S.O.
Member of the Royal Victorian Order (if Class V)	M.V.O.
Member of the Order of the British Empire	M.B.E.
Indian Order of Merit (Military)[2]	I.O.M.
Royal Red Cross[3]	R.R.C.
Distinguished Service Cross	D.S.C.
Military Cross	M.C.
Distinguished Flying Cross	D.F.C.
Air Force Cross	A.F.C.
Associate, Royal Red Cross[3]	A.R.R.C.
Order of British India[2]	O.B.I.
Distinguished Conduct Medal	D.C.M.
Conspicuous Gallantry Medal	C.G.M.
George Medal	G.M.
Distinguished Conduct Medal of the Royal West African Frontier Force and the King's African Rifles[3]	D.C.M.

[2] See p. 83 for note.
[3] See p. 83 for note.

Indian Distinguished Service Medal[1]	I.D.S.M.
Distinguished Service Medal	D.S.M.
Military Medal	M.M.
Distinguished Flying Medal	D.F.M.
Air Force Medal	A.F.M.
Medal for Saving Life at Sea	S.G.M.
Indian Order of Merit (Civil)[1]	I.O.M.
Colonial Police Medal for Gallantry	C.P.M.
Queen's Gallantry Medal	Q.G.M.
British Empire Medal[2]	B.E.M. (not part of the Order of the British Empire, and shown separately)
King's Police Medal	K.P.M.[3]
King's Police and Fire Service Medal	K.P.F.S.M.[3]
Queen's Police Medal	Q.P.M.[4]
Queen's Fire Service Medal	Q.F.S.M.[4]
Colonial Police Medal for Meritorious Service	C.P.M.
Meritious Service Medal[1]	M.S.M. (not awarded after 20th July 1928)
Army Emergency Reserve Decoration	E.R.D.
Volunteer Officer's Decoration[1]	V.D.
Territorial Decoration	T.D.
Efficiency Decoration	E.D.
Decoration for Officers of the Royal Naval Reserve	R.D.
Decoration for Officers of the Royal Naval Volunteer Reserve[1]	
Air Efficiency Award	A.E.

[1] No longer bestowed.
[2] Since 1974 no recommendations for Gallantry were made for the B.E.M. A new medal for this purpose was instituted in that year, the Queen's Gallantry Medal (Q.G.M.).
[3] The designation of medals already awarded does not change from King's to Queen's during the present reign.
[4] The change from King's to Queen's was made on 19 May 1954.

Canadian Forces Decoration	C.D.

ORDER OF CANADA

The formation of the Order of Canada was announced in 1967.

The Order, of which the Queen is Sovereign, is divided into the following grades according to its last revised constitution:

C.C. Companion of the Order of Canada. With precedence after V.C. and G.C. before all other letters.

O.C. Officer of the Order of Canada. With precedence after C.C.

C.M. Member of the Order of Canada. With precedence after O.C.

The Cross of Valour, The Star of Courage and The Medal of Bravery have no letters.

ORDER OF AUSTRALIA

The Order of Australia was established in 1975.

The Order, of which The Queen is Sovereign, consists of a General Division and a Military Division and is divided into the following classes:

A.K. Knight of the Order of Australia. With precedence after the Order of Merit.

A.D. Dame of the Order of Australia. With the same precedence as Knight of the Order of Australia.

A.C. Companion of the Order of Australia. With precedence after Knight Grand Cross of the Order of the British Empire.

A.O. Officer of the Order of Australia. With precedence after Knight Bachelor.

A.M. Member of the Order of Australia. With precedence after the Distinguished Service Order.

O.A.M. Medal of the Order of Australia. With precedence after the Royal Red Cross (2nd class).

THE QUEEN'S SERVICE ORDER OF NEW ZEALAND

This Order was established in 1975. The Order, of which The Queen is Sovereign, is divided into two parts, for Community Service and for Public Services.

There are two divisions:

Q.S.O.   Companions of The Queen's Service Order. With precedence after Officer of the Order of the British Empire.

Q.S.M.   The Queen's Service Medal. With precedence after Queen's Gallantry Medal, and before British Empire Medal.

Untitled Gentleman

It is for the writer to decide whether one should be addressed as John Brown, Esq. or Mr. John Brown. For the history of these descriptions see Sir Anthony Wagner, *English Genealogy*, 1960, pp. 104–6. The former style is now customary in most walks of life in Great Britain and Ireland but in the United States,[1] Canada, Australia, and New Zealand, the style of Mr. is generally used. John Brown is considered impolite, except for schoolboys. (See below.)

BEGINNING OF LETTER

Formal	(Dear) Sir[2]
Social	Dear Mr. Brown

ENDING OF LETTER

Formal	Yours faithfully (see also p. 2)
Social	Yours sincerely

ENVELOPE

John Brown Esq.[3]
Mr. John Brown

VERBAL ADDRESS AND DESCRIPTION IN CONVERSATION

Mr. Brown.

On formal occasions the following distinction is often made, unless a prefix, such as 'Captain', makes this unnecessary:

Head of the family	Mr. Brown
Others	Mr. John Brown
Employee Status	Sir

[1] See also Usage in the United States, p. 358.
[2] See p. 51, note [1].
[3] Esqre, now regarded as an old-fashioned form, may be used if preferred.

Schoolboys

The usual style of addressing the envelope is 'John Brown', but at Eton and some other public schools they are often given 'Esq.' after the name. The style of 'Master John Brown', at one time given to boys up to the age of 12 or 13, has largely gone out of fashion. If adopted at all, it is now restricted to small boys up to the age of about 8 years, but is generally disliked by them.

Untitled married lady

It is incorrect for a widow to be addressed by her own christian names or initials, as this implies that her marriage was dissolved. This mistake is frequently made.

If the christian name of the lady's husband (living or dead) is unknown, it is considered better to address her as Mrs. Brown[1] rather than Mrs. Mary Brown.[1]

If the senior lady of the family has a title (e.g. Lady Mary Brown), this is sufficient identification for the next senior lady to be known as Mrs. Brown.[1]

BEGINNING OF LETTER

Formal	(Dear) Madam[2]
Social	Dear Mrs. Brown[1]

ENDING OF LETTER

Formal	Yours faithfully (see also p. 2)
Social	Yours sincerely

ENVELOPE

(a) Wife or widow of the head of the family (provided no senior widow is living):

Mrs. Brown[1]

(b) Wives or widows of other members of the family:

Mrs. John Brown[1] *or* Mrs. J. W. Brown[1] (her husband's initials)

(c) Divorced ladies:

Mrs. Mary Brown[2] *or*, as is usually preferred, Mrs. M. J. Brown[1] (her initials)

[1] Ladies, especially those engaged in business or the professions, who prefer not to disclose their marital status, have recently taken to using the prefix 'Ms' (pronounced 'Muz') in lieu of 'Mrs' or 'Miss'. In 1976 the Speaker of the House of Commons agreed to lady Members of Parliament styling themselves 'Ms' if they so wished. This terminology should not be used unless a lady has indicated this preference, because it offends many more than it pleases.
[2] See p. 29, note [1].

VERBAL ADDRESS AND DESCRIPTION IN CONVERSATION

Mrs. Brown.[1]

On formal occasions the following distinction is usually made:

   (a) Wife or widow of the head of the family, and
        divorced ladies:
            Mrs. Brown[1]
   (b) Wives of younger sons:
            Mrs. John Brown[1]
            Mrs. Edward Brown[1]

Employee Status   Madam

The old description of a married lady as 'Mistress Brown' (i.e. Mrs.) is still prevalent in rural Scotland.

Junior branches of a family

Although the relationship of an individual to the head of the family would not be known to most acquaintances, the custom of restricting the use of the surname alone (e.g. Mrs. Waynflete) to the wife of the head of the family (or, if still living, the widow of the previous head), is still followed socially, especially in the country. In some families, where the various branches keep in touch with the senior line, wives of all these cousins style themselves by their husbands' christian names, e.g. Mrs. William Waynflete, and not as Mrs. Waynflete. As so many families are scattered, and in consequence relationships not maintained, this custom is not kept up as much as in the past.

Untitled unmarried lady

BEGINNING OF LETTER

Formal	(Dear) Madam[2]
Social	Dear Miss Brown[1]

ENDING OF LETTER

Formal	Yours faithfully (see also p. 2)
Social	Yours sincerely

ENVELOPE

Eldest unmarried daughter of the senior generation

            Miss Brown[1]

Otherwise   Miss Mary Brown[1]

[1] See p. 88, note [1].
[2] See p. 29, note [1].

VERBAL ADDRESS AND DESCRIPTION IN CONVERSATION

Social   Miss Brown[1]

On formal occasions, if she is not the senior unmarried lady:
  Miss Mary Brown.[1 and 2]

Employee Status   Madam

Scottish Titles and Territorial Designations

According to Scots law there are some special titles which are recognized by the Crown.

These fall into two divisions:

1. Those pertaining to the Peerage of Scotland with the title of Master. See *Scottish Title of Master* (p. 58).
2. Recognized chiefly styles and territorial designations of chieftains and lairds, which are strictly speaking part of their surname (p. 91). These are under the jurisdiction of the Lord Lyon King of Arms. By statute these form part of the name, and should always be used.

These titles are as follows:
  Chiefs of clans (Highlands)
  Chiefs of names (Lowlands)
  A few independent Heads of considerable houses who are recognized as chiefs (e.g. Fraser of Lovat, Macdonald of Clanranald, Macdonald of Sleat)
  Chieftains (branch chiefs)
  Lairds

Some of the above are feudal barons, in addition, with precedence before esquires. They may be known by their baronial status (usually on the Continent, where baronets and the other designations mentioned above are not understood). For this reason the fifth grade in Peerage of Scotland is a Lord of Parliament and *not* a Baron as in other Peerages. There is no English equivalent for the formal style of William Stirling, Baron of Keir.

The traditional prefix to which chiefs, chieftains, and lairds are entitled is 'The Much Honoured', which is not much used today.

---

[1] See p. 88, note 1.
[2] If a younger branch adopts a family name to distinguish them from the senior line, the same rule applies. If members of this branch are known as the Berkeley Browns, the senior unmarried lady is Miss Berkeley Brown. Others are known as Miss Joan Berkeley Brown, etc. It is probable, however, that these details will not be known except to those in the same circle.

A chief wears on ceremonial occasions three eagle's feathers, so he normally uses for his bonnet badge a circlet consisting of his crest and motto, surmounted by three silver feathers. A chieftain has two feathers.

Chiefships and chieftaincies descend to the nearest heir of the blood and name, unless there is a family settlement with a different line of succession. The ruling chief, may, if he thinks fit, nominate his successor, but in such a case Crown confirmation through the Lord Lyon's permitting such a successor to matriculate the chiefly Arms must be obtained.

Where a chiefship has long been dormant, and no heir can prove his right to the succession, Lyon in his ministerial capacity may grant and confirm the chiefly Arms to a suitable person of the name who thus is officially recognized as chief (usually after a petition from the leading men of the clan), subject to challenge by an heir coming forward and proving his claim within twenty years.

If the name of a laird is recognized it does not necessarily imply that the estate is now in possession of the laird concerned, e.g. MacDonell of Glengarry. Subsequent owners with the same surname must use some other designation. In the case of Glengarry, for example, he must make this stipulation against all future purchasers, even of other surnames, in the deed of sale. Someone could become 'Black of Kintail', but no Mackenzie, except the Chief, can become by purchase 'Mackenzie of Kintail'.

Scottish Chief, Chieftain or Laird

CHIEF, CHIEFTAIN OR LAIRD

Surnames were adopted by the Anglo-Normans in the twelfth and thirteenth centuries from either placenames or nicknames. In the Lowlands, Braes, and part of the Highlands, territorial surnames were adopted to match (e.g. Sir Matthew of Moncreiffe). The chief as head of the family and owning the name-place, described himself as 'Sir John of Moncreiffe of that Ilk' (which became standardized in charter Latin as 'dominus Johannes de Moncreiffe de eodem'). By the sixteenth century the 'of' became omitted before Moncreiffe (William Moncreiffe of that Ilk).

By the second half of the sixteenth century, Highland chiefs were styled by the Crown as 'of that Ilk', to make their chiefly status clear, and they so styled themselves (e.g. MacGregor of that Ilk). Some varied between this form and a territorial designation (e.g. Maclean of Duart).

After the Union of 1707, Highland chiefs moved to a straightforward re-duplification of the name (e.g. Macdonald of Macdonald) because of the difficulty in explaining 'of that Ilk' in England. Most other families have since followed suit.

In recent years the Lord Lyon has recognized landless chiefs as 'of that Ilk', though their ancestors never bore that designation.

For centuries some chiefs have abbreviated their style, and adopted the initial 'The', e.g. Chisholm of Chisholm is known as 'The Chisholm', and Macnab of Macnab as 'The Macnab'. Others use 'The' as well as the clan or territorial designation, e.g. The Maclaren of MacLaren, The MacKinnon of MacKinnon, and The Macneil of Barra. The use of 'The' by certain chiefs, in place of the christian name, is officially recognized by the Lord Lyon.

Macdonald of Clanranald is formally styled The Captain of Clanranald, 'Captain' being a mediaeval word for 'Chief', literally 'Headman'. Similarly, the Mackintosh chief of Clan Chattan is formally styled The Captain of Clan Chattan (pronounced Hattan).

The use of 'The' arose in two ways. Occasionally 'le' was a corruption of 'de', e.g. Robert of Bruce was incorrectly called Robert the Bruce. Usually it implied *The* Chief of the Clan or Name, much in the same way as today we speak of '*The* Mr. Ford'. Though this form was used both in the Highlands and Lowlands, its survival is now restricted to chiefs of Highland clans.

In Scotland the following chiefly designations are used:

1. *Direct re-duplification of the name*, e.g.
   Henry Borthwick of Borthwick
   The MacKinnon of MacKinnon
2. *Single designation*
   The Menzies (pronounced Ming-iz)
3. *'Of that Ilk'*
   Sir Iain Moncreiffe of that Ilk, Bt.
4. *Territorial designation*
   Colonel Donald Cameron of Lochiel
   The Macneil of Barra

Biographies of Chiefs of Clans and Names appear in DEBRETT. Chieftains (branch chiefs) and lairds have the appropriate territorial designation following their christian and surnames.

FORMS OF ADDRESS

In Scotland it is normal to write to chiefs, chieftains and lairds by their designation or estate and not by their surname. The English 'Esquire' is not added to the name on the envelope.

BEGINNING OF LETTER

Formal	(Dear) Sir
Social	Dear Chisholm[1]
	Dear Lochiel
	Dear Drum

A member of a Clan or Name writes to his Chief: Dear Chief.

ENVELOPE

The Chisholm
Colonel Donald Cameron of Lochiel, T.D.
The MacNeil of Barra
Henry Forbes Irvine of Drum
Peter Barclay of that Ilk

VERBAL ADDRESS

By clan or territorial designation, and not by the surname.
Lochiel
Mackintosh

On introduction, 'The' can be used, if applicable (e.g. The Macnab), or simply 'This is Lochiel'.

DESCRIPTION IN CONVERSATION

As for Verbal Address, except for those styled 'The' (e.g. The Chisholm) are so described.

CHIEF, CHIEFTAIN OR LAIRD (WOMAN)

There is no separate feminine equivalent for a lady who is a chief, chieftain, or laird, and a woman has exactly the same status as a man, except that one does not write to her by her estate only. See also *Wife of a Chief*, p. 94.

---

[1] A non-Scotsman who writes to a Chief or Laird with a Service rank, especially when younger or junior in rank, would write socially to The Mackintosh as 'Dear Admiral Mackintosh of Mackintosh'. This style is not incorrect as it includes the clan or territorial designation which is the essential part of the name.

BEGINNING OF LETTER

Formal	(Dear) Madam
Social	Dear Madam Maclachlan of Machlachlan *or* Dear Mrs. Maclachlan of Machlachlan (whichever form is adopted, see *Wife of a Chief, etc.* below)
	Dear Miss Rose of Kilravock

If she possesses a title, she is addressed as such. A letter to the Chief of Clan MacLeod, will be addressed 'Dear Dame Flora (MacLeod of MacLeod)'.

ENVELOPE

Madam Maclachlan of Maclachlan *or* Mrs. Stewart of Ardvorlich (whichever form is adopted, see *Wife of a Chief, etc.* below)

If she possesses a title, then as such, e.g.:

Dame Flora MacLeod of MacLeod, D.B.E.

Miss Rose of Kilravock

WIFE OF A CHIEF, ETC.

Until the end of the eighteenth century, a wife of a chief or laird was invariably described as 'Lady', followed by her husband's territorial designation, e.g. the wife of Cameron of Lochiel was called Lady Lochiel.

As the difference between 'Lady' plus the estate, and 'Lady' plus the surname (e.g. a knight's wife), was not understood by English officials, this title for a chief's wife died out early last century, becoming restricted to the peerage, baronetage and knightage. For the same reason, a chief's or laird's wife came to adopt her husband's full surname, and not just the territorial designation part.

Today, some wives of chiefs or chieftains use the designation of 'Mrs.'; others have adopted the Irish style of 'Madam', e.g. Madam Chisholm, which has met with the Lord Lyon's approval. To be certain of the designation preferred, one needs to check with an individual family.

WIDOW OF A CHIEF, ETC.

The style of the Dowager Madam (*or* Mrs.) Maclean of Ardgour is now seldom used, but when the widow of a previous chief, etc., is under the same roof as the wife of the current chief, this identification is useful.

ELDEST SON AND HEIR APPARENT OF A CHIEF

He is known by his father's territorial designation, with the addition of 'younger', abbreviated to 'yr.' (so that it will not be mistaken for a surname). This may either follow the surname, but it is more usually placed after the territorial designation, e.g.:

Ranald Macdonald of Castleton, yr., *or*

Ranald Macdonald, yr. of Castleton

If the christian name of the heir apparent is different from his father, 'yr.' may be omitted.

WIFE OF THE ELDEST SON

She is known by her husband's style, i.e. with 'yr.', but without his christian name, e.g. Mrs. MacGregor of MacGregor, yr., unless she is sufficiently distinguished from her mother-in-law, e.g. Lady Mary MacGregor of MacGregor.

OTHER SONS

They are not known by their father's territorial designation but as an esquire, e.g. John Macdonald, Esq., unless they are recognized as lairds in their own right, e.g. Sir Thomas Innes of Learney's younger son is Malcolm Innes of Edingight, being laird of that old family estate.

ELDEST DAUGHTER

As an unmarried daughter she uses the territorial designation of her house without her christian name, e.g. Miss MacLeod of Glendale, unless a senior lady is still living, such as an unmarried daughter of a previous chief, etc., when she will use her christian name as well as the territorial designation, as for younger daughters.

OTHER DAUGHTERS

All other unmarried daughters bear the designation of their house e.g. Miss Janet MacLeod of Glendale.

SIGNATURE

By statute, lairds were prevented from signing themselves like peers without a first name. It was laid down that they should sign with first name and surname including designation, e.g. Donald Cameron of Lochiel.

Irish Chieftainries

Chieftains of Irish Tribes and Septs are known by their titles.

About the beginning of the nineteenth century, some of the representatives of the last holders of these chieftainries resumed the appropriate designations which had lapsed with the destruction of the Gaelic order.

The use of 'The' as a prefix, though convenient and generally used, lacks official recognition by the Chief Herald of Ireland.

The descent of the following by primogeniture in the male line from the last inaugurated or *de facto* chieftain has been examined by the Genealogical Office, Dublin Castle. Subject in some cases to the possible survival of senior lines at present unidentified, they are recorded at the Genealogical Office as Chiefs of the Name, and are recognized by courtesy. Certain chieftains or chiefs (the terms are synonymous in Ireland) whose pedigrees have not been finally proved, are included in the following list on account of their prescriptive standing:

The O'Neill of Clanaboy	O'Neill (descended from the Kings of Ulster)
The O'Brien of Thomond (*Lord Inchiquin*)	O'Brien (descended from the Kings of Munster)
The McMorrough Kavanagh	Dormant (descended from the Kings of Leinster)
O'Conor Don[1]	O'Conor (descended from the Kings of Connaught)
The MacDermot, Prince of Coolavin[2]	MacDermot
The MacDermot Roe	Dormant since 1917
The McGillycuddy of the Reeks	McGillycuddy
The O'Callaghan	O'Callaghan
The O'Donel of Tirconnell	O'Donel
The O'Donoghue of the Glens	O'Donoghue
The O'Donovan	O'Donovan
The O'Grady of Kilballyowen[3]	O'Grady
The O'Kelly of Gallagh and Tycooly[4]	O'Kelly

[1] Does not use the prefix 'The'.
[2] The word 'Prince' is not normally used.
[3] Often abbreviated to 'The O'Grady'.
[4] Often abbreviated to 'The O'Kelly'.

The O'Morchoe	O'Morchoe
O'Sionnaigh (called The Fox since 1552)	Dormant
The O'Toole of Fer Tire (*Comte O'Toole*)	Dormant since 1965

BEGINNING OF LETTER

Formal	(Dear) Sir
Social	Dear O'Conor[1]

ENVELOPE

Armed Forces rank precedes the style, e.g.
  Lieut-Colonel The O'Grady, M.C.

VERBAL ADDRESS

  O'Conor
On introduction the full title is used, e.g.:
  The O'Conor Don

DESCRIPTION IN CONVERSATION

By the title, e.g.:
  The O'Conor Don

SIGNATURE

As a peer, e.g.:
  O'Grady

WIFE OF AN IRISH CHIEFTAIN

She is referred to and addressed as Madam, e.g.: Madam O'Donoghue.

The form of Madam probably originated because several Roman Catholic chieftains of Jacobite sympathies left Ireland in the eighteenth century to live abroad. They usually spoke French through entering service abroad, being prevented as Catholics from holding commissions in the British Army. In France 'Madame' is the equivalent of both 'Lady' and 'Mrs.'.

---

[1] A non-Irishman who writes to a Chieftain with a Service rank, especially when he is younger or junior in rank, would write 'Dear Colonel The O'Grady'.

CHILDREN OF AN IRISH CHIEFTAIN

They do not have any special form of address.

IRISH HEREDITARY KNIGHTS

There are three Irish hereditary Knights, feudal dignities which were conferred upon the FitzGerald family, viz. The Knight of Kerry (the Green Knight), The Knight of Glin (the Black Knight), and The White Knight. The last of these, whose surname became fixed as FitzGibbon, is dormant, though there is a claimant. The Knight of Kerry, who is a baronet, prefers to be addressed 'The Knight of Kerry', his older title.

BEGINNING OF LETTER

Formal	Dear Sir
Social	Dear Knight

ENVELOPE

> The Knight of Glin
> Major the Knight of Kerry, Bt., M.C.

VERBAL ADDRESS

> Knight

DESCRIPTION IN CONVERSATION

> The Knight of Glin
> The Knight of Kerry

WIFE OF AN IRISH HEREDITARY KNIGHT

She is addressed as the wife of an Irish chieftain, viz.:
> 'Madam' before her surname

The wife of the Knight of Kerry (who is also a Baronet) is addressed as Lady FitzGerald.

JOINT FORM OF ADDRESS

> The Knight of Glin and Madam FitzGerald
> The Knight of Kerry and Lady FitzGerald

Position of Letters After the Name

The abbreviations 'Bt.' or 'Bart.' (for a Baronet) and 'Esq.', if applicable, precede all other letters.

The series of other letters are grouped either by regulations or by custom as follows:

1. Orders and Decorations conferred by the Crown.

2. Appointments in the following order, Privy Counsellor, Aide de Camp to Her Majesty, Honorary Physician to The Queen, Honorary Surgeon to The Queen, Honorary Dental Surgeon to The Queen, Honorary Nursing Sister to The Queen, and Honorary Chaplain to The Queen, viz. P.C., A.D.C., Q.H.P., Q.H.S., Q.H.D.S., Q.H.N.S. and Q.H.C.

3. University Degrees.

4. (a) Religious Orders,
   (b) Medical Qualifications.

5. (a) Fellowships of Learned Societies,
   (b) Royal Academicians and Associates,
   (c) Fellowships, Memberships, etc., of Professional Institutions, Associations, etc.,
   (d) Writers to the Signet.

6. Appointments (other than 2 above), in the following order, Queen's Counsel, Justice of the Peace, Deputy Lieutenant and Member of Parliament, viz. Q.C., J.P., D.L., M.P.

7. Membership of one of the Armed Forces, such as R.N. or R.A.F.

—————

The following notes are given for guidance.

It is important to keep the group order, even if the individual series of letters in Groups 3, 4, and 5 present difficulties. For further details see the appropriate section.

The nature of the correspondence determines which series of letters should normally be included under Groups 3, 4, and 5. For instance, when writing a professional letter to a doctor of medicine one would normally add more medical qualifications than in a social letter.

On a formal list all the appropriate letters are usually included after each name.

Those who have letters signifying Crown Honours and Awards are usually given only the principal letters in Groups 3, 4, and 5 (e.g. M.D., F.R.C.S., F.R.S.).

A peer who is a junior officer in the Armed Forces, is not usually addressed by his Service rank in social correspondence, unless he so wishes, or a letter is forwarded to him at a Service address or club.

1. ORDERS AND DECORATIONS

All the appropriate letters are obligatory in correspondence and lists. The order is laid down for Knights (p. 75), Dames (p. 78), and others (p. 83).

2. PRIVY COUNSELLORS AND APPOINTMENTS TO THE QUEEN

For peers the letters P.C. are obligatory. For other Privy Counsellors, 'Rt. Hon.' before the name is sufficient identification (see p. 80). As the other appointments to the Crown (Q.H.P., Q.H.S., etc.) are held for a limited period only, they are not always used by recipients.

3. UNIVERSITY DEGREES

Doctorates in the faculties of Divinity and Medicine (D.D., M.D.) and Masters degrees in the latter (e.g. M.S.) are given in all correspondence. Other Divinity degrees (e.g. B.D.) are sometimes included.

Other degrees in medicine (e.g. M.B., B.S.) are sometimes included, especially in professional correspondence, but if one progresses in the same degree only the higher is given.

Doctorates in other faculties are sometimes given, especially if the correspondence concerns the particular profession or subject (e.g. LL.D., D.Sc.). Alternatively, except for surgeons, the envelope may be addressed as 'Doctor' before his name, without giving his (or her) degrees.

Other degrees are seldom, and M.A. and B.A. never, used in social correspondence, but they are generally included in a formal list.

For further information see *Medical Section* and *Academic Section*.

4 (a) RELIGIOUS ORDERS

Letters for members of religious communities, when used, should be included, e.g. S.J. Some Members of the Order of St. Benedict do not normally use the letters O.S.B. as the prefix of 'Dom' or 'Dame' is held to be a sufficient identification.

(b) MEDICAL QUALIFICATIONS

Fellowships are given in all correspondence (e.g. F.R.C.P., F.R.C.S.)

Other qualifications are sometimes given, especially those which are the highest held. They are usually included when writing professionally.

When all letters signifying qualifications are included, as for example in a nominal list, they should appear in the following order. (*Note:* Fellows and Members of each category precede the next category):

> Medicine
> Surgery (except M.R.C.S.)
> Obstetrics, Gynaecology and other specialities
> Qualifying diplomas (e.g. M.R.C.S., L.R.C.P.)
> Other diplomas (e.g. D.P.H., D.Obst. R.C.O.G.)

In practice, a maximum of three series of letters including M.D. (see Group 3 above) is usually sufficient in ordinary correspondence (e.g. M.D., M.S., F.R.C.S.). See also *Medical Section*.

5. (a) FELLOWSHIPS OF LEARNED SOCIETIES

Fellowships fall into two categories:

> (a) honorific, i.e. nomination by election,
> (b) nomination by subscription.

Normally only honorific fellowships are used in social correspondence (e.g. F.R.S., F.B.A.). Fellowships by subscription are generally restricted to correspondence concerning the same field of interest, e.g. a writer to a Fellow of the Zoological Society on the subject of zoology will include F.Z.S. after the name.

There is no recognized order for placing these letters. Strictly speaking, they should be arranged according to the date of foundation or incorporation of the societies concerned, but some hold that those with a Royal Charter should precede others.

In practice the following is usually adhered to:

(1) Where one society is indisputably of greater importance than another, the letters may be placed in that order; or alternatively the fellowship of the junior society may be omitted.

(2) If such precedence cannot be determined, the letters may be placed in order of conferment. Where this is not known, they may be placed in alphabetical order.

(3) Where a fellow is pre-eminent in a particular subject, his fellowship of a society connected with this interest may either be placed first, or his other fellowships omitted.

The following are some of the principal learned societies, with their dates of incorporation:

Fellow of The Royal Society	F.R.S.	1662
Fellow of The Society of Antiquaries	F.S.A.	1707
Fellow of The Royal Society of Edinburgh	F.R.S.E.	1783
Fellow of The Royal Society of Literature	F.R.S.L.	1823
Fellow of The British Academy	F.B.A.	1901

Presidents of some societies have special letters to signify their appointment, e.g. The President of the Royal Society has P.R.S. after his name, but these letters are only used within the particular society.

The Royal Society of Literature bestows an award limited to ten recipients, the Companion of Literature. The letters C.Lit. are placed before the Fellowship.

(b) ROYAL ACADEMY OF ARTS, THE ROYAL SCOTTISH ACADEMY, ETC.

It is not suggested that Royal Academicians yield in precedence to fellows of learned societies. In practice the two lists do not coincide.

The President and Past Presidents are indicated as follows:

President of the Royal Academy	P.R.A.
Past President of the Royal Academy	P.P.R.A.
President of the Royal Scottish Academy	P.R.S.A.
Past President of the Royal Scottish Academy	P.P.R.S.A.

Royal Academicians and Associaties are included as follows:

Royal Academician	R.A.
Royal Scottish Academician	R.S.A.
Associate of the Royal Academy	A.R.A.
Associate of the Royal Scottish Academy	A.R.S.A.

Similarly with other Academies, e.g. President Royal Hibernian Academy (P.R.H.A.) and Academicians (R.H.A.).

Honorary Academicians and Associates do not normally use the relevant letters.

(c) FELLOWSHIPS AND MEMBERSHIPS OF PROFESSIONAL INSTITUTIONS, ASSOCIATIONS, ETC.

These letters are usually restricted to correspondence concerning the particular profession.

It is not suggested that professional societies as such yield precedence to learned societies, but in point of fact the two groups do not coincide to any great extent. Most of the senior learned societies which elect fellows are senior in age and importance to the professional. Those whose fellowships are by subscription are generally only used in the particular field of interest. For example, if Mr. John Smith is a Chartered Engineer and a Fellow of the Royal Historical Society, he would normally be described professionally as John Smith, Esq., C.Eng., F.I.Mech.E. When corresponding on historical subjects he is normally described as John Smith, Esq., F.R.Hist.S. If both series of letters are placed after his name, it is usual to place first those which concern the particular function or subject.

As there is no recognized order for placing qualifications awarded by different bodies, a recipient usually places these letters on headed paper, business cards, etc. in order of importance to his particular profession.

Council of Engineering Institutions

The Council of Engineering Institutions (C.E.I.) which was granted a Royal Charter in 1965, is a federation of fifteen chartered engineering institutions (see below). The object of the Council is to promote and maintain in the public interest the unity, integrity and quality of the engineering profession. It is responsible for maintaining and enhancing the standards of engineering as a profession and administers the qualification structure which leads to chartered status.

In 1971 the Privy Council approved changes to the Council's Charter so that C.E.I. could set up the Engineers' Registration Board (E.R.B.) which enables chartered engineers, technician engineers, and technicians to be registered and to use the designatory letters C.Eng., T.Eng.(C.E.I.), and Tech.(C.E.I.), respectively. These titles are based on nationally recognised academic examinations, training and experience.

The designatory letters C.Eng., denoting chartered engineer, follow immediately after an individual's name and are followed in turn by the letters F. (Fellow) or M. (Member) identifying him with the particular institution(s) to which he belongs. Thus J. Smith, C.Eng., F.I.C.E., M.I.Mech.E., is a chartered engineer who is a Fellow of the Institution of Civil Engineers and a Member of the Institution of Mechanical Engineers.

Note : Some chartered engineers are also Masters of Engineering (a university degree). They are shown as M.Eng., C.Eng., etc.

The constituent members of C.E.I. are the Royal Aeronautical Society, Institution of Chemical Engineers, Institution of Civil Engineers, Institution of Electrical Engineers, Institution of Electronic and Radio Engineers, Institute of Fuel, Institution of Gas Engineers, Institute of Marine Engineers, Institution of Mechanical Engineers, Institution of Mining Engineers, Institution of Mining and Metallurgy, Institution of Municipal Engineers, Royal Institution of Naval Architects, Institution of Production Engineers, and Institution of Structural Engineers.

Chartered Societies of the Land

Three chartered societies of the land, viz. :

> The Royal Institution of Chartered Surveyors
> The Chartered Land Agents' Society
> The Chartered Auctioneers' and Estate Agents' Institute

united in June 1970 to become the Royal Institution of Chartered Surveyors. Fellows and Professional Associates respectively have the letters F.R.I.C.S. and A.R.I.C.S.

Incorporated Society of Valuers and Auctioneers

The Incorporated Society of Auctioneers and Landed Property Agents united in April 1968 with The Valuers Institution to form The Incorporated Society of Valuers and Auctioneers, with the letters F.S.V.A. and A.S.V.A.

(d) WRITERS TO THE SIGNET

It is customary for the letters W.S. to follow the name after University degrees and those which signify Fellowship or Membership of a Society or Institution, despite the fact that the W.S. Society (an ancient Society of Solicitors in Scotland) is frequently considerably older than many Institutions. This is a way of indicating the profession. It is not customary for the letters W.S. to be used socially.

6. APPOINTMENTS

The letters M.P. are always shown for a Member of Parliament.

The letters Q.C. are always shown for a Queen's Counsel including a County Court Judge, but *not* a High Court Judge.

The letters J.P. for a Justice of the Peace and D.L. for a Deputy Lieutenant may be included *in that order*.[1] In practice they are often omitted for a peer, or for one with several honours and awards.

Note: There is no official abbreviation for a Lord-Lieutenant, H.M. Lieutenant or a Vice-Lieutenant, see Local Government Section.

7. MEMBERSHIP OF ONE OF THE ARMED FORCES

Royal Navy.—The letters 'R.N.' (or 'Royal Navy', which this Service prefers) are placed after the names of serving officers of and below the rank of Captain. They are also placed after the names of retired Captains, Commanders, and Lieutenant-Commanders where they are prefixed by Naval rank. The letters R.N.R. are likewise used by officers of the Royal Naval Reserve.

Army.—The appropriate letters which signify a Regiment or Corps may be placed after the name for officers on the active list of and below the rank of Lieutenant-Colonel, but are often omitted in social correspondence. These letters are not used for retired officers.

Corps have letter abbreviations (e.g. R.E., R.A.M.C., R.A.O.C., R.A.P.C.). Most regiments are written in full.

Royal Air Force.—The letters R.A.F. are placed after serving and retired officers, except for Marshals of The Royal Air Force. Officers above the rank of Group Captain do not often use these letters. Similarly with R.A.F.V.R.

Royal Marines.—The letters 'R.M.' (or 'Royal Marines' which some officers prefer) are placed after the names of serving and retired officers of and below the rank of Lieutenant-Colonel. Similarly R.M.R. (Royal Marines Reserve).

For further information, e.g. Women's Services, see *Armed Forces Section.*

---

[1] One regrets to see how often these letters are placed in the wrong order after the names of deceased in the 'Deaths' column of *The Times* and *Daily Telegraph*; not to mention the number of holders of both offices who do not, apparently, know that J.P. should be placed *before* D.L.

The Aga Khan

The Aga Khan received the personal title of His Highness from The Queen in 1957 on succeeding his grandfather His Highness the late Rt. Hon. the Aga Khan, G.C.S.I., G.C.I.E., G.C.V.O., and is therefore styled 'His Highness the Aga Khan.' The wife of the Aga Khan is styled 'Her Highness Begum Aga Khan.'

The widow of the late Aga Khan is styled 'Her Highness Begum Sultan Mohamed Aga Khan.'

Indian Princes

The principal Indian Princes and Chiefs, and their wives, may by courtesy be styled His *or* Her Highness, though the Princely Order in India was abolished by a presidential decree on 31st Dec., 1971.

The Maltese Nobility

The Nobility of Malta consists of titles of the following degrees: Marquis, Count, and Baron. They take precedence among themselves according to the date of creation as a noble, irrespective of title. They are all addressed 'The Most Noble' followed by the title.[1] If the title of Marquis is of Italian origin, the Italian form comprising 'Marchese' is sometimes used in place of 'Marquis'.

The eldest sons and heirs apparent of nobles have the courtesy title of 'Marchesino', 'Contino', or 'Baroncino' before the title, depending on its degree. If the heir be a daughter, she has the courtesy title of 'Marchesina', 'Contina', or 'Baroncina'. They are addressed by these titles, which are untranslatable, followed by the family title (e.g. Marchesino St. George).

The younger sons and all daughters of nobles are styled by courtesy 'The Noble' before the christian name and title.

Other members of a noble's family are styled 'dei Marchesi', 'dei Conti', or 'dei Baroni,' followed by their christian name and surname or title. When a woman who has succeeded to a title marries an untitled commoner named Smith, she is addressed 'The Most Noble Countess Smith Montalto'. When a daughter, with the style of 'The Noble', marries Mr. Smith, she is styled 'The Noble Mrs. Smith'.

These titles are no longer recognized by the Republic of Malta.[2]

---

[1] Queen Victoria recognized the prefix of 'Most Noble,' which was communicated to the Governor of Malta by The Earl Granville on 23rd February, 1886.

[2] Before the Constitution of Independence, 1964, all titles were controlled by the Crown, but subsequently, until the establishment of Malta as a Republic within the Commonwealth, 1974, they were regulated by the Committee of Privileges, Malta, as the First Court, and the Civil High Court, Malta, in the case of an appeal.

The Canadian Nobility

There is one French title which is recognized by the British Crown, the Baron de Longueüil (of Longueüil in the Province of Quebec). This was created in 1700 by King Louis XIV for the services rendered in Canada by Charles Le Moyne, whose descendants still hold it.

Commonwealth Sovereigns

In Southern Africa there are the Kingdoms of Lesotho (previously Basutoland) and Swaziland, and in the Pacific the Kingdom of Tonga. The Supreme Head of Malaysia has the style of 'His Majesty'. He is elected for a term of five years by the rulers of the Malay States from among their number. Other rulers include the Sultan of Brunei and the Head of State of Western Samoa.

Kings are addressed as His Majesty, and both the Sultan of Brunei and the Head of State of Western Samoa as 'His Highness'.

Part IV

STYLES BY OFFICE

STYLES BY OFFICE

CHURCHES SECTION

Retired officers of the Armed Forces who enter Holy Orders in any Church within the United Kingdom are not addressed by their Service rank, either in the body of the letter or on the envelope,[1] but this practice is customary in Australia and Canada.

Church of England and Associated Churches in the Anglican Communion

As a result of the Lambeth Conference 1968, under the guidance of the Archbishop of Canterbury, a simplified form of Address for the clergy of the Church of England was announced as given in this section.

Ordained clergymen of the Church of England, and other Churches within the Anglican Communion, do not receive the accolade of knighthood, though the letters signifying an order of knighthood are placed after the name, e.g. The Right Reverend[2] the Lord Bishop of Brompton, K.C.V.O.

Doctorate Degrees should be added on the envelope where appropriate.

If a clergyman succeeds to a title or has a courtesy title or style, the ecclesiastical style precedes the temporal, e.g.:

---

[1] When it is desired to show that a clergyman has served in the Armed Forces, e.g. in a list of retired officers, the following form is used: The Reverend John Smith, Commander, Royal Navy.

[2] Often abbreviated to 'The Rt. Rev.'. Some clergymen prefer 'The Reverend' to be written in full. Others prefer the abbreviation 'The Revd.' but 'The Rev.' is usually adopted. When abbreviations are used within the Church of England some hold that the last letter does not need a full stop when it is also the last letter of a word, thus Rev., Ven., but Revd, St and Rt, with no stop. Although the typographical practice is to abolish full stops wherever possible, this usage is optional.

1. The Venerable Sir John Jones, Bt.
2. The Reverend the Hon. John Brown.
3. The Very Reverend the Earl of Southend.

Wives of the clergy do not have any special form of address.

ARCHBISHOPS OF CANTERBURY AND YORK

They are Privy Counsellors, and accordingly are addressed 'The Most Reverend and Right Honourable . . .' and have seats in the House of Lords. The Archbishop of Canterbury is Primate of all England and Metropolitan. The Archbishop of York is Primate of England and Metropolitan.

BEGINNING OF LETTER
Dear Archbishop[1]

ENDING OF LETTER
Yours sincerely

ENVELOPE
The Most Reverend and Right Hon. the Lord Archbishop of Canterbury/York

VERBAL ADDRESS
Formal	Your Grace
Social	Archbishop

DESCRIPTION IN CONVERSATION
The Archbishop (of York)

SIGNATURE, see p. 128.

ARCHBISHOPS OF THE CHURCH OF IRELAND AND OTHER PROVINCES

There are two Archbishops of the Church of Ireland: Armagh (Primate of all Ireland) and Dublin (Primate of Ireland).

BEGINNING OF LETTER
Dear Archbishop[1]

[1] Prior to October 1968, the formal style in use was 'My Lord Archbishop', which may still be adopted if preferred. (It is usual to adopt the formal style for announcement at a public function.)

ENDING OF LETTER
>   Yours sincerely

ENVELOPE
>   The Most Reverend the Lord Archbishop of Blank

VERBAL ADDRESS

Formal	Your Grace
Social	Archbishop

DESCRIPTION IN CONVERSATION
>   The Archbishop (of Blank)

RETIRED ARCHBISHOPS

On retirement, Archbishops revert to the status of a Bishop. The former Archbishop of Canterbury is usually created a Peer. Dr. Michael Ramsey was created Lord Ramsey of Canterbury. So far no Archbishop of York has retired.

BEGINNING OF LETTER
>   See Retired Bishops (*Note*, the Right Reverend and Right Hon. Lord Ramsey of Canterbury prefers to be addressed Dear Bishop Ramsey)

ENDING OF LETTER
>   See Retired Bishops

ENVELOPE
>   See Retired Bishops (*Note*, Lord Ramsey of Canterbury prefers to be addressed The Right Reverend and Right Hon. Dr. A. M. Ramsey)

VERBAL ADDRESS
>   See Retired Bishops (*Note*, Lord Ramsey of Canterbury prefers to be called 'Bishop', or 'Bishop Ramsey')

DESCRIPTION
>   See Retired Bishops, e.g. Bishop Ramsey

BISHOP OF LONDON

He is always a Privy Counsellor, and accordingly is addressed as
"Right Reverend and Right Honourable . . .".

BEGINNING OF LETTER

>Dear Bishop[1]

ENDING OF LETTER

>Yours sincerely

ENVELOPE

>The Right Reverend and Right Hon. the Lord Bishop of
>London

VERBAL ADDRESS

>Bishop[1]

DESCRIPTION IN CONVERSATION

>The Bishop (of London)

SIGNATURE, see p. 128.

BISHOPS, DIOCESAN AND SUFFRAGAN, CHURCH OF ENGLAND AND THE CHURCH IN WALES

The Bishops of London, Durham, and Winchester have seats in
the House of Lords. Until 1841 all the other Diocesan Bishops of
the Church of England, except the Bishop of Sodor and Man, also
had seats, but since that date, only 21 sit in the Upper House.
When a vacancy arises it is filled by the senior Diocesan Bishop
without a seat, and the vacated See is then placed at the foot of the
list of those awaiting seats. Translation of a Bishop from one See to
another does not affect his right to sit in the House of Lords. The
Bishop of Sodor and Man is an ex-officio member of the Legislative
Council of the Isle of Man.

In each Diocese of the Church of England, Suffragan Bishops
are appointed on the recommendation of the Bishop to assist him.
These are styled by the name of some ancient town within the
See. While enjoying full episcopal rights, they do not qualify for
membership of the House of Lords.

[1] Prior to October 1968, the formal style was 'My Lord', which may still be adopted if
preferred. It is usual to adopt the formal style for announcement at a public function.

There has been some controversy as to whether a Suffragan Bishop is entitled to the style of 'Lord' Bishop (i.e. whether this title is ecclesiastical or temporal), but although the prefix is usually given by custom or courtesy, he is not so styled in an official document.

The Church in Wales became a separate Province of the Anglican Communion as a result of disestablishment in 1920. The office of Archbishop of Wales is held by one of their six Diocesan Bishops.

BEGINNING OF LETTER
> Dear Bishop[1]

ENDING OF LETTER
> Yours sincerely

ENVELOPE
> The Right Reverend the Lord Bishop of Blank
> *or* The Right Reverend the Bishop of Blank

VERBAL ADDRESS
> Bishop[1]

DESCRIPTION IN CONVERSATION
> The Bishop (of Blank)

SIGNATURE, see pp. 128–129.

ASSISTANT AND RETIRED BISHOPS

BEGINNING OF LETTER
> Dear Bishop[2]

ENDING OF LETTER
> Yours sincerely

ENVELOPE
> The Right Rev. John Smith
> If a Privy Counsellor (e.g. a retired Bishop of London), The Right Rev. and Right Hon. John Smith.

VERBAL ADDRESS
> Bishop[2]

---

[1] Prior to October 1968, the formal style for a Diocesan Bishop was 'My Lord', and for other Bishops 'My Lord' or 'Right Reverend Sir'. The latter alternative was used by those who did not agree that a non-Diocesan Bishop should be described as a 'Lord Bishop'. These forms may still be adopted if preferred. It is usual to adopt the formal style for announcement at a public function.
[2] Prior to October 1968, the formal style was 'My Lord' or 'Right Reverend Sir', which may still be adopted if preferred. It is usual to adopt the formal style for announcement at a public function. See *Bishops, Diocesan and Suffragan,* above.

DESCRIPTION IN CONVERSATION
The Bishop, *or* by name, e.g. Bishop Smith

BISHOPS, EPISCOPAL CHURCH IN SCOTLAND

Since the Episcopal Church is not the State Church of Scotland a Bishop has no *official* precedence and recognition. He is therefore addressed as 'The Right Rev. John Smith, Bishop of X', and not as 'The Right Rev. the Bishop of X'.

Socially he is styled as for a Diocesan Bishop of the Church of England (p. 114), except for the Primus of Scotland who acts as the Presiding Bishop. He is elected by the other bishops and has no Metropolitan power. He is styled 'Most Reverend the Primus'.

The following is the form of address for the Primus:

BEGINNING OF LETTER
Dear Primus

ENDING OF LETTER
Yours sincerely

ENVELOPE
The Most Reverend the Primus

VERBAL ADDRESS
Primus

DESCRIPTION IN CONVERSATION
The Primus

SIGNATURE, see p. 129.

BISHOPS, CHURCH OF IRELAND

The Church of Ireland was united with the Church of England by the Act of Union 1800, but was disestablished in 1869.

Bishops are styled as Diocesan Bishops in the Church of England (p. 114), with the following exception:

The Bishop of Meath (Premier Bishop of the Church of Ireland) is styled 'The Most Reverend' instead of 'The Right Reverend'.

For signatures of Bishops, see p. 129.

BISHOPS OF OVERSEAS CHURCHES

They are styled as for Bishops in the Church of England (p. 114).

The Presiding Bishop of the Protestant Episcopal Church in the United States has the following style:

> The Most Reverend the Presiding Bishop

Certain Bishops of Churches Overseas have the style 'in' or 'on' instead of 'of', e.g.:

> The Bishop on the Niger Delta
> The Bishop in Egypt
> The Bishop in Iran
> The Bishop in Argentina and Eastern South America with the Falkland Islands

DEAN

A Dean is the incumbent of a cathedral or collegiate church, except when he is a Provost, see p. 118. The style is also used in certain colleges (see *Academic Section*).

BEGINNING OF LETTER

> Dear Dean[1]

ENDING OF LETTER

> Yours sincerely

ENVELOPE

> The Very Reverend the Dean of Ely[2]

VERBAL ADDRESS

> Dean[3]

DESCRIPTION IN CONVERSATION

> The Dean (of Ely)

RETIRED DEAN

After retirement, he is addressed as are other clergy, i.e. 'The Reverend' instead of 'The Very Reverend' as above, unless he

---

[1] Prior to October 1968, the formal style was 'Very Reverend Sir', and the social style was 'Dear Mr. Dean', which may still be adopted if preferred.
[2] For abbreviation of Reverend see p. 111, note [2].
[3] Prior to October 1968, the verbal address was 'Mr. Dean', which may still be adopted if preferred. It is usual to adopt the formal style for announcement at a public function.

remains an Archdeacon, Canon or Prebendary, or is appointed to emeritus rank, when he is addressed according to the appropriate rank. The word 'emeritus' is only used in official documents.

PROVOST

The incumbent of a cathedral which has been so created out of a parish church and whose responsibilities in consequence carry additionally something in the nature of Rector or Vicar is usually appointed a Provost and not a Dean. Where a cathedral has a Provost rather than a Dean, the freehold and the patronage is normally vested in the Provost for the time being, and not in the Chapter as would be normal where the appointment of Dean existed. In other respects his duties are the same as a Dean's. The style is also used in certain non-ecclesiastical appointments, such as the Heads of certain colleges (see *Academic Section*).

BEGINNING OF LETTER

Dear Provost[1]

ENDING OF LETTER

Yours sincerely

ENVELOPE

The Very Reverend the Provost of Coventry

VERBAL ADDRESS

Provost[2]

DESCRIPTION IN CONVERSATION

The Provost (of Coventry)

RETIRED PROVOST

After retirement he is addressed as other clergy, i.e. 'The Reverend', instead of 'The Very Reverend' (p. 111), unless he remains an Archdeacon, Canon or Prebendary, or is appointed to emeritus rank, when he is addressed as such. The word 'emeritus' is only used in official documents.

[1] Prior to October 1968, the formal style was 'Very Reverend Sir', and the social style, 'Dear Mr. Provost', which may still be adopted if preferred.
[2] Prior to October 1968, the verbal style was 'Mr. Provost', which may still be adopted if preferred. It is usual to adopt the formal style for announcement at a public function.

ARCHDEACON

An Archdeacon is a senior clergyman whose duty it is to supervise his brother clergy, and to administer part of a diocese, hence his territorial designation. As well as his visitation duties he is in charge of the fabric of parish churches and their contents.

BEGINNING OF LETTER
> Dear Archdeacon[1]

ENDING OF LETTER
> Yours sincerely

ENVELOPE
> The Venerable[2] the Archdeacon of Exeter

VERBAL ADDRESS
> Archdeacon[3]

DESCRIPTION IN CONVERSATION
> The Archdeacon (of Exeter)

RETIRED ARCHDEACON

After retirement he is addressed as other clergy, i.e. 'The Reverend' in place of 'The Venerable' as above, unless he remains a Canon or Prebendary, or is appointed to emeritus rank, when he is addressed accordingly. The word 'emeritus' is only used in official documents. He is often incorrectly referred to as 'Archdeacon Smith' but the word 'archdeacon' signifies an office not a rank. Strictly speaking, there cannot be an Archdeacon Emeritus though the title is often used.

CANON

A Canon is either residentiary, with duties in his cathedral, or honorary. The latter is usually given to incumbents with a record of honourable service in the diocese.

[1] Prior to October 1968, the formal style was 'Venerable Sir' and the social style was 'Dear Mr. Archdeacon', which may still be adopted if preferred. It is usual to adopt the formal style for announcement at a public function.
[2] Often abbreviated to 'The Ven.'.
[3] Prior to October 1968, the verbal address was 'Mr. Archdeacon', which may still be adopted if preferred. It is usual to adopt the formal style for announcement at a public function.

A Minor Canon is a cleric attached to a cathedral or collegiate church to assist in the daily services. He is addressed as are other clergy (p. 121).

BEGINNING OF LETTER
> Dear Canon *or*
> Dear Canon Smith

ENDING OF LETTER
> Yours sincerely

ENVELOPE
> The Reverend Canon John Smith

VERBAL ADDRESS
> Canon *or*
> Canon Smith

DESCRIPTION IN CONVERSATION
> The Canon *or*
> Canon Smith

RETIRED CANON

After his retirement he is addressed as other clergy (p. 121) unless he is appointed a Canon Emeritus when he is addressed as previously. The word 'emeritus' in only used in official documents.

Honorary Canons usually retain their title unless they specifically resign it on leaving the diocese or retiring from the Church.

PREBENDARY

Prebendaries have a Prebendal Stall in certain cathedrals or collegiate churches. The appointment is similar to a nonresidentiary Canon.

BEGINNING OF LETTER
> Dear Prebendary *or*
> Dear Prebendary Smith

ENDING OF LETTER
> Yours sincerely

ENVELOPE

The Reverend Prebendary John Smith

VERBAL ADDRESS

Prebendary *or*
Prebendary Smith

DESCRIPTION IN CONVERSATION

Prebendary *or*
Prebendary Smith

RETIRED PREBENDARY

After retirement he is addressed as other clergy (below) unless he is appointed to emeritus rank. In this case he continues to be addressed as Prebendary. The word 'emeritus' is only used in official documents.

RURAL DEAN

No special form of address but he is often an honorary canon— see *Canon* (p. 129) or *Other Clergy* (below), as applicable.

OTHER CLERGY

BEGINNING OF LETTER

Dear Mr. Smith *or*
Dear Father Smith, according to personal preference.
When writing to beneficed clergy, the form 'Dear Rector' or 'Dear Vicar' may be used.[1]

ENDING OF LETTER

Yours sincerely,

ENVELOPE

The Reverend John Smith[2]
The form 'The Reverend Smith' or 'Reverend Smith' is incorrect and should never be used.

[1] The difference between a Rector and a Vicar is now purely nominal. A Rector was in receipt of greater and lesser tithes, and a Vicar of the lesser tithes only. Tithes were virtually abolished in 1936. Vicars are appointed to all new livings.
[2] For abbreviation of Reverend, see p. 111, note [2].

VERBAL ADDRESS

'Mr. Smith' *or* 'Father Smith', according to his personal preference.

DESCRIPTION IN CONVERSATION

'Mr. Smith' *or* 'Father Smith', according to his personal preference, or 'The Rector' or 'The Vicar', if applicable.

RELIGIOUS COMMUNITIES, CHURCH OF ENGLAND (MEN)

Ordained members of Religious Orders are addressed as Father, and lay members as Brother except in the case of the Society of St. Francis, all of whose members are called Brother.

The letters signifying the Religious Orders are given on p. 125.

The head of a Community may be:

The Right Reverend the Abbot
The Reverend the Prior
The Reverend Superior-General
The Reverend Pro-Superior
The Reverend Superior

BEGINNING OF LETTER

Superior

By his office, e.g.:

Dear Father Abbot
Dear Father Prior
Dear Father Superior (including Superior-General and Pro-Superior)

Other Ordained Members

Dear Reverend Father (this covers all ordained members) alternatively, the name may be used, e.g.:
Dear Father Smith
Dear Father David (for Orders where surnames are not used)
Dear Dom Andrew (Benedictine)
Dear Brother John (Franciscan)
Dear Father (all Orders where the name is not known)

Lay Members

Dear Brother Andrew
Dear Brother (all Orders where the name is not known)
Dear Dom Andrew (Benedictine)

ENDING OF LETTER

    Yours sincerely

ENVELOPE

By his office, followed by the letters to denote his Order,[1] e.g.:

    The Right Reverend the Lord Abbot, O.S.B.

    The Reverend the Prior, C.G.A.

Note.—A few communities do not have letters.

Other Ordained Members

    The Reverend Andrew Thompson, O.G.S., *or*

    The Reverend Fr. Andrew Thompson, O.G.S.

    The Reverend Fr. Andrew C.G.A. (if the surname is not
        used).

    The Reverend Dom John Smith, O.S.B. (Benedictine)

    Brother George, S.S.F. (Franciscan)

Lay Members

    Brother John (with his surname, if used by his Order)

    Dom John Smith, O.S.B. (Benedictine)

VERBAL ADDRESS

Superior

    Father Abbot

    Father Prior

    Father Superior (including Superior-General and Pro-
        Superior)

Other Ordained Members

    Father David (with his surname, if used by his Order)

    Dom John Smith, Dom John, *or* Father Smith (Benedictine)

    Brother George (Franciscan)

Lay Members

    Brother John *or*

    Brother

    Dom John (Benedictine)

    The surname or religious name may be used if distinction is
necessary or on introduction.

DESCRIPTION IN CONVERSATION

Superior

    The Abbot

    The Prior (or appropriate office)

[1] For the appropriate letters for Religious Orders, see p. 125.

Other Ordained Members
>Father Smith
>Father David
>Dom Andrew Smith (Benedictine)
>Brother Philip (Franciscan)

Lay Members
>Brother Andrew (and his surname if used by his Order)
>Dom John Smith

RELIGIOUS COMMUNITIES, CHURCH OF ENGLAND (WOMEN)

For the appropriate letters for Religious Orders, see p. 125.

BEGINNING OF LETTER

Superiors by their office, e.g.:
>Dear Mother Superior (including an Abbess)
>Dear Prioress
>Dear Reverend Mother
>Dear Sister Superior

Other Sisters
>Dear Sister Agnes
>Dear Dame Mary (Benedictine, having taken final vows)
>Dear Sister Mary (Benedictine)

ENVELOPE

Superiors
By office, followed by the letters of their Order (a few Communities do not have letters), such as:
>The Right Reverend the Abbess, O.S.B.
>The Reverend the Prioress
>The Reverend Mother Superior
>The Reverend Mother
>The Reverend Mother General
>The Reverend Sister Superior
>The Reverend Mother Audrey Mary

Other Sisters
>Sister Agnes, followed by the letters of her Order
>The Reverend Dame Mary Smith O.S.B. (Benedictine, having taken final vows)
>Sister Mary Smith O.S.B. (Benedictine)

VERBAL ADDRESS

Superiors by office, e.g.:
    Reverend Mother (in some communities 'Mother')
Other Sisters
    Sister Agnes (in some communities 'Sister')

DESCRIPTION IN CONVERSATION

Superiors by office, e.g.:
    The Lady Abbess
Other Sisters
    Sister Agnes
    Dame Mary Smith (Benedictine, if final vows have been
       taken)
    Sister Mary Smith (Benedictine)

RELIGIOUS ORDERS, CHURCH OF ENGLAND

(with recognized abbreviations)

Men

C.M.P.	Company of Mission Priests[1]
C.R.	Community of the Resurrection (Mirfield, Yorks.)
C.S.W.G.	Community of the Servants of the Will of God (Crawley Down, Sussex)
O.G.S.[1]	Oratory of the Good Shepherd (Greenford, Middlesex)
O.S.B.	Benedictine Community of Nashdom Abbey (Burnham, Bucks)
O.S.P.	Order of St. Paul (Alton)
S.S.F.	Society of St. Francis (Cerne Abbas)
S.S.J.E.	Cowley Fathers (Society of Mission Priests of St. John the Evangelist, Oxford)
S.S.M.	Society of the Sacred Mission (Willen, Milton Keynes)

Men and Women

C.G.A.	Community of the Glorious Ascension (Burton-on-Trent)

Women

C.A.H.	Community of All Hallows (Bungay, Suffolk)
C.B.V.M.	Community of the Blessed Virgin Mary (Rottingdean, Sussex)

[1] Not in the strict sense a Religious community, so does not come under the Advisory Council for Religious Communities.

C.E.	Community of the Epiphany (Truro)
C.H.C.	Community of the Holy Cross (Haywards Heath, Sussex)
C.H.F.	Community of the Holy Family (St. Leonards-on-Sea)
C.H.N.	Community of the Holy Name of Jesus (Malvern)
C.H.R.	Community of the Holy Rood (Middlesbrough)
C.J.G.S.	Community of the Companions of Jesus the Good Shepherd (Newton Abbot)
C.P.	Community of the Presentation (Hythe)
C.R.	Community of the Resurrection of Our Lord (Grahamstown, S. Africa and London)
C.R.J.B.S.	Community of Reparation to Jesus in the Blessed Sacrament (London)
C.S.A.	Community of St. Andrew (London)
C.S.C.	Community of Servants of the Cross (Lindfield, Sussex)
C.S.C.	Community of the Sisters of the Church (Ham Common, Surrey)
C.S.Cl.	Community of St. Clare (Freeland, Oxon.)
C.S.D.	Community of St. Denys (Warminster, Wilts.)
C.S.F.	Community of St. Francis (S. Petherton, Somerset)
C.S.J.B.	Community of St. John the Baptist (Clewer, Windsor)
C.S.K.	Community of St. Katharine of Egypt (Henley-on-Thames)
C.S.L.	Community of St. Laurence (Belper)
C.S.M.V.	Community of St. Mary the Virgin (Wantage)
C.S.P.	Community of St. Peter (Woking)
C.S.P.	Community of the Sacred Passion (Tanzania and East Hanningfield, Chelmsford)
C.S.P.H.	Community of St. Peter (Horbury, Yorks.)
C.S.W.	Community of St. Wilfrid (Exeter)
F.S.J.M.	Franciscan Servants of Jesus and Mary (Posbury St. Francis, Crediton)
N.S.S.J.D.	Community of Nursing Sisters of St. John the Divine (Hastings)
O.H.P.	Order of the Holy Paraclete (Whitby)
O.S.E.H.	Order of St. Elizabeth of Hungary (Heathfield)
S.C.	Servants of Christ (Burnham, Bucks.)
S.C.	Sisters of Charity (Bristol)
S.H.T.	Society of Holy Trinity (Ascot)

S.L.G.   Community of the Sisters of the Love of God (Oxford)

S.P.B.   Society of the Precious Blood (Burnham Abbey, Taplow)

S.S.B.   Sisters of Bethany (Bournemouth)

S.S.P.   Community of St. Peter the Apostle, Westminster (Laleham Abbey, Middlesex)

CHAPLAINS TO H.M. FORCES

A chaplain serving with H.M. Forces is addressed by his ecclesiastical rank, and never in speech by his relative Service rank, which is only for administrative purposes. It is not necessary or usual to write the Service rank, but when used formally it must appear in brackets after the ecclesiastical title and before the chaplain's christian name or initials.

The Chaplain of the Fleet, the Chaplain General to the Forces, Army, and the Chaplain-in-Chief, Royal Air Force, are Archdeacons, and therefore 'The Venerable' is placed before the name. Letters begin with the appointment or name, e.g. 'Dear Chaplain General' or 'Dear Archdeacon Smith'. Envelopes are addressed accordingly, e.g. 'The Chaplain of the Fleet', 'The Chaplain General', 'Chaplain-in-Chief' or 'The Venerable John Smith', followed by his appointment. Verbally they are addressed by their appointment or as Archdeacon, as may be appropriate.

The Deputy Chaplain General to the Forces, Army, the Principal Chaplain, Church of Scotland and Free Churches, Royal Navy, or Royal Air Force and the Principal Roman Catholic Chaplain, Royal Navy, Army or Royal Air Force are addressed in correspondence by name, or by appointment. Principal Roman Catholic Chaplains are Monsignori, and are addressed accordingly: see *Roman Catholic Church*.

Other chaplains are addressed by name or by appointment in correspondence as may be appropriate, e.g. 'Dear Canon Jones', 'Dear Mr. Jones', 'Dear Assistant Chaplain General', etc. When the name is used, the appointment held should be placed after the name, e.g.:

    The Reverend John Jones, O.B.E., M.A., C.F.
        Assistant Chaplain General,
            H.Q., Blankshire Command.

The letters R.N. and R.A.F. are placed after the names of chaplains to these Services, following any letters for decorations, etc. Army chaplains have the letters 'C.F.' after the name (following any letters for decorations, etc.). Verbally a chaplain may be addressed by name, or by appointment or by ecclesiastical title or, informally, as 'Padre'.

When the chaplain's name is not known, correspondence should be addressed to e.g.:

> The Church of England Chaplain,
>> R.A.F. Station,
>>> Blanktown.
>
> The Roman Catholic Chaplain,
>> H.M.S. Blankshire, etc.

Correspondence to a Jewish Chaplain is addressed, e.g.:

> The Reverend David Smith, C.F.,
>> Senior Jewish Chaplain,
>>> Blanktown Garrison, etc.

Verbally he is addressed as 'Rabbi', as 'Minister' or 'Padre' as may be appropriate.

ARCHBISHOPS' AND BISHOPS' SIGNATURES

CHURCH OF ENGLAND

Archbishops and Bishops sign, after a cross, by their christian names followed by their Province or See, sometimes in Latin, or a Latin abbreviation (see below), e.g.:

> + Donald Cantuar
> + Robin Worcester

The following sign, after the christian name, as below. Other Sees are accorded the usual spelling.

Archbishops

Canterbury	Cantuar
York	Ebor

Bishops

Carlisle	Carliol
Chester	Cestr
Chichester	Cicestr
Durham	Dunelm
Ely	Elien
Gloucester	Gloucestr
London	Londin
Norwich	Norvic
Oxford	Oxon
Peterborough	Petriburg

Rochester	Roffen
Salisbury	Sarum
Truro	Truron
Winchester	Winton

Retired Bishops
They sign their name after a cross, followed by Bishop.

CHURCH IN WALES

The Archbishop and Metropolitan signs, after a cross, his christian name followed by 'Cambrensis'. A Bishop signs, after a cross, his christian name and diocese. The Bishop of Llandaff signs as 'Landav' and others by the usual spelling of the diocese.

EPISCOPAL CHURCH IN SCOTLAND

Bishops, including the Primus, sign, after a cross, their christian name, followed by their dioceses, except that the Bishop of Moray, Ross and Caithness signs 'Moray' and the Bishop of St. Andrews, Dunkeld and Dunblane signs 'St. Andrews'—without the other dioceses.

The Bishop of Edinburgh signs by his christian name followed by 'Edenburgen'.

CHURCH OF IRELAND

Archbishops sign, after a cross, their christian name, followed by their Province; Bishops sign, after a cross, their christian name, followed by the first diocese in their title.

CHANCELLORS, DIOCESAN (See *Legal Section*).

The Church of Scotland

This is the Established Church in Scotland, and is Presbyterian by constitution. The Supreme Court of the Church is the General Assembly which meets annually in May and is presided over by a Moderator, who is appointed each year by the Assembly. The Sovereign either attends in person or is represented by the Lord High Commissioner to the General Assembly who is appointed by the Crown. The same styles are used whether a man or woman is appointed to this office.

THE LORD HIGH COMMISSIONER TO THE GENERAL ASSEMBLY

BEGINNING OF LETTER
Your Grace
This form of address is adhered to even when the Lord High Commissioner is a member of the Royal Family, with the sole exception of the Duke of Edinburgh who would be referred to as his Royal Highness in all references, having senior precedence to the Lord High Commissioner.

ENDING OF LETTER
I have the honour to remain,
Your Grace's most devoted and obedient servant.

ENVELOPE
His (or Her) Grace the Lord High Commissioner

VERBAL ADDRESS
Your Grace

DESCRIPTION IN CONVERSATION
The Lord High Commissioner

MODERATOR OF THE GENERAL ASSEMBLY

BEGINNING OF LETTER
Formal   Dear Sir *or*
                Dear Moderator
Social   Dear Mr. (Dr.) Smith *or*
                Dear Moderator

ENDING OF LETTER
Formal   Yours faithfully (see also p. 2)
Social   Yours sincerely

ENVELOPE
The Rt. Rev. the Moderator of the General Assembly of the Church of Scotland, *or*
The Rt. Rev. John Smith

VERBAL ADDRESS
Moderator

DESCRIPTION IN CONVERSATION
    The Moderator

FORMER MODERATORS

After his year of office a former Moderator is styled, The Very Reverend John Smith. Otherwise as for *Other Clergy* (Church of Scotland) below.

THE DEAN OF THE CHAPEL ROYAL AND THE DEAN OF THE THISTLE

They are styled 'The Very Reverend' (See *Dean, Church of England*, p. 117). Sometimes both appointments are held by one person.

OTHER CLERGY

BEGINNING OF LETTER

Formal	Dear Sir *or*
	Dear Minister
Social	Dear Mr. Smith *or*
	Dear Minister

ENDING OF LETTER

Formal	Yours faithfully (see also p. 2)
	Yours sincerely

ENVELOPE
    The Reverend John Smith
    The Minister of Blanktown (if a Minister of a Parish)
  If a lady be ordained she would be styled 'The Reverend Mary Smith.' (Mrs. or Miss is not used.)

VERBAL ADDRESS
    Mr. Smith *or*
    Minister

DESCRIPTION IN CONVERSATION
    Mr. Smith *or*
    The Minister

CHAPLAIN TO THE FORCES

See pp. 127-128.

The Methodist Church, the Baptist Union of Great Britain and Ireland, and Free Churches of Other Denominations

(See also *United Reformed Church* (p. 133), *the Presbyterian Church of Wales* (p. 134), and *in Ireland* (p. 134), *The Salvation Army* (p. 134) and the *Moravian Church in Great Britain and Ireland* (p. 136).)

MINISTERS

BEGINNING OF LETTER

Formal	Dear Sir or Madam
Social	Dear Dr., Mr., Mrs. *or* Miss Smith

ENDING OF LETTER

Formal	Yours faithfully (see also p. 2)
Social	Yours sincerely

ENVELOPE

The Reverend John Smith (The Reverend Dr. John Smith, *or* with the appropriate letters signifying a Doctor's degree). Lady Ministers are addressed as, The Reverend Mary Smith ('Mrs.' or 'Miss' is not used.)

VERBAL ADDRESS

Mr. (or Dr.) Smith

On the platform the President of the Methodist Church, the Methodist Church in Ireland, etc., and the President of the Baptist Union of Great Britain and Ireland (who may be a layman) are referred to as Mr. President.

The Congregational Federation consists of those members of the Congregational Church in England and Wales who did not join the United Reformed Church (see p. 133). The Chairman of the Congregational Union in Scotland is referred to as Mr. (or Madam) Chairman.

DESCRIPTION IN CONVERSATION
   Mr., Dr., Mrs., or Miss Smith *or*
   The Minister, The Pastor, The President, etc.

CHAPLAINS TO THE FORCES
See pp. 127-128.

DEACONESSES OF THE METHODIST CHURCH
She is referred to as Sister Jane Smith, and is known in her community as Sister Jane, but in a written description she may be referred to as Deaconess Jane Smith which distinguishes her from a nursing sister.

United Reformed Church of England and Wales

The United Reformed Church came into being 5th October, 1972, by the Union of the Presbyterian Church of England with the Congregational Church in England and Wales.

THE MODERATOR OF THE GENERAL ASSEMBLY OF THE UNITED REFORMED CHURCH IN ENGLAND AND WALES

BEGINNING OF LETTER

Formal	Dear Moderator (or Mr. Moderator)
Social	Dear Moderator (or Mr. Moderator)

ENDING OF LETTER

Formal	Yours faithfully (see also p. 2)
Social	Yours sincerely

ENVELOPE
   The Rt. Rev. John Smith

VERBAL ADDRESS
   Moderator (or Mr. Moderator)

DESCRIPTION IN CONVERSATION
   The Moderator

FORMER MODERATORS

After his year of office, a Moderator reverts to 'The Rev.'.

MINISTERS

As for the Church of Scotland, Other Clergy (p. 131), except that the form 'Dear Minister' is not used. Verbal address is Mr. Smith.

If a lady, she is styled The Rev. Mary Smith (Mrs. or Miss is not used).

The Presbyterian Church of Wales

Moderators of the General Assembly of the Presbyterian (or Calvinistic Methodist) Church of Wales continue to be styled 'The Reverend'.

It is not customary to address the Moderator of this Church by name.

BEGINNING OF LETTER

    Dear Moderator

Ministers are styled as for the United Reformed Church.

The Presbyterian Church in Ireland

Moderators of the General Assembly of the Presbyterian Church in Ireland are addressed as for the Presbyterian Church of England, viz. The Right Reverend.

Former Moderators are styled 'The Very Reverend'.

BEGINNING OF LETTER

    Dear Doctor Smith *or*
    Dear Moderator

Ministers are styled as for the United Reformed Church.

The Salvation Army

After a two years' residential course as a cadet, a student is commissioned as an officer, as the Movement terms its Ministers. Ranks are as follows:

    General
    Commissioner
    Colonel

Lieutenant-Colonel
Major
Captain
Lieutenant

N.B. The rank of Brigadier, junior to that of Lieutenant-Colonel, is now being phased out, and no further promotions to that rank are being made.

One Commissioner is appointed to be Chief of the Staff of the Salvation Army.

The senior officer of the Movement within other countries is the territorial commander, or officer commanding in smaller territories, who holds the rank of Commissioner, Colonel or Lieutenant-Colonel.

The senior officer of the whole Movement is the General of the Salvation Army who is elected by the High Council.

Married Officers

Commissioned officers marry within the commissioned ranks of the Salvation Army. If they marry outside these ranks they opt out of officership of the Salvation Army, though they may continue as lay members.

BEGINNING OF LETTER

According to their rank, as follows:

Dear General
Dear Chief (i.e. Chief of the Staff)
Dear Commissioner
Dear Colonel (includes Lieutenant-Colonel)
Dear Major
Dear Captain
Dear Lieutenant

An officer's wife may be referred to by her name (e.g. Mrs. Smith) or by her husband's rank (e.g. Mrs. Major Smith).

ENVELOPE

According to the exact rank held (e.g. Major John Jones or Captain Mary Brown), except for married ladies.

Married ladies take their husband's rank on marriage, e.g. the wife of Major Frank Briggs is addressed on the envelope 'Mrs. Major Frank Briggs'.

The Moravian Church in Great Britain and Ireland
Within this Church the term 'Brother' (including a Bishop) or
'Sister' may be used in general correspondence

BISHOP
BEGINNING OF LETTER
Dear Brother or Dear Bishop, followed by his surname

ENDING OF LETTER
Formal   Yours faithfully (see also p. 2)
Social   Yours sincerely

ENVELOPE
The Rt. Rev. John Smith

VERBAL ADDRESS AND DESCRIPTION IN CONVERSATION
Bishop Smith or Brother

PRESBYTERS AND DEACONS
(See *Ministers of the Methodist Church* (p. 132).)

The Roman Catholic Church
The territorial designation and the term 'My Lord' are not
officially recognized within the United Kingdom, and accordingly
are not used in official communications and documents. Hence in
these communications Archbishops, Bishops, Abbots and Priors
are addressed by name and not by their Province, Diocese, etc.
Letter endings tend to be more informal than in the past. For the
Order of St. Benedict and *The Society of Jesus* see these sections
(pp. 148–154).

THE POPE
BEGINNING OF LETTER
Your Holiness *or*
Most Holy Father

ENDING OF LETTER
For Roman Catholics   I have the honour to be,
                                  Your Holiness's most devoted
                                      and obedient child (or 'most
                                      humble child')

For non-Roman Catholics	I have the honour to be (or 'to remain'), Your Holiness's obedient servant

ENVELOPE
>His Holiness
>>The Pope

VERBAL ADDRESS
>Your Holiness

DESCRIPTION IN CONVERSATION
>His Holiness *or*
>The Pope

CARDINAL

If appointed to a See, he may be addressed by his appointment, e.g. 'His Eminence the Cardinal Archbishop of Westminster', otherwise as 'His Eminence Cardinal Smith'. The territorial designation is not *officially* used (see p. 136), when such letters are addressed to the person and not territorially to his Province or Diocese.

BEGINNING OF LETTER

Formal	Your Eminence (usual) *or* My Lord Cardinal
Officially Recognized	Your Eminence
Social	Dear Cardinal Smith

ENDING OF LETTER
Very Formal

Roman Catholic	I have the honour to be (or 'to remain'), My Lord Cardinal Your Eminence's devoted and obedient child

Roman Catholics in Holy Orders write 'servant' instead of 'child'

Formal	I remain, Your Eminence ('My Lord Cardinal' is sometimes used in place of 'Your Eminence'), Yours faithfully

Officially Recognized	I have the honour to be (*or* 'to remain'), Your Eminence's obedient servant
Social	Yours sincerely

ENVELOPE
Formal and Social

(if an Archbishop)	His Eminence the Cardinal Archbishop of Westminster
(if not an Archbishop)	His Eminence Cardinal Smith
Officially Recognized	His Eminence Cardinal Smith

VERBAL ADDRESS

Formal	Your Eminence
Social	Cardinal (Smith)

DESCRIPTION IN CONVERSATION

Formal	His Eminence
Social	The Cardinal *or* Cardinal Smith

ARCHBISHOP

On retirement from his office, a Roman Catholic Archbishop is appointed to a titular See, and is then normally addressed by name.[1]

BEGINNING OF LETTER

Formal	My Lord Archbishop
Officially Recognized	Most Reverend Sir
Social	Dear Archbishop

ENDING OF LETTER

Very Formal (Roman Catholic)	I have the honour to be (or 'to remain'), Your Grace's devoted and obedient child

Roman Catholics in Holy Orders write 'servant' instead of 'child'

[1] See p. 139, note [1]. A titular See is not normally used in ordinary correspondence, but if desired, it may be given on the next line of the envelope, e.g.:
The Right Reverend John Smith,
Bishop of Laodicea.

Formal	I remain,
	Your Grace,
	Yours faithfully *or*
	Yours faithfully (see also p. 2)
Officially Recognized	I have the honour to be,
	Most Reverend Sir,
	Your obedient servant
Social	Yours sincerely

ENVELOPE
Formal and Social	His Grace the Archbishop of Sydney
Officially Recognized	The Most Reverend Archbishop Smith
Titular Archbishop	The Most Reverend Archbishop Smith[1]

VERBAL ADDRESS
Formal	Your Grace
Social	Archbishop

DESCRIPTION IN CONVERSATION
Formal	His Grace
Social	The Archbishop (of Blank)

BISHOP

Roman Catholic Bishops are styled 'Right Reverend', except in Ireland, where they are styled 'Most Reverend'.

In lists prepared by non-Roman Catholic organizations, a Roman Catholic Bishop should be mentioned by his name (e.g. The Right Reverend Bishop Brown). If the territorial designation is given, and there is an Anglican Bishop whose See has the same name, it should be stated 'Roman Catholic Bishop of Lancaster'.

Letter endings have tended to be more informal than in the past.

On retirement from his See or office, a Bishop is appointed to a titular See, and addressed by name. Though it is not the usual practice, the titular See may be appended on the envelope after the name if desired.[1]

---

[1] By tradition a retiring Bishop is given the honorary title of a disused Diocese. In the past former Christian Sees in Asia Minor and Africa were used, with the Latin phrase 'in partibus infidelium'. Today English-speaking retired Bishops are assigned to titular English-speaking dioceses which have fallen into abeyance, and the Latin phrase discontinued. In 1969, for example, the retired Bishop of Rochester N.Y., was appointed titular Archbishop of Newport (Monmouthshire), a See which was replaced by Cardiff in 1916.

BEGINNING OF LETTER

Formal	My Lord (usual) *or* My Lord Bishop
Officially Recognized	Right Reverend Sir (*Note,* 'Most Reverend Sir' for an Irish Bishop)
Social	Dear Bishop *or* Dear Bishop Smith

ENDING OF LETTER

Very Formal

Roman Catholic	I have the honour to be, Your Lordship's obedient child

Roman Catholics in Holy Orders write 'servant' instead of 'child'.

Formal	I remain, My Lord, Yours faithfully ('My Lord Bishop' may be used in place of 'My Lord') *or* Yours faithfully (see also p. 2)
Officially Recognized	I have the honour to be (or 'to remain'), Right Reverend Sir, Your obedient servant (*Note,* 'Most Reverend Sir' for an Irish Bishop)
Social	Yours sincerely

ENVELOPE

Formal and Social	His Lordship the Bishop of Blank *or* The Right Reverend John Smith, Bishop of Bramber (*Note,* 'Most Reverend' for an Irish Bishop) The Right Reverend John Smith Auxiliary Bishop of . . .
Officially Recognized	The Right Reverend Bishop Smith

In Ireland the word 'Dr.' is included on the envelope before the name, e.g. 'The Most Reverend Dr. John Smith, Bishop of Kildare'.

VERBAL ADDRESS
Formal	My Lord (usual) *or*
	My Lord Bishop
Social	Bishop

DESCRIPTION IN CONVERSATION
Formal	His Lordship
Social	The Bishop

ABBOT
(See also *Order of St. Benedict,* pp. 149-150.)

BEGINNING OF LETTER
Formal	My Lord Abbot *or*
	Right Reverend and dear Father Abbot
Officially Recognized	Right Reverend Sir
Social	Dear Father Abbot

ENDING OF LETTER
Very formal	I beg to remain, my Lord Abbot, Your devoted and obedient servant,
Formal	Yours faithfully (see also p. 2)
Social	Yours sincerely

ENVELOPE
Formal and Social	The Right Reverend the Abbot of Blank (followed by the initials of his Order)
Officially Recognized	The Right Reverend John Smith (followed by the initials of his Order)

VERBAL ADDRESS
Formal	Father Abbot
Social	Abbot

DESCRIPTION IN CONVERSATION
The Abbot (of Blank)

MONSIGNOR

This title is held by virtue of a particular office, a Protonotary Apostolic, a Prelate of Honour or a Chaplain to His Holiness the Pope. By a recent pronouncement, Monsignori are addressed as The Reverend instead of the Right Reverend or The Very Reverend.

BEGINNING OF LETTER

Formal	Reverend Sir
Social	Dear Monsignor Smith (usual) *or*
	Dear Monsignore

ENDING OF LETTER

Formal	Yours faithfully (see also p. 2)
Social	Yours sincerely

ENVELOPE

 The Reverend Monsignor[1] John Smith *or*
 The Reverend Monsignore
If he is a Canon:
 The Very Reverend Monsignor[1] (Canon) John Smith

VERBAL ADDRESS

 Monsignor Smith (usually adopted) *or*
 Monsignore
If he is a Canon, he is usually known as 'Monsignor Smith'.

DESCRIPTION IN CONVERSATION

 Monsignor Smith

PROVINCIAL

The Provincial is the Superior of a Province in a Religious Order, such as the Dominicans, the Franciscans, or the Jesuits.

BEGINNING OF LETTER

Formal	Very Reverend Father Provincial
	or
	Very Reverend Father
Social	Dear Father Provincial *or*
	Dear Father Smith

[1] Often abbreviated to Mgr.

CONCLUSION OF LETTER
Formal   Yours faithfully (see also p. 2)
Social   Yours sincerely

ENVELOPE
> The Very Reverend Father Provincial (followed by the letters of his Order) *or*
> The Very Reverend Father Smith (followed by the letters of his Order)

VERBAL ADDRESS
> Father Provincial

DESCRIPTION IN CONVERSATION
> Father Provincial

PRIOR

(See also *Order of St. Benedict*, p. 150.)

BEGINNING OF LETTER
Very formal   Very Reverend and Dear Father
                         Prior
Formal and social   Dear Father Prior

ENDING OF LETTER
Formal   Yours faithfully (see also p. 2)
Social   Yours sincerely

ENVELOPE
> The Very Reverend the Prior of Blank *or*
> The Very Reverend John Smith
> (followed by the initials of his Order)

VERBAL ADDRESS
> Father Prior

DESCRIPTION IN CONVERSATION
> The Prior (of Blank)

PROVOST

The form of address is as for a Canon, with the substitution of Provost for Canon. See *Canon*, p. 144.

CANON

If he is a Monsignor, see *Monsignor* (p. 142).

BEGINNING OF LETTER

Formal	Very Reverend Sir
Social	Dear Canon Smith *or*
	Dear Canon

ENDING OF LETTER

Formal	Yours faithfully (see also p. 2)
Social	Yours sincerely

ENVELOPE

The Very Reverend Canon John Smith

VERBAL ADDRESS

Canon Smith

DESCRIPTION IN CONVERSATION

Canon Smith

PRIEST

A Regular (member of a Religious Order) or Secular Priest is addressed as 'Father'. (See also *Order of St. Benedict*, p. 151, *Friar,* p. 153, and *Society of Jesus,* pp. 153-154.)

BEGINNING OF LETTER

Formal	Dear Reverend Father
Social	Dear Father Smith

ENDING OF LETTER

Formal	Yours faithfully (see also p. 2)
Social	Yours sincerely

ENVELOPE

The Reverend John Smith (usual) *or*
The Reverend Fr. Smith
If a Regular, the initials of his Order should be inserted after his name.

VERBAL ADDRESS
    Father
    The surname may be used if distinction is necessary or on introduction *or* Father John (for Regulars where only the christian or religious name is used).

DESCRIPTION IN CONVERSATION
    Father Smith *or*
    Father John (for Regulars where only the christian or religious name is used).

LAY BROTHERS
They are verbally addressed as 'Brother' and referred to as 'Brother John'. (See also *Order of St. Benedict*, Monks not Priests p. 151, and *Friar,* p. 153.)

CHAPLAIN TO THE FORCES

See pp. 127-128.

Religious Communities (Women)

The appropriate letters of the Orders are placed after the name.
    Although previously a religious name was usually adopted on taking vows, and the christian name and surname not used, it is becoming the practice in some Orders to retain both christian name and surname.
    An Abbess is addressed 'The Lady Abbess' and in some Orders 'The Right Reverend and Lady Abbess'.
    (See also *Order of St. Benedict*, pp. 152-153.)

REVEREND MOTHER OR REVEREND SISTER SUPERIOR

BEGINNING OF LETTER
According to her office:
    Dear Reverend Mother *or*
    Dear Sister Superior

ENVELOPE
According to her office:
    The Reverend Mother Prioress
    The Reverend Mother
    The Sister Superior

VERBAL ADDRESS

According to her office:
Reverend Mother
Sister Superior

DESCRIPTION IN CONVERSATION

According to her office:
The Mother Prioress
The Reverend Mother
The Sister Superior

SISTER OF ORDERS

BEGINNING OF LETTER

Dear Sister Mary

ENVELOPE

The Reverend Sister Mary, D.C.
The Reverend Sister Mary O'Brien, with letters of her Order

VERBAL ADDRESS

Sister Mary

DESCRIPTION IN CONVERSATION

Sister Mary (O'Brien)

RELIGIOUS ORDERS, CONGREGATIONS, SOCIETIES, ETC. (ROMAN CATHOLIC) IN ENGLAND AND WALES
(See also *Brothers*, p. 148.)

A.A.	Assumptionists
C.I.C.M.	Scheut Fathers
C.J.	Josephites
C.M.	Vincentians
C.M.F.	Claretians
C.P.	Passionists
C.R.I.C.	Canons Regular of the Immaculate Conception
C.R.L.	Canons Regular of the Lateran
C.R.P.	
(or O.Praem)	Canons Regular of Prémontré
C.S.Sp.	Holy Ghost Fathers

C.SS.R.	Redemptorists (Congregation of the Most Holy Redeemer)
F.D.P.	Sons of Divine Providence
F.M.I.	Sons of Mary Immaculate
F.S.C.J.	Verona Fathers (Sons of the Sacred Heart)
I.C.	Institute of Charity, (Rosminians)
I.M.C.	Consolata Fathers
M.H.M.	Mill Hill Missionaries
M.I.C.	Marian Fathers
M.S.	Missionaries of La Salette
M.S.C.	Missionaries of the Sacred Heart
M.S.F.S.	Missionaries of St. Francis de Sales (Fransalians)
O.A.R.	Augustinian Recollects
O.Carm.	Calced Carmelites
O.Cart.	Carthusians
O.C.R.	Cistercians
O.D.C.	Discalced Carmelites
O.F.M.	Franciscans (Friars Minor)
O.F.M.Cap.	Franciscans (Friars Minor Capuchin)
O.F.M.Conv.	Franciscans (Friars Minor Conventual)
O.M.I.	Oblates of Mary Immaculate
O.P.	Dominicans
O.Praem.	See C.R.P.
O.S.A.	Augustinians
O.S.B.	Benedictines
O.S.Cam.	Camillians
O.S.M.	Servites
P.I.M.E.	P.I.M.E. Fathers (Pontifical Foreign Mission Institute of Milan)
P.S.S.C.	Pious Society of St. Charles
S.A.	Franciscan Friars of the Atonement
S.C.A.	Pallottines Fathers (Society of Catholic Apostolate)
S.C.J.	Sacred Heart Fathers
	Betharram Fathers (Priests of the Sacred Heart)
S.D.B.	Salesians (of Don Bosco)
S.D.S.	Salvatorians (Society of the Divine Saviour)
S.J.	Jesuits (Society of Jesus)
S.M.	Marists
S.M.A.	African Missions Society
S.M.B.	Bethlehem Fathers
S.M.M.	Montfort Missionaries (Company of Mary)

s.P.	Servants of the Holy Paraclete
S.P.S.	Society of St. Patrick
SS.CC.	Picpus Fathers
S.S.E.	Fathers of St. Edmund
S.S.P.	Society of St. Paul
S.S.S.	Blessed Sacrament Fathers
S.V.D.	Divine Word Missionaries
S.X.	Xaverian Fathers
W.F.	White Fathers (Society of Missionaries of Africa)

BROTHERS

C.F.A.	Alexians
C.F.C.	Brothers of Charity
C.F.X.	Xaverian Brothers
F.D.M.	Brothers of Mercy
F.I.C.	Brothers of Christian Instruction (Ploermel)
F.M.C.	Marist Brothers
F.S.C.	De la Salle Brothers
F.S.C.H.	Christian Brothers
O.H.	St. John of God (Order of Hospitallers)
S.C.	Brothers of Sacred Heart
S.S.G.	Brothers of St. Gabriel

WOMEN

They seldom use letters of abbreviation. Many Orders or Congregations do not have established abbreviations.

Order of St. Benedict

As the result of recent developments within the Order of St. Benedict, monks, whether clerical or lay, are to be addressed as 'Dom'. The style of 'Reverend' is to be extended to lay brothers by courtesy. At the present time all Benedictine monasteries have not yet adopted this system. Custom varies considerably from congregation to congregation and even from monastery to monastery.

The following notes are intended as a guide for use in Great Britain. American Benedictines of the two American Congregations do not use 'Dom' but are styled 'The Reverend John Smith, O.S.B.'.

Lay brothers are referred to as claustral brothers.

The form of addressing 'Juniors' (or 'Clerics', as they are called in some monasteries), i.e. monks studying for the priesthood, varies according to the monastery. In one the new monk is 'Dom John' from his novitiate until his ordination, when he becomes 'Father John'. In another, the student monk is 'Reverend Father John' until his ordination, when he becomes 'Dom John'.

Today, monks who are priests could be addressed verbally, and in informal letters as 'Father'; those who are not priests as 'Brother'. In formal letters and usage, 'Dom' may be applied to all. Many Benedictines are content not to have O.S.B. appended to the name, 'Dom' being sufficient distinction.

BENEDICTINE ABBOT

Benedictine Abbots in Great Britain are not 'Lord' Abbots. The head of a Benedictine Congregation is generally referred to as the Abbot President.

BEGINNING OF LETTER

To the Abbot President	Dear Father President
To other Abbots	Dear Father Abbot

ENVELOPE

To the Abbot President	The Right Reverend The Abbot President, X Abbey
To other Abbots	The Right Reverend The Abbot of Y, *or*
	The Right Reverend Father Abbot, *or*
	by name, The Right Reverend Dom A.S., Abbot of Y.

VERBAL ADDRESS

The Abbot President	Father President
Other Abbots	Father Abbot

DESCRIPTION IN CONVERSATION

The Abbot President	As such
Other Abbots	The Abbot (of Buckfast)

TITULAR ABBOTS

It is customary, though not invariably so, for a retired Abbot to take the title of an extinct Abbey. Titular Abbacies may also be conferred on individual monks. Such Abbots, if they have a local title, may be addressed as 'The Right Reverend the Abbot of X', but by practice and custom in the English Congregation they are usually addressed 'The Right Reverend Dom John Smith'. Letters may begin 'Dear Father Abbot', 'Dear Father John', or even 'Dear Abbot John'.

It has hitherto been customary to refer to Abbots by their surnames, e.g. Abbot Smith, but the more recent practice is to refer to them by the religious name 'Abbot John'. This practice is invariably adopted among American Benedictines.

ABBOT VISITOR OR ABBOT GENERAL

Where these offices exist, they are so addressed.

VERBAL ADDRESS
Father Abbot.

PRIOR

Priors, whether Conventual Priors (superiors of independent monasteries) or Claustral Priors (second in command to the Abbot in an Abbey) have the style Very Reverend.

A Conventual Prior is thus addressed on the envelope:

The Very Reverend the Prior
X Priory
or
The Very Reverend the Prior of X

A Claustral Prior is addressed on the envelope:

The Very Reverend the Prior,
X Abbey.

Letters begin 'Dear Father Prior'; and the address in conversation is 'Father Prior'.

TITULAR PRIORS

In the English Benedictine Congregation there are a number of titular Priors, bearing the titles of ancient Cathedral Monasteries. They are formally addressed or referred to as 'The Very Reverend the Prior of X', but by practice and custom in the congregation 'The Very Reverend Dom John Smith' is most usual. Letters begin 'Dear Father Prior', or, less formally, 'Dear Father John'.

PRIESTS

BEGINNING OF LETTER
Formal   Dear Dom Julian
Social   Dear Father Julian
                            Dear Father, if the name is not
                              known

ENDING OF LETTER
   Yours sincerely

ENVELOPE
   The Reverend Dom Julian Smith, O.S.B.
The use of 'The Reverend' and 'O.S.B.' is optional.

VERBAL ADDRESS
Formal   Dom John
Social   Father
                            If distinction is necessary or on
                              introduction 'Father Smith'.
He may be called by those who know him 'Dom', but this is
not usual.

In the Solesmes (French) Congregation, which includes Quarr
Abbey, Isle of Wight, 'Dom' is reserved to priest-monks. The
christian name is not normally used, but only the surname, as
'Dom Tissot'. 'Dom' is treated as an official style such as in
official occasions and notices, title pages of books, etc. but in
ordinary conversation 'Père' is used. Thus, in the former instance,
he would be known as 'Dom Tissot', described in conversation as
'le Père Tissot', and would be addressed in conversation as 'mon
Père'.

DESCRIPTION IN CONVERSATION
   Dom John Smith
Parochially he is often referred to as Father Smith.

MONKS WHO ARE NOT PRIESTS

This includes both monks who are preparing for priesthood and
those who are not going to take Orders.

Novices should always be addressed as 'Brother', and it is usual
in the English Congregation for this style to be used for those not
yet in Solemn or final Vows.

ENVELOPE

ENVELOPE

The Reverend Brother Julian Smith, O.S.B.

The use of 'The Reverend' and 'O.S.B.' is optional.

'Dom' may be used as appropriate in these cases, as for Priests.

DESCRIPTION IN CONVERSATION

Brother Julian

Benedictine Nuns

The following refers principally to the practice of the English Benedictine Congregation. In other Benedictine monasteries of nuns there is considerable diversity of practice.

ABBESS

She is formally referred to as Lady Abbess, though in one monastery at least, 'Mother Abbess' has replaced this.

BEGINNING OF LETTER

Dear Lady Abbess (or Mother Abbess)

ENVELOPE

The Lady Abbess (or Mother Abbess)

X Abbey.

The courtesy style of 'The Right Reverend' is not normally used.

VERBAL ADDRESS

Lady Abbess *or* Mother Abbess

DESCRIPTION IN CONVERSATION

The Lady Abbess *or* Mother Abbess

PRIORESS

A Prioress may be either a Conventual Prioress or a Claustral Prioress (corresponding to Conventual or Claustral Priors), though at present there are no Conventual Prioresses in the English Congregation. Prioresses are addressed and referred to as 'Mother Prioress'.

NUN IN FINAL VOWS

The formal style of address and reference is 'Dame' (corresponding to 'Dom' for a monk), but in ordinary use 'Sister' is now common.

BEGINNING OF LETTER
> Dear Dame Jane

ENVELOPE
> Dame Jane Smith

VERBAL ADDRESS
> Dame Jane *or* Sister Jane

DESCRIPTION IN CONVERSATION
> Dame Jane *or* Sister Jane

NOVICES, JUNIORS AND EXTERN SISTERS

They are addressed as Sisters.
> The envelope is addressed:
> Sister Jane Smith
> X Abbey

Friar

Members of certain Religious Orders, especially the Mendicant Orders of Franciscans (Grey Friars), Dominicans (Black Friars), Augustinians (Austin Friars) and Carmelites (White Friars) are known as friars and not monks, primarily due to their flexibility of movement within the Order. Each order is organized with a Father Provincial for each Province, and a Father Prior (or Father Guardian in the case of the Franciscan Order) for each House. Though friar means brother, the term covers all priests and lay brothers. Forms of address are as for those of other Religious Orders.

The Society of Jesus

Jesuits do not normally accept ecclesiastical dignities. To do so would be contrary to the views expressed by their founder, St.

Ignatius Loyola. The General, Provincials, Vice-Provincials and Major Superiors (normally those in charge of a mission area) are entitled to the prefix 'The Very Reverend'. All others are addressed as 'The Reverend'.

An exception to the above is when a Jesuit receives an episcopal appointment in special circumstances, e.g. as an Archbishop or Bishop. He then takes the appropriate ecclesiastical style for such Office.

Members of the Order append S.J. after their names. The Order is restricted to men.

The Jewish Community
The Orthodox Synagogues
They include the United Synagogue.

THE CHIEF RABBI
His appointment is Chief Rabbi of the United Hebrew Congregation of the British Commonwealth of Nations.

BEGINNING OF LETTER
Formal	Dear Sir, *or*
	Dear Chief Rabbi
Social	Dear Chief Rabbi

ENDING OF LETTER
Formal	Yours faithfully (see also p. 2)
Social	Yours sincerely

ENVELOPE
    The Chief Rabbi Dr. Immanuel Jakobovits
    The prefix 'The Very Reverend' is formally correct, but is not used by the present Chief Rabbi.

VERBAL ADDRESS
    Chief Rabbi

DESCRIPTION IN CONVERSATION
    The Chief Rabbi

THE CHIEF RABBI EMERITUS
As for the Chief Rabbi, but with the addition of 'Emeritus'.
    The Prefix 'The Very Reverend' is formally correct, but is not normally used.

ENVELOPE

> Chief Rabbi Emeritus Sir Israel Brodie, K.B.E.

RABBI

BEGINNING OF LETTER

Formal	Dear Sir
Social	Dear Rabbi Wiseman
	Dear Dr. Wiseman (if a doctor)

ENDING OF LETTER

Formal	Yours faithfully (see also p. 2)
Social	Yours sincerely

ENVELOPE

> Rabbi J. Wiseman
> Rabbi Dr. J. Wiseman (if a doctor).
> The 'Reverend' before Rabbi is not now used.

VERBAL ADDRESS

> Rabbi Wiseman
> Dr. Wiseman (if a doctor)

DESCRIPTION IN CONVERSATION

> Rabbi Wiseman
> Dr. Wiseman (if a doctor)

MINISTER

Readers and Cantors also use the title The Reverend.

BEGINNING OF LETTER

Formal	Dear Sir *or*
	Reverend Sir
Social	Dear Mr. Wiseman
	Dear Dr. Wiseman (if a doctor)

ENDING OF LETTER

Formal	Yours faithfully (see also p. 2)
Social	Yours sincerely

ENVELOPE

The Reverend David Wiseman
The Reverend Dr. David Wiseman (if a doctor)

VERBAL ADDRESS

Mr. Wiseman
Dr. Wiseman (if a doctor)

DESCRIPTION IN CONVERSATION

Mr. Wiseman
Dr. Wiseman (if a doctor)

CHAPLAIN TO THE FORCES

(See pp. 127-128.)

The Sephardi Synagogues

The Sephardi (Spanish and Portuguese) Community in Great Britain has several Synagogues. The oldest synagogue in the country is the Spanish and Portuguese Congregation in London, established in Creechurch Lane in the City of London in 1657. All the Sephardi Synagogues in Great Britain, and the Sephardi Community in Salisbury, Rhodesia, are under the spiritual jurisdiction of the Haham, the traditional title of the Chief Rabbi in Great Britain.

There are a number of Sephardi Rabbis who are not Ecclesiastical officials of Congregations.

The form of address for the Haham is as follows:

BEGINNING OF LETTER

Formal and Social   Dear Haham

ENDING OF LETTER

Formal   Yours faithfully (see also p. 2)
Social   Yours sincerely

ENVELOPE

The Very Reverend the Haham, Dr. S. Gaon

For *Rabbis* and *Ministers*, see pp. 155-156.

Reform and Liberal Synagogues

The Reform Synagogues of Great Britain and the Union of Liberal and Progressive Synagogues are separate organizations. However, they have a Council of Reform and Liberal Rabbis whose Chairman for the time being is their Ecclesiastical Representative.

The Ecclesiastical Representative and other Rabbis are addressed identically as Rabbis (p. 155).

Ministers are addressed identically as those on p. 155.

A woman was ordained a Rabbi on 28th June 1975, becoming the first woman outside the United States to be ordained, and the fourth woman in Jewish history to have become a Rabbi.

DIPLOMATIC AND COMMONWEALTH SECTION

A FOREIGN AMBASSADOR ACCREDITED TO THE UNITED KINGDOM AND A COMMONWEALTH HIGH COMMISSIONER

An Ambassador accredited to the Court of St. James's is accorded the style of His/Her Excellency within the United Kingdom and Colonies. A Commonwealth High Commissioner in the United Kingdom is accorded the same style and precedence as an Ambassador.

The wife of an Ambassador or High Commissioner is not entitled to the style of 'Her Excellency' and is referred to and addressed by her name in official documents, but is sometimes called 'Her Excellency' by courtesy, if coupled with her husband's name or in a list of Ambassadors' wives. The term 'Ambassadress' for the wife of an Ambassador is gaining currency in London. It is used in other countries, but *never* for a lady Ambassador.

The husband of a Ambassador is not accorded any style as such.

Precedence within the Diplomatic Corps is accorded to an Ambassador and High Commissioner in a common roll from the time they take up their duties in London. *The London Diplomatic List,* published at two monthly intervals by H.M.S.O., contains, after the alphebetical list, a list of the heads of diplomatic missions in London in order of precedence. See *Precedence section,* p. 309.

It is always correct to describe an Ambassador or High Commissioner by adding the country after the name, e.g. 'His Excellency the Ambassador of Jordan' or 'His Excellency the High

Commissioner for Canada'. (Note the word 'for' in respect of Commonwealth countries.) It is also correct and often preferable to use the adjectival form if of long established use, e.g. 'His Excellency the French Ambassador', but there are semantic or political hazards in several instances. An advantage of the former system is that the full terminology of the Ambassador's country may be used, e.g. 'The Ambassador of the People's Democratic Republic of Yemen', as distinct from his neighbour 'The Ambassador of the Yemen Arab Republic', neither being easily rendered adjectivally. There is a growing use of the name of the country in place of its adjectival equivalent, as for example 'The Jordan Ambassador', rather than 'The Jordanian Ambassador'. 'Netherlands' is used in diplomatic circles, and not 'Dutch'.

In a letter to an Ambassador or High Commissioner, it is usual to mention 'Your Excellency' in the opening paragraph. In a long letter, subsequent references may be made to 'You' or 'Your', e.g. 'I am most grateful to you for your assistance', but 'Your Excellency' is again stated in the closing section.

BEGINNING OF LETTER

Formal	Your Excellency
Social	(My) dear Ambassador
	(My) dear High Commissioner

ENDING OF LETTER

Formal for an Ambassador	I have the honour to be, with the highest consideration, Your Excellency's obedient servant
Formal for a High Commissioner	As above, with the omission of 'with the highest consideration'.
Social for an Ambassador	Believe me, My dear Ambassador Yours (very) sincerely
Social for a High Commissioner	Believe me, Yours (very) sincerely

ENVELOPE

His (Her) Excellency always precedes all other styles, titles or ranks, Señor, etc. precedes Don or Doctor. An Armed Forces rank immediately follows His Excellency, e.g.:

His Excellency General . . .
His Excellency Doctor . . .
His Excellency Monsieur, Mr., Herr, Signor, Sẽnor,
Senhor . . . etc.

See *Foreign Equivalents of 'Mr.'*, pp. 384-386.

If an Ambassador is His/Her Royal Highness, His/Her Highness or His/Her Serene Highness, 'His/Her Excellency' is unnecessary.

'Esquire' cannot be used after 'His Excellency'.

Formal and Social	His Excellency
	The Ambassador of Finland
	or
	His Excellency
	The Finnish Ambassador

Alternatively, the envelope may be addressed to 'His Excellency Mr. A.B.C.', followed by post-nominal letters if known, especially if British Orders of Chivalry have been received. In such a case, where a recipient also has foreign honours, 'etc., etc.' may be added, for the latter. This alternative form is to be preferred when the address that follows is not that of the Embassy or when the letter is purely private.

VERBAL ADDRESS

Formal	Your Excellency should be mentioned at least once in conversation, thereafter 'Sir' (Madam) *or* by name
Social	Ambassador, *or* by name
	High Commissioner *or* by name
	'Mr. Ambassador' and 'Ambassador Smith' are foreigners' English but not objectionable.

DESCRIPTION IN CONVERSATION

Formal	His Excellency
Social	The French Ambassador *or*
	The Ambassador of the Ivory Coast *or*
	The Ambassador *or*
	by name (as applicable)
	The Canadian High Commissioner *or*

The High Commissioner for
 Canada *or*
The High Commissioner
or by name (as applicable)

JOINT FORM OF ADDRESS
 His Excellency the French Ambassador and Madame le
 Blanc (or appropriate title)
Similarly for a High Commissioner and his wife.

BRITISH AMBASSADOR ACCREDITED TO A FOREIGN COUNTRY

A British Ambassador accredited to a foreign country is known as
'His/Her Excellency' *within the country to which he/she is accredited* and often by courtesy when travelling outside it on duty, but
not in the United Kingdom. Similarly an Ambassador who is
Head of a United Kingdom Mission abroad (e.g. to the United
Nations) is styled 'His/Her Excellency'.

A lady Ambassador is called Ambassador, and *not* Ambassadress.
Her husband is not accorded any style as such.

The wife of an Ambassador is not entitled to the style of 'Her
Excellency'. She is addressed and referred to by her name, or
conversationally as the Ambassadress.

BEGINNING OF LETTER
Formal   Sir/Madam
Social   (My) dear Ambassador

ENDING OF LETTER
Formal   I have the honour to be
                                              Sir/Madam
                                              Your Excellency's obedient
                                                  Servant,
Social   Believe me,
                                              My dear Ambassador
                                              Yours (very) sincerely,

ENVELOPE
Peer   His Excellency the Viscount
                                              Flintshire, K.C.M.G.[1]

---

[1] If desired 'H.M. Ambassador' may be added. Either form should be followed by 'British
Embassy', except where the residence is not within the Embassy.

Privy Counsellor	His Excellency the Rt. Hon. John Jones, C.M.G.[1]
Knight	His Excellency Sir William Smith[1]
Esquire	His Excellency Mr. John Smith, C.M.G.[1]
	His Excellency Major-General John Brown, C.M.G.[1]
	'Esq.' is not used with His Excellency.

VERBAL ADDRESS

Formal	Your Excellency should be mentioned at least once in conversation, thereafter, Sir, *or* by name
Social	Ambassador, *or* by name

DESCRIPTION IN CONVERSATION

Formal	His Excellency
Social	The British Ambassador, *or* The Ambassador *or* by name (as applicable)

BRITISH HIGH COMMISSIONER IN A COMMONWEALTH COUNTRY

A High Commissioner is accorded the same style and precedence as an Ambassador, and is styled 'His Excellency'.

A Deputy High Commissioner is usually appointed, but has no prefix. A letter may be addressed by name or Dear Deputy High Commissioner.

MINISTER

It used to be normal practice to establish a Legation headed by a Minister, instead of an Embassy headed by an Ambassador, in foreign capitals of less than primary importance. Today it is very rare, having been widely replaced by the accreditation of Ambassadors resident elsewhere. There is now but one British Legation overseas, headed by Her Majesty's Minister accredited to the

[1] If desired 'H.M. Ambassador' may be added. Either form should be followed by 'British Embassy', except where the residence is not within the Embassy.

Holy See, who is styled His Excellency and addressed in other respects like an Ambassador with the substitution of Minister.

In London all the Diplomatic Missions are Embassies or High Commissions.

However the old practice gave rise to the use of the terms Minister Plenipotentiary, Minister and Minister-Counsellor to denote both appointments and grades in the diplomatic world, coming between Ambassador and Counsellor. There are many such in London, and they may be addressed either by name or by appointment, more commonly by name.

In the British Diplomatic Service the terms Minister Plenipotentiary and Minister-Counsellor are not used, but in the larger British diplomatic missions abroad there are Ministers who assist the Ambassador. They are normally addressed by name, but may be referred to as the Minister, the Minister (Economic), etc.

DEPUTY HIGH COMMISSIONER

Within the Commonwealth it is usual to appoint a Deputy High Commissioner to assist the High Commissioner, and act for him in his absence. He may be addressed and referred to by name or, perhaps more commonly, as Deputy High Commissioner.

CHARGÉ D'AFFAIRES AND ACTING HIGH COMMISSIONER

In the temporary absence of the permanent head of a diplomatic mission, or between appointments as such, a Chargé d'Affaires ad interim (a.i.) is generally appointed to conduct business. Within the Commonwealth he is generally appointed as and styled Acting High Commissioner. A Chargé d'Affaires en titre is occasionally accredited as a permanent head of mission when there is no present intention to accredit an Ambassador.

Chargés d'Affaires and Acting High Commissioners represent their government rather than their Head of State and are not accorded the style of Excellency.

An Acting High Commissioner is usually addressed by name, but it is not incorrect to address him/her by appointment thus, 'My dear Acting High Commissioner'.

BEGINNING OF LETTER

Formal	Sir
Social	(My) dear Chargé d'Affaires
	or by name

CONCLUSION OF LETTER

Formal	I have the honour to be, Sir,
Foreign	with high consideration, Your obedient Servant
British	I have the honour to be, Sir, Your obedient Servant
Social	Yours sincerely

ENVELOPE

John Brown, Esq.,
Chargé d'Affaires,
British Embassy, . . .

Monsieur Georges Van
    Cleef,
Chargé d'Affaires
. . . Embassy

John Brown, Esq.,
Acting High Commissioner,
British High Commission, . . .

Shri K. Singh,
Acting High Commissioner,
. . . High Commission

VERBAL ADDRESS

Chargé d'Affaires
or by name

DESCRIPTION IN CONVERSATION

The Guatamalan Chargé d'Affaires, *or*
The Chargè d'Affaires of Guatamala
The British Chargé d'Affaires
or by name (as applicable)

The Acting High Commissioner for Sri Lanka
or by name

OTHER MEMBERS OF DIPLOMATIC STAFFS, INCLUDING SERVICE ATTACHÉS

Ministers Plenipotentiary, Ministers, Minister-Counsellors, Counsellors, Advisers, First, Second and Third Secretaries, Attachés, etc. i.e. Diplomats who are not head of their mission, are usually addressed by name, but Consuls and Consul-Generals are usually addressed as such (see below).

CONSUL-GENERAL, CONSUL, OR VICE-CONSUL

A Consul-General, Consul, or Vice-Consul who holds Her Majesty's Commission is entitled to the letters 'H.M.' before the appointment. The formal style of 'H.B.M.' (Her Britannic Majesty) is not now used.

Other Consuls, Vice-Consuls, and Consular Agents, appointed other than by the Crown, are known as the British Consul, Vice-Consul, etc., and do not have the prefix 'H.M.'.

The officer in charge of a Consular appointment, during the absence of the incumbent, takes for the time being the rank of the incumbent, but is addressed as 'The Acting British Consul-General, Consul', etc.

Consuls of the other Commonwealth Countries are addressed as 'The Australian Consul', etc.

ENVELOPE

> John H. Brown, Esq., C.M.G.,
> H.M. Consul-General,
> British Consulate-General

> William Smith, Esq.,
> H.M. Consul,
> British Consulate

> William Jones, Esq.,
> British Consul,
> British Consulate

Otherwise as an Esquire or appropriate style.

For precedence *vis-a-vis* officers of the Armed Forces, see Part V.

AGENT-GENERAL

Each Province in Canada and each State of Australia is represented in London by an Agent-General.

Lieutenant	Captain	Flight Lieutenant
Sub-Lieutenant	Lieutenant	Flying Officer
	Second Lieutenant	Pilot Officer

Officers of the same rank, rank with each other according to their seniority.

Royal Navy

'ROYAL NAVY' or 'R.N.' PLACED AFTER THE NAME

All officers of the Royal Navy below the rank of Rear-Admiral are entitled to the words 'Royal Navy' or 'R.N.' after their name proceeded by decorations, etc. whether on the active or retired lists. The Royal Navy prefer this to be written in full, but the abbreviation 'R.N.' is customarily used.

ADMIRAL OF THE FLEET

This is a rank held for life. (See also *Titled Officers*, p. 167.)

BEGINNING OF LETTER

According to his title (he would almost certainly be a peer, baronet, or knight).

Formal

| If a Peer | My Lord |
| Otherwise | (Dear) Sir |

Social

If a Peer, Baronet, or Knight	Dear Lord Blank
	Dear Sir John (the surname may be added if the acquaintanceship is slight)
Otherwise	Dear Admiral Smith

ENDING OF LETTER

| *Formal* | Yours faithfully (see also p. 2) |
| *Social* | Yours sincerely |

ENVELOPE

According to rank, with the appropriate letters after his name, e.g.:
Admiral of the Fleet the Earl of Flintshire, G.C.B., K.B.E.
Admiral of the Fleet Sir John Brown, G.B.E., K.C.B.

VERBAL ADDRESS

According to his title[1]:

Lord Brown

Sir John

He may prefer to be known by his naval rank, which is socially abbreviated to 'Admiral'.

A younger man, or a more junior officer in any of the Armed Forces addresses him as 'Sir'.

DESCRIPTION IN CONVERSATION

Lord Flintshire

Sir John Brown

If reference is made to his rank, Admiral of the Fleet is used in full.

ADMIRAL, VICE-ADMIRAL, REAR-ADMIRAL

All three ranks are known socially as Admiral. The exact rank is given within the Royal Navy, on the envelope or in a formal description.

(See also *Titled Officers*, p. 167.)

BEGINNING OF LETTER

Formal	(Dear) Sir
Social	
If a Knight	Dear Sir William[1] (the surname may be added if the acquaintanceship is slight)
Otherwise	Dear Admiral Robinson

CONCLUSION OF LETTER

Formal	Yours faithfully (see also p. 2)
Social	Yours sincerely

ENVELOPE

This is addressed to the exact rank, with the appropriate letters following the name, e.g.

Admiral Sir William Smith, G.C.B.

Vice-Admiral Sir John Brown, K.B.E., M.V.O.

Rear-Admiral John Robinson, V.C., C.B., O.B.E.

[1] If he prefers his Naval rank to be used, letters begin 'Dear Admiral Blank', and the verbal address is 'Admiral Blank' or 'Admiral'. (See also *Use of an Officer's Rank Without His Surname*, p. 168.)

VERBAL ADDRESS

If a Knight	Sir William[1]
Otherwise	Admiral Robinson

A younger man, or a more junior officer in any of the Armed Forces addresses him as 'Sir'.

DESCRIPTION IN CONVERSATION

If a Knight	Sir William Smith
Otherwise	Admiral Robinson

Should social reference be made to only one Admiral, Vice-Admiral, or Rear-Admiral he may be called informally 'the Admiral'.

COMMODORE[2] OR CAPTAIN

BEGINNING OF LETTER

Formal	(Dear) Sir
Social	Dear Commodore Smith
	Dear Captain Smith

These ranks should not be abbreviated.

ENDING OF LETTER

Formal	Yours faithfully (see also p. 2)
Social	Yours sincerely

ENVELOPE

Commodore John Smith, C.B.E., Royal Navy (or R.N.)
Captain John Brown, C.B., Royal Navy (or R.N.)
These ranks should not be abbreviated.

VERBAL ADDRESS

Commodore Smith
Captain Smith

A younger man, or a more junior officer in any of the Armed Forces, addresses him as 'Sir'.

DESCRIPTION IN CONVERSATION

Commodore Smith
Captain Smith

---

[1] If he prefers his Naval rank to be used to that appropriate for his knighthood, letters begin 'Dear Admiral Blank', and the verbal address is 'Admiral Blank' or 'Admiral'. (See *Titled Officers*, p. 167, and *Use of an Officer's Rank Without His Surname*, p. 168.)
[2] See p. 168, note 1.

COMMANDER OR LIEUTENANT-COMMANDER

In the Royal Navy he is styled Commander or Lieutenant-Commander, as applicable, but socially both are styled Commander. The exact rank is given on the envelope or in a list.

BEGINNING OF LETTER
Formal   (Dear) Sir
Social   Dear Commander Smith (this rank should
                                   not be abbreviated)

ENDING OF LETTER
Formal   Yours faithfully (see also p. 2)
Social   Yours sincerely

ENVELOPE
     Commander John Smith, O.B.E., Royal Navy (or R.N.)
     Lieutenant-Commander John Jones, Royal Navy (or R.N.)
These ranks should not be abbreviated.

VERBAL ADDRESS
     Commander Smith
     A younger man, or a more junior officer in any of the Armed Forces addresses him as 'Sir'.

DESCRIPTION IN CONVERSATION
     Commander Smith

LIEUTENANT

As for a Commander, with the substitution of Lieutenant.

SUB-LIEUTENANT[1]

BEGINNING OF LETTER
Formal   (Dear) Sir
Social   Dear Mr. Smith

ENDING OF LETTER
Formal   Yours faithfully (see also p. 2)
Social   Yours sincerely

---

[1] The ranks of Commissioned Warrant Officer (e.g. Commissioned Signal Boatswain) and Warrant Officer (e.g. Warrant Telegraphist) have been abolished. Those that remain on the retired list do not normally use their ranks.

ENVELOPE
> Sub-Lieutenant John Smith, Royal Navy (or R.N.)
> This rank should not be abbreviated.

VERBAL ADDRESS
> Mr. Smith

DESCRIPTION IN CONVERSATION
> Mr. Smith

MIDSHIPMAN

A Midshipman is addressed as for a Sub-Lieutenant, with the exception of the envelope which is addressed according to his rank, i.e.:

> Midshipman John Smith, Royal Navy (or R.N.)
> There is now no rank of Cadet Royal Navy. Those who join the Britannia R.N. College Dartmouth have the rank of Midshipmen.

MEDICAL, DENTAL AND INSTRUCTOR OFFICERS[1]

The ranks of naval Medical Officers are preceded by 'Surgeon', e.g. Surgeon Rear-Admiral Sir John Green, K.B.E.

The ranks of naval Dental Officers are preceded by 'Surgeon' and suffixed '(D)', e.g. Surgeon Lieutenant (D) Richard Green, R.N.R.

The ranks of naval Instructor Officers are preceded by 'Instructor', e.g. Instructor Commander James Smith, Royal Navy.

WOMEN MEDICAL AND DENTAL OFFICERS

These are officers of the Royal Navy and are addressed accordingly (i.e. *not* as if they were members of the Women's Royal Naval Service).

RETIRED AND FORMER OFFICERS

Admirals of the Fleet remain on the active list for life and so continue to hold this rank. Other officers of the rank of lieutenant-commander and above customarily use, and are addressed by, their rank after being placed on the retired list. More junior officers who are no longer actively employed do not do this.

The word 'retired' (abbreviated to 'Ret' or 'Rtd') should *not* be added after an officer's name in ordinary correspondence or in

---

[1] The ranks of Engineer and Paymaster have been abolished. However, a few of the former continue to style themselves, e.g. Engineer Captain, on the retired list.

lists, but only when it is specifically necessary to indicate that an officer is on the retired list, e.g. one employed in a civilian capacity in a Ministry of Defence establishment where it facilitates postal arrangements.[1]

For retired officers who take Holy Orders, see p. 111 note [1].

ROYAL NAVAL RESERVE

Forms of address are as for the Royal Navy except for 'Royal Naval Reserve' (or 'R.N.R.') after the name. But most officers only use their ranks when under training or when called up for service with the Royal Navy. (The Royal Naval Volunteer Reserve (R.N.V.R.) was merged with the R.N.R. shortly after World War Two.)

CHAPLAINS TO THE ROYAL NAVY

(See *Chaplains to H.M. Forces*, pp. 127-128.)

NON-COMMISSIONED RATES

The principal rates,[2] excluding technical and specialist rates, are as follows:

> Fleet Chief Petty Officer (F.C.P.O.)
> Chief Petty Officer (C.P.O.)
> Petty Officer (P.O.)
> Leading Seaman (Ldg. Smn.)
> Able-Bodied Seaman (A/B)

BEGINNING OF LETTER

Dear Mr. Smith (for a Fleet Chief Petty Officer), otherwise according to rate, e.g. Dear Chief Petty Officer Smith.

ENVELOPE

According to rate.

Rates should not be abbreviated to prevent confusion with initials of christian names.

VERBAL ADDRESS

According to rate.

---

[1] One regrets to see how often the word 'retired' (or an abbreviation of it) is wrongly included after the name of an officer when his death is announced in *The Times* or *Daily Telegraph*.
[2] These rates are customarily used only by men actively employed; not, e.g. by pensioners.

Royal Marines

Forms of address are as for the Army.

Those of the rank of Lieutenant-Colonel and below place R.M. (some prefer 'Royal Marines' in full) after their name.

Retired Royal Marine Officers may place Royal Marines or R.M. after their names.

NON-COMMISSIONED RANKS

The principal ranks[1] are as follows:
    Warrant Officer Class 1 (W.O. I)
    Warrant Officer Class 2 (W.O. II)
    Colour Sergeant (C.Sgt.)
    Sergeant (Sgt.)
    Corporal (Cpl.)
    Lance Corporal (L.Cpl.)
    Marine (Mne.)

BEGINNING OF LETTER
    Warrant Officer   Dear Mr. Smith
    Colour Sergeant   Dear Colour Sergeant Smith
  Otherwise, as for the Army.

ENVELOPE
According to rank.

VERBAL ADDRESS
As for beginning of letter (omitting 'Dear').

The Army

FIELD MARSHAL

This rank is held for life.
  (See also *Titled Officers*, p. 167.)

BEGINNING OF LETTER
According to his title (he would almost certainly be a peer, baronet, or knight).[2]
Formal
    If a Peer   My Lord
    Otherwise   (Dear) Sir

---

[1] These ranks are customarily used only by men actively employed; not, e.g. by pensioners.
[2] When he prefers his Military rank to be used, letters are commenced 'Dear Field Marshal Blank'. (See also *Use of an Officer's Rank Without His Surname*, p. 168.)

Social
If a Peer	Dear Lord Blank
Otherwise	Dear Sir John (the surname may be added if the acquaintanceship is slight)

ENDING OF LETTER

Formal	Yours faithfully (see also p. 2)
Social	Yours sincerely

ENVELOPE

According to rank with the appropriate letters after his name, e.g.:

Field Marshal (the Rt. Hon.) the Lord Blank, G.C.B.
Field Marshal Sir John Brown, K.C.B.

VERBAL ADDRESS

According to his title:[1]

Lord Blank
Sir John

A younger man, or a more junior officer in any of the Armed Forces, addresses him as 'Sir'.

DESCRIPTION IN CONVERSATION

Lord Horsham
Sir John Brown *or* The Field Marshal

If reference is made to his rank, Field Marshal is used in full.

GENERAL, LIEUTENANT-GENERAL, MAJOR-GENERAL OR BRIGADIER-GENERAL

All four ranks are referred to as General, except on the envelope, or formally, such as in a list, when the exact rank is given.

The rank of Brigadier-General was abolished in the United Kingdom in 1921. It is included because a few retired Brigadier-Generals are still living. The rank of Brigadier-General (in place of Brigadier) has recently been restored to the Canadian Armed Forces. (See *Commonwealth Armed Forces*, p. 195.)

(See *Titled Officers*, p. 167.)

---

[1] When he prefers his Military rank to be used, the verbal address is 'Field Marshal Blank' or 'Field Marshal'. (See also *Use of an Officer's Rank Without His Surname*, p. 168.)

BEGINNING OF LETTER
Formal   (Dear) Sir
Social
    If a Knight   Dear Sir John[1] (the surname may be
                       added if the acquaintanceship is slight)
    Otherwise   Dear General Smith

ENDING OF LETTER
Formal   Yours faithfully (see also p. 2)
Social   Yours sincerely

ENVELOPE
According to the exact rank, with the appropriate letters after
the name, e.g.:
    General Sir Edward Jones, G.C.B.
    Lieutenant-General Sir John Smith, K.C.B.
    Major-General John Jones, C.B., C.B.E.
    Brigadier-General William Robinson, C.I.E., D.S.O.
    The ranks should not be abbreviated.

VERBAL ADDRESS
If a Knight   Sir John[1]
Otherwise   General Jones *or* General
    A younger man, or a more junior officer in any of the Armed
Forces, addresses him as 'Sir'.
    (See *Titled Officers*, p. 167.)

DESCRIPTION IN CONVERSATION
If a Knight   Sir John Smith[2]
Otherwise   General Jones
    Should social reference be made to only one General Officer,
he may be called 'the General'.

BRIGADIER

This rank was adopted in 1928.

BEGINNING OF LETTER
Formal   (Dear) Sir
Social   Dear Brigadier Smith[2]
    This rank should not be abbreviated.

If he prefers his military rank to be used letters begin 'Dear General Blank', and the verbal
address is 'General Blank', or 'General'. (See also *Use of an Officer's Rank Without His Surname*,
p. 168.)
[2] See also *Use of an Officer's Rank Without the Surname*, p. 168.

ENDING OF LETTER

Formal	Yours faithfully (see also p. 2)
Social	Yours sincerely

ENVELOPE

Brigadier John Brown, D.S.O., M.C.
This rank should not be abbreviated.

VERBAL ADDRESS

Brigadier Brown *or* Brigadier
A younger man, or a more junior officer in any of the Armed Forces, addresses him as 'Sir'.

DESCRIPTION IN CONVERSATION

Brigadier Brown
Should social reference be made to only one Brigadier he may be called 'the Brigadier'.

COLONEL OR LIEUTENANT-COLONEL

Both ranks are referred to as Colonel, except on the envelope, or in a formal description, such as a list when the exact rank is given.

BEGINNING OF LETTER

Formal	(Dear) Sir
Social	Dear Colonel Robinson[1]

This rank should not be abbreviated.

ENDING OF LETTER

Formal	Yours faithfully (see also p. 2)
Social	Yours sincerely

ENVELOPE

The Regiment or Corps (or abbreviations) may be added to an officer on the active list.

Lieutenant-Colonel Edward Black, M.C.,
Grenadier Guards
These ranks should not be abbreviated.

[1] See also *Use of an Officer's Rank Without His Surname*, p. 168.

VERBAL ADDRESS
> Colonel Brown *or* Colonel

A younger man, or a more junior officer in any of the Armed Forces, addresses him as 'Sir'.

DESCRIPTION IN CONVERSATION
> Colonel Brown

MAJOR OR CAPTAIN

The form of address is as for a Colonel, with the substitution of Major or Captain.

LIEUTENANT OR SECOND LIEUTENANT

BEGINNING OF LETTER

Formal	(Dear) Sir.
Social	Dear Mr. Jones

ENDING OF LETTER

Formal	Yours faithfully (see also p. 2)
Social	Yours sincerely

ENVELOPE
The Regiment or Corps may be added on the next line, as for a Lieutenant-Colonel.
> John Brown, Esq.,
> Grenadier Guards[1]

VERBAL ADDRESS
> Mr. Brown

The verbal use of the terms 'Cornet' for a 2nd Lieutenant of The Blues and Royals, and 'Ensign' for a 2nd Lieutenant of Foot Guards is restricted to within the Household Division.

DESCRIPTION IN CONVERSATION
> Mr. Brown

WOMEN MEDICAL AND DENTAL OFFICERS

These are officers of the R.A.M.C. or R.A.D.C., but forms of address are as for the Women's Royal Army Corps (see p. 190).

[1] It is now the practice in some regiments to include the rank of the officer on the envelope to a military address, e.g. '2nd Lieutenant John Brown, . . . Regt.'.

OFFICER CADET

The form of address is as for a Lieutenant, but the envelope is addressed as follows:

Professional	Officer Cadet John Jones
Social	John Jones, Esq.

RETIRED AND FORMER OFFICERS

Field Marshals remain on the active list for life and so continue to use this rank. Other regular officers of the rank of major and above may use, and be addressed by, their rank after being placed on the retired list. More junior officers who do so are lacking in *savoir vivre,* which applies also to temporary officers of *all* ranks (e.g. those with war service only).

The word 'retired' (abbreviated to 'Retd') should *not* be added after an officer's name in ordinary correspondence or in lists, but only when it is specifically necessary to indicate that an officer is on the retired list, e.g. one employed in a civilian capacity in a Ministry of Defence establishment, when it facilitates postal arrangements.[1]

For retired officers who take Holy Orders, see p. 111 note 1.

TERRITORIAL, AUXILIARY AND VOLUNTEER RESERVE

Officers should only use, and be addressed by, their ranks on correspondence, etc. relevant to their T.A. and V.R. role. Forms of address are then as for the Army.

CHAPLAIN

(See *Chaplains to H.M. Forces*, pp. 127-128.)

NON-COMMISSIONED RANKS

Full stops between letters of abbreviation are no longer used within the Service, e.g. CSM.

Some ranks vary according to the Regiment or Corps.[2]

The Household Division, which comprises The Household Cavalry and The Guards' Division, differs considerably from the rest of the Army, see below.

The principal ranks in the British Army (apart from the Household Division) are:

---

[1] See also p. 174, note 1.
[2] Normally only used by men actively employed; not, e.g. by pensioners.

Warrant Officer Class I (e.g. Regimental Sergeant Major (RSM), Staff Sergeant Major (SSM), Conductor or Sub Conductor RAOC, etc.)

Warrant Officer Class II (e.g. Regimental Quartermaster Sergeant (RQMS), Company Sergeant Major (CSM), Staff Quartermaster Sergeant (SQMS), Quartermaster Sergeant (QMS), etc.)

Staff Sergeant (SSgt) and Colour Sergeant (CSgt)

Sergeant (Sgt)

Corporal (Cpl)

Lance Corporal (LCpl) or Lance Bombardier (LBdr)

Private (Pte) or equivalent rank (e.g. Gunner (Gnr), Sapper (Spr), Fusilier (Fus), Rifleman (Rfn), Signalman (Sig), Driver (Dvr), Craftsman (Sig), Ranger (Rgr)).

BEGINNING OF LETTER

Ranks are not abbreviated.

Warrant Officer Class I	Dear Mr. Smith
Warrant Officer Class II	Dear Sergeant Major Smith
Staff Sergeant	Dear Staff Sergeant Smith
Sergeant	Dear Sergeant Smith
Corporal and Lance Corporal	Dear Corporal Smith
Private and equivalent ranks	Dear Private (Gunner, etc.) Smith

ENVELOPE

According to rank, which may be abbreviated. Initials rather than a christian name are used, e.g.:

RSM J. Jones, M.C., M.M.

CSM W. Jones

Sgt J. Brown

VERBAL ADDRESS

According to Corps and Regimental custom.

A Warrant Officer Class I is called 'Mr. Smith'. If he has the appointment of Regimental Sergeant Major, he may be called either 'Regimental Sergeant Major' or 'RSM Jones'.

A Warrant Officer Class II who has the appointment of Company Sergeant Major, may be called either 'Sergeant Major' or 'CSM Brown'. Other Warrant Officers Class II by their appointment, e.g. 'RQMS Brown'.

NCOs are called according to their rank. A Lance Corporal is called 'Corporal'. These ranks may be used with or without the surname.

For Privates or equivalent rank, the surname must always be added.

THE ARMY, HOUSEHOLD DIVISION

This comprises the Household Cavalry and The Guards' Division.

(a) *Household Cavalry* (The Life Guards, and The Blues and Royals).

 The principal ranks are as follows:
 Warrant Officer Class I, Regimental Corporal Major (RCM)
 Warrant Officer Class II, Squadron Corporal Major (SCM)
 Staff Corporal (SCpl)
 Corporal of Horse (CoH)
 Corporal (Cpl)
 Lance Corporal (LCpl)
 Trooper (Tpr)

BEGINNING OF LETTER

Ranks or appointments are not abbreviated.

Warrant Officer Class I, (Regimental Corporal Major)	Dear Mr. Smith
Warrant Officer Class II, (Squadron Corporal Major)	Dear Corporal Major Smith
Corporal of Horse	Dear Corporal Smith

Otherwise as for the Army in general.

ENVELOPE

According to rank, which may be abbreviated, e.g. CMS.

VERBAL ADDRESS

As for beginning of letter (omitting 'Dear'). NCOs may be addressed with or without their surname. Troopers are always addressed with their surname.

(b) *The Guards' Division* (*formerly The Brigade of Guards*)

 The principal ranks are as follows:
 Warrant Officer Class I (RSM)
 Warrant Officer Class II (CSM, etc.)

> Colour Sergeant (CSgt) and Company Quartermaster
> Sergeant (CQMS)
> Sergeant (Sgt)
> Lance Sergeant (LSgt)
> Lance Corporal (LCpl)
> Guardsman (Gdsm)

BEGINNING OF LETTER

Ranks or appointments are not abbreviated.

Regimental Sergeant Major	Dear Sergeant Major Brown
Other Warrant Officers	By their appointment, and name
Colour Sergeant and Company Quartermaster Sergeant	By their rank and name
Sergeant and Lance Sergeant	Dear Sergeant Smith
Lance Corporal	Dear Corporal Smith

ENVELOPE

According to rank, which may be abbreviated, e.g. Sgt.

VERBAL ADDRESS

As for beginning of letter (omitting 'Dear'). Alternatively some ranks may be abbreviated (e.q. CQMS Brown).

N.C.O.s may be addressed with or without their surname. Guardsmen are always addressed with their surname.

The Royal Air Force

MARSHAL OF THE ROYAL AIR FORCE

This rank is held for life. (See also *Titled Officers*, p. 167.)

BEGINNING OF LETTER

According to his title (he would almost certainly be a peer, baronet or knight).[1]

Formal

If a Peer	My Lord
Otherwise	(Dear) Sir

Social

If a Peer	Dear Lord Blank
Otherwise	Dear Sir John (the surname may be added if the acquaintanceship is slight.)

[1] When he prefers his Air Force rank to be used, letters begin 'Dear Air Marshal Blank, and the verbal address is 'Air Marshal Blank' or 'Air Marshal'. The Style of 'Marshal' is also used, but is unofficial (see also *Use of an Officer's Rank Without His Surname*, p. 168.)

ENDING OF LETTER
Formal   Yours faithfully (see also p. 2)
Social   Yours sincerely

ENVELOPE
    Marshal of the Royal Air Force (the Rt. Hon.) Viscount
       Dorking, G.C.B.
    Marshal of the Royal Air Force Sir John Jones, G.C.B.

VERBAL ADDRESS
According to his title[1]:
    Lord Dorking
    Sir John
  A younger man, or a more junior officer in any of the Armed
Forces, addresses him as 'Sir'.

DESCRIPTION IN CONVERSATION
    Lord Dorking
    Sir John Jones

AIR CHIEF MARSHAL, AIR MARSHAL, OR AIR VICE-MARSHAL

All these ranks are referred to as Air Marshal except on the
envelope or in a formal description, such as in a list, when the
exact rank is given.
  (See also *Titled Officers*, p. 167.)
  The letters R.A.F. may follow the name, and any letters signifying orders, etc.

BEGINNING OF LETTER
Formal   (Dear) Sir
Social
    If a knight   Dear Sir John[1] (the surname may be
                    added if the acquaintanceship is slight)
    Otherwise   Dear Air Marshal Smith

ENDING OF LETTER
Formal   Yours faithfully (see also p. 2)
Social   Yours sincerely

[1] When he prefers his Air rank to that appropriate for his knighthood, letters begin 'Dear Air Marshal Brown', (See also *Use of an Officer's Rank Without His Surname*, p. 168.)

ENVELOPE

According to the exact rank, with the appropriate letters after the name, e.g.:

Air Chief Marshal Sir John Brown, G.B.E., R.A.F.
Air Vice-Marshal Edward Grey, C.B., C.B.E., R.A.F.
These ranks should not be abbreviated.

VERBAL ADDRESS

| If a Knight | Sir John[1] |
| Otherwise | Air Marshal Grey |

A younger man, or a more junior officer in any of the Armed Forces, addresses him as 'Sir'.

DESCRIPTION IN CONVERSATION

| If a knight | Sir John Brown |
| Otherwise | Air Marshal Grey |

Should social reference be made to only one Air Chief Marshal, Air Marshal, or Air Vice-Marshal he may be called 'the Air Marshal'.

AIR COMMODORE, GROUP CAPTAIN, WING COMMANDER, SQUADRON LEADER OR FLIGHT LIEUTENANT

These ranks are always used in full. The letters R.A.F. follow the name, and any letters which signify Orders, etc.

BEGINNING OF LETTER

Formal	(Dear) Sir
Social[2]	Dear Air Commodore Davis
	Dear Group Captain Smith
	Dear Wing Commander Jones
	Dear Squadron Leader Robinson
	Dear Flight Lieutenant Brown

ENDING OF LETTER

| *Formal* | Yours faithfully (see also p. 2) |
| *Social* | Yours sincerely |

[1] When he prefers his Air rank to that appropriate for his knighthood, the verbal address is 'Air Marshal Brown' or Air Marshal'. (See also *Use of an Officer's Rank Without His Surname*, p. 168.)
[2] See *Use of an Officer's Rank Without His Surname*, p. 168.

ENVELOPE
>   Air Commodore David Davis, C.B., R.A.F.
>   Group Captain John Smith, C.B.E., R.A.F.
>   Wing Commander John Jones, D.F.C., R.A.F.
>   Squadron Leader Richard Robinson, M.B.E., R.A.F.
>   Flight Lieutenant John Brown, R.A.F.

VERBAL ADDRESS
>   Air Commodore Davis
>   Group Captain Smith
>   Wing Commander Jones
>   Squadron Leader Robinson
>   Flight Lieutenant Brown

A younger man, or more junior officer in any of the Armed Forces, addresses him as 'Sir'.

DESCRIPTION IN CONVERSATION
As for verbal address

FLYING OFFICER OR PILOT OFFICER

The letters R.A.F. follow the name, and any letters which signify orders, etc.

BEGINNING OF LETTER

Formal	(Dear) Sir
Social	Dear Mr. Smith

ENDING OF LETTER

Formal	Yours faithfully (see also p. 2)
Social	Yours sincerely

ENVELOPE
>   John Smith, Esq., A.F.C., R.A.F. *or*
>   Flying Officer John Smith A.F.C., R.A.F.

VERBAL ADDRESS
>   Mr. Smith

DESCRIPTION IN CONVERSATION
>   Mr. Smith

WOMEN MEDICAL AND DENTAL OFFICERS

Women officers in the Medical and Dental branches are members of the R.A.F., and accordingly have the letters R.A.F. after their names. To avoid confusion in addressing correspondence to a woman medical or dental officer, a christian name may be used (e.g. Flight Lieutenant Marion G. Broad, M.B., Ch.B., R.A.F.) instead of the initials customary in the case of a W.R.A.F. officer. Otherwise, the conventions are the same as those applicable to the W.R.A.F.

OFFICER CADET

There is now no rank of Officer Cadet in the Royal Air Force. Entrants to the R.A.F. College, Cranwell, are commissioned on arrival.

RETIRED AND FORMER OFFICERS

Marshals of the Royal Air Force remain on the active list for life and so continue to use this rank. Other officers of the rank of Flight Lieutenant and above may use, and be addressed by, their rank after being placed on the retired list.

The word 'retired' (or the abbreviation 'Retd.') need not be added after an officer's name, but officially it has been the practice for the Ministry of Defence to use the abbreviation 'Retd.' for officers on the retired list.

For retired officers who take Holy Orders, see p. 111 note 1.

ROYAL AIR FORCE VOLUNTEER RESERVE

Officers should only use, and be addressed by, their ranks when under training or when called up for service. Forms of address are then as for the Royal Air Force except that the letters R.A.F.V.R. follow the name (in lieu of R.A.F.).

CHAPLAIN TO THE ROYAL AIR FORCE

(See *Chaplains to H.M. Forces*, pp. 127-128.)

NON-COMMISSIONED RANKS[1]

The principal ranks are as follows:

- Warrant Officer
- Flight Sergeant (Flt. Sgt.)
- Chief Technician (Chief Tech.)
- Sergeant (Sgt.)
- Corporal (Cpl.)
- Junior Technician (Jnr. Tech.)
- Senior Aircraftman (S.A.C.)
- Leading Aircraftman (L.A.C.)
- Aircraftman (A.C.)

BEGINNING OF LETTER

Warrant Officer (formally)	Dear Warrant Officer Smith
(otherwise)	Dear Mr. Smith
Other ranks	According to rank

ENVELOPE

According to rank, with 'R.A.F.' (or R.A.F.V.R.) after the name.

VERBAL ADDRESS

As for beginning of letter (omitting 'Dear').

Women's Services, Relative Ranks

W.R.N.S.	*W.R.A.C.*	*W.R.A.F.*
Commandant[2]	Brigadier[3]	Air Commodore[4]
Superintendent	Colonel	Group Captain
Chief Officer	Lieutenant-Colonel	Wing Commander
First Officer	Major	Squadron Leader
Second Officer	Captain	Flight Lieutenant
Third Officer	Lieutenant	Flying Officer
Probationary Third Officer	2nd Lieutenant	Pilot Officer

Women's Royal Naval Service

Titled officers are addressed as such, e.g. Dear Dame Mary, or if the acquaintanceship is slight, Dear Dame Mary Green, unless the recipient is unknown to the writer in which case her Service rank should be used, e.g. Dear Commandant Green. All other officers

[1] These ranks customarily only used by men actively employed; not, e.g. by pensioners.
[2] The Director W.R.N.S. holds this rank.
[3] The Director W.R.A.C. holds this rank.
[4] The Director W.R.A.F. holds this rank.

are addressed by their rank which sould not be abbreviated. The letters W.R.N.S. should always be added since some ranks are identical with the Merchant Navy. Socially, an officer may be called by her Service rank if she so wishes, but when off duty it is usual for her to be called in writing and in speech, Miss (Mary) Brown or Mrs. (John) Smith. Subject to the above:

BEGINNING OF LETTER

Formal	Dear Madam *or* Dear First Officer Smith[1]
Social	Dear First Officer Smith *or* Dear Miss Smith

ENDING OF LETTER

Formal	Yours faithfully (see also p. 2)
Social	Yours sincerely

ENVELOPE

Initials, rather than christian names, are customarily used, e.g. Chief Officer M. Brown, W.R.N.S.

VERBAL ADDRESS

According to rank[2]

DESCRIPTION IN CONVERSATION

According to rank

RETIRED AND FORMER OFFICERS

Officers placed on the retired list, or who leave the Service earlier for some other reason (e.g. on marriage), do not normally continue to use their ranks.

NON-COMMISSIONED RATES

There are five rates:
> Fleet Chief Wren
> Chief Wren
> Petty Officer Wren (P.O. Wren)
> Leading Wren
> Wren

BEGINNING OF LETTER AND VERBAL ADDRESS

Dear Miss *or* Mrs. Smith for a Fleet Chief Wren, otherwise according to rate.

---

[1] Within the Women's Services those junior to her write 'Dear Ma'am'.
[2] Within the Women's Services those junior to her address her as 'Ma'am'.

ENVELOPE

According to rate, omitting Miss or Mrs. The letters W.R.N.S. are not added after the name.

VERBAL ADDRESS

Miss *or* Mrs. Smith for Fleet Chief Wren, otherwise according to rate.

Women's Royal Army Corps

Titled officers are addressed as such, e.g. Dear Dame Mary, or if the acquaintanceship is slight, Dear Dame Mary Green, unless the recipient is unknown to the writer in which case her Service rank should be used, e.g. Dear Brigadier Green. Otherwise all officers are addressed by their rank (except where mentioned below) which should not be abbreviated. The letters W.R.A.C. are always added to distinguish them from male officers whose ranks are identical.

BEGINNING OF LETTER

Formal	Dear Madam *or* Dear Colonel Smith[1]
Social	Dear Colonel Smith *or* Dear Colonel (for majors and above)

ENDING OF LETTER

Formal	Yours faithfully (see also p. 2)
Social	Yours sincerely

ENVELOPE

Initials, rather than christian names, are customarily used, e.g. Major M. Brown, W.R.A.C.

VERBAL ADDRESS

According to rank, except for Lieutenants and 2nd Lieutenants who are referred to as Miss (or Mrs.) Jones.[2]

DESCRIPTION IN CONVERSATION

According to rank.

[1] See p. 189, note [1].
[2] See p. 189, note [2].

RETIRED AND FORMER OFFICERS

Officers placed on the retired list, or who leave the Service earlier for some other reason (e.g. on marriage), do not normally continue to use their ranks.

NON-COMMISSIONED RANKS

They have Army ranks, see pp. 180-182

BEGINNING OF LETTER

Warrant Officers   Dear Miss (or Mrs.) Smith
Others according to rank, e.g. Dear Corporal Jones

ENVELOPE

Address according to rank, with W.R.A.C. after the name. Initials are normally used in preference to christian name.

VERBAL ADDRESS

Warrant Officers   Miss (or Mrs.) Smith
Others according to rank.

Women's Royal Air Force

Titled officers are addressed as such, e.g. Dear Dame Mary, or if the acquaintanceship is slight, Dear Dame Mary Green, unless the recipient is unknown to the writer in which case her Service rank should be used, e.g. Dear Air Commodore Green. Otherwise all officers are addressed by their rank which should not be abbreviated. The letters W.R.A.F. should be added after the name (or W.R.A.F.R.O., or W.R.Aux.A.F. for officers of the Reserve and Auxiliaries respectively).

BEGINNING OF LETTER

Formal   Dear Madam *or* Dear Group Captain Smith[1]
Social   Dear Group Captain Smith *or* Dear Group
              Captain (for Squadron Leaders and above)

ENDING OF LETTER

Formal   Yours faithfully (see also p. 2)
Social   Yours sincerely

[1] See p. 189, note [1].

ENVELOPE
Initials rather than christian names are customarily used, e.g.
Wing Commander M. Brown, W.R.A.F.

VERBAL ADDRESS
According to rank (including Flying Officers and Pilot Officers in
which respect they differ from male officers).[1]

RETIRED AND FORMER OFFICERS

Officers placed on the retired list, or who leave the Service earlier
for some other reason (e.g. on marriage) do not normally continue
to use their ranks.

NON-COMMISSIONED RANKS

Warrant Officers, as for R.A.F., (p. 188) with the equivalent
alternative Dear Miss (or Mrs.) Smith.

Others according to rank which are as for R.A.F. (p. 188) except:

Senior Aircraftwoman (S.A.C.W.)
Leading Aircraftwoman (L.A.C.W.)
Aircraftwoman (A.C.W.)

Queen Alexandra's Royal Naval Nursing Service

An officer of Queen Alexandra's Royal Naval Nursing Service
adds the letters Q.A.R.N.N.S. after her name and any letters
signifying Orders, etc.

The ranks are as follows:
Matron-in-Chief
Principal Matron
Matron
Superintending Sister
Senior Nursing Sister
Nursing Sister

BEGINNING OF LETTER
Formal   (Dear) Madam
Social   Dear Miss (Mrs.) Smith

ENDING OF LETTER
Formal   Yours faithfully (see also p. 2)
Social   Yours sincerely

[1] See p. 189, note [2].

ENVELOPE

Professional	Miss Rosemary Smith,
	Matron, Q.A.R.N.N.S.
Private	Miss Rosemary Smith, Q.A.R.N.N.S.

VERBAL ADDRESS
    Miss Smith[1]

DESCRIPTION IN CONVERSATION
    Miss Smith[1]

SENIOR and JUNIOR RATINGS

The rates of nurses are as follows:

    Head Naval Nurse
    Assistant Head Naval Nurse
    Senior Naval Nurse
    Naval Nurse
    Probationary Naval Nurse

They are all referred to at the beginning of a letter as 'Dear Nurse Smith', but envelopes are addressed to their rate, followed by Q.A.R.N.N.S. They are also referred to verbally by their rate.

Queen Alexandra's Royal Army Nursing Corps

Officers of Queen Alexandra's Royal Army Nursing Corps have Army ranks, with the letters Q.A.R.A.N.C. after the name. They are always addressed by their Service rank. Relative ranks are the same as for the W.R.A.C. (see p. 190).

    The ranks are as follows:
        Brigadier—held by the Matron-in-Chief and Director of Army Nursing Service
        Colonel—held by the Deputy Director of Army Nursing Service
        Lieutenant-Colonel—held by an Assistant Director of Army Nursing Service
        Major ⎫
        Captain ⎬—held by Matrons and Sisters
        Lieutenant ⎭

[1] A Matron or Sister may also be so addressed and described.

Forms of address are as for the Women's Royal Army Corps (see pp. 191–192) except that in speech Matrons and Sisters may be so addressed and described instead of by their military rank.

NON-COMMISSIONED RANKS

They have Army ranks *see Women's Royal Army Corps,* p. 191.

VERBAL ADDRESS AND CORRESPONDENCE
As for the Women's Royal Army Corps, p. 191.

Princess Mary's Royal Air Force Nursing Service

An officer of Princess Mary's Royal Air Force Nursing Service adds the letters P.M.R.A.F.N.S. after her name, preceded by any letters signifying Orders, etc.

The appointments and ranks are as follows:

Director of R.A.F. Nursing Services and Matron-in-Chief	Air Commandant
Deputy Director of R.A.F. Nursing Services	Group Officer
Senior Matron	Wing Officer
Deputy Matron or Ward Sister	Squadron Officer
Nursing Sister	Flight Officer Flying Officer

Air Commandant equates to Air Commodore and all other ranks are equivalent to those of the Royal Air Force with the same prenoms.

BEGINNING OF LETTER

Formal	(Dear) Madam
Social	
Professional	Dear Wing Officer Smith (or appropriate rank)
Private	Dear Miss Smith

ENDING OF LETTER

Formal	Yours faithfully (see also p. 2)
Social	Yours sincerely

ENVELOPE

Professional	Squadron Officer Mary Smith, A.R.R.C., P.M.R.A.F.N.S.
Private	Miss Mary Smith, A.R.R.C.

VERBAL ADDRESS

Professional	Squadron Officer Smith[1]
Private	Miss Smith

DESCRIPTION IN CONVERSATION
As for verbal address.

NON-COMMISSIONED RANKS

All non-commissioned ranks of the P.M.R.A.F.N.S. take air women's rank see p. 192.

Commonwealth Armed Forces

The names and decorations are followed by the abbreviation of the appropriate service for Naval and Air Force Officers.

Royal Australian Navy
Captain John Brown, R.A.N.
Royal Australian Air Force
Squadron Leader John Brown, R.A.A.F.
Royal New Zealand Navy
Commander William Smith, D.S.C., R.N.Z.N.
Royal New Zealand Air Force
Group Captain John Robinson, D.F.C., R.N.Z.A.F.

CANADA

On 1st February, 1968, the Canadian Armed Forces adopted new rank titles common to all three Services. However, serving members of the former Royal Canadian Navy were allowed to continue using their traditional Naval ranks.

The ranks and decorations of all personnel are now followed by the letters C.F. (Canadian Forces).

The new ranks are as follows:
General

[1] A Matron or Sister may also be so addressed and described instead of by her Air Force rank,

Lieutenant-General
Major-General
Brigadier-General
Colonel
Lieutenant-Colonel
Major
Captain
Lieutenant
2nd Lieutenant

Officers of the Naval Operations Branch may use traditional Naval ranks when employed in what can be clearly described as 'Navy' jobs, to match the ranks used in most of the world's navies.

Reserves follow the pattern set by the Regular Forces.

The Corporation of Trinity House

The Corporation of Trinity House is the General Lighthouse Authority for England, Wales and the Channel Islands, controlling over 90 lighthouses, over 20 light vessels, and maintaining a fleet of steam and motor vessels. It is also the principal pilotage authority in the United Kingdom, and is responsible for 41 districts. Active Elder Brethren also sit with the Judges of the Admiralty Division of the High Court of Justice to act as Nautical Assessors in marine cases tried by that Court.

The Active Elder Brethren of the Corporation of Trinity House are accorded the style and title of Captain, which they retain for life, according to the Royal Warrant issued on 20th December, 1912. On social and ceremonial occasions they have precedence immediately after that accorded to Captains in the Royal Navy.

No person is eligible to fill the office of an Active Elder Brother unless he has served afloat in command of one or more of H.M. ships for at least two years after having attained the rank of Commander, Royal Navy, or unless he has held command in the Mercantile Marine on foreign voyages for at least three years.

An Elder Brother does not have letters after his name to signify his office. The form of address is as for a Captain in the Royal Navy unless he is of more senior naval rank.

The title Captain is also accorded to the Lighthouse Service Superintendents and Pilotage Superintendents. In the case of the former, the description is Captain T.H.S. (Trinity House Service). These letters are placed after his name and decorations (if any) on the envelope.

POLITICAL AND CIVIL SERVICE SECTION

All Cabinet Ministers of the United Kingdom Parliament are members of the Privy Council. Other Ministers outside the Cabinet may also be admitted to the Privy Council. They accordingly have the prefix 'The Rt. Hon.' before their names. (N.B.— The Rt. Hon. takes the place of Mrs. or Miss before a lady's name.) In addition there are those Privy Counsellors of Northern Ireland appointed before the Council was abolished in 1973. See *Privy Council* (p. 80).

All Members of the House of Commons of the United Kingdom have the letters M.P. following their names. See *Letters After the Name* (p. 99).

There is no special form of address for the wife of either a Privy Counsellor or a Member of Parliament.

There are several junior Ministers of an administration who are not admitted to the Privy Council. Most of these are Members of Parliament, but a few may have seats in the House of Lords.

Member of Her Majesty's Government

BEGINNING OF LETTER

He is addressed as for an Esquire:

Formal   (Dear) Sir
Social   Dear Mr. Blake, or appropriate rank

If the writer knows the Minister concerned, and the subject of his letter broadly concerns his department, it is permissible to write to him by his appointment, e.g.:

> Dear (Mr.) Prime Minister
> Dear Lord Chancellor (see *Legal Section* p. 206)
> Dear Lord Privy Seal
> Dear (Mr.) Chancellor
> Dear (Mr.) Minister
> Dear Lord President [of the Council]
> Dear (Mr.) President [of the Board of Trade]

> Dear Home/Foreign Secretary, *or* Dear Secretary of State
> Dear Solicitor General
> Dear Attorney General
> Dear Lord Advocate
> Dear Chief Secretary
> Dear Under-Secretary

This form is not used when the name of the appointment is cumbersome.

The inclusion of 'Mr.' before certain officers is now becoming archaic except in very formal correspondence. 'Dear Mr. Secretary' has long passed out of use. 'Dear Secretary of State' is customarily used in the United States, where it is followed by the surname.

The very formal style, viz. 'Sir' *or* 'Madam' is occasionally used officially within the Civil Service and the Armed Forces, but seldom outside.

ENDING OF LETTER

Formal	Yours faithfully (see also p. 2)
Social	Yours sincerely

When writing to a Minister by his appointment (e.g. Dear Minister), the letter is ended, 'Yours sincerely'.

For a very formal letter, the following is the ending:

> I have the honour to be,
>   Sir,
>   Yours faithfully

'Your obedient servant' has become obsolete.

ENVELOPE

Personal Letter

A letter to a Minister sent to his department, normally includes both his name and appointment, e.g.:

> The Rt. Hon. Sir Michael Blank, K.B.E., M.P.,
> Secretary of State for Foreign Affairs

Ministerial Letter

A letter sent to a Minister as the head of his department is addressed by his appointment only, e.g.:

> The Secretary of State for Foreign Affairs

For a minor departmental matter, see *Government Departments* (p. 199).

VERBAL ADDRESS AND DESCRIPTION IN CONVERSATION
By appointment or name.

The Speaker of the House of Commons

'Mr. Speaker' is his customary designation on Parliamentary matters, otherwise according to his rank.

Government Departments (Civil Service)

BEGINNING OF LETTER
He or she is addressed as for an Esquire or the feminine equivalent:

Formal   Dear Sir *or* Dear Madam
Social   Dear Mr. Byron, Dear Miss Byron, *or* appropriate rank

The alternative style of writing by the appointment is not normally employed when this is cumbersome, e.g. Dear Permanent Under-Secretary.

The very formal style, viz. 'Sir' *or* 'Madam' is used within the Civil Service on specific official matters, but only very occasionally outside.

ENDING OF LETTER
Formal   Yours faithfully (see also p. 2)
Social   Yours sincerely

When writing to a member of the Civil Service by his appointment (e.g. Dear Under-Secretary), the letter is ended, 'Yours sincerely'.

For a very formal letter, the following is the ending:

    I have the honour to be,
        Sir,
            Yours faithfully

'Your obedient servant' has become obsolete.

ENVELOPE
Personal Letter
A letter to a member of the Civil Service sent to his department, normally includes both his name and appointment.
Official Letter
This is addressed by appointment only.

If a letter relates only to a minor matter, it is usually addressed to 'The Secretary' of the appropriate department rather than to its Ministerial head.

By appointment or name.

Members of Commonwealth Parliaments

The letters which are placed after the names of Members of Parliament vary according to the country, state or province and the name of the respective House.

In *Canada* Parliament consists of the Senate and the House of Commons. Members of the latter House place M.P. after the name. Members of the Legislative Assemblies of Canadian Provinces place M.L.A. after the name, except the Province of Quebec, where the appropriate letters are M.A.N. (Membre de l'Assemblée Nationale du Québec) and Ontario, where the letters are M.P.P. (Member of Provincial Parliament).

In *Australia* Parliament consists of the Senate and the House of Representatives. Members of the latter House place M.P. after the name. Parliament of the Australian States consists of two chambers, apart from Queensland. Members of the Legislative Council (the Upper House) place M.L.C. after the name. In South Australia and Tasmania the Lower House is known as the House of Assembly. In South Australia Members are accorded the letters M.P., and in Tasmania the letters M.H.A. In the other states the Lower House is the Legislative Assembly, and Members place M.L.A. after the name.

In *New Zealand* Members of the House of Representatives are designated M.P. The Legislative Council was abolished in 1951.

Senators in Canada are described as The Hon. before the name, as appropriate, without the word 'Senator'.

Senators in Australia are addressed as such before the name, e.g. Senator the Hon. John Smith, or Senator John Smith, as applicable.

For the title 'Honourable' before the name in the Commonwealth see pp. 201-205.

The title of 'The Honourable' in Commonwealth Countries

Holders of certain offices are styled 'The Honourable' in some countries of the Commonwealth, either for life or for tenure of office, but not their spouses. If they are members of the Privy Council of the United Kingdom they are styled 'The Right Honourable'.

The appropriate countries are listed below. Apart from Canada where there are additional offices with this style, those in countries over which The Queen reigns are the following:

Members of Executive Councils

Members of Legislative Councils

Speaker of Lower House of the Legislatures

The following may personally be recommended by the Governor General, or, in the case of Australian states, the Governor, for Her Majesty's permission to retain the title on retirement:

1. Members of Executive Councils who have served for at least three years as Ministers, or one year as Prime Minister or, in the case of Australian States, as Premier.

2. Presidents of Senates and Legislative Councils, and Speakers of Legislative Assemblies on quitting office, after having served three years in their respective offices.

3. Senators and Members of Legislative Councils on retirement or resignation after a continuous service of not less than ten years.

In Canada Speakers of the House of Commons on retirement are eligible to be granted permission to retain the title of Honourable by the Governor General on behalf of Her Majesty The Queen. In New Zealand Her Majesty in 1974 waived the prerequisite that Members of the Executive Council and the Speaker of the House of Representatives had to serve three years in office.

The title is also borne be certain categories of Judges (see *Legal Section,* pp. 220-225).

Within the Commonwealth, the title of Honourable is granted in the following countries, whether Member or Associated States.

CANADA, FEDERAL

For Life

Members of the Queen's Privy Council for Canada, including Members of the Federal Cabinet

Members of the Senate

For Tenure of Office

Speaker of the Senate

Speaker of the House of Commons

CANADIAN PROVINCES

For Life

Lieutenant-Governors (also styled His/Her Honour)

For Tenure of Office
> Members of Executive Councils
> Presidents and Speakers of the Legislatures

AUSTRALIA, COMMONWEALTH OF
For Life
> Members of the Federal Executive Council (Ministers and Assistant Ministers become Members on appointment to office)

For Tenure of Office
> President of the Senate (sometimes described as the Upper House of Parliament)
> Speaker of the House of Representatives (sometimes described as the Lower House of Parliament)

AUSTRALIAN STATES
For Life
> Members of Executive Council of Victoria

For Tenure of Office
> Members of Executive Councils of States other than Victoria whilst holding Ministerial Office
> Members of Legislative Councils (*Note*: Queensland has only one House, the Legislative Assembly)
> Speaker of the Lower House of the Legislatures (Legislative Assemblies)

NEW ZEALAND
> Members of the Executive Council (Ministers)
> Speakers of the House of Representatives

ANTIGUA
> Members of the Senate
> Members of the House of Representatives

BAHAMAS
> Ministers and Members of the Senate (inside and outside)
> Members of the House of Assembly (inside the House only)

BARBADOS
> Members of the Privy Council (of Barbados)
> Government Ministers
> (*Note*: The Speaker of the House of Assembly is styled 'His Honour')

BELIZE
Members of the House of Senate (inside and outside)
Members of the House of Representatives (inside and outside)

BERMUDA
Cabinet Ministers
Members of the Legislative Council

BOTSWANA
Members of Parliament
Cabinet Ministers
Assistant Ministers

BRITISH VIRGIN ISLANDS
Members of the Executive Council (official and elected)

DOMINICA
Cabinet Ministers and Members of the House of Assembly
(inside and outside)

FALKLAND ISLANDS
Members of the Executive Council
Members of the Legislative Council

FIJI
Members of the House of Representatives

THE GAMBIA
Cabinet Ministers

GIBRALTAR
Members of the Council
Elected Members of the House of Assembly

GILBERT ISLANDS
Council of Ministers
Speaker of the House of Assembly

GRENADA
Government Ministers (The Prime Minister is called Dr. the
Hon. . . .)
Members of the Senate
Speaker of the House of Representatives

HONG KONG
Members of the Executive Council
Members of the Legislative Council

MAURITIUS
> Members of the Legislative Assembly

MONTSERRAT
> Official and Elected Members of the Executive Council
> Elected and Nominated Members of the Legislative Council
> (inside and outside)

PAPUA NEW GUINEA
> Members of National Parliament (during sessions)
> Prime Minister and other Ministers (inside and outside)

ST. HELENA
> Members of the Executive Council

ST. KITTS-NEVIS-ANGUILLA
> Members of the House of Assembly, both elected and
> nominated
> Speaker of the House of Assembly

ST. LUCIA
> Members of the House of Assembly, both elected and
> nominated
> Speaker of the House of Assembly

ST. VINCENT
> Members of the House of Assembly, both elected and
> nominated
> Speaker of the House of Assembly

SEYCHELLES
> Members of the House of Assembly

SIERRA LEONE
> Government Ministers

SINGAPORE
> Government Ministers

SOLOMON ISLANDS
> Members of the Legislative Assembly (inside) including
> Ex-officio Members
> Members of the Council of Ministers (inside and outside)
> including Ex-officio Members

SWAZILAND
> Ministers and Members of Parliament (The Prime Minister
> has the title of Right Honourable)

TONGA
Ministers of the Crown
Governors and Nobles of the Realm

TRINIDAD AND TOBAGO
Members of the Senate
Members of Parliament

WESTERN SAMOA
Prime Minister
Ministers
Speaker of the Legislative Assembly
Holders of tama-a-aiga titles (except the Head of State, who is
  His Highness)

ZAMBIA
Members of the Central Committee of the Party
Cabinet Ministers (Secretary General of the Party is styled
  His Honour, and the Prime Minister Right Honourable)

The Title of 'The Honourable' outside the Commonwealth

THE REPUBLIC OF SOUTH AFRICA
The Prime Minister
The Chief Justice
Members and former Members of the Executive Council
The President of the Senate
The Speaker of the House of Assembly and Deputy Ministers
Administrators of the several Provinces and the Administrator
  of South West Africa
Judges of the Supreme Court of South Africa and Com-
  missioners-General
Senators

The following persons, on relinquishing office, are eligible
to be recommended for permission to retain the title of 'Honourable':

Chief Justices, Deputy-Ministers, Judges of the Supreme
  Court of South Africa and Commissioners-General.

Presidents of the Senate and Speakers of the House of
  Assembly after holding office for a period of not less than
  three years.

Administrators of the Provinces and the Administrator of South West Africa after holding office for a continuous period of not less than five years.

Senators after holding office for a continuous period of not less than ten years.

UNITED STATES OF AMERICA

See Part VI *American Usage* (pp. 343-368).

LEGAL SECTION

England and Wales

LORD CHANCELLOR

The Lord High Chancellor of Great Britain, colloquially called 'the Lord Chancellor', is the chief judicial officer in England, and receives a peerage on appointment. He is also a member of the Privy Council and of the Cabinet. He is Speaker of the House of Lords where he sits on the Woolsack, President of the House of Lords sitting in its judicial capacity as the highest Court of Appeal in the United Kingdom, and President of the Court of Appeal and of the Chancery Division of the High Court. He vacates office with the Government.

A letter concerning his Department should be addressed to The Rt. Hon. the Lord Chancellor.

Correspondence on these matters may be addressed:

Formal	My Lord
Social	Dear Lord Chancellor

Otherwise according to his rank in the peerage.

The letters Q.C. do not appear after his name.

LORD CHIEF JUSTICE OF ENGLAND

He is the head of the judges of the Queen's Bench Division, and takes precedence over all other judges of this Division. He also presides in the Court of Appeal (Criminal Division). He is a Privy Counsellor, and on appointment is raised to the peerage.

A letter concerning his office may be addressed to The Rt. Hon. the Lord Chief Justice of England.

Correspondence may begin:

Formal   My Lord
Social   Dear Lord Chief Justice
   Otherwise according to his rank in the peerage.
   The letters Q.C. do not appear after his name.

MASTER OF THE ROLLS

The Master of the Rolls sits and presides over the Court of Appeal (Civil Division), and has third place in legal seniority after the Lord Chancellor and the Lord Chief Justice.
   He is knighted, and is a member of the Privy Council.
   He is addressed according to his judicial rank.

PRESIDENT OF THE FAMILY DIVISION

The President presides over the Family Division of the High Court. In legal precedence his place is next after the Master of the Rolls.
   He is knighted and is a member of the Privy Council.
   He is addressed according to his judicial rank.

LORDS OF APPEAL IN ORDINARY

Lords of Appeal in Ordinary, who are always Members of the Privy Council, are created peers for life.[1] They preside over appeals in the House of Lords in its judicial capacity.
   The letters Q.C. are not used after the name of a Lord of Appeal in Ordinary.

LORD JUSTICE OF THE COURT OF APPEAL

Sixteen Lord Justices are appointed to sit in the Court of Appeal with the Master of the Rolls. Such a judge is admitted to the Privy Council as a member of the Judicial Committee, and normally will have received a knighthood as a Judge of the High Court of Justice. The christian name is not used as a form of address except where there is more than one Lord Justice with the same surname. Then the senior is not referred to by his christian name, but the christian name of a junior is used on all occasions (e.g. Lord Justice Davies and Lord Justice Edmund Davies).
   The letters Q.C. do not appear after his name.
   A retired Lord Justice is addressed 'The Rt. Hon. Sir John Blank'.

---

[1] A Lord of Appeal in Ordinary is appointed a peer under Section 6 of the Appellate Jurisdiction Act 1876, by virtue of which he is entitled during his life to rank as a baron. That he is not in law a baron is demonstrated by the fact that it required a Royal Warrant, which was not issued until 1897, to give his children precedence next after the children of a baron.

BEGINNING OF LETTER

Formal	My Lord
Social	Dear Lord Justice

ENDING OF LETTER

Formal	Yours faithfully (see also p. 2)
Social	Yours sincerely

ENVELOPE

The Rt. Hon. Lord Justice Smith

VERBAL ADDRESS

Formal	My Lord *or* Your Lordship[1]
Social	Lord Justice

DESCRIPTION IN CONVERSATION

Formal and Social	The Lord Justice, *or* Lord Justice Brown
Judicial Matters, especially on the Bench	His Lordship

JUDGE OF HIGH COURT

The High Court of Justice is that part of the Supreme Court of Judicature which does not comprise the Court of Appeal or the Crown Court, and is divided into three Divisions, Queen's Bench, Chancery, and Family. High Court Judges are styled 'The Hon. Mr. Justice' and are known as Puisne Judges, which literally means 'younger'.

A Judge of the High Court is normally knighted on appointment. The letters Q.C. do not appear after his name.

See also *Judge of High Court (Lady)*, p. 209.

BEGINNING OF LETTER

Formal	(Dear) Sir,
Judicial Matters	My Lord
Social	Dear Judge (excluding the surname)

ENDING OF LETTER

Formal	Yours faithfully (see also p. 2)
Social	Yours sincerely

[1] See p. 34, note 4.

ENVELOPE

Formal and Judicial Matters	The Hon. Mr. Justice Smith (excluding the christian name). If there is more than one Judge of the High Court with the same surname the senior judge is referred to by his surname alone, and the christian name of the junior judge is used on all occasions (e.g. Mrs. Justice Lane, and Mr. Justice Geoffrey Lane)
Social	Sir John Smith ('The Honourable' is not used in conjunction with 'Sir John Smith')

VERBAL ADDRESS

Formal	Sir
Judicial Matters and on the Bench	My Lord *or* Your Lordship[1]
Social	Sir John (Smith), e.g. Sir John and Lady Smith. Members of the Bar may address a High Court Judge as 'Judge'

DESCRIPTION IN CONVERSATION

Formal and Social	The Judge, *or* Mr. Justice Smith, *or* Sir John (Smith), e.g. Sir John and Lady Smith
Judicial Matters especially on the Bench	His Lordship

JUDGE OF HIGH COURT (LADY)

She is created a Dame just as her male counterpart receives a knighthood. The letters Q.C. do not appear after her name.

BEGINNING OF LETTER

Formal	(Dear) Madam
Social	Dear Dame Elizabeth (Lane)

ENDING OF LETTER

Formal	Yours faithfully (see also p. 2)
Social	Yours sincerely

[1] See p. 34, note [2].

ENVELOPE

Formal	The Hon. Mrs. Justice Lane
Social	Dame Elizabeth Lane ('The Honourable' is not used in conjunction with 'Dame Elizabeth')

VERBAL ADDRESS

Formal	Madam
Judicial Matters and on the Bench	My Lady *or* Your Ladyship[1]
Social	Dame Elizabeth (Lane). Members of the Bar may address her as 'Judge'

DESCRIPTION IN CONVERSATION

Formal and Social	The Judge *or* Mrs. Justice Lane, *or privately*, 'Dame Elizabeth'
Judicial Matters, especially on the Bench	Her Ladyship

JUDGE OF HIGH COURT (RETIRED)

Since the passing of the Judicial Pensions Act 1959, High Court Judges retire at the age of 75 years. Those appointed before the passing of the Act retire according to their wishes.

The prefix 'The Hon. Mr. Justice' is dropped on retirement.

BEGINNING OF LETTER

Formal	(Dear) Sir
Social	Dear Judge (excluding the surname)[1] *or* Dear Sir John
	Dear Sir John Brown (if of slight acquaintance)

ENDING OF LETTER

Formal	Yours faithfully (see also p. 2)
Social	Yours sincerely

ENVELOPE

Formal and Social	Sir John Brown

[1] See p. 39, note 2.

VERBAL ADDRESS
Formal   Sir
Social   Judge (excluding the surname)[1] *or*
                       Sir John (Brown)

DESCRIPTION IN CONVERSATION
Formal and Social   The Judge[1] *or*
                       Sir John (adding the surname if necessary)

CIRCUIT JUDGE

If he or she was a Queen's Counsel when at the Bar, the letters
Q.C. should follow the name in correspondence.

BEGINNING OF LETTER
Formal and Judicial
   Matters   (Dear) Sir *or* (Dear) Madam
Social   Dear Judge

ENDING OF LETTER
Formal   Yours faithfully (see also p. 2)
Social   Yours sincerely

ENVELOPE
Formal and Social   His (*or* Her) Honour Judge Smith (ex-
                       cluding the christian name). If more
                       than one Circuit Judge of the same
                       surname are assembled together at the
                       same address, the christian name may
                       be added in brackets

  If a Knight:
Formal   His Honour Judge Sir John Smith
Social   Sir John Smith

VERBAL ADDRESS
Formal   Sir (or Madam)
Judicial Matters and
  on the Bench   Your Honour
Social   Judge (excluding the surname). If he is a
                       knight, he may also be called privately,
                       Sir John (Smith), e.g. Sir John and
                       Lady Smith

[1] Retained only by courtesy.

DESCRIPTION IN CONVERSATION

Formal and Social	The Judge, *or* Judge Smith
Judicial Matters and on the Bench	His (*or* Her) Honour

CIRCUIT JUDGE (RETIRED)

The prefix 'His (or Her) Honour' is retained on retirement from office, but 'Judge' is dropped.[1]

BEGINNING OF LETTER

Formal	(Dear) Sir (or Madam)
Social	Dear Judge[1] *or*
	Dear Mr. *or* Mrs. Brown

ENDING OF LETTER

Formal	Yours faithfully (see also p. 2)
Social	Yours sincerely

ENVELOPE

Formal and Social	His Honour John Brown *or*
	Her Honour Mary Brown
If a Knight	His Honour Sir John Brown

VERBAL ADDRESS

Formal	Sir (or Madam)
Social	Judge (excluding the surname) *or*
	Mr. Brown, Mrs. Brown, Miss Brown

If a knight, he is officially called Sir John (Brown)

DESCRIPTION IN CONVERSATION

Formal and Social	The Judge, *or* Judge Brown *or*
	Mr. Brown

ATTORNEY GENERAL AND SOLICITOR GENERAL

They are Law Officers of the Crown, advise the Government on legal matters of importance, and represent the Crown in Court in certain of the more serious or important cases. Both are political appointments.

[1] Retained only by courtesy.

The Attorney General is head of the Bar in England, and takes precedence over all barristers. The Solicitor General is junior in precedence to the Attorney General, and is a Queen's Counsel. A Solicitor General is also appointed for Scotland.

(See also p. 198.)

RECORDERS

Apart from the full-time Recorders of London, Liverpool and Manchester, their duties were changed under the Courts Act 1971. Previously, they presided at the Courts of Quarter Sessions. The new style Recorders are not appointed of a specific place. Liverpool and Manchester each have Circuit Judges who retain the Honorary title of Recorder during their lifetime. Some local authorities have continued the previous office of Recorder of . . . . . as Honorary Recorder of . . . . .

BEGINNING OF LETTER

Formal	(Dear) Sir
Official Business	Dear Mr. Recorder
	(Note.—In this instance 'Mr.' is always included)
Social	As for an Esquire, or applicable rank

ENDING OF LETTER

Formal	Yours faithfully (see also p. 2)
Social	Yours sincerely

ENVELOPE

Formal and Social	As for an Esquire

Otherwise as for an Esquire, but whilst on the Bench he is addressed as 'Sir'.

QUEEN'S COUNSEL AND BARRISTERS

Barristers are divided into Queen's Counsel and Junior Counsel. When a Barrister becomes a Q.C., he is said to 'take silk', from the silk gown that he wears.

The letters Q.C. are placed after the name of Queen's Counsel while they are at the Bar or after appointment to the Circuit Bench. They are not used, however, after the names of High Court Judges or persons holding other higher legal appointments. Those who were appointed King's Counsel changed the letters K.C. to Q.C. at the beginning of the present reign.

For the position of the letters see *Letters After the Name*, p. 99.

Barristers are no longer termed 'Barrister-at-law' but 'Barrister' on the direction of the Bar Council.

JUSTICE OF THE PEACE AND MAGISTRATE

Justices of the Peace are appointed by the Crown for every metropolitan and non-metropolitan county. See *Local Government section* p. 232.

While on the Bench he or she is addressed as 'Your Worship' and described as 'His *or* Her Worship'. Otherwise as an Esquire or feminine equivalent. He or she may use the letters 'J.P.' after the name, but this is not obligatory. The letters J.P. precede D.L. as the former is a Crown appointment, and the latter a Lord Lieutenant's appointment. See also *Letters After the Name*, p. 99.

If a Justice of the Peace has been transferred to the Supplemental List at the age of 70, he may still have the letters J.P. placed after his or her name.

STIPENDIARY MAGISTRATE

These are whole time paid appointments, held by barristers or solicitors.

While on the Bench he or she is addressed as a Magistrate, otherwise as an Esquire, followed by the appointment. A Stipendiary Magistrate is not accorded J.P. after his name.

CORONER

He is addressed as an Esquire, and is known as 'Sir' in court.

HIGH SHERIFF (see p. 235)

DIOCESAN CHANCELLOR

The Diocesan Chancellor is usually appointed for life by the Bishop of his Diocese. He acts as the legal adviser to the Bishop and is Judge of the Consistory Court.

The following instructions are for writing to the Diocesan Chancellor in his official capacity only.

BEGINNING OF LETTER

Formal	Dear Mr. Chancellor *or* Dear Sir
Social	Dear Chancellor

ENDING OF LETTER

Formal	Yours faithfully (see also p. 2)
Social	Yours sincerely

ENVELOPE

The Worshipful Chancellor Peter (or P.) Smith
If in Holy Orders: The Reverend Chancellor Peter Smith

VERBAL ADDRESS

Formal	Mr. Chancellor
Social	Chancellor
In Court	Sir *or* Worshipful Sir (*not* Your Worship)

DESCRIPTION IN CONVERSATION

The Chancellor (*or if necessary* The Diocesan Chancellor)

DIOCESAN CHANCELLOR (LADY)[1]

As above, with the following exceptions

BEGINNING OF LETTER

Formal	Dear Madam Chancellor *or* Dear Madam
Social	Dear Chancellor

ENVELOPE

The Worshipful Chancellor Miss Sheila Cameron

VERBAL ADDRESS

Formal	Madam Chancellor
Social	Chancellor
In Court	Madam, *or* Worshipful Madam, (*not* Your Worship)

Scotland

LORD JUSTICE-GENERAL

On taking his seat on the bench he receives a Judicial title (see *Lord of Session*, p. 217) but is always described by his office. He is invariably a Privy Counsellor.

[1] In 1970 a lady was appointed Chancellor of the Diocese of Colchester.

BEGINNING OF LETTER

Formal	My Lord
Social	Dear Lord Justice-General

ENDING OF LETTER

Formal	Yours faithfully (see also p. 2)
Social	Yours sincerely

ENVELOPE

The Rt. Hon. the Lord Justice-General

VERBAL ADDRESS

Formal	My Lord
Social	Lord Justice-General

DESCRIPTION IN CONVERSATION

Lord Justice-General

RETIREMENT

On retirement from office, he is known by his Judicial title, with the prefix 'The Right Honourable'.

WIFE OR WIDOW OF LORD JUSTICE-GENERAL

As for the wife or widow of a Lord of Session.
(See p. 218.)

LORD JUSTICE-CLERK

On taking his seat on the bench he receives a Judicial Title (see *Lord of Session*, p. 217), but is always described by his office.

BEGINNING OF LETTER

Formal	My Lord
Social	Dear Lord Justice-Clerk

ENDING OF LETTER

Formal	Yours faithfully (see also p. 2)
Social	Yours sincerely

ENVELOPE

The Rt. Hon. the Lord Justice-Clerk if a Privy Counsellor, otherwise The Hon. the Lord Justice-Clerk

VERBAL ADDRESS

Formal	My Lord
Social	Lord Justice-Clerk

DESCRIPTION IN CONVERSATION

Lord Justice-Clerk

RETIREMENT

If he retires from office he is known by his Judicial title, with the prefix 'The Right Hon.', if a Privy Counsellor, otherwise 'The Hon.'.

WIFE OR WIDOW OF LORD JUSTICE-CLERK

As for the wife or widow of a Lord of Session. (See p. 218.)

LORD OF SESSION

A Senator (Judge) of the College of Justice in Scotland is known as a Lord of Session. On taking his seat on the bench he is given a Judicial title by which he is known both in office and on retirement. The Lord Justice-General and the Lord Justice-Clerk are addressed for all purposes by their appointments and not by the Judicial Titles with which they take their seats on the bench (see *Lord Justice-General* or *Lord Justice-Clerk*, pp. 215-216).

COMMENCEMENT OF LETTER

Formal	My Lord
Social	Dear Lord Cameron

CONCLUSION OF LETTER

Formal	Yours faithfully (see also p. 2)
Social	Yours sincerely

ENVELOPE

The Hon. Lord Cameron
If a Privy Counsellor, The Rt Hon. Lord Wylie.

VERBAL ADDRESS

Formal	My Lord
Social	Lord Cameron

DESCRIPTION IN CONVERSATION

By their Judicial title, e.g. Lord Cameron, The Lord Justice-General and The Lord Justice-Clerk are known by their appointments.

RETIREMENT

As in office.

CHAIRMAN OF SCOTTISH LAND COURT

On appointment as Chairman he receives a Judicial title by which he is always known, both in office and on retirement. He is treated as a Lord of Session (see *Lord of Session*, p. 217).

WIFE OR WIDOW OF A LORD OF SESSION AND OF THE CHAIRMAN OF SCOTTISH LAND COURT

A wife or widow of a Lord of Session (including Lord Justice-General and Lord Justice-Clerk) and of the Chairman of the Scottish Land Court is addressed by her husband's Judicial title, preceded by 'Lady'.

She has no prefix before 'Lady', but in other respects she is addressed as the wife of a Baron.

CHILDREN OF A LORD OF SESSION AND OF CHAIRMAN OF SCOTTISH LAND COURT

They receive no courtesy rank or style.

LORD ADVOCATE

The Lord Advocate is the principal Law Officer of the Crown in Scotland, corresponding to the Attorney General in England. He is one of the four Law Officers of the Crown, and as such a Minister of the Crown. He may be either a Member of Parliament or a member of the House of Lords, but need not necessarily be either. He is invariably admitted to the Privy Council on taking office as he is a member of the Scottish Universities Committee of the Council.

BEGINNING OF LETTER
Formal

If a Peer	My Lord
Otherwise	(Dear) Sir

Social   By name, but if connected with his department, 'Dear Lord Advocate'

ENDING OF LETTER

Formal	Yours faithfully (see also p. 2)
Social	Yours sincerely

ENVELOPE
> The Rt. Hon. the Lord Advocate, Q.C. M.P. *or*
> The Rt. Hon. John Smith, Q.C. M.P.

SHERIFF, SCOTLAND

The office of Sheriff in Scotland is now principally a judicial one. The Sheriff Courts have a very wide criminal and civil jurisdiction—considerably wider than the jurisdiction of the Crown Courts and the County Courts in England.

The holder of the office of Sheriff Principal is, however, the direct descendant of the King's peace-keeping officer of feudal times and continues to exercise administrative and executive functions within his Sheriffdom.

Scotland is divided into six Sheriffdoms, each having its own Sheriff Principal. Most Sheriffdoms are divided into Sheriff Court districts, each having one or more Sheriff(s). Within his own Sheriffdom, the Sheriff Principal takes precedence immediately after the Lord-Lieutenant.

The Sheriffs Principal are all senior Queen's Counsel and are appointed on a full-time basis. All the Sheriffs are either Advocates or Solicitors and are also appointed on a full-time basis.

All Sheriffs Principal and Sheriffs are addressed as 'My Lord' *or* 'My Lady', on the bench, and as 'Sheriff Smith' formally and socially.

Northern Ireland

The Lord Chief Justice, if a knight, is addressed by his christian name and surname, e.g. 'The Right Honourable Sir Robert Lowry, Lord Chief Justice of Northern Ireland'.

The remainder of the Judiciary are addressed as in England and

Wales. (*Note*: County Court Judges in Northern Ireland still continue at the time of going to press, and are addressed similar to Circuit Judges in England and Wales).

Canada

The Chief Justice of Canada is styled 'The Right Honourable' for life.

The following Judges are styled 'The Honourable' during tenure of office, and on retirement, if approval is given.

Judges of the Supreme and Federal Courts of Canada.

Chief Justices and Judges of the following Courts:

Alberta Newfoundland New Brunswick Nova Scotia Ontario Prince Edward Island	The Supreme Court
Quebec	The Court of Appeal, and the Superior Court
British Columbia	The Court of Appeal and the Supreme Court
Manitoba Saskatchewan	The Court of Appeal and the Court of Queen's Bench
Northwest Territories Yukon Territory	The Supreme Court

N.B. The spellings of 'Honourable' and 'Honour' are officially adopted in Canada, but 'Honorable' and 'Honor' are sometimes used.

THE CHIEF JUSTICE OF CANADA

BEGINNING OF LETTER

Formal	(Dear) Sir
Social	Dear Chief Justice
Envelope	The Rt. Hon. the Chief Justice of Canada *or*
	The Rt. Hon. (followed by his name), The Chief Justice of Canada

THE CHIEF JUSTICE OF SUPREME COURTS AND OTHER HIGH COURTS

BEGINNING OF LETTER

Formal	(Dear) Sir
Social	Dear Chief Justice

ENDING OF LETTER

Formal and Social	Yours (very) truly

ENVELOPE

> The Hon. the Chief Justice of . . .
> The Rt. Hon. the Chief Justice of . . . (if a Member of the Privy Council) *or*
> The Hon John Smith
> The Chief Justice of . . .

JUDGES OF SUPREME COURTS AND OTHER HIGH COURTS

> The Hon. Mr. Justice (surname)
> see *High Court Judges,* p. 208
> On the bench Judges are referred to as 'Your Lordship'.

JUDGES OF LOWER COURTS

Judges of County and District Courts in Canadian Provinces are referred to and addressed 'His Honour'.

Australia

The highest court is the Federal Court of Australia, known as the High Court. Each State in Australia has its own Supreme Court. The High Court, as well as having an original jurisdiction, sits on appeals from the Supreme Court of the States. The members of the High Court are referred to as Justices and not Judges.

The Chief Justice of Australia and some Justices of the High Court are admitted to the Privy Council and are known for life as 'The Right Honourable'. The remainder in the following list are styled 'The Honourable' during tenure of office, and may be permitted to retain the style on retirement if approval is given:

Justices of the High Court of Australia
The Chief Justice of the Australian Industrial Court
The President and Deputy Presidents of the Australian Conciliation and Arbitration Commission
Judges of the Federal Court of Bankruptcy
The Chief Judge and Judges of the Family Court of Australia
The Chief Justice, President of Court of Appeal, Judges of Appeal and Puisne Judges of Supreme Court, New South Wales
The Chief Justice and Puisne Judges of the Supreme Courts of:
    Victoria
    Queensland
    South Australia
    Western Australia
    Tasmania
Judges of the Supreme Court of Australian Capital Territory
Judges of the Supreme Court of Northern Territory

N.B. The spellings of 'Honourable' and 'Honour' are officially adopted in Australia (e.g. *The Commonwealth Directory*), but 'Honorable' and 'Honor' are sometimes used (e.g. *The Parliamentary Handbook*).

THE CHIEF JUSTICE OF AUSTRALIA

The Chief Justice of Australia, as a Member of the Privy Council, is styled 'The Right Honourable' for life.

BEGINNING OF LETTER
Formal   (Dear) Sir
Social   Dear Chief Justice

ENVELOPE
    The Right Honourable (Sir Garfield Barwick, GCMG) Chief Justice of Australia

HIGH COURT OF AUSTRALIA

Judges of the High Court are sometimes knighted and admitted to the Privy Council. They are known both officially and colloquially as Justices. (Since 1973 no Justices of the High Court have been knighted or appointed to the Privy Council, but it is not known at this stage whether the practice will be resumed.)

The forms of address are as follows:

BEGINNING OF LETTER

Formal	(Dear) Sir
Social	Dear Justice

ENVELOPE

If a Privy Counsellor	The Rt. Hon. Mr. Justice Smith
If a Justice has not been admitted to the Privy Council	The Hon. Mr. Justice Smith

Socially the following may be used for other Justices:

The Rt. Hon. Sir John Smith, K.B.E.
The Hon. Sir John Smith, K.B.E. (if not admitted to the Privy Council)

On the bench he is referred to as 'Your Honour'.

SUPREME COURT

BEGINNING OF LETTER

Formal		(Dear) Sir
Social		
	If the Chief Justice	Dear Chief Justice
	Otherwise	Dear Judge

ENDING OF LETTER

Formal	Yours faithfully (see also p. 2)
Social	Yours sincerely

ENVELOPE

If the Chief Justice	The Chief Justice of the Supreme Court of (New South Wales), the Hon. . . .
Otherwise	The Hon. Mr. Justice Smith

Socially the following may be used for other Judges, if knighted:
The Hon. Sir John Smith

If a lady:
The Hon. Justice Mary Smith
On the bench he or she is referred to as 'Your Honour'.

OTHER COURTS

As for a Supreme Court Judge, except the Chief Judge of the Australian Industrial Court, and the Chief Judge of the Family Court of Australia, who are addressed socially as:

> Dear Chief Judge

ENVELOPE

The name of the Judge is followed by the appointment, e.g.

> The Honourable Mr. Justice Smith,
> President (or Deputy President) of the Australian Conciliation and Arbitration Commission

LOWER COURTS

Judges of County and District Courts in the States of Australia are addressed as 'His Honour' and he is referred to on the Bench as 'Your Honour'. See *Circuit Judge* (p. 211).

New Zealand

The Chief Justice of New Zealand and the President and the two other Judges of the Court of Appeal are normally admitted to the Privy Council, and as such are styled 'The Right Honourable' during tenure of office and during retirement. It is usual for the Chief Justice, and for the President and Judges of the Court of Appeal, to be knighted.

The Puisne Judges of the Supreme Court are styled 'The Honourable' during tenure of office, and may be permitted to retain that style during retirement if approval is given. The Senior Puisne Judge is normally knighted. Judges of the Court of Arbitration, of the Compensation Court, and of the Maori Land Court are styled 'Judge' during tenure of office, with the exception of the Chief Judge of the Maori Land Court who is styled 'Chief Judge'.

Judges of the Court of Appeal and of the Supreme Court in New Zealand are referred to and addressed in the same way as High Court Judges in the United Kingdom, i.e. (Dear) Sir, *or* Dear Judge. The envelope is addressed 'The Hon. Mr. Justice Smith', *or* 'The Rt. Hon. Mr. Justice Smith' if admitted to the Privy Council.

A letter to the Chief Justice is addressed 'The Rt. Hon. the Chief Justice', or 'The Rt. Hon. Sir . . ., Chief Justice of New Zealand'. The commencement of the letter is:

'(Dear) Sir', *or*
'Dear Chief Justice'.

There are no Courts in New Zealand which correspond to the British County Courts.

Other Commonwealth Countries

Chief Justices, Judges of the Courts of Appeal and Puisne Judges of the Supreme and High Courts, including Dependent Territories, during office are addressed as The Hon. Mr. Justice before the surname, including knights. Forms of address are as for Judges of the High Court of England and Wales.

Deemsters of the Isle of Man are accorded 'His Honour' before the name, and referred to as 'Deemster' in place of 'Judge'. Bailiffs in Jersey and Guernsey have no Judicial prefix, and are addressed either by office (Dear Bailiff) or name.

MEDICAL SECTION

There are two distinct forms of address, for the broad disciplines of Medicine and Surgery.

Medicine (including General Practice)

A Doctor of Medicine who practises *medicine* is known as 'Doctor'.

A Physician who holds other medical degrees or diplomas (including those which are both medical and surgical, e.g. M.R.C.S., L.R.C.P., M.B., B.S.) is known by courtesy as 'doctor' in speech.

Where one has qualifications in more than one discipline he (or she) is usually addressed according to that which he (or she) practises.

Where one progresses in the same degree, qualification, etc., only the higher is shown, i.e. if a Bachelor of Medicine becomes a Doctor of Medicine he is shown only as M.D. *or* D.M. (according to the University); similarly if a M.R.C.P. becomes a F.R.C.P. only the latter is shown.

An Anaesthetist (F.F.A., R.C.S.), a Pathologist (F.R.C. Path.), and a Radiologist (F.R.C.R.) are all called 'Doctor'.

BEGINNING OF LETTER

Formal	Dear Sir
Social	Dear Doctor Smith
	Dear Sir John

ENDING OF LETTER

Formal	Yours faithfully (see also p. 2)
Social	Yours sincerely

ENVELOPE

John Smith, Esq., M.D., F.R.C.P. *or* Dr. John Smith,
Sir John Smith, M.D., F.R.C.P.
John Brown, Esq., B.M., B.S. *or* Dr. John Brown
William Robinson, Esq., M.R.C.S., L.R.C.P. *or* Dr. William
Robinson

Note.—Those with doctorates, masterships and fellowships should be addressed on the envelope with the appropriate letters. Others who practise medicine, as in the second and third examples, may be addressed on the envelope as Dr. William Robinson if the exact qualifying diplomas (e.g. M.B. or B.M., B.S., B.Chir. or Ch.B.) are not known. See *Letters After the Name*, (p. 227).

VERBAL ADDRESS AND DESCRIPTION IN CONVERSATION

Dr. Smith

Surgery (including Gynaecology)

A Surgeon (usually with a Mastership or Fellowship in Surgery) is known as 'Mr. Smith' in speech.

A Doctor of Medicine who practises surgery is known as 'Mr. Smith' in speech.

Where a doctor has qualifications in more than one discipline, it is usual for him (or her) to be addressed according to that which he (or she) practises. See *Letters After the Name,* (p. 227).

BEGINNING OF LETTER

Formal	Dear Sir,
Social	Dear Mr. Smith
	Dear Sir John

ENDING OF LETTER

Formal	Yours faithfully (see also p. 2)
Social	Yours sincerely

ENVELOPE

John Smith, Esq., M.S., F.R.C.S.
William Jones, Esq., D.M., M.S., F.R.C.S.
Sir John Smith, M.S., F.R.C.S.

An Obstetrician and a Gynaecologist (usually M.R.C.O.G. or F.R.C.O.G.) is addressed as a Surgeon in England and Wales. Elsewhere, including Scotland, Ireland, Australia, Canada, New Zealand, South Africa and the U.S.A., it is the custom for him (or her) to be called 'Doctor'.

VERBAL ADDRESS AND DESCRIPTION IN CONVERSATION

Mr. Smith

Dental Practitioner

If a Dental Surgeon, he is referred to as a Surgeon, i.e. Mr. John Jones, with the appropriate letters signifying his degrees or qualifications.

In general practice he may be referred to as a Doctor if he has a medical degree or qualification in addition to a dental qualification, but not otherwise.

Letters after the name

By custom those denoting medicine follow those of Orders, Decorations, and Medals bestowed by the Crown.

They are usually placed in the following order:

Doctorates
Masterships
Baccalaureates (degrees of Bachelor)
Postgraduate Diplomas (e.g. Fellowships and Memberships except M.R.C.S.)
Qualifying Diplomas (M.R.C.S., L.R.C.P., etc.)

It is the custom for letters indicating Doctorates, Masterships, and Fellowships to be given in correspondence. Baccalaureates, Memberships, and Qualifying Diplomas may be shown if no higher qualifications are held.

It is sufficient for a maximum of three series of letters to be shown, e.g., M.D., F.R.C.S., F.R.C.O.G.

If required for formal lists, the following is the complete list of letters commonly used in medicine in the British Isles.

DOCTORATES
 D.M.—Doctor of Medicine
 M.D.—Doctor of Medicine
 D.Ch.—Doctor of Surgery

MASTERSHIPS
 M.Ch.—Master of Surgery
 M.Chir.—Master of Surgery
 M.S.—Master of Surgery
 Ch.M.—Master of Surgery
 M.D.S.—Master of Dental Surgery
 M.A.O.—Master of the Art of Obstetrics

BACCALAUREATES
 B.M.—Bachelor of Medicine
 M.B.—Bachelor of Medicine
 B.Ch.—Bachelor of Surgery
 B.Chir.—Bachelor of Surgery
 B.S.—Bachelor of Surgery
 Ch.B.—Bachelor of Surgery
 B.D.S.—Bachelor of Dental Surgery
 B.A.O.—Bachelor of the Art of Obstetrics

POSTGRADUATE DIPLOMAS (Fellowships and Memberships except M.R.C.S.)
 F.R.C.P.—Fellow of the Royal College of Physicians
 F.R.C.P. Ed.—Fellow of the Royal College of Physicians of Edinburgh
 F.R.C.P.I.—Fellow of the Royal College of Physicians of Ireland
 F.R.C.P. (Glasg.)—Fellow (*qua* physician) of the Royal College of Physicians and Surgeons of Glasgow
 M.R.C.P.—Member of the Royal College of Physicians
 M.R.C.P. Ed.—Member of the Royal College of Physicians of Edinburgh
 M.R.C.P.I.—Member of the Royal College of Physicians of Ireland
 M.R.C.P. (Glasg.)—Member of the Royal College of Physicians and Surgeons of Glasgow

M.R.C.P. (U.K.)[1]

F.R.C.S.—Fellow of the Royal College of Surgeons

F.R.C.S. Ed.—Fellow of the Royal College of Surgeons of Edinburgh

F.R.C.S.I.—Fellow of the Royal College of Surgeons in Ireland

F.R.C.S. (Glasg.)—Fellow (*qua* surgeon) of the Royal College of Physicians and Surgeons of Glasgow

F.R.C.O.G.—Fellow of the Royal College of Obstetricians and Gynaecologists

M.R.C.O.G.—Member of the Royal College of Obstetricians and Gynaecologists

F.R.C.G.P.—Fellow of the Royal College of General Practitioners

M.R.C.G.P.—Member of the Royal College of General Practitioners

F.R.C.Path.—Fellow of the Royal College of Pathologists[2]

M.R.C.Path.—Member of the Royal College of Pathologists

F.R.C.Psych.—Fellow of Royal College of Psychiatrists (formerly Royal Medico-Psychological Association)

M.R.C.Psych.—Member of Royal College of Psychiatrists

F.R.C.R.—Fellow of the Royal College of Radiologists

F.F.A., R.C.S.—Fellow of the Faculty of Anaesthetists, the Royal College of Surgeons

F.D.S., R.C.S.—Fellow in Dental Surgery, the Royal College of Surgeons

F.F.C.M.—Fellow of the Faculty of Community Medicine

M.F.C.M.—Member of the Faculty of Community Medicine

QUALIFYING DIPLOMAS

M.R.C.S., L.R.C.P.—Member of the Royal College of Surgeons; Licentiate of the Royal College of Physicians

L.R.C.P., L.R.C.S., L.R.F.P.S.—Licentiate of the Royal College of Physicians of Edinburgh, of the Royal College of Surgeons of Edinburgh, and of the Royal Faculty of Physicians and Surgeons of Glasgow[3]

L.R.C.P., L.R.C.S., L.R.C.P.S.—Licentiate of the first two Royal Colleges, and of the Royal College of Physicians and Surgeons of Glasgow[3]

[1] This diploma is now granted by most colleges who have united in this respect. Past Members who were awarded the diploma retain letters as previously.
[2] These letters include those who qualified as F.C.Path.
[3] The Royal Faculty of Physicians and Surgeons of Glasgow has become a Royal College, but those who qualified in the former letters (L.R.F.P.S.), retain them.

L.R.C.P.I. and L.M.—Licentiate of the Royal College of Physicians of Ireland, and Licentiate in Midwifery

L.R.C.S.I. and L.M.—Licentiate of the Royal College of Surgeons in Ireland, and Licentiate in Midwifery

L.S.A.—Licentiate of the Society of Apothecaries

L.M.S.S.A.—Licentiate in Medicine and Surgery, the Society of Apothecaries

OTHER POSTGRADUATE DIPLOMAS

M.M.S.A.—Master of Midwifery, Society of Apothecaries

D.P.H.—Diploma in Public Health

D.O.—Diploma in Ophthalmology

D.O.M.S.—Diploma in Ophthalmic Medicine and Surgery

D.P.M.—Diploma in Psychological Medicine

D.C.P.—Diploma in Clinical Pathology

Dip. Bact.—Diploma in Bacteriology

D.M.R.D.—Diploma in Medical Radio-Diagnosis

D.M.R.T.—Diploma in Medical Radio-Therapy

D.M.R.E.—Diploma in Medical Radiology and Electrology

D.Phys.Med.—Diploma in Physical Medicine

D.A.—Diploma in Anaesthesia

D.C.H.—Diploma in Child Health

D.I.H.—Diploma in Industrial Health

D.L.O.—Diploma in Laryngology and Orology

D.Obst.R.C.O.G.—Diploma in Obstetrics, the Royal College of Obstetricians and Gynaecologists

D.T.M. and H.—Diploma in Tropical Medicine and Hygiene

D.M.J.—Diploma in Medical Jurisprudence

Dip.Soc.Med. Edin.—Diploma in Social Medicine of the University of Edinburgh

NURSING SECTION

The following are the appointments in the Nursing Service:

Regional Nursing Officer
Area Nursing Officer
District (or Chief) Nursing Officer
Divisional Nursing Officer
Principal Nursing Officer
Senior Nursing Officer
Nursing Officer

Charge Nurse (ladies who were previously known as Sisters may retain this title or adopt the newer one of Charge Nurse. Males invariably are known as Charge Nurses)

Staff Nurse

This applies to all nurses working in hospitals within the National Health Service although the old titles (Matron, Sister, etc.) continue to be used in other hospitals and nursing homes.

The term 'Nurse' is protected by Act of Parliament, and the following are entitled to be so called in England and Wales:

State Registered Nurse (S.R.N.)

Registered Mental Nurse (R.M.N.)

Registered Nurse for the Mentally Sub-Normal (R.N.M.S.)

Registered Sick Children's Nurse (R.S.C.N.)

Student Nurses training for the Register

State Enrolled Nurse (S.E.N.)

Pupil Nurses training for the Roll

These titles are different in Scotland, e.g. the equivalent of a State Registered Nurse is Registered General Nurse (R.G.N.).

The teaching grades are as follows:

Director of Nurse Education

Senior Tutor

Tutor

Clinical Teacher

It is now the custom to write to all the above by his or her name. The appointment may follow, if required (e.g. Miss Marion Smith, District Nursing Officer, West Blankshire Hospital). If the name or terminology of the senior appointment is not known correspondence may be addressed to 'Head of the Nursing Services'.

Midwife

The term 'Midwife' is protected by Act of Parliament.

It is customary to write to a State Certified Midwife (S.C.M.) or a Pupil Midwife training for certification by her name.

Nursing Corps and Services

(See *Queen Alexandra's Royal Naval Nursing Service,* pp. 192-193; *Queen Alexandra's Royal Army Nursing Corps,* pp. 193-194; *Princess Mary's Royal Air Force Nursing Service,* pp. 194-195.)

LOCAL GOVERNMENT SECTION

Lord-Lieutenant[1]

ENGLAND AND WALES

A Lord-Lieutenant (the two words should be hyphenated) is appointed by the Crown for each of the following counties. (Those in bold type are **metropolitan counties;** the rest are non-metropolitan):

ENGLAND

Bedfordshire	Lancashire
Berkshire[2]	Leicestershire
Buckinghamshire	Lincolnshire
Cambridgeshire	**Merseyside**
Cheshire	Norfolk
Cleveland	Northamptonshire
Cornwall	Northumberland
Cumbria	North Yorkshire
Derbyshire	Nottinghamshire
Devon	Oxfordshire
Dorset	Salop
Durham	Somerset
East Sussex	**South Yorkshire**
Essex	Staffordshire
Gloucestershire	Suffolk
Greater London[3]	Surrey
Greater Manchester	**Tyne and Wear**
Hampshire	Warwickshire
Hereford and Worcester	**West Midlands**
Hertfordshire	West Sussex
Humberside	West Yorkshire
Isle of Wight	Wiltshire
Kent	

WALES

Clwyd	Gwent
Dyfed	Gwynedd
Glamorgan	Powys

[1] The office can be held by a lady.
[2] Berkshire is a Royal County.
[3] The Lord-Lieutenant of Greater London has no jurisdiction in the City of London where the duties of the Lieutenancy are discharged by the Lord Mayor.

SCOTLAND

The Lord Provosts of Aberdeen, Dundee, Edinburgh and Glasgow are *ex-officio* Lord-Lieutenants of their respective cities.

A Lord-Lieutenant is appointed by the Crown for each of the following counties:

Aberdeenshire	Morayshire
Angus	Nairn
Argyll and Bute	Orkney
Ayr and Arran	Perth and Kinross
Banffshire	Renfrewshire
Berwickshire	Ross and Cromarty
Caithness	Roxburgh, Ettrick and Lauderdale
Clackmannan	
Dumfries[1]	Shetland
Dunbartonshire	Stewartry of Kirkcudbright
East Lothian	Stirling and Falkirk
Fife	Sutherland
Inverness	Tweeddale
Kincardineshire	Western Isles
Lanarkshire	West Lothian
Midlothian	Wigtown

NORTHERN IRELAND

A Lord-Lieutenant[2] is appointed by the Crown for each of the following:

Co. Antrim	Co. Londonderry
Co. Armagh	Co. Tyrone
Co. Down	City of Belfast
Co. Fermanagh	City of Londonderry

A Lord-Lieutenant is the Sovereign's representative in his county, etc. Officially he or she is appointed 'Her Majesty's Lord-Lieutenant of and in the County of . . . ', but the usual style is, e.g. The Lord-Lieutenant of Blankshire.

FORM OF ADDRESS

There is no specific form of address for a Lord-Lieutenant, nor are letters appended after his name. Correspondence may be addressed:

[1] Also known as Nithsdale and Annandale and Eskdale.
[2] Article 2 of the Northern Ireland (Lieutenancy) Order 1975 provided that Her Majesty should appoint a Lord-Lieutenant and one or more Lieutenants for each county and county borough in Northern Ireland.

Formal	Colonel Sir John Brown, K.C.B., D.S.O.
	H.M. Lord-Lieutenant of Blankshire
Otherwise	Colonel Sir John Brown, K.C.B., D.S.O.
	Lord-Lieutenant of Blankshire

In speech a Lord-Lieutenant is referred to as 'My Lord-Lieutenant'. The plural form of Lord-Lieutenant is Lord-Lieutenants.

H.M. Lieutenant

For some counties the Crown also appoints one or more Lieutenants, styled, e.g. Her Majesty's Lieutenant for Blankshire, who also represent the Sovereign. In particular there are, under the Lord-Lieutenant of Glamorgan, three Lieutenants for respectively, Mid Glamorgan, South Glamorgan and West Glamorgan.

There is no specific form of address for a Lieutenant, nor are there any letters for this appointment appended after his name. Official correspondence is addressed:

Formal	George Smith, Esq.,
	H.M. Lieutenant of Blankshire
Otherwise	George Smith, Esq.,
	Lieutenant of Blankshire

In speech a Lieutenant is referred to as 'Her Majesty's Lieutenant'.

Vice Lord-Lieutenant

For his period of office a Lord-Lieutenant appoints a Vice Lord-Lieutenant from among his Deputy Lieutenants, (for whom see p. 235). There is no recognised abbreviation for a Vice Lord-Lieutenant: he continues to use the letters D.L. after his name. Official correspondence is addressed:

Edward Green, Esq., D.L.,
Vice Lord-Lieutenant of Blankshire

Assistant Lieutenant

For his period of office the Lord-Lieutenant of Greater London may also appoint four Assistant Lieutenants from among his Deputy Lieutenants for whom there is likewise no recognised abbreviation, and to whom official correspondence should be addressed:

Robert White, Esq., D.L.,
Assistant Lieutenant of Greater London.

Deputy Lieutenant

A Lord-Lieutenant appoints a number of Deputy Lieutenants, an office held for life. The letters D.L. should be placed after their names, although in social correspondence these are often omitted. *Note*—D.L. *follows* J.P. see *Position of Letters After the Name,* p. 99.

High Sheriff

A High Sheriff is appointed by the Crown annually in March for each of the counties listed above in England, except that the Duke of Cornwall (the Prince of Wales) appoints the High Sheriff of Cornwall, and the Queen, in right of her Duchy of Lancaster, appoints the High Sheriffs for Lancashire, Greater Manchester and Merseyside. High Sheriffs of counties and cities in Northern Ireland and counties in Wales are appointed as listed above, except in the latter country three are appointed for, respectively, Mid Glamorgan, South Glamorgan and West Glamorgan.

Official correspondence may be addressed:

John Smith, Esq.,
High Sheriff of Loamshire.

Sheriff, England, Wales and Northern Ireland

CITY OF LONDON
Two Sheriffs are elected annually by Common Hall. It is customary for an Alderman who has not served the office of Lord Mayor to be elected as one of them.

The Sheriff who is also an Alderman is addressed according to his rank, or simply as 'Mr. Sheriff', but when writing to him in his official capacity the following forms may be used:

BEGINNING OF LETTER
Dear Alderman and Sheriff (omitting the name)

ENVELOPE
Mr. Alderman and Sheriff Smith
Alderman and Sheriff Sir John Brown
Alderman and Sheriff the Rt. Hon. Lord Portsdown
Lieutenant-Colonel, Alderman and Sheriff Jones

In the case of a lady:

Mrs. (or Miss) Alderman and Sheriff White

Alderman and Sheriff Lady Green (being the wife of a baronet or knight)

Alderman and Sheriff the Lady Loamshire (being the wife of a peer)

VERBAL ADDRESS

Mr. Sheriff

The Sheriff who is not an Alderman is addressed as above, but omitting all reference to Alderman.

OTHER CITIES, ETC.

The City of Oxford has the right to elect a Sheriff annually, as have the following which were anciently counties in themselves, or were 'counties corporate':

Berwick-upon-Tweed	Lichfield
Bristol	Lincoln
Canterbury	Newcastle-upon-Tyne
Carmarthen	Norwich
Chester	Nottingham
Durham	Poole
Exeter	Southampton
Gloucester	Worcester
Kingston-upon-Hull	York

These Sheriffs, whose duties are chiefly of a ceremonial kind, are not to be confused with High Sheriffs of counties.

There is no special form of address for these Sheriffs, although the appointment may follow the name in official correspondence.

Under Sheriff

One (or occasionally more) Under Sheriff may be appointed to assist each High Sheriff or to act for him in his absence. He is generally a practising solicitor.

One or two Under Sheriffs are also appointed to assist the Sheriffs for the City of London.

There is no specific form of address, but in official correspondence the appointment is included after the name, e.g.:

Brigadier John Jones, C.B.E.,

Under Sheriff of Salop

Sheriff, Scotland

See *Legal Section* p. 219.

Justice of the Peace

See *Legal Section,* p. 214.

County Council[1]

Each of the counties in England listed above under *Lord-Lieutenant* has a County Council which elects a Chairman, a Vice-Chairman, and, in some cases, a Deputy Chairman. So, too, with the counties in Wales except that there are separate County Councils for Mid Glamorgan, South Glamorgan and West Glamorgan.

The Chairman of the Greater London Council is styled 'The Right Honourable'.

CHAIRMAN

BEGINNING OF LETTER

> Dear Mr. Chairman (even though the office be held by a lady)

ENDING OF LETTER

Formal	Yours faithfully (see also p. 2)
Social	Yours sincerely

ENVELOPE

Formal	The Right Honourable the Chairman of the Greater London Council
	The Chairman of the Salop County Council
Social	By name

VERBAL ADDRESS

> Mr. Chairman (even though the office be held by a lady) *or* by name

[1] Northern Ireland has neither County nor Regional Councils.

DESCRIPTION IN CONVERSATION

The Chairman *or* by name

For Vice-Chairman and Deputy Chairman the above rules apply, except for the omission of 'The Right Honourable' in the case of the Greater London Council.

Regional Council[1]

In Scotland each of the following regions has a Regional or Islands Council. Those asterisked elect a Convenor and a Vice-Convenor, the rest a Chairman and a Vice-Chairman.

Borders*	Lothian*
Central	Orkney
Dumfries and Galloway*	Shetland
Fife	Strathclyde
Grampian	Tayside
Highland	Western Isles*

A Convenor is addressed as for a Chairman; *omitting* 'Mr.'. A Vice-Convenor is addressed as for a Vice-Chairman, omitting 'Mr.'.

County, Regional or Islands Councillor[2]

These are not styled 'Councillor'. Some members of the Greater London Council use the suffix G.L.C. after their names, but there is no official authority for this, neither has the abbreviation C.C. for County Councillor any official standing.

Civic Heads, England and Wales

GREATER LONDON

These are:

    The Lord Mayor of London
    The Lord Mayor of Westminster
    The Mayor of the Royal Borough of Kensington and Chelsea
    The Mayor of the Royal Borough of Kingston-upon-Thames
    The Mayors of the 29 other Boroughs into which the area is divided[3]

---

[1] Northern Ireland has neither County nor Regional Councils.
[2] The office of County Alderman has recently been abolished.
[3] For a full list see *The Municipal Year Book*.

CITIES ELSEWHERE[1]

The following elect *Lord Mayors*:

Birmingham	Newcastle upon Tyne
Bradford	Norwich
Bristol	Nottingham
Cardiff	Oxford
Coventry	Plymouth
Kingston upon Hull	Portsmouth
Leeds	Sheffield
Leicester	Stoke-on-Trent
Liverpool	York
Manchester	

The following elect *Mayors*:

Bath[2]	Lancaster[3]
Cambridge	Lincoln
Canterbury	Peterborough
Carlisle	St. Albans
Chester	Salford
Derby	Southampton
Durham	Swansea
Exeter	Wakefield
Gloucester	Winchester
Hereford	Worcester

The following elect *Chairmen*:

Bangor	Rochester
Chichester	Salisbury
Ely	Truro
Lichfield	Wells
Ripon	

METROPOLITAN DISTRICT AND DISTRICT COUNCILS

For a full list of these see *The Municipal Year Book*. Each of these granted Borough status elects a *Mayor*.[4] The others elect a *Chairman*.

[1] The status of City, which once denoted a cathedral see, is now conferred by the Crown. There are, consequently, cities *without* a cathedral (e.g. Southampton) and towns *with* a cathedral (e.g. Guildford).
[2] Styled 'Chairman and Mayor'.
[3] Styled 'Mayor and Chairman',
[4] Windsor and Maidenhead is a Royal Borough.

PARISH COUNCILS (ENGLAND ONLY) AND COMMUNITY COUNCILS (WALES ONLY)

Those which have adopted the style of City of Town Council elect a *City Mayor* or *Town Mayor*. For a full list see *The Municipal Year Book*.[1] The remainder elect a *Chairman*.

Civic Heads, Northern Ireland

CITIES

Belfast elects a *Lord Mayor*.
Londonderry elects a *Mayor*.

DISTRICT COUNCILS

For a full list of these see *The Municipal Year Book*. Some elect a *Mayor*, others a *Chairman*.

Lord Mayor

The Lord Mayors[2] of London and York have been styled 'The Right Honourable' since time immemorial. Other Lord Mayors are so styled only when granted this privilege by The Sovereign: these are Belfast and Cardiff. The remainder are styled 'The Right Worshipful'.[3] There is no difference in the form of address for a Lord Mayor who is a lady.

BEGINNING OF LETTER
Formal	My Lord Mayor
Social	Dear Lord Mayor

ENDING OF LETTER
Formal	Yours faithfully (see also p. 2)
Social	Yours sincerely

ENVELOPE
Formal and	The Right Honourable the Lord Mayor
Social	of . . ., *or*
	The Right Worshipful the Lord Mayor of . . .

If desired the name, preceded by Councillor may follow the office,[4] but 'The Right Honourable' or 'The Right Worshipful' should always be placed before 'the Lord Mayor'.

---

[1] Caernarvon is a Royal Town.
[2] The correct plural form; *not* Lords Mayor.
[3] The Lord Mayor of Bristol is sometimes styled 'The Right Honourable' but there is no official authority for this.
[4] Not applicable to the Lord Mayor of London.

VERBAL ADDRESS
    My Lord Mayor, *or*
    Lord Mayor

DESCRIPTION IN CONVERSATION
    The Lord Mayor, *or*
    The Lord Mayor of . . .

Lady Mayoress

A Lady Mayoress (i.e. the wife or other chosen female consort, e.g. a daughter, of a Lord Mayor) is not styled 'The Right Honourable' or 'The Right Worshipful'.

BEGINNING OF LETTER
Formal	My Lady Mayoress
Social	Dear Lady Mayoress

ENDING OF LETTER
Formal	Yours faithfully (see also p. 2)
Social	Yours sincerely

ENVELOPE
    The Lady Mayoress of . . .
    If desired the name, preceded by Councillor where applicable, may follow the office.

VERBAL ADDRESS
    My Lady Mayoress *or*
    Lady Mayoress

DESCRIPTION IN CONVERSATION
    The Lady Mayoress *or*
    The Lady Mayoress of . . .

Lord Mayor's Consort

A lady Lord Mayor's husband is so styled, but is addressed by his name.

Deputy Lord Mayor

The rules for addressing a Lord Mayor apply except that he is not styled 'Right Honourable' nor 'Right Worshipful', and the verbal form is 'Deputy Lord Mayor'. *Note* There is no Deputy Lord Mayor of (the City of) London. An Alderman deputising for the Lord Mayor of London is styled Lord Mayor locum tenens.

Deputy Lady Mayoress

The rules for addressing a Lady Mayoress apply except that the verbal form is 'Deputy Lady Mayoress'.

Mayor

The Mayor of a City (see pp. 238-239 above) (including a City Mayor) is styled 'The Right Worshipful'. The Mayors of Hastings, Hythe, New Romney and Rye are also so styled because these are ancient Cinque Ports. (The other three, Dover, Sandwich and Winchelsea, no longer have Mayors.)

All other Mayors (including Town Mayors) are styled 'The Worshipful'.

BEGINNING OF LETTER
Formal   Mr. Mayor
Social   Dear Mr. Mayor

These forms are used even though the Mayor is a peer, or is a lady, though some lady Mayors prefer the form 'Madam Mayor'.

ENDING OF LETTER
Formal   Yours faithfully (see also p. 2)
Social   Yours sincerely

ENVELOPE
    The Right Worshipful the Mayor of (the City of) . . .
    The Worshipful the Mayor of the Royal Borough of . . .
    The Worshipful the Mayor of . . .

If desired the Mayor's name, preceded by Councillor, may follow the office, but 'The Right Worshipful' or 'The Worshipful' should precede 'the Mayor'.

VERBAL ADDRESS
    Mr. Mayor

'Your Worship' is archaic, except when the Mayor is sitting as a magistrate for which he must be a Justice of the Peace.[1] If, however, more than one Mayor is present, 'Your Worships' must be used because there is no acceptable plural form of 'Mr. Mayor'.

[1] All Mayors used to be J.P.s *ex-officio*, but this privilege was abolished in 1969.

DESCRIPTION IN CONVERSATION
> The Mayor *or*
> The Mayor of . . .

Mayoress

A Mayoress (i.e. the wife or other chosen female consort, e.g. a daughter, of a Mayor) is so styled; *not* 'The Right Worshipful' or 'The Worshipful'.

BEGINNING OF LETTER
Formal   Madam Mayoress
Social   Dear Mayoress
> These forms are used, even though the Mayoress is a peeress.

ENDING OF LETTER
Formal   Yours faithfully (see also p. 2)
Social   Yours sincerely

ENVELOPE
> The Mayoress of . . .
> If desired the Mayoress's name, preceded by Councillor (where applicable), may follow the office.

VERBAL ADDRESS
> Mayoress

DESCRIPTION IN CONVERSATION
> The Mayoress *or*
> The Mayoress of . . .

Mayor's Consort

A lady Mayor's husband is so styled, but for all purposes he should be addressed by name.

Deputy Mayor

A Deputy Mayor is so styled; *not* 'The Right Worshipful' or 'The Worshipful'. Otherwise the above rules for addressing a Mayor apply.

Deputy Mayoress

As above for a Mayoress, with the addition of 'Deputy'.

Chairman of District Council or Parish Council

As for the Chairman of a County Council (see p. 237).

Alderman (*Corporation of London only*)[1]

One is elected for each Ward.

BEGINNING OF LETTER
Formal   Dear Alderman
Social   By name

ENDING OF LETTER
Formal   Yours faithfully (see also p. 2)
Social   Yours sincerely

ENVELOPE
Formal

Mr. Alderman (followed by his name)

Alderman Sir (followed by his name etc. for a baronet or knight)

Alderman the Right Hon. Lord (followed by his title, etc. for a peer)

Lieutenant-Colonel & Alderman (followed by his title, name, etc. for one holding a rank in the Armed Forces)

In the case of a lady: Mrs. or Miss Alderman (followed by her name)

Alderman Lady (followed by her name for the wife of a baronet or knight)

Alderman the Lady (followed by her title for the wife of a peer).

Social   By name

VERBAL ADDRESS
As for Description in Conversation

DESCRIPTION IN CONVERSATION
For a man: Alderman, which may be followed by his name and, where applicable, his title.
For a lady: Alderman, which may be followed by her name, preceded by Mrs. or Miss or, where applicable, her title.

[1] Elsewhere the office of Alderman has recently been abolished except for the London Boroughs on whose Councils they will continue to serve until May 1978, pending which they should be addressed as for Councillors, substituting 'Alderman' for 'Councillor'.

Honorary Alderman

Councils may elect Honorary Aldermen for life. They are addressed as for an Esquire, or appropriate rank, except that on the envelope 'Honorary Alderman' may follow the name.

Common Councilman (*Corporation of London only*)

As for an Esquire, or appropriate rank. For a lady, her correct style, whether married, single or widowed. On the envelope the letters C.C. should follow the name, after any orders or decorations. Members of the Court of Common Council are not styled 'Councillor'.

Deputy (*Corporation of London only*)

A Common Councilman in each Ward is appointed Deputy to the Alderman of his Ward. He, or she, is addressed at the beginning of a letter as 'Dear Deputy'; and on the envelope as for an Esquire, or appropriate rank, or in the case of a lady, her correct style, followed by the word 'Deputy'.

City, Borough or District Councillor

BEGINNING OF LETTER

Formal	Dear Councillor, which may be followed by his or her name, preceded where applicable by rank and title or, in the case of a lady, by 'Mrs.' or 'Miss' ('Mr.' is *not* used)
Social	By name

ENDING OF LETTER

Formal	Yours faithfully (see also p. 2)
Social	Yours sincerely

ENVELOPE

Formal	Councillor, followed by his or her name preceded, where applicable, by rank and title and, in the case of a lady, by 'Mrs.' or 'Miss'
Social	By name

> Councillor, which may be followed by his or her name and where applicable, rank, title and, in the case of a lady, 'Mrs.' or 'Miss' ('Mr.' is *not* used)

DESCRIPTION IN CONVERSATION

> As for Verbal Address

Corporation and Municipal Officers

These are normally addressed by their appointment, e.g., at the beginning of a letter 'Dear Chief Executive'[1] and on the envelope 'The Chief Executive (of . . .). Similarly, 'Dear (Mr.) Town Clerk', Dear (Mr.) Chamberlain', 'Dear (Mr.) City Engineer'. Formal letters may, however, begin 'Dear Sir'.

Civic Heads, Scotland

The District Councils of the cities of Aberdeen, Dundee, Edinburgh and Glasgow elect Lord Provosts. The Lord Provosts of Edinburgh and Glasgow are styled The Right Honourable.

Other District Councils elect a Provost, a Chairman or a Convenor. For a full list see *The Municipal Year Book*.

BEGINNING OF LETTER[2]

Formal	My Lord Provost
	Dear Provost
	Dear (Mr.) Chairman
	Dear Convenor
Social	Dear Lord Provost. Otherwise as above

ENDING OF LETTER

Formal	Yours faithfully (see also p. 2)
Social	Yours sincerely

[1] Those who hold the office, previously known as Clerk or Town Clerk in County and District Councils, now usually have the title of Chief Executive.
[2] There is no difference in the form of address for a lady Lord Provost.

ENVELOPE

>The Right Hon. the Lord Provost of Edinburgh[1] *or* Glasgow[2]
>The Lord Provost of Aberdeen *or* Dundee[2]

>The Provost of . . .[3]
>The Chairman of . . .[3]
>The Convenor of . . .[3]

DESCRIPTION IN CONVERSATION

>The Lord Provost (of . . .)
>The Provost (of . . .)
>The Chairman (of . . .)
>The Convenor (of . . .)

VERBAL ADDRESS

>My Lord Provost
>Provost
>Chairman
>Convenor

Lady Provost

The wife (or other chosen lady consort, e.g. a daughter) of a Lord Provost is styled The Lady Provost, but the Lady Provosts of Edinburgh and Glasgow are *not* styled 'The Right Honourable'.

BEGINNING OF LETTER

Formal	My Lady Provost
Social	Dear Lady Provost

ENDING OF LETTER

Formal	Yours faithfully (see also p. 2)
Social	Yours sincerely

ENVELOPE

>The Lady Provost of . . .
>If desired, may be followed by her name

[1] The alternative styled, 'The Right Honourable John Blank, Lord Provost of Edinburgh', is also used.
[2] If desired, may be followed by his or her name.
[3] If desired, may be preceded by his or her name, in which case 'The' is omitted before 'Provost' 'Chairman' or 'Convenor'.

DESCRIPTION IN CONVERSATION
> The Lady Provost (of . . .)

VERBAL ADDRESS
> My Lady Provost *or*
> Lady Provost

Wife of a Provost, Chairman or Convenor

The wife of a Provost, Chairman or Convenor has no style comparable with mayoress. She is addressed by name.

Councillor[1]

The form of address follows English practice (see p. 245).

Municipal Officers

The form of address follows English practice (see p. 246) except for the use of Depute in lieu of Deputy,[2] e.g. Depute Chief Executive.

Australia

A municipality with a population of 5,000 or more and a rateable value of not less than $80,000 is classed as a town. One with a population of 10,000 or more and a rateable value of not less than $160,000 is classed as a city.

The civic head of Australia's capital, the city of Canberra, is the Chairman of the Legislative Assembly. Other cities are:

Adelaide	Hobart	Perth
Brisbane	Melbourne	Sydney
Geelong	Newcastle	Wollongong

All these have Lord Mayors who are styled 'the Right Honourable' except for Geelong whose Mayor is styled 'the Right Worshipful'. All towns have Mayors.

Subject to the above, forms of address are in accordance with the English practice.

---

[1] The office of Bailie has been abolished for a Councillor, and is now only used to describe a magistrate.
[2] Those who hold the office, previously known as Clerk or Town Clerk in Regional, Island and District Councils, now usually have the title of Chief Executive. The District is the lowest level in Scottish local government.

Canada

The smaller municipalities are classed as towns; the more populous ones as cities. Both towns and cities have Mayors who are styled 'The Worshipful' and who, subject to this, should be addressed in accordance with the English practice.

The wife of a Mayor is *not* styled Mayoress; she is addressed by name.

New Zealand

A town whose population reaches 20,000 becomes a city. Both towns and cities have Mayors (i.e. none have Lord Mayors). Forms of address are as in England.

Other Commonwealth Countries

None have Lord Mayors. Most have Mayors for both towns and cities. Forms of address are as in England.

Republic of Ireland

Dublin and Cork elect Lord Mayors who are styled 'The Right Honourable'. Other cities and towns elect Mayors who are styled 'The Worshipful'. Forms of address are as in England.

Other Countries

Space precludes inclusion of the rules distinguishing cities from towns since these vary from country to country. In general terms, however, the smaller municipalities are towns, the larger ones are cities.

Forms of address for certain major countries are given in the following table. For others 'Dear Mr. Mayor' (beginning of letter), 'The Mayor of . . .' (envelope), and 'Mr Mayor' (speech), should be used if the local form is not known.

Outside the Commonwealth, and countries which were formerly within the Commonwealth (e.g. the Republics of Ireland and South Africa), the wife of a civic head has no style comparable with Mayoress. She is, therefore, addressed by name, e.g. Madame Chappelon, Frau von Eisenstein, etc.

CIVIC HEADS ABROAD

	FRANCE	ITALY	GERMANY	SPAIN	USA	USSR
Beginning of letter	Cher M. le Maire	Gentile Signor Sindaco	*Berlin*: Dear Herr Regierender Bürgermeister *Other cities & large towns*: Dear Herr Oberbürgermeister *Small towns*: Dear Herr Bürgermeister	Dear Alcalde	Dear Mr. Mayor *or* Dear Mayor Smith *or* Sir	Dear Mr. Chairman
Envelope	*Paris*: M. le Préfet de la Seine *Elsewhere*: M. le Maire de (name of city or town)	Al Sindaco del Commune di (name of city) or town)	*Berlin*: Herr Regierender Bürgermeister *Other cities & large towns*: Herr Oberbürgermeister *Small towns*: Herr Bürgermeister	El Alcalde de (name of city or town)	The Honorable John Smith, Mayor of Brownton. If of a small city Mr. Richard Green, Mayor of Whitton, but 'The Honorable' is usually given by courtesy.	The Chairman of the (name of city or town) Soviet
Verbal address	*Paris*: 'Monsieur le Préfet' *Elsewhere*: 'Monsieur le Maire' *N.B.* There is no elected mayor of Paris.	'Signor Sindaco'	*Berlin*: 'Sehr verehrter' (or, more familiarly, 'lieber') Herr Regierender *Other cities & large towns*: 'Sehrverehrter (or, more familiarly, 'lieber') Herr Oberbürgermeister' *Small towns*: 'Sehr-verehrter (or, more familiarly, 'lieber') Herr Bürgermeister'	'Alcalde'	Mr. Mayor *or* 'Mayor Smith'	'Mr. Chairman'

POLICE SECTION

Metropolitan Police and City of London Police

COMMISSIONER

BEGINNING OF LETTER

Formal	(Dear) Sir
Social	
If a Knight	Dear Sir John (Smith)
Otherwise	Dear Mr. Smith *or* Commissioner

ENDING OF LETTER

Formal	Yours faithfully (see also p. 2)
Social	Yours sincerely

ENVELOPE

Sir John Jones (followed by Decorations)
John Jones, Esq. (followed by Decorations)
Commissioner of Police of the Metropolis, *or* for the City of
   London

VERBAL ADDRESS

Commissioner, *or* by name

DEPUTY OR ASSISTANT COMMISSIONER

BEGINNING OF LETTER

As for Commissioner, but if by his appointment, Dear Deputy
Commissioner (*or* Assistant Commissioner).

ENVELOPE

Sir John Smith (followed by Decorations)
or John Smith, Esq. (followed by Decorations)
Deputy Commissioner of Police   } of the Metropolis, *or*
or Assistant Commissioner of Police } for the City of London

VERBAL ADDRESS

By appointment *or* by name.

DEPUTY ASSISTANT COMMISSIONER

BEGINNING OF LETTER

Formal	(Dear) Sir
Social	Dear Mr. Smith *or*
	Dear Deputy Assistant Commissioner

ENVELOPE

John Smith Esq. (followed by Decorations)
Deputy Assistant Commissioner, Metropolitan Police

VERBAL ADDRESS

By appointment *or* by name.

COMMANDER, CHIEF SUPERINTENDENT AND SUPERINTENDENT

BEGINNING OF LETTER

Formal	(Dear) Sir (*or* Madam)
Social	Dear Commander Smith (*or* appropriate rank)
	or Dear Mr./Mrs./Miss Smith

ENVELOPE

(Men)   With his rank before his name, followed by 'Metropolitan Police' *or* 'City of London Police', e.g.
> Chief Superintendent J. W. Johnson, M.B.E., Metropolitan Police

or by his name, followed by his appointment, e.g.
> John W. Johnson, Esq., M.B.E., Chief Superintendent, Metropolitan Police

(Women) With her rank before her name, as above, e.g.
> W/Chief Superintendent J. W. Smith, M.B.E., City of London Police

or by her name, followed by her appointment, e.g.
> Miss Julia W. Smith, M.B.E., W/Chief Superintendent, City of London Police

(C.I.D.) 'Detective' is added before Chief Superintendent, Superintendent *or* W/Detective, where appropriate

By the appointment, *or* by name.

CHIEF INSPECTOR, INSPECTOR, POLICE SERGEANT AND POLICE CONSTABLE

At the beginning of a letter the appropriate rank is placed before the name, i.e. Dear Chief Inspector (Inspector, Sergeant or Constable) Smith, with the prefix 'Detective' if a member of C.I.D.

The rank is placed on the envelope before the name. Police Sergeant is often abbreviated to P.S., Police Constable to P.C., Detective Sergeant to D.S. and Detective Constable to D.C.

On the envelope a woman is addressed as under:

Chief Inspector	W/Chief Inspector Smith
Inspector	W/Inspector Smith
Detective Chief Inspector	W/Detective Chief Inspector Smith
Detective Inspector	W/Detective Inspector Smith

A woman Police Sergeant is often abbreviated to W.P.S.

Detective Sergeant	W.D.S.
Police Constable	W.P.C.
Detective Constable	W.D.C.

which are all placed before the name.

'Metropolitan Police' *or* 'City of London Police' follows the name.

Other Police Forces

CHIEF CONSTABLE

BEGINNING OF LETTER
By name, *or* 'Dear Chief Constable'.

ENVELOPE
Sir John Smith *or* John Smith Esq., as appropriate (followed by Decorations)
Chief Constable, Blankshire Constabulary

VERBAL ADDRESS
Chief Constable, *or* by name

DESCRIPTION IN CONVERSATION
The Chief Constable, *or* by name

DEPUTY OR ASSISTANT CHIEF CONSTABLE

As for Chief Constable, with the substitution of the appropriate appointment.

CHIEF SUPERINTENDENT OR SUPERINTENDENT

As for Metropolitan Police, with the substitution of the appropriate Force.

CHIEF INSPECTOR AND OTHER RANKS

Chief Inspector, Inspector, Police Sergeant and Police Constable as for Metropolitan Police with the substitution of the appropriate Force.

MERCHANT NAVY AND AIRLINE OFFICERS SECTION

Merchant Navy

Officer ranks in the Merchant Navy, of which the old name was the Mercantile Marine, vary from company to company.

The Master of the ship always ranks as Captain (i.e. he holds a Master's Certificate and commands, or has commanded a ship). In some companies the senior Captain holds the rank of Commodore, of which there is one per company.

In large ships (mostly passenger) there is a Staff Captain, in addition to the Captain. Other deck officers are as follows:

Chief Officer
Second Officer
Third Officer
Fourth Officer[1]

The old names of First Mate (for Chief Officer), Second Mate (for Second Officer), etc., are still used, mostly in coastal ships.

In the engineering department, the Chief Engineer is sometimes known as Commodore Chief Engineer, otherwise Chief

[1] Some ships carry a Junior Chief Officer. In large ships there can be as many as three First Officers, three Second Officers and three Third Officers. In this case each is known as 'Senior', 'Intermediate', and 'Junior'.

Engineer. The other ranks are Second Engineer Officer, Third Engineer Officer, etc., occasionally down to Eighth Engineer Officer.[1]

Other ship's officers include the Surgeon, Purser, Assistant Purser, Catering Officer (and occasionally Assistant Catering Officer), and Radio Officer.

Further information may be obtained from the General Secretary, Mercantile Marine Service Association, Nautilus House, Mariners Park, Wallasey, Merseyside, L45 7PH.

FORMS OF ADDRESS

The Commodore and Captain are addressed and referred to by these ranks.

The Staff Captain is addressed and referred to as Captain Jones.

These ranks are retained in retirement, but without the word '(retired)' after the name.

All other officers (including the Commodore Chief Engineer), are referred to as Mr. Jones, except the Surgeon, who is known by his medical status, e.g. Dr. Johnson.

BEGINNING OF LETTER

Formal	Dear Sir
Social	Dear Commodore Jones
	Dear Captain Brown
	Dear Mr. Smith

ENDING OF LETTER

Formal	Yours faithfully (see also p. 2)
Social	Yours sincerely

ENVELOPE

Letters signifying Orders, etc., are followed by those indicating the Service (e.g. R.N.R.).

> Commodore John Jones, O.B.E., R.N.R.
> Captain William Smith, M.B.E.
> Captain William Brown
>   Staff Captain, S.S. *Bengal*
> John Robinson, Esq.
>   Third Officer, S.S. *Bengal*

---

[1] As with the deck officers, in large ships there can also be more than one Second Engineer Officer, Third Engineer Officer, etc.

Edward Black, Esq.
Second Engineer Officer, S.S. *Bengal*

VERBAL ADDRESS

Commodore Jones
Captain Smith
Mr. Robinson

DESCRIPTION IN CONVERSATION

As for verbal address.

Airline Officers

The Captain is referred to as Captain Smith, and addressed as Captain John (or J.) Smith.

Other officers vary according to the company, but in the main they are Senior First Officer, First Officer, and Second Officer. They are addressed as John Jones, Esq., and referred to as Mr. Jones.

ACADEMIC SECTION

Chancellor of a University

The Chancellor of a University is addressed according to his rank and name, for which see the applicable section, but if a letter concerns his university, the style 'Dear Chancellor' may be used both formally and socially.

The old style of 'Dear Mr. Chancellor' is becoming archaic, but is still sometimes used in the Universities of Oxford and Cambridge.

In the main, 'Mr. Chancellor' is restricted to formal documents and verbally to formal occasions, such as at an official function.

The following is the form of address used on matters pertaining to his university.

BEGINNING OF LETTER

Formal   My Lord *or* (Dear) Sir (as applicable) *or* Dear Chancellor

Social   Dear Lord Blank, Dear Sir Henry (Smith) *or* Dear Dr. (Mr.) Jones (as applicable) *or* Dear Chancellor—this is a more distant style than by his name

ENDING OF LETTER

Formal	Yours faithfully (see also p. 2)
Social	Yours sincerely

ENVELOPE

Formal	The Chancellor of the University of Huntingdon
Social	Sir John Jones, C.H., K.B.E., LL.D., Chancellor of the University of Huntingdon

VERBAL ADDRESS

Formal	Mr. Chancellor (on a platform, otherwise according to his rank or name, 'My Lord', 'Sir Henry', etc.)
Social	By name, *or* Chancellor

DESCRIPTION IN CONVERSATION

The Chancellor, *or* by name

High Steward of the Universities of Oxford and Cambridge

The High Steward is addressed according to his rank and name. For formal and social correspondence, see the applicable section, but if the subject of the letters concerns his university, the style of 'Dear High Steward' may be used, both in formal and social correspondence.

ENVELOPE

Formal	The High Steward of the University of Oxford *or* The Rt. Hon. the Viscount Blank, High Steward of the University of Oxford
Social	The High Steward of the University of Oxford *or* The Viscount Blank, High Steward of the University of Oxford

Deputy High Steward of the University of Cambridge

The Deputy High Steward is addressed according to his rank and name. If the subject of the letter concerns his university, the form of address is as for the High Steward, with the addition of the word 'Deputy'.

The Executive Head of a University, including Vice-Chancellor

The Executive Head of a University is the generic term which covers the Vice-Chancellor, President, Principal or Rector, irrespective of what the individual title may be.

The Vice-Chancellor, President, etc., of a university is addressed according to his rank and name, but if the subject of the letter concerns his university, the formal and social style of 'Dear Vice-Chancellor', 'Dear President', etc. may be used. In the newer universities it is more usual to write to him by his name.

The old style of Mr. Vice-Chancellor is becoming archaic, but is sometimes used in the Universities of Oxford and Cambridge. The Executive Head of a Scottish University is sometimes jointly appointed Vice-Chancellor and Principal. He is then addressed as Principal.

For the form of address of a Principal, see *Head of University College*, p. 261.

Broadly speaking, for other universities whose executive head is jointly Vice-Chancellor and Principal, e.g. The University of Birmingham, he is addressed as Vice-Chancellor.

(See also *Commonwealth Universities*, p. 260).

BEGINNING OF LETTER

Formal	(Dear) Sir (*or* according to rank) *or* Dear Vice-Chancellor, Principal, Rector, etc. (on a matter concerning his university)
Social	Dear Sir Henry (Jones) Dear Dr. Jones, etc. *or* Dear Vice-Chancellor, Principal, Rector, etc. (on a matter concerning his university; this is a more distant style than by name)

ENDING OF LETTER

Formal	Yours faithfully (see also p. 2)
Social	Yours sincerely

ENVELOPE

Formal

The Vice-Chancellor,
The University of Milton Keynes

Social

Sir Philip Jones, C.B.E., LL.D.,
Vice-Chancellor,
The University of Milton Keynes[1]

For the Universities of Oxford and Cambridge the designations of the Vice-Chancellor are:

The Reverend the Vice-Chancellor of the University of Oxford (irrespective of whether he is in Holy Orders)

The Right Worshipful the Vice-Chancellor of the University of Cambridge

VERBAL ADDRESS

Formal

Mr. Vice-Chancellor (on a platform, etc.)
Vice-Chancellor, *or* by name
Principal, etc. (if applicable), *or* by name
Sir Henry, etc.

Social

Vice-Chancellor, *or* by name
Principal, etc. (if applicable), *or* by name

DESCRIPTION IN CONVERSATION

The Vice-Chancellor, Principal, etc., *or* by name

Deputy Chancellor, Pro-Chancellor, Deputy Vice-Chancellor, or Pro-Vice-Chancellor

The holders of these appointments are addressed by name, but for correspondence on university matters the envelope should include the appointment.

[1] Or Vice-Chancellor of The University of . . .

Commonwealth Universities

It is not possible to formulate any uniform system for the appointments and forms of address within the various universities of the Commonwealth, since there are no generally accepted rules. Reference should be made to the *Commonwealth Universities Yearbook* for lists of academic and administrative offices, but the following information is given of a general nature.

For those who hold the joint appointment of Vice-Chancellor and Principal see *Executive Head of a University*, p. 258.

CANADA

The most usual title for an executive head of a English-language university is 'President and Vice-Chancellor', or in some cases simply 'President', and occasionally, 'Vice-Chancellor and Principal' (or the reverse), but seldom just 'Vice-Chancellor' or 'Principal'. It is usual to begin a letter to the executive head of a university by using the first part of the appointment, e.g. to The Vice-Chancellor and Principal, just as 'Dear Vice-Chancellor', but the whole appointment is stated on the envelope.

In French Canadian universities the executive head is usually a Rector.

The heads of various faculties in a university are usually Deans.

A President or Dean is addressed with the addition of his surname, e.g.:

Dear President Jones
Dear Dean Smith

MALTA

The Executive Head of the University is termed Rector Magnificus.

OTHER COMMONWEALTH COUNTRIES

In Australia, New Zealand, and most other Commonwealth countries the form of address is usually based upon the British system.

Head of a University College

The title of the Head varies from college to college. The following shows the principal titles adopted, together with some examples of colleges, etc. under each appropriate appointment.

Dean

> Christ Church, Oxford[1]
> King's College, Theological Dept., University of London
> School of Pharmacy, University of London
> London School of Hygiene and Tropical Medicine

The Heads of the Medical Schools and Colleges of the University of London.

The Heads of the Institutes of the British Postgraduate Medical Federation.

Director

> London School of Economics and Political Science, University of London
> School of Oriental and African Studies, University of London

Master

> Balliol College, Oxford
> Pembroke College, Oxford
> University College, Oxford
> St. Catherine's College, Oxford
> St. Cross College, Oxford
> St. Peter's College, Oxford
> St. Benet's Hall, Oxford[2]
> Campion Hall, Oxford[2]
> The Colleges of the University of Cambridge *except* King's, Queens' and the Colleges for women.
> Birkbeck College, University of London

Mistress

> Girton College, Cambridge

[1] He is also Dean of Oxford, and has the ecclesiastical title 'The Very Reverend', see p. 117.
[2] He is invariably a clergyman, and is addressed 'The Reverend the Master'.

President

Clare Hall, Cambridge
Corpus Christi College, Oxford
Magdalen College, Oxford
St. John's College, Oxford
Trinity College, Oxford
Wolfson College, Oxford
Lucy Cavendish Collegiate Society, Cambridge
New Hall, Cambridge
Queens' College, Cambridge
University College, Cambridge
University Colleges of Dublin, Cork and Galway
Magee University College, Londonderry

Principal

Brasenose College, Oxford
Hertford College, Oxford
Jesus College, Oxford
St. Edmund Hall, Oxford
Linacre College, Oxford
Mansfield College, Oxford
Regent's Park College, Oxford
The colleges for women, University of Oxford
Newnham College, Cambridge
The Chief Administrative Officer, University of London
The following Schools, University of London:

Bedford College
Chelsea College
Heythrop College
King's College
Queen Elizabeth College
Queen Mary College
Royal Holloway College
Royal Veterinary College (*Principal and Dean*)
Westfield College
Wye College

The Colleges of the University of Durham *except* University,
Collingwood, Grey, Hatfield and Van Mildert
The Colleges of the University of Wales

Provost

>   Oriel College, Oxford
>   Queen's College, Oxford
>   Worcester College, Oxford
>   King's College, Cambridge
>   Trinity College, Dublin
>   University College, London

Rector

>   Exeter College, Oxford
>   Lincoln College, Oxford
>   Imperial College of Science and Technology, University of
>   London

In a Scottish university a Rector has a unique meaning as the students' representative.

Warden

>   All Souls College, Oxford
>   Greyfriars Hall, Oxford[1]
>   Keble College, Oxford
>   Merton College, Oxford
>   New College, Oxford
>   Nuffield College, Oxford
>   St. Antony's College, Oxford
>   Wadham College, Oxford
>   Goldsmith's College[2]

BEGINNING OF LETTER

Formal	(Dear) Sir *or* Madam
Social	By name (Dear Dr. Smith, etc.), *or* by appointment
	Dear Dean, Director, Master, Mistress, President, Principal, Provost, Warden

The old style of placing 'Mr.' before the following appointments: Dean, President, Provost, Warden, is becoming archaic, but is still sometimes used within the Universities of Oxford and Cambridge.

---

[1] He is invariably a clergyman, and is addressed as 'The Very Reverend the Warden'.
[2] An institution with recognized teachers of the University of London. The Heads of the other similar institutions are Principals, but the head of the Royal College of Music is Director.

'Mr. Dean' is also used when a Dean of a college has that ecclesiastical rank, although it is not included in the new form of address used by the Church of England. (See p. 117.)

ENDING OF LETTER

Formal	Yours faithfully (see also p. 2)
Social	Yours sincerely

ENVELOPE

Formal	The Master,
	Pepys' College,
	Cambridge
Social	Sir James Smith, Ph.D.,
	Master of Pepys' College,
	Cambridge

Clergymen

When the head of a college is a clergyman, his ecclesiastical rank is shown before his name or appointment, e.g.:

The Very Reverend the Dean,
Christ Church *or*
The Very Reverend John Smith, D.D.,
Dean of Blank Hall

VERBAL ADDRESS

Formally (at a function) (for Universities of Oxford and Cambridge) 'Mr. Dean', 'Mr. President', 'Mr. Provost', 'Mr. Warden', 'Mr. Principal' and 'Mr. Rector'. The two last named, although used within the University of Oxford, are rarely used outside. This form is inappropriate for Master. Otherwise, Sir *or* Madam, Dean, President, Master, Provost, Warden, etc., *or* by name.

DESCRIPTION IN CONVERSATION

By his appointment, i.e. The Master (of Blank College), *or* by name.

Professor

A Professor is addressed by name, e.g. Professor John Jones. Though he may also hold a doctorate he continues to be addressed as a Professor while he has a chair.

Should a Professor be in Holy Orders he is addressed as the Reverend Professor John Smith and known verbally as Professor Smith.

Should a Professor be a Canon (or have higher ecclesiastical rank) he is sometimes known as Professor Smith, but strictly speaking the ecclesiastical rank supersedes the academic. Thus, a canon should be known as Canon Smith rather than as Professor Smith, but in practice this is a matter of personal choice. The academic style is used more often within a university, and the ecclesiastical style outside.

On the Continent, the style Professor the Reverend . . . is sometimes adopted.

When a Professor retires from his (or her) chair at a university and emeritus rank is conferred, the Professor Emeritus or Emeritus Professor continues to be addressed as previously in correspondence. On the Continent the word 'Emeritus' is sometimes used after Professor.

For the use of the term Professor in America, see p. 358.

BEGINNING OF LETTER

Formal	Dear Sir *or* Madam
Social	Dear Professor Jones (should he be a peer, Dear Lord Kirkcudbright, *or* a knight, Dear Sir Henry (Jones))

ENDING OF LETTER

Formal	Yours faithfully (see also p. 2)
Social	Yours sincerely

ENVELOPE

Professor John Smith

'Professor' precedes any title held, e.g. Professor Lord Blank,[1] or Professor Sir Henry Smith,[1] Professor Dame Mary Smith[1] or Professor the Hon. John Robinson.[1]

Should he be in Holy Orders, the ecclesiastical rank precedes the academic, i.e. The Reverend Professor John Jones.

If a canon: The Reverend Canon Edward Jones, or The

---

[1] It is not customary in *formal* usage to combine the style emanating from other sources, i.e. Professor, with titles conferred by the Sovereign. In social usage this is not uncommon, though deprecated by purists.

Reverend Professor Edward Jones, as desired (usually on a university matter the latter is used, otherwise the former).

The form 'The Reverend Canon Professor Edward Jones' is never used as it is too cumbersome.

VERBAL ADDRESS

Professor Jones

Should he possess a title, he is known as Lord Blank, or Sir John Jones.

If a canon, Canon Jones or Professor Jones, as desired (see also Envelope).

DESCRIPTION IN CONVERSATION

As for Verbal Address.

Doctor

The recipient of a doctorate conferred by a university or other body, such as The Council for National Academic Awards, is entitled to be addressed as 'Doctor'. See *University Degrees* (p. 269) and *Non-University Degrees* (p. 273).

The exception to the above is a surgeon (also in England and Wales, a gynæcologist) who is known as 'Mr.'. See *Medical Section* (p. 226).

The recipient of an honorary doctorate is entitled to the style of 'Doctor', In practice, when a well-known figure outside the academic world receives an honorary doctorate (or doctorates) the recipient does not always use this style if he has other prefixes, e.g. a peer, a high-ranking Service officer, a judge, etc. This, however, is a matter of the recipient's choice.

BEGINNING OF LETTER

Formal	Dear Sir
Social	Dear Doctor Jones
If a peer	Dear Lord Blank
Or a baronet or knight	Dear Sir Henry (Jones)

ENDING OF LETTER

Formal	Yours faithfully (see also p. 2)
Social	Yours sincerely

ENVELOPE

It is a matter of choice whether the appropriate degree(s) should be placed after his (or her) name or to address the doctor as Dr. John *or* Dr. Mary Smith, though by custom, a Doctor of Divinity always has the letters D.D. appended after his name. This arises because many recipients, such as an archbishop or bishop, are not normally addressed as Dear Doctor Blank. See also *Medical Section,* p. 225.

In the University of Oxford the appropriate letters are usually omitted, and the envelope is addressed 'Dr. John Smith', irrespective of the particular doctorate. In the University of Cambridge both forms are used, and in the University of London the letters to signify the particular doctorate are usually given. It is, however, recommended that the letters, where known, are used to distinguish him (or her) from a medical practitioner who is known as 'Doctor', whether or not he is a doctor of medicine. (See *Medical Section,* p. 225.)

> The Very Rev. John Jones, D.D.
> Lord Blank, D.Lit.
> Sir Henry Robinson, Mus.D.
> John Smith, Esq., LL.D.
> Mrs. Joan Smith, Ph.D.

See also *University Degrees* (p. 269) and *Order of Placing Degrees* (p. 270).

VERBAL ADDRESS

> Dr. Smith, unless he is a peer, baronet, or knight, then by his appropriate rank.

DESCRIPTION IN CONVERSATION

As for Verbal Address.

Other Academic Appointments

The following are the usual appointments:

SCHOOLS

Boys

Headmaster, although there are certain variations, e.g.:
> High Master of St. Paul's, Manchester Grammar School, etc.
> Head Master of Westminster
> Master of Dulwich, Marlborough, Wellington, etc.

Rector of Edinburgh and Glasgow Academies, etc.
Warden of Radley, St. Edward's School, Oxford, etc.

Girls
Usually Headmistress or Principal.

Training and Technical Colleges and Schools
Usually Principal or Warden.

Teaching Hospitals, Medical Colleges, Schools and Institutes
Usually Dean.

Adult Education Centres and University Settlements
Usually Warden.

BEGINNING OF LETTER
The Head of a College, School, Educational Centre, etc., may be addressed by his (or her) appointment if the letter concerns his college, etc., but more usually by name.
    If the former style is adopted, then:
        Dear Headmaster,
        Dear Principal,
        Dear Warden, etc.
    Others holding staff appointments are addressed by name.

ENDING OF LETTER
Formal   Yours faithfully (see also p. 2)
Social   Yours sincerely

ENVELOPE
By appointment, i.e.:
        The Headmaster
        The Principal
        The Bursar
        The Secretary to the Principal, etc.
or by name.

VERBAL ADDRESS
        Headmaster, Principal, Warden, Dean, etc., *or* by name

DESCRIPTION IN CONVERSATION
        The Headmaster, Principal, Warden, Dean, etc., *or* by name

University Degrees

Letters which denote a particular degree often vary according to the conferring university (see below). First degrees also vary, but are often B.A. in arts and B.Sc. in science. At the old Scottish Universities of St. Andrews, Glasgow, and Aberdeen, and at Dundee, the first arts degree is that of M.A. The ordinary degree in arts at Edinburgh is now B.A.

In social correspondence it is generally only necessary to place letters after the name to denote a doctor's degree, and even then the term 'Dr. John Smith' is sometimes used on the envelope (see p. 267). Lesser degrees are usually omitted.

An exception is generally made for the inclusion of the degree of Bachelor of Divinity (B.D.), and in the faculty of Medicine, see *Medical Section* (p. 226).

Some graduates add their universities in parentheses after their degrees, such as in a school prospectus, e.g. Mr. John Smith, M.A. (Cantab.). The university is usually omitted in lists of names, etc.

LISTS OF UNIVERSITY GRADUATES

In a formal list, such as of patrons, officers, and directors of societies and firms, *all* degrees may be placed after the name (with the exceptions mentioned below), but if a person has several Crown or other honours and awards, it is a matter of personal choice or discretion which, if any, should be included. This is particularly applicable to well-known public figures who have acquired many honorary degrees.[1]

The following rules are normally applied:

(1) The degree of a Bachelor or Master is not accorded to those who have proceeded to the corresponding second or final degree (e.g. one does not include B.A. *and* M.A., 'B.Sc.' *and* M.Sc., 'M.Sc.' *and* D.Sc. or 'LL.B.' *and* LL.D.).

(2) The degree of M.A. is not accorded to a doctor of the Universities of Oxford and Cambridge, where a doctor's degree is considered to include the M.A. degree.

---

[1] In some lists published by the University of Cambridge (e.g. the Register of the Senate and the Roll of the Regent House), it is the custom to list the highest degree only in the case of doctors. The exception to this rule is the degree of Doctor of Philosophy, which is not a higher doctorate at the university.

ORDER OF PLACING DEGREES

The order of placing the appropriate letters after the name depends upon:

(a) The precedence of faculties within the conferring university.

(b) Whether a particular university places the degrees conferred in 'descending order' (i.e. in order of seniority), or in 'ascending order' (i.e. in the order by which they are taken).

The 'descending order' follows the same system applied to other honours and qualifications. Most universities, however, adopt the 'ascending order' system, which has the advantage of following the sequence of events.

Not only does the position of the appropriate letters vary according to the awarding university but also either the name of the degree or the letters to indicate it:

1.	Doctor of Civil Law	Oxford	D.C.L.
	Doctor of Law	Cambridge	LL.D.
	Doctor of Laws	Other universities	LL.D.
2.	Doctor of Letters	Cambridge Leeds Liverpool Manchester and Sheffield	Litt.D.
	Doctor of Letters	Oxford and other universities	D.Litt.
	Doctor of Literature	London and Belfast	D.Lit.
3.	Doctor of Music	Cambridge and Manchester	Mus.D.
	Doctor of Music	Oxford and other universities	D.Mus.
4.	Doctor of Philosophy	Oxford, Sussex, Ulster and York	D.Phil.
		Other universities	Ph.D.

This variance is particularly marked between degrees conferred at Oxford and Cambridge. When only a few universities existed the difference showed the conferring university.

The order of degrees conferred by four universities are given below as examples, viz:

Oxford
Cambridge
London
Birmingham

Cambridge has adopted the 'descending order'. Oxford, London and Birmingham, and most other universities adopt the 'ascending order', and are included as being representative of those who use this system.

UNIVERSITY OF OXFORD

(Degrees are placed in ascending order)

B.Ed.	M.A.
B.A.	M.Sc.
B.Phil.	M.S.
B.Mus.	D.Phil.
B.Litt.	D.Mus. ⎬ (if also M.A.)
B.S.	D.Sc.
B.M.	D.Litt.
B.C.L.	D.M.
B.D.	D.C.L.
M.Sc. ⎫	D.D.
D.Phil. ⎪	
D.Mus. ⎬ (If not also M.A.)	
D.Sc. ⎪	
D.Litt. ⎪	
D.M. ⎭	

UNIVERSITY OF CAMBRIDGE

(Degrees are placed in descending order)

D.D.	Mus.M.
LL.D.	M.Sc. and M.Litt.
M.D.	M.Phil.
Sc.D. and Litt. D.	M.B.
Mus.D.	B.Chir.
B.D.	LL.B.
Ph.D.	B.A.
M.Chir.	Mus.B.
M.A.	Vet.M.B.
LL.M.	B.Ed.

UNIVERSITY OF LONDON

(Degrees are placed in ascending order)

First Degrees
B.D.
B.A.
LL.B.
B.Mus.
M.B., B.S.
B.D.S.
B.Pharm.
B.Vet.Med.
B.Sc.
B.Sc.(Eng.)
B.Sc.(Econ.)
B.Sc.(Soc.)
B.Ed.
B.H.

M.Sc.
M.Sc.(Econ.) (no longer
    awarded)
M.Ed.

Higher Master's Degree
M.Phil.

Doctorate
Ph.D.

Higher Medical Doctorates
M.D.
M.S.
M.D.S.
D.Vet.Med.

Master's Degrees
M.Th.
M.A.
LL.M.
M.Mus.
M.Vet.Med. (no longer
    awarded)
M.Pharm.

Higher Doctorates
D.D.
D.Lit.
LL.D.
D.Mus.
D.Sc.
D.Sc.(Eng.)
D.Sc.(Econ.)

UNIVERSITY OF BIRMINGHAM

(Degrees are placed in ascending order)

First Degrees
B.Sc.
B.A.
B.Mus.
M.B., Ch.B.
B.D.S.
B.Com.
B.Soc.Sc.
LL.B.
B.Ed.

Master's Degrees
M.Sc.
M.A.
B.D.
M.D.
M.D.S.
M.Com.
M.Soc.Sc.
LL.M.
M.Ed.

Doctorate D.Mus.
Ph.D. D.D.
  M.D.
Higher Doctorates D.Soc.Sc.
D.Sc. LL.D.
D.Litt.

New degrees may be conferred from time to time, according to changes in faculty.

For degrees conferred by other universities, both in the United Kingdom and the Commonwealth countries, the *Commonwealth Universities Yearbook* should be consulted.

HONORARY DEGREES

Recipients of honorary degrees are entitled to the same letters as university graduates.

In certain universities, e.g. Essex, York, and Stirling, an honorary doctorate is conferred 'of the university', according to the system in France, instead of in a particular faculty. The appropriate letters after the name are 'D.Univ.', except Essex where 'D.U.' is used.

NON-UNIVERSITY DEGREES

The most usual of these degrees are those conferred by the Council for National Academic Awards. These are the first degrees of B.A., B.Ed., and B.Sc., those for post-graduate study, M.A., M.Ed., and M.Sc., and for research, M.Phil. and Ph.D. In addition to honorary degrees conferred the higher doctorates of D.Sc., D.Litt. and D.Tech., are awarded for work of high distinction.

The Cranfield Institute of Technology grants the degrees of Doctor and Master in applied science, engineering, technology and management.

The Royal College of Art confers the following degrees:

Doctor DrRCA
Doctor of Philosophy PhD [RCA]
Master of Design MDes [RCA]
Master of Arts MA [RCA]

These letters are placed after the name, e.g. John Smith, Esq., DrRCA. (*Note,* the Royal College of Art does not use points.)

Part V

OFFICIAL AND SOCIAL OCCASIONS

Royal Invitations

Invitations to Official Functions

Invitations to Private Functions

Wedding Invitations

Applications for the Royal Enclosure, Ascot

List of Names on Programmes, Brochures, etc.

Joint Forms of Address

Christmas Cards

Visiting, Professional and Business Cards

Precedence

Table Plans

Specimen Table Plans

Guests Lists

OFFICIAL AND SOCIAL OCCASIONS

Royal Invitations

THE SOVEREIGN

Her Majesty's invitations are sent by:

The Lord Steward of the Household
   to a State Banquet.

The Lord Chamberlain
   to all major Court functions, such as a Garden Party,
   Wedding, Funeral or Memorial Service.

The Master of the Household
   to all domestic functions given by The Queen at Buckingham Palace, or where The Queen is resident.

All invitations from The Queen are *commands*, and a reply
should be so worded, addressed to the member of Her Majesty's
Household who has issued the invitation.

An invitation to a Garden Party is accompanied by an admission
card which states that an acknowledgement is *not* required unless
the guest is unable to attend, in which case the admission card
must be returned.

The Master of the Household

is Commanded by Her Majesty to invite

Mr. and Mrs. John Brown

to an Afternoon Party at Sandringham House

on Thursday, January 10th from 4 to 6.30 o'clock

ACCEPTANCE

'Colonel Sir Henry and Lady Smith present their compliments to the Master of the Household, and have the honour to obey Her Majesty's Command to luncheon on May 10th at 12.30 o'clock.'

NON-ACCEPTANCE

The reason for non-acceptance should be stated. 'A prior engagement' is not considered to be a sufficient reason for failing to obey The Queen's Command.

> 'Colonel and Mrs. John Brown present their compliments to the Master of the Household, and much regret that they will be unable to obey Her Majesty's Command to.........
> ....on...............................owing to the illness of Mrs. John Brown.'

A LETTER OF THANKS

When appropriate, e.g. after a State Banquet, *not* after a Garden Party, this is addressed to the member of the Household who forwarded the invitation, the writer asking him to convey his thanks to Her Majesty for etc.

QUEEN ELIZABETH THE QUEEN MOTHER

Invitations are sent by The Comptroller of the Household to Queen Elizabeth The Queen Mother, except on very formal occasions, such as the wedding of The Princess Margaret, when they were sent by The Lord Chamberlain.

Invitations from The Queen Mother are *commands*, and should be so answered.

---

*The Comptroller of the Household of
Queen Elizabeth The Queen Mother
is Commanded by Her Majesty
to invite
Sir Henry and Lady White*

to............................. at............... on.............

ACCEPTANCE AND NON-ACCEPTANCE

As for The Sovereign.

OTHER MEMBERS OF THE ROYAL FAMILY

Invitations from other members of the Royal Family are not 'commands' and will usually be forwarded by a Member of their Household to whom a reply should be addressed.

In other respects, as for The Sovereign.

INVITATIONS TO MEMBERS OF THE ROYAL FAMILY

(For *Official Functions*, see p. 280.)

An invitation to a member of the Royal Family, i.e. those with the titles of 'His (*or* Her) Royal Highness', is extended by letter through the Private Secretary. The title of a Royal guest is shown in full, e.g.

Her Majesty The Queen
His Royal Highness the Prince Philip, Duke of Edinburgh
Their Royal Highnesses the Duke and Duchess of Kent

A member of a branch of the Royal Family, apart from a Royal Peer or Peeress, is given the appropriate description in all written communications, e.g.

His Royal Highness Prince Michael *of Kent*

A married Princess is shown with her husband's title or name on an invitation and the envelope, e.g.

Her Royal Highness Princess Alexandra, the Hon. Mrs. Angus Ogilvy.

If the invitation includes her husband she is still described as above, e.g.

Her Royal Highness Princess Alexandra, the Hon. Mrs. Angus Ogilvy, and the Hon. Angus Ogilvy.

In these cases the Princess appears *before* her husband.

The word 'The' before 'Prince' (*or* 'Princess') is restricted to the Prince Philip, Duke of Edinburgh and the children of a Sovereign. Other members of the Royal Family without peerages are described as His (*or* Her) Royal Highness Prince (*or* Princess).

OTHER ARRANGEMENTS FOR ROYAL GUESTS AT FUNCTIONS

(See *Official Functions*, p. 280.)

Invitations to Official Functions

For a function given by an organization, society, etc., the invitation is usually issued on a card, which may be engraved in script from a copper plate, or printed (in script or Roman type). This should make clear the following:

(a) *The nature of the function*, e.g. 'For the Opening of . . . by . . .'; 'To mark the Centenary of . . .'; 'For a Dinner', etc.

(b) *Where the function is to be held*, e.g. at The Splendide, Park Lane, W.1. Ballroom entrance.

(c) *The date of the function*.

(d) *The time of the function*, e.g. 12.45 for 1.0 p.m. (for a luncheon); 6.0–8.0 p.m. (for a reception); 7.30 for 8.0 p.m. (for a dinner). When it is desired to indicate the time at which a function will end, there are two alternatives: '8.0 p.m.–Midnight', or '8.0 p.m. Cars (or carriages) at Midnight'. For a formal ceremony, such as the laying of a foundation stone, unveiling a statue, etc., for which an invitation gives only the starting time, e.g. at 3.0 p.m., the card should also bear some such phrase as: 'Guests are requested to be seated by 2.45 p.m.'.

(e) *The dress*. For a day function (including a cocktail hour reception) this need only be specified if it is to be other than lounge suit, e.g. morning dress, academic robes, etc. For an evening function it should always be specified, e.g. evening dress (which means tailcoat with white tie), dinner jacket, lounge suit, uniform, etc. The word 'decorations' is added if these are to be worn with either evening dress or dinner jacket.

To indicate that a member of the Royal Family will be present, one of the following is engraved or printed at the top of the card:

In the gracious presence of Her Majesty The Queen
In the gracious presence of Her Majesty Queen Elizabeth The Queen Mother
In the presence of His (or Her) Royal Highness (the) Prince (or (the) Princess) . . .

Note. The word 'gracious' is included only for The Queen and The Queen Mother. The word 'the' is included only for children of the Sovereign.

If it is particularly desired to indicate that an important non-royal guest will be present, this may be done in the form: 'To meet (or in honour of) the Right Honourable the Lord Mayor of London and the Lady Mayoress'.

Examples :

The President, Sir John Blank, K.B.E., and Council of
The National Society of . . .
request the pleasure of the company of

....

at their Twenty-First Annual Banquet
to be held at the Hotel Magnificent, Manchester, (Oak Suite)
on Saturday 27th February, 1971,
at 7.30 for 8.0 p.m.

Evening Dress   *R.S.V.P.*
    or Dinner Jacket   *The Secretary,*
                                         123, Piccadilly,
Decorations   *Manchester, 1.*

The Chairman and Governors of
The Royal College of . . .
have the honour to invite

....

to the College Hall
at 3.0 p.m. on Saturday 29th February, 1971,
for the Presentation of Awards by
Her Royal Highness the Duchess of . . .

Guests should be   *An answer is*
seated by   *requested to the*
2.45 p.m.   *Bursar before*
                                         20th February.

ADMISSION CARDS

To assist the Toastmaster (announcer), or to prevent gatecrashers, 'Please bring this card with you', may be added at the bottom of the invitation card. Alternatively (especially for an evening function for which a large card cannot be carried easily in a pocket or handbag) the following wording may be added: 'An admission card will be sent on receipt of your acceptance'.

The following is an example of an admission card, which should be printed in Roman type and should not exceed $4\frac{1}{2} \times 3\frac{1}{2}$ inches in size:

Please admit

....

to The Dorchester, Park Lane (Ballroom entrance)
for the Lord Mayor of Westminster's Reception
on Saturday 29th February, 1971,
from 8.0–11.0 p.m.

To be handed
to the announcer.

Note 1.—An admission card to a ceremony may be used to allocate a specific seat.

Note 2.—Separate admission cards should be sent for a husband and his wife, even though they have both been included on the same invitation card.

Note 3.—Additional information or instructions, e.g. about car parking, are best given on a separate sheet sent with the invitation, or with the admission card.

MEMBERS OF THE ROYAL FAMILY

An invitation to a member of the Royal Family is always extended by letter, either through the Lord-Lieutenant of the County or to the Private Secretary, the latter being the general rule in London, the former elsewhere. A printed invitation is not sent except that a specimen may be forwarded to the Private Secretary, if desired.

An informal enquiry as to whether the member of the Royal Family would be likely to give favourable consideration to accepting an invitation is recommended before sending a formal one. This should outline the nature and purpose of the function.

Whether the consort (husband or wife) of a member of the Royal Family should be included in the invitation depends on the nature of the function. This point can be raised with the Lord-Lieutenant or Private Secretary in the informal enquiry.

Only in exceptional circumstances should two or more members of the Royal Family (other than consorts) be invited to the same function.

If an invitation to a member of the Royal Family is declined, it can subsequently be extended to a more junior member, but *never* to a more senior one.

An invitation to a member of the Royal Family having been accepted, the organisers of the function should discuss with the Private Secretary, or with another member of the Royal Household nominated by him, the detailed arrangements in so far as they concern the member of the Royal Family (time of his or her arrival, by whom he or she will be accompanied, dress, which of the guests are to be presented and when, etc.).

NAMES ON INVITATIONS

Invitations to official functions give the host by his office and/or name. This is engraved or printed, with his full title, rank, etc., and followed by his decorations, etc. (Note, invitations to private functions are treated differently, see p. 288). Prefixes such as His Grace, His Excellency, The Right Worshipful, are, however, omitted except:

(a) 'The Right Honourable' is included for a Privy Counsellor who is not a peer.

(b) The prefix 'The Honourable (Hon)' and the suffix 'Esquire' are never used. (In both cases a gentleman is shown as Mr. John Smith.)

The younger sons of a Duke or Marquess are shown as, e.g. Lord John Russell, and the daughters of a Duke, Marquess or Earl as, e.g. Lady Jane Gilbert.

An invitation to a clergyman with the rank of The Reverend should be in the form 'The Reverend John and Mrs. Henderson.'

An invitation to a pair of guests of some relationship other than husband and wife takes one of the following forms:

Brother and sister: Mr. John Brown and Miss Elizabeth Brown.

Mother and son: Mrs. George Carruthers and Mr. William Carruthers. (*Note*: An invitation to an adult son is usually sent separately from that to his parent/s.)

Unmarried sisters: The Misses Smith.

The form 'and Lady' may be used when it is not practicable to ascertain whether a gentleman is married, if it is desired to allow a gentleman to bring, say, his daughter instead of his wife, and if it is desired to allow a bachelor to bring a partner. For ladies invited in their own right, the comparable form is 'and Escort'.

Examples are:

The Right Hon. the Prime Minister (and Mrs. Head)

The Duke and Duchess of Loamshire

The Lord Mayor and Lady Mayoress of Blanktown

The President of the Royal Academy, Sir John Brown, K.B.E. (and Lady Brown)

The President of the Royal Society (and Lady Smith)

The French Ambassador (and Madame Pompadour)

Rear-Admiral the Earl of Nonsuch, C.B., D.S.O. (and the Countess of Nonsuch)

Colonel Sir John Bayonet, Bt., M.V.O. (and Lady Bayonet)

The Master of the Worshipful Company of Holeborers (and Mrs. White)

The Right Honourable William Black, L.L.D., Q.C., M.P.

The Archbishop of Canterbury and Mrs. Church

The Cardinal Archbishop of Westminster

The Earl of Ludlow, O.B.E., M.C. and the Countess of Ludlow

The Dean of Westminster, the Very Reverend James D. Brown, K.C.V.O., M.A., D.D. (and Mrs. Brown)

Professor Albert Blossom, F.R.S., M.A. (and Mrs. Blossom)

Lord and Lady John Russell

Captain and Mrs. George Rifle (*but* Captain George Foremast, Royal Navy, and Mrs. Foremast)

Mr. Justice Wig (and Mrs. Wig)

Judge Mace and Lady

Mr. and Mrs. Paul Neville

Dr. and Mrs. Henry James

Miss Dorothy Trubshaw and Escort

THE NAME ON ADMISSION CARDS

The guest is shown on an admission card by office *or* by name, in the form in which he is to be announced to the host and hostess. If by name, this is limited to his title, rank and name, except that the following prefixes should be included:

His Grace—for the Archbishops of Canterbury and York
His Eminence—for a Cardinal
His Excellency—for Ambassadors and High Commissioners
The Right Honourable, The Right Worshipful, The Worshipful, etc.—for Civic Heads who are so styled

A husband and wife should each be issued with a separate admission card.

Examples are :

The Prime Minister	Mrs. Head
The Right Honourable the Lord Mayor (of London)	The Lady Mayoress (of London)
The President of The Royal Society	
His Excellency[1] the Swedish Ambassador	Madame Blank
The Duke of Loamshire	The Duchess of Loamshire
His Grace the Archbishop of Canterbury	Mrs. Blank
His Eminence the Cardinal Archbishop of Westminster	
The Bishop of Hereford	Mrs. Steele
The Earl of Wessex	The Countess of Wessex
General Sir John Cannon	Lady Cannon
The Dean of Westminster	Mrs. Brown
Professor Albert Blossom	Mrs. Blossom
Lord Russell	Lady Russell
Captain Rifle	Mrs. Rifle
Mr. Justice Wig	Mrs. Wig
Judge Mace	Miss Single

[1] May be abbreviated to H.E.—but *not* by the announcer.

Mr. Neville	Mrs. Neville
Dr. James	Mrs. James
Miss Trubshaw	Mr. Johnson

THE ENVELOPE

An invitation to an official function should normally be addressed only to the husband if sent to his official address, even though his wife is also invited. He is given his full prefix, title, rank, decorations, etc. as for a formal letter. If the invitation is sent to the home address, the wife's name appears on the envelope. *See the appropriate section.*

REPLIES

These, which should be on headed paper to show the sender's address, are best illustrated by examples:

(a) Mr. and Mrs. William Brown thank the President and Council of the National Society of . . . for their kind invitation for Saturday, 29th February, which they accept with much pleasure (*or* which they have the honour to accept).

(b) Lord and Lady White thank the Master of the Worshipful Company of Holeborers for his kind invitation for Saturday, 29th February, which they much regret being unable to accept. (A reason may be given, e.g. owing to a previous engagement; because of absence abroad, etc.).

(c) The Reverend John and Mrs. White thank the Dean and Chapter of . . . for their kind invitation for Saturday, 29th February. They accept with much pleasure for the service in the Abbey but regret that they are unable to accept for the subsequent reception.

The date is placed underneath.

Note.—The prefix 'The Honourable' is never included in the reply before either the host's or guest's name.

REPLY CARDS

The organization of a large function is greatly facilitated by the use of reply cards (printed in Roman type) which are sent out with the invitations. These should be of small postcard size and may be numbered serially for ready reference to the invitation list, which it is seldom practicable to draw up in alphabetical order.

An example is:

Serial No.

The Lord Mayor of Birmingham's Civic Banquet
Tuesday 29th February, 1971

Name(s) ....
(Block letters, please.)

*Has/have much pleasure in accepting the invitation
of the Lord Mayor and Lady Mayoress
*Regret(s) being unable to accept the invitation of the
Lord Mayor and Lady Mayoress

*Please delete whichever is not applicable.

A reply card may also be used to obtain other information, e.g. 'I shall/I shall not* require car parking facilities'.

A guest should *always* use the printed card for his reply. Should he wish to add anything, such as an explanation for his inability to accept, this should be done by a separate letter.

The reply to an invitation which takes the form '. . . and Lady', or '. . . and Escort', should always give the name of the chosen lady or escort.

Note. . . Because postage is now so expensive the considerate host or organiser of an official function for which it is only necessary to know the approximate number who will be attending (e.g. for an afternoon party or for an evening reception) will request replies only from those able to accept, i.e. by adding to the specimen invitation cards on p. 281, below the words requesting an answer, 'only if able to accept', and also by deleting the asterisks, the line beginning 'Regrets' and the footnote on the specimen reply card on p. 287.

Invitations to Private Functions

There are two kinds of invitations to formal functions, which (unless time is short) are prepared on cards engraved in script from a copper plate, viz.

(a) For formal luncheon and dinner parties.
(b) 'At Home' invitations for all other parties, e.g. dances, receptions, garden parties, luncheons, dinners and suppers.

Invitations to informal functions may be extended by letter, telephone, etc.

(a) *Invitations to formal luncheon and dinner parties.*

Major and Mrs. John Brown

Sir John and Lady Brent

request the pleasure of * *your company*
at Dinner
on Tuesday, 29th February
at 8 for 8.30 o'clock

R.S.V.P.
   2300, *Cadogan Square*,   *Black tie*
   *S.W.*1.

---

* *or* 'honour of'

Example 1

These are engraved on a card of good texture, usually about $6 \times 4\frac{1}{2}$ inches in size (or slightly larger if necessary), and are prepared in the name of both the host and hostess, see Example 1. If time is short, they may be printed. They contain some of the information as for an official function (p. 280) but with certain important exceptions, which are given on pages 292–294.

Alternatively, the more old-fashioned style of 'request the pleasure of the company of', may be adopted, the guests' names being added on the next line, in place of the top left-hand corner.

If the luncheon or dinner takes place at an address other than that to which the replies are to be sent, e.g. at an hotel, this is

---

Dr. and Mrs. Edward Shaw

Lady White

requests the pleasure of * *your company*

for Dinner

----

on Wednesday, 18th May

----

at Claridge's

R.S.V.P.   *8 for 8.30 p.m.*
6004 *Berkeley Street,*   *Black tie* †
   W.1.

---

   * *or* 'honour of'   † if desired to include dress

Example 2

---

stated on a line after the date. The time may be placed either after the date, or at the bottom right hand corner before, or in place of, the dress.

It often happens that a host or hostess keeps a stock of invitation cards engraved in script from a copper plate. The occasion, date, time, and also place (if away from home) are then added. See

Example 2. This card may also be prepared with the wording 'request the pleasure of the company of', the guests' names being added.

If the luncheon or dinner is not a very formal one, an 'at Home' card may be used. See Example 5. The time, e.g. '12.45 for 1.15 o'clock' (*or* p.m.) or '8 for 8.30 o'clock' (*or* p.m.) is usually sufficient indication of the occasion.

(b) *'At Home' Invitations.*

These invitations, which for formal occasions are usually engraved on a card of good texture about $6 \times 4\frac{1}{2}$ inches in size (or

---

Mr. and Mrs. Crispin Ashburnham

Mrs. Hugh Harrington

at Home

Wednesday, 30th June

R.S.V.P.	*6.45 p.m.*
2555 Cumberland	*Mercers' Hall,*
Terrace,	*Ironmonger Lane,*
N.W.1.	*E.C.2.*

Please bring this card with you.

Example 3

slightly larger if necessary), are prepared in the name of the hostess only, in the case of married couples. If the time of the function is not a sufficient indication as to its nature, the latter may be stated on the card, e.g. 'Dancing 10 o'clock'. If the invitation extends from say 6 o'clock to 8.30, the description 'cocktails', 'wine', or 'sherry' etc. is unnecessary, though it is often included. See Examples 3 and 4.

For many 'at Home' functions *except dances*, a smaller card may be used, usually $4\frac{1}{2} \times 3\frac{1}{2}$ inches, on which is engraved (or printed) the hostess's name, 'at Home', R.S.V.P. and her address. A stock of these cards is purchased for various functions. Other details are completed by the hostess. See Example 5.

Commander and Mrs John Eyre-Butler

Lady Elizabeth Berkeley

at Home

Monday, June 1st

R.S.V.P.
   Faversham Hall,   *Dancing*
   Tinbury,   10.30 *p.m.*
   Essex.

Example 4

For small informal parties a basic stock of 'at Home' cards may be purchased, which merely have 'at Home' and 'R.S.V.P.'

Miss Barbara Worth

Mrs. Richard Greene

at Home

Monday, May 12th

R.S.V.P.
   16, *Argyll Lane,* Cocktails
   W.8.   6. 30 o'clock

Example 5

engraved (or printed) on them. They are usually of the identical size of the above cards, $4\frac{1}{2} \times 3\frac{1}{2}$ inches. The hostess then adds her name, address, date, time, name of guests, and other necessary information.

HOST AND HOSTESS
The exact rank in the peerage of the host and/or hostess is given on all types of invitation. The word 'The' before a title is usually omitted for the ranks of Marquess and Earl, and always for those of Viscount and Baron (e.g. Marchioness of Flintshire, Viscountess Longhurst).

No prefixes appear before the name, such as 'The Right Honourable', 'The Honourable' 'His Excellency', 'The Worshipful'.

No letters are placed after the name, such as those which signify decorations or degrees, or the letters 'Bt.'.

JOINT HOSTESSES
If there is more than one hostess, their names are placed one under the other. The first name corresponds to the address to

---

Miss Davina Firebrace and Partner

Mrs. Henry Waterhouse

Lady Black

Mrs. Sebastian Jones

at Home

for * Elizabeth, Henrietta and Fiona

Wednesday, June 6th

The Hyde Park Hotel

R.S.V.P.   Dancing
  757, Bedford Square,   10 o'clock
    W.C.1.
            Please bring this card with you.

---

* 'for their daughters', if applicable, may be inserted.

Example 6

which the replies are to be sent. See Example 6. If a joint party is to be held at a hostess's house and the replies are to be sent to her, her name is placed first on the invitation, irrespective of any title held.

If the hostesses are to deal with replies separately, their addresses are placed from left to right at the foot of the card, in the same order as their names.

OTHER INFORMATION ON THE INVITATION

'Decorations' on a *private* invitation implies that a member of the Royal Family is expected to be present. (*Note*, the word does not have this meaning on an official invitation).

For functions where the hostess considers it to be necessary to indicate the dress expected to be worn, 'White tie' may be added for evening dress, "Black tie" for dinner jackets, or 'Afternoon Dress' or 'Informal' for lounge suits. Otherwise she is content to leave this to the discretion of her guests.

If it is necessary to keep out gatecrashers, 'Please bring this card with you' may be added at the foot of the card.

If there is no information to the contrary, it is understood that the function is to be held at the address to which a reply is requested.

If the function takes place in the country, a map is often placed on the back of the card, or on a separate sheet.

ENCLOSURES

A separate slip is often sent, with times of trains, and such requests as 'Are you coming by road or rail?' or 'Do you want to be included in a dinner party, or a dinner party and house party?'

SENDING OUT INVITATIONS

If an invitation is extended and accepted verbally, e.g. by telephone, it should be confirmed by an invitation card on which 'R.S.V.P.' has been deleted, and 'To remind' substituted. This is not normally acknowledged.

NAMES OF GUESTS

These are written in the top left corner, except for formal luncheon/dinner invitations designed to include them in the middle of the card. See also *Official Invitations* (p. 280), but the following should be noted.

(a) No prefixes, such as 'The Right Honourable', 'The Honourable', 'His Excellency', 'The Worshipful' are given.

(b) No letters after the name, such as those which signify decorations or degrees, or the letters 'Bt.' are given.

(c) All peers and peeresses, apart from Dukes and Duchesses, who are referred to by these titles, are given in the form of 'Lord and Lady Blank'. This is the established custom for all functions except the very important, when the exact rank in the peerage may be given.

(d) Grown-up sons and daughters are usually sent separate invitations, even when they live at home, but when their exact names, or their availability, are not known, it is permissible to add 'and family' after their parents' names.

(e) The addition 'and escort' *or* 'and partner' (*not* 'and friend') may be added to allow a guest to bring an unspecified escort or partner with her/him.

(f) During Ascot week and other similar occasions and festivals for which house parties are given, invitations may show after the names of the guests 'and house party'.

Examples of showing guests are:

The Lord Mayor (and Lady Mayoress) of London
The Swedish Ambassador (and Madame Blank)
The Duke (and Duchess) of Loamshire
The Archbishop of Canterbury (and Mrs. Jones)
Lord (and Lady) Wessex
General Sir John (and Lady) Cannon
Air Commodore (and Mrs.) John Plane
Professor (and Mrs.) Albert Blossom
The Dean of Rochester (and Mrs. Proudie)
The Archdeacon of Exeter (and Mrs. Pugh)
Canon (and Mrs.) John Porter
The Reverend John (and Mrs.) Henderson
Dr. (and Mrs.) John Homer
Mr. (and Mrs.) John Brown
Miss Dorothy Brown

For other relationships, see p. 283. For the ranks of officers in the Services, see pp. 167–192.

ENVELOPE

An invitation to both husband and wife is addressed to the wife only. A guest is given his (*or* her) full prefix, title, rank, decorations, etc., as for a formal letter.

REPLIES

These are sent on writing paper with the address, as for *Official Functions* (p. 280). They are addressed to the hostess even when the invitation is a joint one from the host and hostess.

When invitations are extended to unnamed guests such as 'and partner', 'and family', the reply should contain the names of those who will attend. The substitution of a named guest is only allowed by permission of the hostess.

Wedding invitations

Wedding invitations by custom are engraved and consist of four pages, the size being usually standardized at $5\frac{1}{2} \times 7$ inches.

The wording, which depends upon who is the host and/or hostess, and their relationship to the bride, is given below. If desired, 'honour' can be used in place of 'pleasure' in all the examples.

If the church is too small to accommodate all the guests, the invitation should be worded to read 'at the Reception to be held after the marriage of their daughter Caroline to Mr. Christopher Henry Herbert, at The Old Manor House, Little Wotton, Gloucestershire, on Wednesday, 14th March 1971'. In this case a leaflet should be placed inside the invitation to give the reason, e.g.:

'Owing to the small size of Little Wotton Church it is only possible to ask a very few guests to the Service. We hope you will forgive this invitation being to the Reception only'.

In no circumstances is a guest invited to the wedding but not to the reception.

For the ranks of officers in the Services, see pp. 167–192.

For Host, Hostess, and Bridegroom, see Host and Hostess (p. 292). 'The Honourable' is never used.

The names of guests are written on the top left-hand of the invitation, as for other invitations (see pp. 293–294).

1.   *The following is a specimen invitation where both parents of the bride are the host and hostess:*

Miss Rosemary Wallop

Lieutenant-Colonel and Mrs. John Standish

request the pleasure of

your company at the marriage

of their daughter

Caroline

to

Mr. Christopher Henry Herbert

at St. Paul's Church, Knightsbridge,

on Wednesday, 14th March, 1971

at 3 o'clock

and afterwards at

The Hyde Park Hotel

R.S.V.P.

Charlford Manor,

Washington,

Sussex.

---

2. *The bride's mother is the only hostess*

> Mrs. John Standish
> requests the pleasure of
> your company at the marriage
> of her daughter
> Caroline, etc.

3. *The bride's father is the only host*

> Mr. John Standish
> requests the pleasure of
> your company at the marriage
> of his daughter
> Caroline, etc.

4. *The bride's mother and stepfather are the host and hostess*

The bride's surname may be included if desired if she has not adopted her stepfather's.

> Mr. and Mrs. John Forsyte
> request the pleasure of
> your company at the marriage
> of her daughter
> Caroline, etc.

5. *The bride's father and stepmother are the host and hostess*

> Mr. and Mrs. John Standish
> request the pleasure of
> your company at the marriage
> of his daughter
> Caroline, etc.

6. *The bride's stepmother is the hostess*

> Mrs. John Standish
> requests the pleasure of
> your company at the marriage
> of her stepdaughter
> Caroline, etc.

7. *The bride's parents have been divorced, but they are the joint host and hostess*

If the bride's parents have married again, the subsequent husband and wife do not play a prominent part at the wedding.

Mr. John King
and
Mrs. George Tremayne[1]
request the pleasure of
your company at the marriage
of their daughter
Sybil, etc.

8. *The bride's relatives, guardians or god-parent(s) are the host and hostess*

The bride's surname may be added if it is different from the host's and hostess's.

Admiral Sir John and Lady Fortescue
request the pleasure of
your company at the marriage
of their niece/ward/his (her) god-daughter
Alexandra, etc.

9. *The bride's relatives who are not a husband and wife are the host and hostess or joint hostesses (e.g. brother and sister, brother and sister-in-law, or sisters)*

As in Example 8, but the surname should be repeated (except for unmarried sisters), e.g.

Captain John Buckfast and Lady Buckfast
Mr. John Buckfast and Mrs. Henry Lowndes
Mr. John Buckfast and Mrs. Edward Buckfast
The Misses Buckfast
Miss Maria Buckfast and Mrs. William Bagshot

10. *The bride is the hostess*

Miss Emily Grattan
requests the pleasure of your company
at her marriage to Mr. John FitzGerald.

This style is preferred to the following alternatives:

(a) The pleasure of your company is requested at the marriage of Miss Emily Grattan and Mr. John Fitz-Gerald . . .

    or

(b) Mr. John FitzGerald and Miss Emily Grattan request the pleasure of your company at their marriage . . .

[1] 'Mrs. Frances King', if she has not remarried.

11. *Second and subsequent marriages*

As in Examples 1 to 9, as applicable, but when the bride is a widow she is described as 'Fleur, widow of Mr. Michael Mont', or if her marriage has been dissolved as 'Mrs. Fleur Mont'. If she has reverted to her maiden name, only her christian name is necessary.

If the bride is hostess, then as in Example 10, with her name as Mrs. John Smith or Mrs. Mary Smith, as applicable.

12. *Invitation to the reception only*

The wording is amended to read:

>   request(s) the pleasure of your company
>   at the reception following the marriage
> of their daughter Ann to .... at .... on ....

If the bride is hostess, the wording should read:

>   . . . at the reception following her marriage, etc.
>   to .... at .... on ....

POSTPONEMENTS AND CANCELLATIONS

A card, generally, $4\frac{1}{2} \times 3$ inches, is usually sent, with the wording printed on the following lines:

1. *Indefinite postponement*

'Owing to the recent death of Colonel Samuel Braithwaite, Mr. and Mrs. John Blank deeply regret that they are obliged to cancel the invitations to the marriage of their daughter Elizabeth to Mr. Mark Braithwaite on . . .'

Invitations are sent out again when the new date is fixed.

2. *Postponement to a later date*

'Owing to the illness of Mrs. Victor Scott, Mr. and Mrs. John Blank deeply regret that they are obliged to postpone the invitations to the marriage of their daughter Anne to Mr. John Scott at St. Margaret's Church, Westminster, from Thursday, 14th December 1970 to Wednesday, 2nd February 1971'.

3. *Cancellation of invitations because the wedding is to take place quietly*

'Owing to the recent death of her husband, Mrs. John Black much regrets that she is obliged to cancel the invitations to the marriage of her daughter Elizabeth to Captain Jonathan Trelawny, which will now take place very quietly on Wednesday 10th October, 1971'.

Invitations are then sent out by letter to near relations and close friends only.

4. *Cancellation of the wedding—engagement broken off*
'Sir John and Lady Hopley announce that the marriage of their daughter Emma to Mr. Christopher Camberley, which was arranged for Wednesday 4th June, 1971, will not now take place'.

ENVELOPES AND REPLIES

These are as for invitations to private functions (p. 295).

Applications for the Royal Enclosure, Ascot

Admittance to the Royal Enclosure, Ascot, lies within the jurisdiction of Her Majesty's Representative, The Marquess of Abergavenny. The number of those to whom the privilege of receiving vouchers is accorded is not disclosed; nor are the reasons why vouchers have been given, or withheld, explained.

Applications are submitted to Her Majesty's Representative from January until the end of April. After that date no further applications are considered.

It does not matter whether the wife or her husband applies for vouchers, but each application should include only members of a family; friends should make a separate application. The method of application, with the respective names, is given below. Applications signed by proxy will not be accepted.

If vouchers are required by young people between the ages of sixteen and twenty-five inclusive at the date of the Royal Meeting, the age should be stated in brackets after the name, because their vouchers are issued at a reduced price. Children below the age of sixteen are not admitted to the Royal Enclosure, except on Friday of the Royal Meeting, when children between the ages of ten and fifteen are admitted with a responsible adult at a reduced rate. No prior application is required for young children.

New applicants are eventually required to be sponsored.

Visitors with overseas passports should apply for vouchers for the Royal Enclosure to their respective Ambassadors or High Commissioners and not to Her Majesty's Representative.

THE APPLICATION

'Colonel John Francis presents his compliments to Her Majesty's Representative and wishes to apply for vouchers to the Royal

Enclosure for his wife Mrs. John Francis, his son Mr. William Francis (aged 22), his daughter Miss Philippa Francis (aged 19) and himself'.

ENVELOPE

> Her Majesty's Representative,
> Ascot Office,
> St. James's Palace,
> London, S.W.1.

List of Names on Programmes, Brochures, etc.

Names are usually listed in order of precedence.

Members of the Royal Family are always shown with the Royal Style, usually in full (e.g. 'Her Royal Highness . . .'). Others should be treated consistently, either in the formal or social style, whichever is adopted, e.g.

Formal style	*Social style*
His Grace the Duke of Blank	The Duke of Blank
Her Grace the Duchess of Blank	The Duchess of Blank
Her Grace Mary, Duchess of Blank	Mary, Duchess of Blank
The Rt. Hon. the Earl of Blank	The Earl of Blank
The Rt. Hon. the Lord Blank	The Lord Blank
His Grace the Archbishop of Blank, *or* The Most Reverend the Lord Archbishop of Blank[1]	The Lord Archbishop of Blank
The Right Reverend the Lord Bishop of Blank	The Lord Bishop of Blank
The Very Reverend the Dean of Blank	The Dean of Blank
The Reverend John Smith	The Reverend John Smith
The Rt. Hon. John Brown	The Rt. Hon. John Brown

There is no rule for the position of 'the' in lists of peers. 'Rt. Hon. the Earl of Blank', 'the Rt. Hon. Viscount Blank', or 'Rt. Hon. Lord Blank' are not wrong, but the above usage is recommended. Similarly it is not laid down whether one should use upper or lower case for the first letter of 'the' within a sentence, except that the former must always be accorded to The Queen and to Queen Elizabeth The Queen Mother.

[1] An archbishop is often listed as 'His Grace the Archbishop of Blank' (*Lord* is then deemed unnecessary), though in letters he is styled 'The Most Reverend'. 'His Grace' is a simplified reference, particularly as the Archbishops of Canterbury and York are also Privy Counsellors. If 'The Most Reverend' is chosen as the prefix, the letters P.C. may be given after the name (if other letters are also listed) in place of 'the Right Honourable'. P.C. may similarly be accorded to the Bishop of London (e.g. 'The Right Reverend the Lord Bishop of London, P.C.' in place of 'The Right Reverend and Right Honourable the Lord Bishop of London').

Peers and Peeresses are only given the territorial designation if this forms an integral part of the title (e.g. Viscount Montgomery of Alamein).

Peers and Peeresses by courtesy and former wives of Peers are not accorded 'The' or the formal prefix of Most Hon. or Rt. Hon.

Untitled men are either consistently shown as 'John Smith, Esq.' *or* as 'Mr. John Smith', and doctors (holders of academic degrees) as 'John Smith, Esq., D.Sc.' *or* 'Dr. John Smith' (*not* 'Dr. John Smith, D.Sc.').

For the *position of letters after the name*, see p. 99. For other information see the appropriate section.

Joint Forms of Address

Christmas cards (and letters to close relatives, e.g. from a son to his father and mother) may have a joint address.

The use of the joint form for invitations to *public* functions is growing, although these should be addressed to the husband (if sent to his official address), and also to *private* functions, although these should be addressed to the wife at the home address.

The chief difficulty in addressing a joint envelope arises where the husband and wife are differently styled. The following is a guide. (Initials may, of course, be used instead of christian names, if desired.)

> Lieutenant-Colonel the Hon. John and Mrs. Smith
> Major John and the Hon. Mrs. Smith
> The Reverend John and Mrs. Smith
> The Hon. Guy and Lady Moira Black
> The Hon. Guy and Mrs. White.
> Mr. Donald Home and the Countess of Blackadder
> Mr. John and Lady Barbara Jones
> Mr. John and the Hon. Mrs. Green
> Mr. and Mrs. Thomas Brown

Christmas Cards

On a Christmas card it is customary for the husband's name to be given before his wife's, but this is a matter of personal choice.

A card should be inscribed from, 'John and Mary Smith', not from 'Mr. and Mrs. John Smith'. If the names are printed, the surname should be crossed through on cards sent to those on christian name terms. See also *Joint Forms of Address* (above).

Cards, Visiting, Professional and Business

These are of two kinds:

    (a) Visiting cards (which are now rarely used)
    (b) Professional and Business cards

VISITING CARDS

These are engraved from a copper plate. A gentleman's card is usually 3 inches long by $1\frac{1}{2}$ inches wide. They should give no more than a title, rank, private or Service address (two if desired), and club. In particular, telephone numbers are never included.

A lady's card is traditionally larger than a gentleman's, and is usually $3\frac{1}{4}$ by $2\frac{1}{4}$ inches, though $3\frac{1}{2}$ by $2\frac{1}{2}$ inches is sometimes used. Some ladies prefer a smaller card of the same size as a gentleman's.

Joint cards, e.g. for a husband and wife, or a mother and her unmarried daughters, are now seldom seen.

TITLES

The name of a peer or peeress is shown by his or her grade, but with no prefix, not even 'The', e.g. Duke of Norfolk, Earl of Lonsdale. Courtesy styles derived from a peerage are shown in the form Lord John Jones, Lady Emily Jones, etc., but 'Honourable' is not used: those so styled are shown as Mr., Mrs., or Miss, as applicable (Lady plus surname, if married to a baronet or knight).

BARONETS AND KNIGHTS

A baronet or knight is shown as Sir John Jones, i.e. without the suffix 'Bt.' or 'Bart.', and his wife as Lady Jones.

OTHER STYLES

The only other prefixes used on a card are ecclesiastical titles, ranks in the Armed Forces, and Doctor or Professor. Other gentlemen precede their name with 'Mr.', followed by their christian name or initials, except that the head of a family may style himself Mr. Forsyte.

A married lady uses her husband's christian name or initials, e.g. Mrs. John Forsyte, or Mrs. J. W. Forsyte, except that the senior married lady in her family may style herself Mrs. Forsyte.

A widow uses the same style as during her husband's lifetime, e.g. Mrs. John Forsyte. She should not use her own christian name or her own initials.

A divorced lady uses either her own christian name or her own initials.

The senior lady of her family, if unmarried, is styled Miss Forsyte. Other unmarried ladies use the style Miss June Forsyte.

SUFFIXES

These are never used on a visiting card, except those which indicate membership of the Armed Forces (see below).

ECCLESIASTICAL RANK

An Archbishop, Bishop, Dean or Archdeacon shows his territorial appointment, e.g. The Archbishop of Canterbury, The Bishop of Bath and Wells, The Dean of Lichfield, *or* The Archdeacon of Lincoln.

A Canon or Prebendary is usually so styled *without* 'The Reverend', e.g. Canon John Jones *or* Prebendary J. W. H. Jones.

A retired Bishop is styled by his prefix, e.g. 'The Right Reverend John Jones'. The style 'Bishop Jones' is not normally used.

An Archdeacon Emeritus is styled Archdeacon Jones, with the personal choice of adding christian name(s) or initial(s). Alternatively, he may use the prefix 'The Venerable', in which case the use of christian name(s) or initial(s) is obligatory.

Other Clergymen are styled The Reverend John Jones *or* The Reverend J. W. Jones.

Note.—The Reverend may be abbreviated to The Revd. or The Rev., see *Churches Section*, p. 111.

ARMED FORCES

Officers in the Armed Forces use their rank in full, i.e. abbreviations such as Lieut.-Col. should be avoided. Exceptions are Naval Officers below the rank of Lieutenant, Army and Royal Marine Officers below the rank of Captain, and Royal Air Force Officers below the rank of Flight Lieutenant, all of whom are styled 'Mr.'.

A Naval Officer below the rank of Rear-Admiral places 'Royal Navy' *or* 'Royal Naval Reserve' below and slightly to the right of his name.

An Army or Royal Marine Officer on the active list below the rank of Colonel, places his Regiment or Corps (or its accepted abbreviation) below his name.

A Royal Air Force Officer below the rank of Air Commodore places Royal Air Force (which may be abbreviated to R.A.F.) below and slightly to the right of his name.

Retired Officers do *not* include 'Retired' or 'Retd.' with the exception of the Royal Navy, where 'Retd.' is occasionally added below and slightly to the right of the name if there is a special reason for doing so. A retired Army or Royal Marine Officer omits his former Regiment or Corps.

WOMEN'S SERVICES

Officers in the Women's Services are usually styled Mrs. or Miss, with the appropriate letters indicating their Corps or Service below and slightly to the right of their names. Officers of the rank of Major or its equivalent and above may, however, use their rank.

EXAMPLES OF CARDS

Mrs. John Berkeley

65 *Pont Lane,*   *Little Stoneley,*
     *S.W.*1.   *Uppingham,*
                                                 Rutland.

Mr. Francis Fortescue

Little Pigeons,
     Shiplake,   *Athenæum.*
          Oxon.

Captain Richard Quarterdeck

Royal Navy

H.M.S. Invincible.

Major Jack Pull-Through

Grenadier Guards

Wellington Barracks,   *Guards' Club.*
S.W.1.

Air Vice-Marshal Sir Thomas Plane

Lodge House,
Silbury,
Bedfordshire.

The Dean of Winchester

The Deanery.

Dame Katherine Carruthers,
W.R.N.S.

Ministry of Defence,   *6 Orpington Mansions,*
Whitehall, S.W.1.   *Kew, Surrey.*

Mr. John Bollard,
Royal Navy

Britannia R.N.C.,
Dartmouth.

PROFESSIONAL AND BUSINESS CARDS

These are used only for professional or business purposes. They are usually printed (using Roman type), or may be engraved (using script) if desired.

A business card being intended to show the bearer's qualifications, the appropriate letters are suffixed to his name, e.g. F.R.I.B.A. The card should indicate the firm by whom the bearer is employed or which he represents, and give his business address and telephone number. His home address and telephone number may be added. Punctuation may be included or omitted as desired.

It is not necessary to prefix the name with any title, rank, Mr., Mrs., or Miss, but this is sometimes done, especially if the card is engraved, to be similar in appearance to a visiting card. If a retired officer from one of the Armed Forces gives his rank, 'Retd.' should be added to the right of and slightly below his name (or where applicable after Royal Navy, etc.).

EXAMPLES OF CARDS

ANTHONY BARKER
BALUCHISTAN NEWS SERVICE

LONDON BUREAU
8000, FLEET ST., E.C.4
TELEPHONE: 01-234-5678.

HOME
10, ALBANY TERRACE,
REGENTS PARK, N.W.1.
TELEPHONE 01-876-5432

Captain William Mainsail,
Royal Navy (Retd.)

Rockets & Starshell Ltd.,
899 High Road,
Greenwich, S.E.10.   *01-235 1234.*

PRECEDENCE SECTION

The only person whose precedence is absolute is the Sovereign. The precedence of all others is the Sovereign's prerogative. Even the precedence of those who appear in the official Tables of Precedence varies from time to time. Moreover, there are many varieties of precedence, national and local;[1] and it not infrequently happens that, in the relationship between host and guests, the requirements of courtesy and hospitality override any strict order of precedence.

Tables of Precedence

These Tables are particularly valuable for placing the holders of various offices in their correct order, e.g. The Speaker of the

---

[1] Thus, for example, the High Steward of Westminster (a Westminster Abbey appointment) is given special precedence on relevant occasions within that city (the Lord Mayor of Westminster is Deputy High Steward). So, too, is the Master Cutler given special precedence in the City of Sheffield.

House of Commons ranks above the Bishop of London. They contain, nonetheless, many traps for the unwary: it is, for example, easy to overlook the fact that Baron X—— (so created for his services) was born the younger son of a Duke of Y——, so that he has the latter precedence rather than the former, and should be placed above the Bishop of London, instead of below him.

The Tables for use in England and Wales and in Scotland are arranged in two lists, one for gentlemen, the other for ladies. Wives of the holders of certain offices do not derive a title from their husbands (e.g. Bishops, Ministers of the Crown, etc.) and so do not appear in the ladies' Table: they are nonetheless accorded the same precedence as their husbands when both attend a function. It may also be desirable to accord them their husbands' precedence at a function at which they are not present.

PRECEDENCE IN ENGLAND AND WALES

GENTLEMEN

[THE SOVEREIGN]
The Heir Apparent[1]
The Sovereign's Younger Sons
[The Sovereign's Grandsons]
The Sovereign's Nephew
Archbishop of Canterbury
Lord High Chancellor
Archbishop of York
Prime Minister
Lord High Treasurer (when existing)
Lord President of the Council
Speaker of the House of Commons
Lord Privy Seal
Ambassadors and High Commissioners
Lord Great Chamberlain[2]
Lord High Constable (when existing) ⎫
Earl Marshal   ⎪ Above all Peers
Lord Steward of the Household   ⎬ of their own
Lord Chamberlain of the Household   ⎪ degree
Master of the Horse   ⎭

---

[1] By Royal Warrant dated 18th September, 1952, it was declared that H.R.H. the Duke of Edinburgh was henceforth to have precedence next to H.M. The Queen, thus having place before the Heir Apparent.
[2] When in actual performance of official duty.

Dukes of England
Dukes of Scotland
Dukes of Great Britain
Dukes of Ireland
Dukes of the United Kingdom and Ireland since the Union[1]
Eldest Sons of Dukes of the Blood Royal
Marquesses of England
Marquesses of Scotland
Marquesses of Great Britain
Marquesses of Ireland
Marquesses of the United Kingdom and Ireland since the Union[1]
Eldest Sons of Dukes
Earls of England
Earls of Scotland
Earls of Great Britain
Earls of Ireland
Earls of the United Kingdom and Ireland since the Union[1]
Younger Sons of Dukes of the Blood Royal
Marquesses' Eldest Sons
Dukes' Younger Sons
Viscounts of England
Viscounts of Scotland
Viscounts of Great Britain
Viscounts of Ireland
Viscounts of the United Kingdom and Ireland since the Union[1]
Earls' Eldest Sons
Marquesses' Younger Sons
Bishop of London
Bishop of Durham
Bishop of Winchester
Other English Diocesan Bishops according to seniority of consecration
Suffragan Bishops according to seniority of consecration
Secretaries of State, if of Baronial rank.
Barons of England
Lords of Parliament, Scotland
Barons of Great Britain

[1] See p. 25.

Barons of Ireland
Barons of the United Kingdom and Ireland since the Union[1]
   including Life Barons and Lords of Appeal in Ordinary
Lords Commissioners of the Great Seal (when existing)
Treasurer of the Household
Comptroller of the Household
Vice-Chamberlain of the Household
Secretaries of State, under Baronial rank
Viscounts' Eldest Sons
Earls' Younger Sons
Barons' Eldest Sons
Knights of the Garter
Privy Counsellors
Chancellor of the Exchequer
Chancellor of the Duchy of Lancaster
Lord Chief Justice of England
Master of the Rolls
President of the Family Division
Lord Justices of Appeal, according to seniority of appointment
Judges of the High Court of Justice, according to seniority
   of appointment
Viscounts' Younger Sons
Barons' Younger Sons
Sons of Life Peers and Lords of Appeal in Ordinary
Baronets, according to date of Patent
Knights of the Thistle[2]
Knights Grand Cross of the Bath
Knights Grand Commanders of the Star of India
Knights Grand Cross of the Order St. Michael and St·
   George
Knights Grand Commanders of the Indian Empire
Knights Grand Cross of the Royal Victorian Order
Knights Grand Cross of the Order of the British Empire
Knights Commanders of the Bath
Knights Commanders of the Star of India
Knights Commanders of St. Michael and St. George
Knights Commanders of the Indian Empire
Knights Commanders of the Royal Victorian Order
Knights Commanders of the Order of the British Empire
Knights Bachelor

[1] See p. 25.
[2] Knights of the Thistle have no relative precedence accorded to them by Statute, but are
customarily placed here. In Scotland they follow Knights of the Garter. (See Scottish Table.)

Circuit Judges in England and Wales, as follows:

(a) Vice-Chancellor of Co. Palatine of Lancaster
(b) Circuit Judges who immediately before 1st Jan. 1972, held office as Official Referees to Supreme Court
(c) Recorder of London
(d) Recorders of Liverpool and Manchester according to priority of appointment.
(e) Common Serjeant
(f) Circuit Judges who immediately before 1st Jan. 1972, held office as Additional Judge of the Central Criminal Court, Assistant Judge of the Mayor's and City of London Court, County Court Judge, Whole time Chairman or Deputy Chairman of courts of quarter sessions for Greater London, Cheshire, Durham, Kent and Lancashire, according to priority of appointment.
(g) Other Circuit Judges, according to priority of appointment

Companions of the Order of the Bath
Companions of the Order of the Star of India
Companions of the Order of St. Michael and St. George
Companions of the Order of the Indian Empire
Commanders of the Royal Victorian Order
Commanders of the Order of the British Empire
Companions of the Distinguished Service Order
Members of the Royal Victorian Order (4th class)
Officers of the Order of the British Empire
Companions of the Imperial Service Order
Eldest Sons of the Younger Sons of Peers
Eldest Sons of Baronets
Eldest Sons of Knights of the Garter
Eldest Sons of Knights of the Thistle[1]
Eldest Sons of Knights of the Bath[2]
Eldest Sons of Knights of the Star of India[2]
Eldest Sons of Knights of the Order of St. Michael and St. George[2]
Eldest Sons of Knights of the Indian Empire[2]
Eldest Sons of Knights of the Royal Victorian Order[2]
Eldest Sons of Knights of the Order of the British Empire[2]
Eldest Sons of Knights Bachelor
Members of the Royal Victorian Order (5th class)

[1] See p. 311 note [2].
[2] Eldest sons of Knights Grand Cross take precedence of eldest sons of Knights of the 2nd degree.

Members of the Order of the British Empire
Younger Sons of Baronets
Younger Sons of Knights
Esquires
Gentlemen

LADIES[1]

THE QUEEN
The Queen Mother
[The Princess of Wales]
The Sovereign's Daughter
[Wives of the Sovereign's Younger Sons]
[The Sovereign's Granddaughters (with style of H.R.H.)]
[Wives of the Sovereign's Grandsons]
The Sovereign's Sister
Wives of the Sovereign's Uncles
The Sovereign's Niece
Duchesses of England
Duchesses of Scotland
Duchesses of Great Britain
Duchesses of Ireland
Duchess of the UK and Ireland since the Union
Wives of the Eldest Sons of Dukes of the Blood Royal
Marchionesses of England
Marchionesses of Scotland
Marchionesses of Great Britain
Marchionesses of Ireland
Marchionesses of the UK and Ireland since the Union
Wives of the Eldest Sons of Dukes
Daughters of Dukes
Countesses of England
Countesses of Scotland
Countesses of Great Britain
Countesses of Ireland
Countess of the UK and Ireland since the Union
Wives of the Younger Sons of Dukes of the Blood Royal
Wives of the Eldest Sons of Marquesses
Daughters of Marquesses
Wives of the Younger Sons of Dukes

[1] If appointments are held by ladies, e.g. Secretaries of State, High Court, or Circuit Judges they should be assigned a corresponding place as in Gentlemen's Table.

Viscountesses of England
Viscountesses of Scotland
Viscountesses of Great Britain
Viscountesses of Ireland
Viscountesses of the United Kingdom and Ireland since the Union[1]
Wives of the Eldest Sons of Earls
Daughters of Earls
Wives of the Younger Sons of Marquesses
Baronesses of England
Ladies of Parliament, Scotland
Baronesses of Great Britain
Baronesses of Ireland
Baronesses of the United Kingdom and Ireland since the Union, including Life Baronesses and Wives of Life Barons and Lords of Appeal in Ordinary
Wives of the Eldest Sons of Viscounts
Daughters of Viscounts
Wives of the Younger Sons of Earls
Wives of the Eldest Sons of Barons
Daughters of Barons
Wives of Knights of the Garter
Privy Counsellors (Women)
Wives of the Younger Sons of Viscounts
Wives of the Younger Sons of Barons
Wives of Sons of Life Peers
Wives of Baronets, according to their husband's Patents
Wives of Knights of the Thistle (see note on Gentlemen's Table)
Dames Grand Cross of the Order of the Bath
Dames Grand Cross of the Order of St. Michael and St. George
Dames Grand Cross of the Royal Victorian Order
Dames Grand Cross of the Order of the British Empire
Wives of Knights Grand Cross of the Bath
Wives of Knights Grand Commanders of the Star of India
Wives of Knights Grand Cross of St. Michael and St. George
Wives of Knights Grand Commanders of the Indian Empire
Wives of Knights Grand Cross of the Royal Victorian Order
Wives of Knights Grand Cross of the Order of the British Empire

[1] See p. 25.

Dames Commanders of the Order of the Bath
Dames Commanders of the Order of St. Michael and St. George
Dames Commanders of the Royal Victorian Order
Dames Commanders of the Order of the British Empire
Wives of Knights Commanders of the Bath
Wives of Knights Commanders of the Star of India
Wives of Knights Commanders of St. Michael and St. George.
Wives of Knights Commanders of the Indian Empire
Wives of Knights Commanders of the Royal Victorian Order
Wives of Knights Commanders of the Order of the British Empire
Wives of Knights Bachelor
Companions of the Order of the Bath
Companions of the Order of St. Michael and St. George
Commanders of the Royal Victorian Order
Commanders of the Order of the British Empire
Wives of Companions of the Bath
Wives of Companions of the Star of India
Wives of Companions of the Order of St. Michael and St. George
Wives of Companions of the Indian Empire
Wives of Commanders of the Royal Victorian Order
Wives of Commanders of the Order of the British Empire
Wives of Companions of the Distinguished Service Order
Members of the Royal Victorian Order (4th class)
Officers of the Order of the British Empire
Wives of Members of the Royal Victorian Order (4th class)
Wives of Officers of the Order of the British Empire
Companions of the Imperial Service Order
Wives of Companions of the Imperial Service Order
Wives of the Eldest Sons of the Younger Sons of Peers
Daughters of the Younger Sons of Peers
Wives of the Eldest Sons of Baronets
Daughters of Baronets
Wives of the Eldest Sons of Knights of the Garter
Wives of the Eldest Sons of Knights
Daughters of Knights
Members of the Royal Victorian Order (5th class)
Members of the Order of the British Empire
Wives of Members of the Royal Victorian Order (5th class)

Wives of Members of the Order of the British Empire
Wives of the Younger Sons of Baronets
Wives of the Younger Sons of Knights
Wives of Esquires
Wives of Gentlemen

PRECEDENCE IN SCOTLAND

GENTLEMEN

[THE SOVEREIGN]
Lord High Commissioner to the General Assembly of the Church of Scotland (during sitting of General Assembly)[1]
Duke of Rothesay[2]
The Sovereign's Younger Sons
The Sovereign's Nephew
Lord-Lieutenants of Counties[3]
Lord Provosts of Cities who are *ex-officio* Lord-Lieutenants (see p. 233)
Sheriffs Principal[4]
Lord Chancellor of Great Britain
Moderator of the General Assembly of the Church of Scotland (during office)
The Prime Minister
Keeper of the Great Seal of Scotland (Secretary of State for Scotland) (if a Peer)
Keeper of the Privy Seal of Scotland (if a Peer)
Hereditary High Constable of Scotland
Hereditary Master of the Household in Scotland
Dukes (as in English Table)
Eldest Sons of Dukes of the Blood Royal
Marquesses (as in English Table)
Eldest Sons of Dukes
Earls (as in English Table)
Younger Sons of Dukes of the Blood Royal
Eldest Sons of Marquesses
Younger Sons of Dukes
Keeper of the Great Seal (Secretary of State for Scotland) (if not a Peer)
Keeper of the Privy Seal (if not a Peer)

[1] By Royal Warrant dated 18th September, 1952, it was declared that H.R.H. the Duke of Edinburgh was henceforth to have precedence next to H.M. The Queen, thus having place before the Lord High Commissioner.
[2] The eldest son of The Sovereign in the Peerage of Scotland (i.e. The Prince of Wales).
[3] Lord Lieutenants within the limits of their jurisdiction have precedence before the Sheriffs Principal having concurrent jurisdiction.
[4] In Scotland Sheriffs exercise judicial functions.

Lord Justice-General
Lord Clerk Register
Lord Advocate
Lord Justice-Clerk
Viscounts (as in English Table)
Eldest Sons of Earls
Younger Sons of Marquesses
Barons or Lords of Parliament Scotland (as in English Table)
Eldest Sons of Viscounts
Younger Sons of Earls
Eldest Sons of Barons or Lords of Parliament, Scotland
Knights of the Garter
Knights of the Thistle
Privy Counsellors
Senators of the College of Justice (Lords of Session), including the Chairman of the Scottish Land Court
Younger Sons of Viscounts
Younger Sons of Barons or Lords of Parliament, Scotland
Sons of Life Peers
Baronets
Knights Grand Cross and Knights Grand Commanders of Orders (as in English Table)
Knights Commanders of Orders (as in English Table)
Solicitor-General for Scotland
Lyon King of Arms
Sheriffs Principal (when not within own County)
Knights Bachelor
Sheriffs
Companions of the Order of the Bath
Thence as in English Table

LADIES

THE QUEEN
The Queen Mother
[Duchess of Rothesay] (see Duke of Rothesay)
The Sovereign's Daughters
The Sovereign's Sisters
[The Sovereign's Aunts]
Wives of Sovereign's Uncles
The Sovereign's Niece
Duchesses (as in English Table)
Wives of the Eldest Sons of Dukes of Blood Royal
Marchionesses (as in English Table)

Wives of Eldest Sons of Dukes
Daughters of Dukes
Wives of Younger Sons of Dukes of Blood Royal
Wives of Eldest Sons of Marquesses
Daughters of Marquesses
Wives of Younger Sons of Dukes
Countesses (as in English Table)
Viscountesses (as in English Table)
Wives of Eldest Sons of Earls
Daughters of Earls
Wives of Younger Sons of Marquesses
Baronesses, or Ladies of Parliament, Scotland (as in English Table)
Wives of Eldest Sons of Viscounts
Daughters of Viscounts
Wives of Younger Sons of Earls
Wives of Eldest Sons of Barons or Lords of Parliament, Scotland
Daughters of Barons or Lords of Parliament (Scotland)
Wives of Knights of the Garter
Privy Counsellors (Women)
Wives of Younger Sons of Viscounts
Wives of Younger Sons of Barons
Wives of Sons of Life Peers
Wives of Baronets
Wives of Knights of the Thistle
Dames Grand Cross of Orders (as in English Table)
Wives of Knights Grand Cross and Knights Grand Commanders of Orders (as in English Table)
Dames Commanders of Orders (as in English Table)
Wives of Knights Commanders of Orders (as in English Table)
Wives of Knights Bachelor and Wives of Senators of the College of Justice (Lords of Session) including the wife of the Chairman of the Scottish Land Court[1]
Companions of the Order of the Bath
Thence as in English Table

PRECEDENCE IN NORTHERN IRELAND

In the light of extensive changes in the Government of Northern Ireland, the official Table requires considerable amendment. At the time of publication The Queen has not approved a new one. The following, based on the previous list, and the omission of

[1] Taking precedence among themselves according to the dates of their husbands' creation as Knights or appointment as Senators of the College of Justice, respectively.

those appointments which have not been filled, is merely included as a guide.

The Office of Governor of Northern Ireland was abolished by Section 32 (1) of the Northern Ireland Constitution Act 1973. Most of his functions are now discharged by the Secretary of State for Northern Ireland.

There is no Prime Minister, Privy Council or Cabinet (though Privy Counsellors still retain that rank). Section 8 of the 1973 Act creates a Northern Ireland Executive, presided over by the Chief Executive, but during the period of direct rule created by the Northern Ireland Act 1974, there are no appointments to the Executive.

There is no Parliament of Northern Ireland; the Northern Ireland Assembly is still in existence but stands dissolved; its Presiding Officer is no longer alive; the Clerk to the Assembly remains in office despite dissolution.

Various changes have been made in the structure of central government in Northern Ireland and the Ministries of Northern Ireland have been re-named Departments. The list of Departments now reads: Finance, Health and Social Services, Education, Agriculture, Commerce, Environment, Manpower Services and Civil Service. These changes are noted after the respective appointments.

Noblemen and Gentlemen who have personal precedence above that of their official rank take the higher precedence.

Officials of the United Kingdom not mentioned in this Table rank according to the Table of Precedence for England and Wales (or Scotland) when in Northern Ireland.

A lady whose husband's precedence is governed by his official rank should be granted that precedence, unless she is entitled to higher precedence in her own right. In all other cases the Table of Precedence in England is followed.

THE SOVEREIGN

> Heir Apparent (The Prince of Wales)[1]
> Relatives of The Sovereign (as in English Table)
> Lord-Lieutenants of Counties and of the Cities of Belfast and Londonderry, and the High Sheriffs of Counties at large within the bounds of their respective jurisdictions.

[1] By Royal Warrant dated 18th September, 1952, it was declared that H.R.H. the Duke of Edinburgh was henceforth to have precedence next to H.M. The Queen, thus having place before the Heir Apparent.

Primates of Ireland and other Archbishops according to the dates of their consecration or translation; and the Moderator of the General Assembly of the Presbyterian Church in Ireland according to the date of election.

Lord Mayor of Belfast and the Mayors of Districts in Northern Ireland within their own bounds; but if within the precincts of their City Halls they shall be granted precedence next after the Royal Family.

Honorary Recorders at civic functions within their own areas of jurisdiction.

High Sheriffs of Belfast and Londonderry at civic functions within the bounds of their Cities.

Peers and their Sons (as in English Table, except the Sons mentioned below), but after Younger Sons of Marquesses and before Barons of England appear all Bishops of the Church of Ireland and all Roman Catholic Bishops in Ireland, according to the date of consecration.

Lord Chief Justice of Northern Ireland.

Eldest Sons of Viscounts

Younger Sons of Earls

Eldest Sons of Barons

Knights of the Garter

Knights of the Thistle

Privy Counsellors

Senior Naval Officer In Charge in Northern Ireland waters, the General Officer Commanding Northern Ireland, and the Air Officer Commanding Northern Ireland, their relative rank and precedence being determined by the *Queen's Regulations* on the subject

Attorney General of Northern Ireland[1]

Lord Justices of Appeal in Northern Ireland

Judges of the High Court of Justice in Northern Ireland

Honorary Recorders within their own areas of jurisdiction other than at civic functions

High Sheriffs of Belfast and Londonderry within the bounds of their own Cities other than at civic functions

Younger Sons of Viscounts

Younger Sons of Barons

Baronets

Knights Grand Cross and Commanders, Knights Commanders, and Knights Bachelor (as in English Table)

---

[1] By Section 10 of the 1973 Act the Attorney-General for England and Wales is, by virtue of that office, also Attorney-General for Northern Ireland.

Town Clerk and the City Chamberlain of Belfast and other Town Clerks in Northern Ireland within their own bounds[1]

Judges of County Courts in Northern Ireland (including Honorary Recorders outside their own areas of jurisdiction)

Companions, Commanders and Officers of Order of Chivalry, Eldest Sons of Younger Sons of Peers, Eldest Sons of Baronets, Knights of the Garter and Knights, Members of the Royal Victorian Order, Members of the Order of the British Empire, Younger Sons of Baronets and Baronets and Knights (as in English Table)

Head of Civil Service[2]

Permanent Secretary to the Department of Finance of Northern Ireland[2]

Permanent Secretary to the Department of Health and Social Services of Northern Ireland

Permanent Secretary to the Department of Education of Northern Ireland

Permanent Secretary to the Department of Commerce of Northern Ireland

Permanent Secretary to the Department of the Environment of Northern Ireland

Permanent Secretary to the Department of Manpower Services of Northern Ireland

Permanent Secretary to the Department of the Civil Service

Comptroller and Auditor-General of Northern Ireland

Legislative Draftsman of Northern Ireland

Crown Solicitor of Northern Ireland

Queen's Counsel of Northern Ireland

Chief Constable of the Royal Ulster Constabulary

Esquires

Gentlemen

Notes on the Tables of Precedence

THE ROYAL FAMILY

Certain Members of the Royal Family are assigned places in the Tables of Precedence according to their relationship to The Queen, viz:

[1] Town Clerks are still unofficially so styled, but their legal title is now that of Clerk, in accordance with Section 41 (1) of the Local Government Act (Northern Ireland) 1972. It will be noted that Belfast has retained this office instead of adopting the title Chief Executive as has been done by the larger Councils in England and Wales.

[2] The post of Head of the Civil Service is now separate from that of Permanent Secretary to the Department of Finance. The Head of the Civil Service ranks above the Permanent Secretaries of Departments.

Gentlemen	*Ladies*
The Duke of Edinburgh	Queen Elizabeth The Queen Mother
The Prince of Wales	The Princess Anne, Mrs. Mark Phillips
	The Princess Margaret, Countess of Snowdon
	Princess Alice, Duchess of Gloucester

Those not specifically mentioned by their relationship to The Queen are:

The Duke of Gloucester	The Duchess of Gloucester
The Duke of Kent	The Duchess of Kent
Prince Michael of Kent	Princess Alexandra, the Hon. Mrs. Angus Ogilvy
	Princess Alice, Countess of Athlone

These are customarily placed before all non-Royal guests.

AMBASSADORS AND HIGH COMMISSIONERS

Precedence within the Diplomatic Corps is accorded to an Ambassador or High Commissioner in a common roll from the time they take up their duties in London. See Diplomatic and Commonwealth Section (p. 157).

The Apostolic Delegate, the Representative of the Pope to the Roman Catholic Hierarchy of Great Britain (but not of Northern Ireland) by courtesy is given precedence among other heads of Diplomatic Missions. He is accorded the prefix of His Excellency.

Chargés d'Affaires rank after all Ambassadors and High Commissioners. If two or more be present they rank among themselves in accordance with the precedence accorded to their respective Ambassadors.

Other members of the Diplomatic Corps of equal rank are usually placed in alphabetical order of their names, but the relative importance of their countries may be taken into consideration.

PEERS AND BARONETS, THEIR WIVES AND CHILDREN

Peers and Peeresses rank among themselves in each degree in the following order: those created (1) of England, (2) of Scotland, (3) of Great Britain, (4) of Ireland, and (5) of the United Kingdom and of Ireland created since the Union, according to the dates of their respective patents.

Baronets rank among themselves according to the dates of their respective patents *only*.

Precedence of ladies is always derived from the father or husband, except in the case of a peeress in her own right.

A dowager peeress, or widow of a baronet, takes precedence of the wife of the incumbent of the title only while remaining a widow.

The children of a living peer, or baronet, have precedence above the children of the previous possessor, or possessors, of the title. If the daughter of a peer marries a peer she takes her husband's rank and precedence, but if she marries the eldest or a younger son of a peer she ranks *either* according to her own inherent precedence (i.e. as the daughter of her father), *or* according to that of her husband (i.e. as the wife of the eldest or younger son of a duke, marquess, earl, etc.), whichever happens to be the higher, no matter what the courtesy title may be. Daughters rank immediately after the wives of their eldest brothers.[1]

ESQUIRES AND GENTLEMEN

Although these ranks appear in the Tables, their definition is now only of academic interest. Sir Charles Young, Garter King of Arms, in his *Order of Precedence*, 1851, stated under *Esquires*, 'it is extremely difficult to define accurately or satisfactorily the persons included by, or entitled to, this designation. Lord Coke, in his exposition of the Statute I Hen. V, cap. 5, of *Additions*, said—"The Sons of all the Peers and Lords of Parliament in the life of their Fathers are in law Esquires, and so to be named." By this statute the Eldest Son of a Knight is an *Esquire* (2 Inst. 667).' Young proceeded to refer to Sir William Blackstone's opinions in his *Commentaries on the Laws of England*. Camden categorised them into four sorts: '1. The Eldest Sons of Knights, and their Eldest Sons in perpetual succession. 2. The Eldest Sons of Younger Sons of Peers, and their Elder Sons in like perpetual succession. 3. Esquires created by the King's letters patent, or other investiture, and their Eldest Sons. 4. Esquires by virtue of their offices; as Justices of the Peace, and others who bear any office of trust under the Crown.' For *Gentlemen*, Young wrote, 'there is no defined priority. Littleton says, "every son is as great a gentleman as the eldest".' See *English Genealogy*, by Sir Anthony Wagner, Garter King of Arms (1960) for the history of Esquires and Gentlemen.

[1] Common sense must nonetheless be used in deciding the precedence to be accorded to peers, peeresses and their children. It is often necessary to take age and other factors into account. For example, it is usually unwise to seat the younger son of a Marquess above a Baron, simply because this is how he ranks in the Table of Precedence, when the former is a youth of 18 and the latter an old gentleman of 80. Again it may be best to sit a high ranking officer in the Armed Forces, or the Chairman and Managing Director of a large firm, with a low place in the Table of Precedence, above a peer who, although he has a much higher place in the Table is only a junior officer or employee.

FOREIGN NOBILITY
Foreign titles of nobility borne by British subjects afford their holders no *official* precedence in Great Britain.

ORDER OF MERIT AND COMPANION OF HONOUR
The Order of Merit and the Order of the Companion of Honour do not confer precedence upon their recipients.

LORD-LIEUTENANT (AND LIEUTENANT)
Although assigned no place in the Table of Precedence for England and Wales, by Royal Warrant in 1904 a Lord-Lieutenant (or Lieutenant) when so acting, has precedence within his own County immediately after the Sovereign (except on civic premises: see below).

This does *not* apply to a Vice-Lieutenant, Assistant Lieutenant, or Deputy Lieutenant.

CIVIC HEADS
Although not mentioned in the Tables of Precedence:

(a) The Lord Mayor of London has precedence throughout his City immediately after the Sovereign, i.e. before other Members of the Royal Family. Outside the City of London he should be placed immediately after Earls.

(b) A Lord Mayor or Mayor in England and Wales and a Lord Provost or Provost in Scotland, has precedence immediately after the Royal Family on his own civic premises (City Hall, etc.), and immediately after the Lord-Lieutenant elsewhere within his city or borough. Outside his city or borough he has no precedence other than that which courtesy may require.

(c) A Deputy Lord Mayor or Deputy Mayor is accorded the same precedence as his Lord Mayor or Mayor *when representing him*. Otherwise he has no precedence except on his own civic premises where he is placed after the Lord Mayor or Mayor, see the *Recorder or Honorary Recorder,* p. 325.

(d) The Chairman of a Metropolitan District Council or District Council has precedence immediately after the Royal Family on his own civic premises, and immediately after the Lord-Lieutenant elsewhere within his District. Outside his District he has no precedence other than that which courtesy may require.

(e) A City Mayor or Town Mayor has no precedence except within his own city or town. There he has precedence after the Chairman of the District Council *except* where the District Council concerned has decided that a City Mayor or Town Mayor shall have precedence over their Chairman.[1]

(f) Except on their own civic premises, the precedence accorded to other Civic Heads (e.g. Chairmen of County Councils) is a matter for local custom.

CIVIC HEADS IN GREATER LONDON

These have the following precedence among themselves:

The Lord Mayor or Mayor in whose City or Borough the function is held

The Lord Mayor of London

The Chairman of the Greater London Council

The Lord Mayor of Westminster

The Mayor of the Royal Borough of Kensington and Chelsea

The Mayor of the Royal Borough of Kingston upon Thames

The Mayors of other London Boroughs in alphabetical order of their Boroughs

RECORDER OR HONORARY RECORDER

Within the City of London the Recorder of London takes precedence immediately after the Aldermen who have 'passed the Chair', i.e. those who have served as Lord Mayor.

An Honorary Recorder is customarily accorded precedence at civic and other functions within his own area of jurisdiction immediately after the Lord Mayor or Mayor.

For Northern Ireland, see the relevant Table of Precedence (pp. 318-321).

HIGH SHERIFF

Although assigned no place in the Table of Precedence for England and Wales, by Royal Warrant in 1904 a High Sheriff when so acting has precedence within his own County after the Lord-Lieutenant.

[1] For example, the Chairman of the Leominster District Council (which covers north Hereford & Worcester) takes precedence before the Town Mayor of Leominster. But South Shropshire District Council, which has its offices in Ludlow, ten miles to the north of Leominster, recognises the ancient office of Mayor of Ludlow by according its Town Mayor precedence within Ludlow before their Chairman.

High Sheriffs have been known to claim that this means *immediately after*. The point has never been clarified. But the usual interpretation is that a High Sheriff takes precedence after the Civic Head and The Recorder of the place in which the function is being held. For a justification for this, see the Table of Precedence for Northern Ireland in which High Sheriffs are specifically mentioned.

CLERGY

Except for those specifically mentioned in the Tables of Precedence, clergy and their wives have no precedence assigned to them.

A clergyman of the Church of England subsequently appointed a knight of one of the Orders of Chivalry has precedence as such although he is not eligible to receive the accolade. Likewise his wife has the precedence of a Knight's wife although she is addressed as e.g. Mrs. John Smith.

In England and Wales it is customary to accord precedence to Roman Catholic Archbishops and Bishops immediately after those of the Anglican Communion.[1] The Heads of other Churches, e.g. the Chief Rabbi, should be similarly recognised.

OFFICERS OF THE ARMED FORCES, OF THE FOREIGN AND COMMONWEALTH SERVICE, AND THE CIVIL SERVICE

Except for those specifically mentioned in the Tables of Precedence, these have no precedence assigned to them. Senior officers who are peers, knights or members of an Order of Chivalry can be placed accordingly. Others of senior rank should be placed before more junior officers who are nonetheless covered by the Tables e.g. a Major-General with no more than an O.B.E. should be placed before a Brigadier with a C.B.E.

PRECEDENCE OF CONSULAR OFFICERS AND OFFICERS OF THE ARMED FORCES

Consuls General rank with but after	Rear-Admirals
	Major-Generals
	Air Vice-Marshals
Consuls rank with but after	Captains, R.N.
	Colonels
	Group Captains

[1] It is not always easy to interpret this custom. For example, at a function held in London attended by the Archbishop of Canterbury, the Cardinal Archbishop of Westminster and the Bishop of London, they should be placed in that order. But if only the Cardinal Archbishop of Westminster and the Bishop of London be present, it is not clear who should rank first. (It is therefore advisable to consult their respective secretaries or chaplains.)

Vice-Consuls rank with but after	Lieutenant-Commanders
	Majors
	Squadron Leaders
Consular Agents rank with but after	Lieutenants, R.N.
	Captains (Army)
	Flight Lieutenants

The officer in charge of a consular post, during the absence of the titular holder, takes the rank of that officer.

IMPORTANT PEOPLE IN INDUSTRY, THE PROFESSIONS, AND THE ARTS

Except for those who have received honours mentioned in the Tables of Precedence, these have no official precedence. Their placing should nonetheless recognise their importance in their respective fields.

MEMBERS OF PARLIAMENT

Except for those specifically mentioned in the Tables of Precedence, these have no official precedence assigned to them. The Member of Parliament for the Constituency in which a function is held should nonetheless be appropriately recognised and seated.

LIST OF PATRONS

When listing the Patrons of a charity, or when compiling any similar list, it is sometimes difficult to be sure of placing them in their correct order of precedence. The acceptable solution is to list them in alphabetical order *except* that the Sovereign and other Members of the Royal Family must come first.

Table Plans

ROYAL GUESTS

When The Queen attends a function the host always surrenders his place to her, he himself being seated on her right.

Other Members of the Royal Family (i.e. The Queen Mother and those entitled to the prefix Royal Highness) are given special precedence, see *Precedence* (pp. 321-322). The husband of a lady member of the Royal Family is accorded precedence immediately after her when both attend a function. If he attends alone, he retains his own precedence, unless he is the principal guest, see *Official Functions*, p. 328.

The Suite in attendance on a Member of the Royal Family should be placed reasonably near to him or her.

No guest should leave a function before a Member of the Royal

Family, except in special circumstances when prior permission should be obtained.

This rule may be honoured in the breach rather than in the observance at Charity Balls, etc. which continue after midnight.

The organiser of an evening function may seek (through the Private Secretary) 'blanket' permission for guests who may have transport difficulties if they do not leave by a certain hour (e.g. to catch the last train), to do so before the Member of the Royal Family leaves.

A guest holding an official position whose duties require him to leave a function before the Member of the Royal Family in order to keep another engagement, should seek permission to do so (through the Private Secretary) in advance of the function.

OFFICIAL FUNCTIONS

The principal guest is placed on the host's right (except for The Queen for whom see above). The principal guest's wife is usually placed on the host's left, the host's wife being placed on the right of the principal guest. If wives are not present the second most important guest is placed on the host's left.

When the principal guest is The Queen (or other Head of State), a Member of the Royal Family, a Prime Minister, a Member of the Cabinet, or someone of comparable importance, the need to invite also some or all of the following, and their wives, should be considered, bearing in mind that those who accept (and their wives) should be placed in this order of precedence after such principal guest:

1. The Lord-Lieutenant of the County
2. The Lord Mayor, Lord Provost, Mayor or Provost of the City, Borough, etc.
3. The High Sheriff of the County (see p. 235).
4. The Chairman of the County Council

Note.—On relevant occasions these guests may, as a courtesy, yield their prime places to a 'guest of honour', or e.g. to an archbishop at a church function, to the Lord Chancellor and the Speaker of the House of Commons at a Parliamentary function, to the Lord Chief Justice or Master of the Rolls at a legal function, etc.

Ambassadors, High Commissioners and Chargés d'Affaires should be placed at the top table, their relative precedence being strictly observed.[1] See p. 322.

---

[1] As a general rule Diplomatic representatives from countries which do not enjoy diplomatic relations with each other should not be invited to the same function. When, as sometimes happens, it is necessary to invite them, care should be taken to avoid placing them near to each other.

Ministers of the Crown and Privy Counsellors should be placed at the top table.

Important dignatories of the Established Church are placed high among the guests in accordance with the Tables of Precedence, see p. 309. High dignitaries of other Churches should, as a courtesy, be placed next after those of the same rank from the Established Church.

When a function takes place within premises belonging to some organisation other than the host's, a senior representative of that organisation should be invited and placed high among the guests.

Other important guests are placed to order of precedence and importance,[1] subject to the following general rules:

(a) Important members of the inviting body should be interspersed among the principal guests.

(b) Wives should be placed according to the precedence of their husbands (except when they have a superior precedence in their own right).

(c) It is up to the host to decide whether husbands and wives are to be seated together, *or* apart. The former is easier to arrange; the latter (which is always followed at private functions) gives husbands and wives a chance to meet 'new faces'.

SEMI-OFFICIAL FUNCTIONS

The host must decide whether a semi-official function, e.g. a society or firm's annual dinner, is to be a formal one, with precedence observed (as at an official function) or whether, as tends to be the case today, it should be a less formal one with less regard for precedence. Even so the members of the host organisation (and their wives) should be interspersed among the other guests: on no account should the former be seated in one block and the latter in another.

SPECIMEN TABLE PLANS

The following examples show possible, but not necessarily the only ways of seating guests at typical functions.

(a) *A Civic function* (in England or Wales) at which the Lord Mayor and Lady Mayoress of a city are host and hostess,

---

[1] Age has sometimes to be considered: placing Midshipman the Duke of Loamshire above Admiral of the Fleet Sir Horatio Hornblower is no more likely to improve the Admiral's temper than it is to advance the Duke's naval career.

using only one side of the top table and with husbands and wives seated together.

Principal guests:
- The Queen[1]
- The Lord-Lieutenant of the County and his wife
- The High Sheriff of the County and his wife
- The Chairman of the County Council and his wife
- The Ruritanian Ambassador (*not married*)
- The Marquess and Marchioness of Portsdown
- The Anglican Bishop of the Diocese and his wife
- The Home Secretary and his wife

- Bishop[2]
- Bishop's wife[2]
- Ruritanian Ambassador[2]
- High Sheriff's wife
- High Sheriff
- Lady Mayoress (*Hostess*)
- Lord Mayor (*Host*)
- THE QUEEN
- Lord-Lieutenant
- Lord-Lieutenant's wife
- Chairman of County Council[2]
- Chairman of County Council's wife[2]
- Marquess of Portsdown[2]
- Marchioness of Portsdown[2]
- Home Secretary[2]
- Home Secretary's wife[2]

CENTRE ←——————→

(b) *A formal function by a Company* at which the Chairman is the host, using only one side of the top table, wives not invited:

[1] The top table plan of any function attended by The Queen or other member of the Royal Family must be submitted for prior approval to the Private Secretary, from whom the names of the Suite in attendance should be obtained.

[2] If desired the Chief Executive and the Leader of the City Council (and their wives) may be seated among these guests.

Principal guests: The Mayor of the Borough
The Prime Minister
The High Commissioner for Nonsuch
The Duke of Loamshire
The Chairman of the Parent Company
The Member of Parliament for the Constituency
The Chief Executive of the District Council
The Leader of the District Council

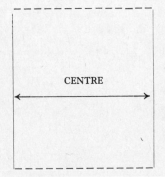

Chief Executive
Chairman of Parent Company
High Commissioner for Nonsuch
Prime Minister
Chairman of Company (*Host*)
Mayor[1]
Duke of Loamshire
Member of Parliament
Leader of Council

(c) *As for* (*b*) but including wives and using both sides of the top table.

Member of Parliament
Duchess of Loamshire

Prime Minister
Chairman's wife (*Hostess*)
Mayor
High Commissioner's wife
Chairman of Parent Company (*not married*)
Leader of Council's wife

Leader of Council
Wife of Chief Executive
High Commissioner for Nonsuch
Mayoress
Chairman of Company (*Host*)
Prime Minister's wife
Duke of Loamshire

Wife of Member of Parliament

Chief Executive

[1] This assumes the Mayor's agreement to waive his precedence as First Citizen as a courtesy to the Prime Minister.

(d) *A function given by a Society* at which the President is the host, accompanied by his wife, using both sides of the top table.

Principal guests: Their Royal Highnesses The Duke and Duchess of Kent[1]

The Lord-Lieutenant of the County and his wife

The Mayor and Mayoress of the Borough

The Vice-Chancellor of the local University and his wife

The Naval Flag Officer of the area and his wife

A Roman Catholic Bishop

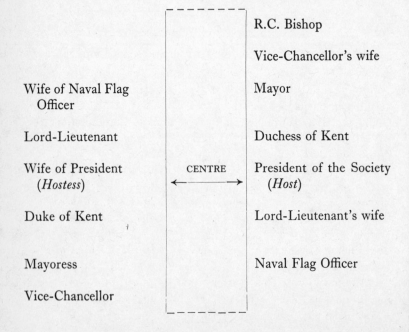

	R.C. Bishop
	Vice-Chancellor's wife
Wife of Naval Flag Officer	Mayor
Lord-Lieutenant	Duchess of Kent
Wife of President (*Hostess*)	← CENTRE →	President of the Society (*Host*)
Duke of Kent	Lord-Lieutenant's wife
Mayoress	Naval Flag Officer
Vice-Chancellor	

[1] See p. 330, note 1.

(f) *A function given by a Society*, as for (d), using only one side of the top table:

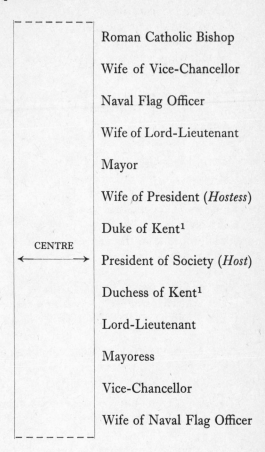

CENTRE

Roman Catholic Bishop

Wife of Vice-Chancellor

Naval Flag Officer

Wife of Lord-Lieutenant

Mayor

Wife of President (*Hostess*)

Duke of Kent[1]

President of Society (*Host*)

Duchess of Kent[1]

Lord-Lieutenant

Mayoress

Vice-Chancellor

Wife of Naval Flag Officer

GUESTS LISTS

Guests may be shown where they are placed at table in various ways:

(a) For a party not exceeding, say, 30, a seating plan may be displayed on a table or board.
(b) For a larger party, up to, say, 100, a numbered drawing of the table may be displayed with a list of the guests alongside it in alphabetical order, each with his seat number.

[1] See p. 330, note 1.

(c) For larger parties than (b), each guest should be provided with a printed table plan, with the names listed in alphabetical order, or with a table diagram with his seat ringed or arrowed.

The following rules are customarily observed: where an alternative is shown, this is at the host's discretion, subject to observing consistency throughout the list.

Any guest invited by virtue of office should be so indicated, e.g. Fenchurch, Sir William, K.B.E., President of the Society of . . .

Peers and Peeresses are shown by their exact rank in the peerage, e.g. Middlesex, The Earl of, K.B.E.; Flintshire, The Countess of, etc. The word 'The' is optional for Viscounts, Barons, their wives and widows. They must all be treated identically, except for peers by courtesy who do not have the prefix 'The' (see below). The prefix appropriate to the grade of peer may be shown if desired, viz:

His or Her Grace	Duke or Duchess
The Most Hon.	Marquess or Marchioness
The Right Hon.	Other Peers and Peeresses

Again, a decision has to be taken whether this prefix is to be used. If it is, all peers and peeresses, apart from those by courtesy (see below), should be treated similarly.

Peers and Peeresses by Courtesy, and former wives of Peers have no peerage prefix, i.e. neither 'The Right Hon.', etc., nor 'The'. (See p. 44.)

Courtesy Styles: those with the prefix 'Lord' or 'Lady' before their christian names do not have the prefix 'The'.

The Courtesy Style of 'The Hon.' is shown.

Privy Counsellors are given the prefix 'The Right Hon.', but not the suffix 'P.C.' (except for peers and peeresses, when these letters *are* shown) (see p. 80).

Baronets are shown with the suffix of 'Bt.' or 'Bart.'.

Honours, Decorations and Degrees, should be included; also the principal other awards, such as Fellowships of learned societies.

Male guests without title or rank should be styled as 'Mr.'. This is especially true when both husbands and wives are invited: the solecism of mixing the styles, e.g. John Brown, Esq., and Mrs. John Brown, must be avoided.

PLACE CARDS

These should be brief, honours, decorations, degrees, etc. being omitted. So too is the formal prefix for peers, who are shown as, e.g. 'The Earl of Blank' or 'Lord Blank', but 'The Right Hon.' is retained for Privy Counsellors who are not peers, and the suffixes R.N., Q.C. and M.P. for those so entitled.

Any office held should be omitted, except that important guests should be indicated by their office instead of their name, e.g. The Swiss Ambassador, The Lord Mayor, etc.

'The Hon.' is usually shown before the name at a public function, but omitted at a private party.

'Mr.' invariably takes the place of 'Esq.'

Other rules are as for *Guests Lists* (p. 333).

GRACE

Grace is usually said before a meal, and sometimes afterwards, in which case it precedes the Loyal Toast(s).

There is no Preamble to Grace. The Toastmaster announces only: 'Pray silence for Grace by your President', or 'by Canon John Jones', 'The Reverend John Jones', etc. (The description of his living, etc. should not be mentioned).

A Bishop may be asked to say Grace except that, if his Chaplain is present, it is customary for him to do so.

THE LOYAL TOASTS

The first and principal Loyal Toast, as approved by The Queen, is: 'The Queen'. It is incorrect to use such forms as: 'I give you the Loyal Toast of Her Majesty The Queen'. To obtain the necessary silence, the Toastmaster may say, without Preamble, e.g.: 'Pray silence for your President'.

The second Loyal Toast, which, if given, immediately follows the first, is likewise limited to: 'Queen Elizabeth The Queen Mother, The Prince Philip, Duke of Edinburgh, The Prince of Wales, and the other Members of the Royal Family'.

Guests do not smoke until after the Loyal Toast(s). The announcement 'Ladies and Gentlemen, you may now smoke' is superfluous unless The Queen or The Queen Mother be present, when it is necessary to announce: 'Ladies and Gentlemen, you have Her Majesty's permission to smoke'.

The Loyal Toast in Lancashire, Greater Manchester and Merseyside follows the traditional wording used in the old County of Lancaster. The Queen intimated on the reorganisation of the county boundaries in 1974 that she hoped that those who wished to do so would feel free to continue to give the Loyal Toast in the traditional form: 'The Queen, Duke of Lancaster' throughout the north west of England or at Lancastrian organisations elsewhere. In Jersey the toast of 'The Queen, our Duke' (i.e. Duke of Normandy) is local and unofficial, and used when only Islanders are present. This toast is not used in the other Channel Islands.

TABLE PLANS FOR PRIVATE FUNCTIONS

The host is customarily seated at one end of the table, the hostess at the other end. Alternatively, the host may be seated in the centre of one side of the table, and the hostess immediately opposite to him[1]. The latter follows the custom at Court and invariably on the Continent.

The principal male guest is placed on the right of the hostess, and his wife on the right of the host. The other seating is largely a matter for the hostess to decide according to the mutual interests of the guests. Strict order of precedence need not be observed, but should not be ignored. The latter is especially true of High Commissioners and Ambassadors whose diplomatic precedence must be respected, see under *Official Functions* (p. 328).

Speeches

THE PREAMBLE

It is impossible to give a list of those who should be mentioned in the Preamble of a speech, since this depends so much on those present at a particular function. In general, however, the list should be kept as short as possible, subject to avoiding any omission which would cause justifiable offence.

The speaker does not, of course, include himself in his preamble.

THE QUEEN AND QUEEN ELIZABETH THE QUEEN MOTHER

Should The Queen or Queen Elizabeth The Queen Mother be present, a Preamble begins: 'May it please Your Majesty'.

[1] Exceptionally, if the party number *eight*, the hostess may give up her place to the chief male guest: otherwise it is impracticable to preserve the rule of seating the sexes alternately. If a party numbers six or ten (i.e. in multiples of four in addition to the host and hostess), the table is easier to arrange, by alternately placing men and women, but today this custom is not too rigidly applied.

THE HOST

With the above exception, a Preamble begins with the host, who is referred to by his office, e.g.:

Mr. President
Mr. Chairman
Mr. Vice-Chancellor
Master
Mr. Prime Warden, etc.

PRESIDENT

If a Member of the Royal Family, he or she is referred to as: 'Your Royal Highness and President'.

If a non-Royal Duke or Duchess, as: 'Your Grace and President'.

If a peer other than a Duke, as: 'My Lord and President'. ('My Lord President' is incorrect, except for the Lord President of the Council).

If a lady, either titled or untitled, with the exception of a Member of the Royal Family or a Duchess, as: 'Madam President'.

If a gentleman below the rank of peer, as: 'Mr. President'.

VICE-PRESIDENT

When a Vice-President takes the Chair, he or she may be referred to as 'Mr. Vice-President' or, 'Madam Vice-President' (with the relevant prefix mentioned under *President*), but he or she is more usually referred to as 'Mr. Chairman', or 'Madam Chairman'.

CHAIRMAN

A Chairman is called 'Mr. Chairman', or 'Madam Chairman', irrespective of his or her rank, with the exception of a Member of the Royal Family, who is referred to as 'Your Royal Highness'. A peer should *not* be called 'My Lord Chairman'.

If a Vice-Chairman, Managing Director, or other officer of the organization takes the Chair, he or she is still referred to as 'Mr. Chairman' or 'Madam Chairman', i.e. the use of these expressions is not restricted to the actual Chairman of the organization.

OTHER IMPORTANT GUESTS

The following list gives the form in which various persons should be included in a Preamble, in order of precedence, after those already mentioned above:

Your Royal Highness

My Lord Mayor (My Lord Provost, Mr. Mayor, Provost, etc.) (see *Note 1* below).

Mr. Recorder (outside London)

Mr. Chairman of the Greater London Council (within Greater London), or,

Mr. Chairman of the . . . County Council (outside Greater London)

My Lord Chancellor

Prime Minister (or more formally 'Mr. Prime Minister') (see *Note 2*).

Your Excellency(ies) (see *Note 3*).

Your Grace(s) (see *Note 4*)

My Lord(s) (see *Note 5*)

Ladies and Gentlemen (see *Note 6*)

Note 1.—This applies only to the Civic Head of the City, Borough etc. in which the function takes place. If desired to mention a Civic Head from elsewhere who is present, this should be done after 'My Lords'. More than one Lord Mayor (or Lord Provost) may be covered either by 'My Lord Mayors' (or 'My Lord Provosts'), or by naming each (e.g. 'My Lord Mayor of York, My Lord Mayor of Plymouth, My Lord Provost of Aberdeen'). There is no plural for 'Mr. Mayor': the form 'Your Worships' should be used although 'Your Worship' is archaic.

Note 2.—Also:

My Lord President (i.e. of the Privy Council)

My Lord Privy Seal

Mr. Chancellor (of the Exchequer or of the Duchy of Lancaster)

Minister(s) (more formally Mr. Minister). (This covers a Secretary of State. The terms 'Mr. Secretary of State' and 'Mr. Secretary' are archaic. Other Ministers are not mentioned in a Preamble when the Prime Minister attends a function.)

Note 3.—High Commissioners and Ambassadors.

Note 4.—This covers Dukes and Duchesses. Should the Archbishop of Canterbury be present, 'Your Grace' (or 'Your Graces' if a Duke or Duchess is also attending) should be mentioned before 'My Lord Chancellor'. Similarly, the Archbishop of York is covered by including 'Your Grace' immediately after 'My Lord Chancellor', i.e. both Archbishops rank before 'Your Excellencies'.

Note 5.—For peers, other than Dukes, peers by courtesy, for diocesan Bishops by right, and for other Bishops by courtesy. In the absence of any peers, the form 'My Lord Bishops' may be used.

Note 6.—When as sometimes happens only one lady is present the form should be 'Lady (My Lady if titled), and Gentlemen', or 'Mrs. (Lady) Blank, Gentlemen': *never* 'Madam and Gentlemen'.

GENERAL NOTES

Roman Catholic Archbishops and Bishops

A Cardinal Archbishop may be included in the form 'Your Eminence', placed by courtesy after 'Your Graces'. Other Archbishops and Bishops are by courtesy mentioned in the same way as those of the Anglican Church.

Clergy

Clergy, other than Archbishops and Bishops, should not be included.[1] In particular the forms, 'Reverend Sir' and 'Reverend Father' are archaic.

Guest of Honour

When the guest of honour is not covered by one of the above terms, he is included in the Preamble by his office, e.g. 'Mr. President', 'Mr. Chairman', etc. immediately before 'Ladies and Gentlemen'. This specific mention also applies when a President, Vice-Chancellor, etc. is providing the building in which the function takes place.

Aldermen and Sheriffs

Within the City of London it is customary to refer to these as 'Mr. Alderman' or 'Aldermen', and 'Mr. Sheriff' or 'Sheriffs' immediately before 'Ladies and Gentlemen'. Elsewhere, Councillors' may be included at civic functions immediately before 'Ladies and Gentlemen'.

The Ending

A speaker proposing a toast should make this clear at the end of his speech in some such form as, 'I give you the toast of . . .', or, 'I ask you to rise and drink to the toast of your . . .'. This obviates any need for the Toastmaster to say, 'The Toast is . . .'.

---

[1] Exceptionally 'Mr. Dean', 'Mr. Provost', or 'Archdeacon' may be included.

Toastmaster

The Toastmaster should be given the form in which he is to make all announcements in writing, and not left to devise his own often exaggerated forms.

For the first speaker the announcement should have a Preamble, as for his speech, followed by, 'Pray silence for . . .'. For subsequent announcements the Preamble should be omitted.

A speaker is announced by his name, followed by his office where applicable, e.g. 'The Right Honourable John Smith, Her Majesty's Secretary of State for . . .'. Suffixes such as 'Companion of the Distinguished Service Order', 'One of Her Majesty's Justices of the Peace', etc. should *not* be used.

Part VI

AMERICAN USAGE

AMERICAN USAGE

Within the United States British custom is usually followed, but there are several important differences.

The Title of Honorable
The title of Honorable is used officially by the following when they are addressed by name:

American Ambassadors

American Ministers (including those with personal rank)

American Representatives on International Organizations

Deputy and Assistant Heads of Independent Government Agencies

Assistant Secretaries of Executive Departments and Officers of comparable rank

Assistants and Special Assistants to the President[1]

Boards, Members of equal rank

Cabinet Officers

Clerk of United States House of Representatives

Commissioners

The Commissioner of the District of Columbia[2]

Counsellor of the Department of State

Foreign Ministers

Governors of States and Territories

Heads of major organizations within the Federal Agencies, i.e. The Federal Bureau of Investigation, Immigration and Naturalization Service, etc.

Heads of International Organizations (unless entitled to His Excellency, by reason of a position previously held), Alternates, Deputies and Assistant Heads

---

[1] Titles of Presidential Assistants vary with each Administration, 'The Honorable' is given usually to the ranking Presidential advisers and assistants.
[2] Popularly known as 'Mayor'.

High officers of State Governments

Judges (Justices of the Supreme Court excepted)

Legal Adviser and officers of comparable rank

Mayors of Cities

Ministers Resident

President of the United States (if addressed by name)

Press Secretary to The President

Public Printer

Secretary of United States Senate

Senators

Sergeant at Arms of United States Senate and House of Representatives

State Cabinet and Legislative officials

Under Secretaries and Officers of comparable rank of Executive Departments

United States Representatives, Alternates and Deputies of International Organizations and organs of such organizations

Vice-President (if addressed by name)

'The Honorable' appears on the first line of the envelope, above the christian and surname on the second line, and a little to the left. The title is not used in conjunction with the prefix of Mr., Mrs., Miss, Dr., a rank in the Services or an academic degree, e.g. The Honorable John Smith, The Honorable Mary Smith. More informally it may be abbreviated to 'The Hon.' or 'Hon.' before the name.

Normally the title is continued for life. Consuls, but not Honorary Consuls, are given the courtesy title of 'Honorable' in official correspondence if they do not qualify from a previous appointment.

The word 'Honorable' is not used in issuing or answering invitations.

The Title of His/Her Excellency

Though this title is not officially used by the Department of State it is the usual form of address for Roman Catholic Archbishops and Bishops, and is often the *social* form for State Governors and American Ambassadors. Foreign Presidents, Ambassadors and others officially and socially bear this style.

It is the usual practice to write 'His/Her Excellency' in full on the line above the name and a little to the left. More informally it may be abbreviated to 'H.E.' before the name.

His/Her Excellency is not used when issuing or answering invitations.

Order of Precedence

There is no officially established list of Order of Precedence in the United States. Unofficially, however, there has been one since 1776. The question of who outranks whom has always been important to Americans, as it is to other nationalities. The people who are at the top of the Protocol List in the United States are the leading politicians. The rules of protocol are considered of great importance and every detail of protocol is followed carefully.

For purposes of protocol the wives of officials have the rank of their husbands at all times. American men, whose wives have political posts, are in the same position. Widows of men who had political posts have no rank, but it is usual for them to be considered as they were during their husband's lifetime at all official receptions, especially at the White House. Widows of Presidents and Vice-Presidents have always had a definite position.

No surnames are used when one speaks to an official: only the title is used. This is not the case when one addresses an Associate Justice of the Supreme Court as there are several men who hold this position. It is correct to address all of these gentlemen, after one is engaged in conversation, by 'Sir'.

UNOFFICIAL TABLE OF PRECEDENCE

The President of the United States
The Vice-President of the United States
The Speaker of the House of Representatives
The Chief Justice of the United States
Former Presidents of the United States
The Secretary of State
The Secretary General of the United Nations
Ambassadors of Foreign Powers
Widows of Former Presidents of the United States
Ministers of Foreign Powers (Chiefs of Diplomatic Missions)
Associate Justices of the Supreme Court of the United States
The Cabinet
    The Secretary of the Treasury
    The Secretary of Defense
    The Attorney General
    The Secretary of the Interior

The Secretary of Agriculture
The Secretary of Commerce
The Secretary of Labor
The Secretary of Health, Education and Welfare
The Secretary of Housing and Urban Development
The Secretary of Transportation
Director, Office of Management and Budget
The United States Representative to the United Nations
Members of the Senate
Governors of States
Former Vice-Presidents of the United States
Members of the House of Representatives
Chargés d'Affaires of Foreign Powers
The Under Secretaries of the Executive Departments and the Deputy
Administrator, Agency of International Development
Director, United States Arms Control and Disarmament Agency
Secretaries of the Army, the Navy, and the Air Force
Chairman, Council of Economic Advisers
Chairman, Council on Environment Quality
Chairman, Joint Chiefs of Staff
Chiefs of Staff of the Army, the Navy, and the Air Force (ranked according to date of appointment)
Commandant of the Marine Corps
(5 Star) Generals of the Army and Fleet Admirals
The Secretary General, Organization of American States
Representatives to the Organization of American States
Director of Central Intelligence
Administrator, General Services Administration
Director, United States Information Agency
Administrator, National Aeronautics and Space Administration
Chairman, Civil Service Commission
Chairman, Atomic Energy Commission
Director, Defense Research and Engineering
Director, Office of Emergency Preparedness
Director of ACTION
Director, Office of Science and Technology
Director, Office of Economic Opportunity
Director, Office of Telecommunications Policy
Administrator, Environmental Protection Agency

Assistants to the President
Deputy Under Secretaries of State
Commandant of the Coast Guard
Assistant Secretaries of the Executive Departments
Chief of Protocol of the United States
Members of the Council of Economic Advisers
Active or Designate United States Ambassadors and Ministers (Career rank, when in the United States)
Under Secretaries of the Army, the Navy and the Air Force
(4 Star) Generals and Admirals
Assistant Secretaries of the Army, the Navy, and the Air Force
(3 Star) Lieutenant Generals and Vice Admirals
Former United States Ambassadors and Ministers to Foreign Countries
Ministers of Foreign Powers (Serving in Embassies, not accredited)
Deputy Assistant Secretaries of the Executive Departments
Deputy Chief of Protocol
Counsellors of Embassies or Legations of Foreign Powers
(2 Star) Major Generals and Rear Admirals
(1 Star) Brigadier Generals and Commodores
Assistant Chiefs of Protocol

THE EXECUTIVE DEPARTMENTS OF THE UNITED STATES

In order of precedence they are:
The Department of State
The Department of the Treasury
The Department of Defense
The Department of Justice
The Department of the Interior
The Department of Agriculture
The Department of Commerce
The Department of Labor
The Department of Health, Education and Welfare
The Department of Housing and Urban Development
The Department of Transportation

The President of the United States

BEGINNING OF LETTER
My Dear Mr. President

ENDING OF LETTER

Social	Respectfully yours *or* Sincerely yours
Business	I have the honor to remain, Most respectfully yours

ENVELOPE

The President

VERBAL ADDRESS

Mr. President. In conversation he may subsequently be called Sir

JOINT FORM OF ADDRESS

The President and Mrs. Washington

The Wife of the President

The First Lady is addressed, verbally and in writing as to any other married woman, Mrs. Washington.

When one has attended a dinner or other function at the White House, one writes a 'thank you' letter to the First Lady.

Vice-President of the United States

BEGINNING OF LETTER

My dear Mr. Vice-President

ENDING OF LETTER

Social	Sincerely yours
Business	Very truly yours *or* Respectfully yours

ENVELOPE

The Vice-President

VERBAL ADDRESS

Mr. Vice-President

JOINT FORM OF ADDRESS

The Vice-President and Mrs. Rockefeller

The Speaker of the House of Representatives

BEGINNING OF LETTER

My dear Mr. Speaker

ENDING OF LETTER

Social	Sincerely yours
Business	Very truly yours

ENVELOPE

The Honorable
(full name)
The Speaker of the House of Representatives

VERBAL ADDRESS

Mr. Speaker, or by name

JOINT FORM OF ADDRESS

The Speaker
and Mrs. (surname)

The Chief Justice of the United States

BEGINNING OF LETTER

My dear Mr. Chief Justice

ENDING OF LETTER

Social	Sincerely yours
Business	Very truly yours

ENVELOPE

The Chief Justice

VERBAL ADDRESS

Mr. Chief Justice, or by name

JOINT FORM OF ADDRESS

The Chief Justice
and Mrs. (surname)

Ambassadors of the United States

The official form of address is 'The Honorable', unlike Foreign Ambassadors, who are always accorded 'His Excellency'. See *Foreign Ambassadors in Washington*, p. 350. The term 'Honorable' continues to be used away from his/her Embassy, and in retirement, when the term 'Ambassador' is also continued. Socially, however, American Ambassadors are styled 'His/Her Excellency'.

Officially an Ambassador is termed of 'the United States', and similarly with an Embassy, but informally 'The American Ambassador' and 'American Embassy' are often used.

American Ambassadors accredited to countries in Central and South America are never referred to as 'the American Ambassador' but as 'the Ambassador of the United States'.

Wives of Ambassadors are not accorded any special style.

BEGINNING OF LETTER

My dear Mr. Ambassador/My dear Madam Ambassador
If an Ambassador has a rank in the Armed Forces in addition, then as above *or* My dear General Smith. The two styles are never used together.

ENDING OF LETTER

Social	Sincerely yours
Business	Very truly yours

ENVELOPE

Official
> The Honorable
> John Brown
> Ambassador of the United States[1] *or* the American
>   Ambassador
> Embassy of the United States[1] *or* American Embassy

If away from the country to which he is accredited
> The Honorable
> John Brown

Social
> His Excellency
> the American Ambassador *or* the United States Ambassador[1]

[1] Invariably used in Central and South America.

VERBAL ADDRESS
Official	Mr./Madam Ambassador or by name
Social	Your Excellency or Mr./Madam Ambassador

JOINT FORM OF ADDRESS
> The Ambassador of the United States
> and Mrs. Blank

or less formally

> The Honorable and Mrs. Henry Blank (away from the country to which he is accredited).

A lady Ambassador, with her husband, is addressed just 'The American Ambassador and Mr. Armstrong.'

Foreign Ambassadors in Washington

Foreign Ambassadors in Washington are ranked according to the time they have spent in Washington without interruption.

BEGINNING OF LETTER
> Your Excellency

ENDING OF LETTER
Social	Sincerely yours
Business	Very truly yours

ENVELOPE
> His Excellency
> Full name
> The Ambassador of (country)

If the Ambassador is titled in his own right, he would be referred to as 'His Excellency The Duke of . . .'.

VERBAL ADDRESS
> Your Excellency *or*, Mr. Ambassador, *or* by name

JOINT FORM OF ADDRESS
> His Excellency
> The Ambassador of (country)
> and Mrs. (surname)

The Associate Justices of the Supreme Court

BEGINNING OF LETTER
> My dear Mr. Justice Frankfurter

ENDING OF LETTER

Social	Sincerely yours
Business	Very truly yours

ENVELOPE

Mr. Justice Frankfurter

VERBAL ADDRESS

Mr. Justice Frankfurter

JOINT FORM OF ADDRESS

Mr. Justice Frankfurter
and Mrs. Frankfurter

The Cabinet of the United States

BEGINNING OF LETTER

My dear Mr. Secretary/Madam Secretary

ENDING OF LETTER

Social	Sincerely yours
Business	Very truly yours

ENVELOPE

The Honorable
Jeremy Smith
The Secretary of State

VERBAL ADDRESS

Mr. Secretary/Madam Secretary
The only exception is the Attorney General whom one addresses
as 'Mr. Attorney General'.

JOINT FORM OF ADDRESS

The Honorable
The Secretary of State
and Mrs. Smith
If the Member of the Cabinet is a woman
The Honorable
The Secretary of State
and Mr. Smith
In speaking to a Member of the Cabinet, one never uses his or
her surname.

The Wife of a Cabinet Minister

When one writes to, speaks or begins a letter to the wife of a Cabinet Minister, one uses the same form as any married woman in America, i.e. Mrs. Smith.

Members of the Senate

When several Senators are at the same function the Senator who has served the longest period in the United States Senate takes precedence.

A Senator does not use this appointment on issuing invitations, nor on visiting cards, but the name of the State represented is engraved in the lower right hand side of the card.

A Senator's wife is addressed as Mrs. Doolittle.

BEGINNING OF LETTER

My dear Senator Doolittle

ENDING OF LETTER

Social	Sincerely yours
Business	Very truly yours

ENVELOPE

The Honorable
   James Doolittle
   United States Senate
The Honorable
   Jane Smith
   United States Senate

VERBAL ADDRESS

Senator *or*
Senator Doolittle

JOINT FORM OF ADDRESS

The Honorable
   James Doolittle
   and Mrs. Doolittle
If the Senator is a woman
   Mr. John Smith
   and the Honorable Jane Smith[1]

---

[1] Only when the wife holds office, in very senior appointments, such as an Ambassador, Member of the Cabinet, or Governor, does her *appointment* precede her husband's names. This also applies to announcing guests at a function.

Governors of States

The position of a Governor is very important. No one except the President or the Vice-President of the United States ranks higher than the Governor in his own state. However, when away from his home State, the Governor ranks below a Senator.

The order of precedence of Governors depends on the date that the State in question entered into the Union. For example, the Governor of Delaware (Delaware was admitted December 7th, 1787) takes precedence over all other Governors.

The Governor is officially designated the Honorable, but in many States he is known as 'His Excellency the Governor.'

BEGINNING OF LETTER

My dear Governor Patterson

ENDING OF LETTER

Social   Sincerely yours
Business   Very truly yours

ENVELOPE

The Honorable
James Patterson
Governor of Georgia
or

Social   His Excellency the Governor of Georgia
(inside his State, His Excellency the
Governor)

VERBAL ADDRESS

Governor *or*
Governor Patterson

JOINT FORM OF ADDRESS

The Governor
and Mrs. Hardie
or

Social   His Excellency the Governor (of New
York)
and Mrs. Hardie

Members of the House of Representatives

BEGINNING OF LETTER
>   My dear Mr. House

ENDING OF LETTER

Social	Sincerely yours
Business	Very truly yours

ENVELOPE
>   The Honorable
>   Richard L. House
>   United States House of Representatives

VERBAL ADDRESS
>   Mr. House

JOINT FORM OF ADDRESS
>   The Honorable
>   Richard L. House
>   and Mrs. House
> If the Representative is a woman
>   Mr. John Smith
>   and the Honorable Jane Smith[1]

Under Secretaries and Assistant Secretaries of the Executive Department, and Holders of other Government Offices

For those with lengthy titles of office, such as an Under Secretary of State, the name of the holder is used in preference to the office.

BEGINNING OF LETTER
>   My dear Mr. Richards

ENDING OF LETTER

Social	Sincerely yours
Business	Very truly yours

[1] See p. 353, note 1.

ENVELOPE

    The Honorable John Richards
        Under Secretary of State
to home   The Honorable John Richards

VERBAL ADDRESS

    Mr. Under Secretary, or by name

JOINT FORM OF ADDRESS

    The Honorable and Mrs. John Richards
If the wife holds office
    Mr. John Richards
    and the Honorable Jane Richards

Mayor

BEGINNING OF LETTER

    Dear Mayor Smith *or*
    Sir *or*
    Dear Mr. Mayor

ENDING OF LETTER

Social   Sincerely yours
Business   Very truly yours

ENVELOPE

    The Honorable[1]
    John Smith,
    City Hall

VERBAL ADDRESS

    Mayor Smith *or*
    Your Honor

The Armed Forces

The Under Secretaries, as well as the Assistant Secretaries of the Army, the Navy and the Marine Corps, rank under the Under Secretaries and Assistant Secretaries of the Executive Departments.

    The Chairman of the Joint Chiefs of Staff ranks above the

[1] A Mayor is described by courtesy as 'The Honorable' if not officially entitled to the prefix.

Chief of Staff of the Air Force, the Chief of Staff of the Army and the Chief of Naval Operations. The last three are of equal rank.

In the United States, the Air Force and the Marine Corps have identical commissioned ranks as in the Army. All ranks are preferably written in full on the envelope.

After the name it is permissible to abbreviate the Service— U.S.N. (United States Navy), U.S.A. (United States Army), U.S.A.F. (United States Air Force), U.S.M.C. (United States Marine Corps). For Reserve officers the applicable abbreviations are, U.S.N.R. (United States Naval Reserve), A.U.S. (Army of the United States), A.F.U.S. (Air Force United States) and U.S.M.C.R. (United States Marine Corps Reserve).

It is incorrect to write to officers by their rank without their name, such as Dear Colonel. Verbally, a General, Lieutenant General, Major General and Brigadier General are all called General. Similarly an Admiral, Vice Admiral and Rear Admiral are all called Admiral. This is the same as the British practice. They are addressed socially as General Robert Brown or Admiral John Smith, and this is the invariable practice in a joint communication with their wives.

Unlike in Britain, junior Naval and Marine officers, viz. Lieutenant Commanders and Lieutenants, are written to as 'Dear Mr. Smith', although the exact rank is shown on the envelope.

On introduction a junior officer is referred to by his exact rank, and thereafter, as 'Mr. . . .'.

First and Second Lieutenants in the Army and Air Force are addressed as 'Mr.', but by modern usage they are often addressed as Lieutenant, both in the commencement of a letter (Dear Lieutenant Smith) and on the envelope (Lieutenant John Smith, A.U.S.).

Chaplains, unlike British practice, are known by their Forces rank, and are so introduced, but subsequently referred to as Chaplain Smith or Father Smith. Correspondence is addressed as follows:

Chaplain John Smith,
Captain U.S.N.

Officers of the Medical and Dental Corps are known as Doctor Brown.

Warrant Officers, Midshipmen and Petty Officers are called Mr.

Sergeants, Corporals and Privates are written as such.

See also pp. 366–367.

Women

Married women adopt their husband's christian names, as in Britain, e.g. Mrs. John Henry Smith. A divorced woman takes her maiden surname before her surname, e.g. Mrs. Howard Edwards, but a letter to her begins 'Dear Mrs. Edwards', and she is introduced as such. An unmarried woman is addressed and referred to as 'Miss Mary Jones', unless she is the senior unmarried woman of the family, when she is addressed on the envelope as 'Miss Jones,' as in Britain.

Mr.

This is the generally accepted prefix in the United States.

Esquire

The word Esquire, usually contracted to Esq., as in Britain, is customarily used in social correspondence especially in the eastern part of the United States, but not in business circles. In the Department of State, the term is reserved for Foreign Service Officers serving abroad, and is not abbreviated.

Professor

Those with a Doctor's degree are generally known as 'Dr. . . .', otherwise as 'Mr . . .' The term 'Professor' is regarded by some as old fashioned.

Doctor of Medicine

Although he is referred to as 'Doctor' verbally and at the beginning of a letter, he is addressed on the envelope, 'John K. Smith, M.D.'.

The use of Numerals, Senior, and Junior after a Name

This practice for important families is widespread in the United States. When a father, who was not previously known as Junior (Jr.) or by a numeral, has a son who is given the same christian name, the son is called Jr. The father may be referred to as Sr. after his name (e.g. Mr. John Howard Sr. and Mr. John Howard Jr.), but some consider that in the best American usage, 'Sr.', is not used by a man, who would continue to be known as Mr. John Howard. His widow might then add 'Sr.' to distinguish her from her daughter-in-law.

When the first John Howard dies, his son drops his Jr. (after a limited time to prevent confusion), unless he decides to retain it out of courtesy to his father's widow. If John Howard Jr. has a son named John who was born during the first John Howard's lifetime, he is known as John Howard III.

Hereafter the usage is optional. If John III has a son born during the lifetime of the first two Johns, the child would be known as John IV. Upon the death of John Sr., leaving behind both a Jr. and a III, the Jr. might become known as Sr., but the III would not normally use Jr. It is common for the III to retain his numeral until his parents' and grandparents' deaths, after which time he would drop his numeral. John IV then has the option of deciding whether to continue with his numeral or to be known as John Jr.

A few families maintain their numerals for several generations with impressive results. There is a John Bishop VI, and until recently there was a Henry Peter Borie VIII, who retained that style until his father the VII decided to become Sr. instead, when the VIII reverted to the style of Henry Peter Borie Jr.

As explained above, the usage of II is not adopted by the Sr.'s son (Jr.), but refers to some other relative of the same christian and surname, often a grandson or nephew, not necessarily in direct succession. Henry Ford's grandson is Henry Ford II, the intervening generation not having the same christian name. Since the numerals and Sr./Jr. for distinguishing purposes do not form part of the name, they tend to be dropped after a period of time when no confusion would result. However, usage varies according to the family concerned.

Letters are addressed to:

Mr. John D. Brown III (Mrs. John D. Brown III)
Mr. John D. Brown, Jr. (Mrs. John D. Brown, Jr.)

Visiting Cards

In the United States of America visiting cards are always engraved and until recent years it was not considered correct to use initials, but it is now normal to do so. The residence appears in the lower right hand corner.

It is possible to use a personal card for business, but not the reverse.

Mr. and Mrs., etc., always precede the name.

Formal Invitations

Mr. and Mrs. Josiah Z. Battle

request the pleasure of the company of

Mr. and Mrs. Falconer

at a reception

Thursday, July fourth
Six to nine o'clock

R.s.v.p.   *The Rocks, Easthampton*

On this type of invitation, the name of the guest is always written in, but the rest of the card is engraved. Invitations must never be printed.

Engraved invitations, which may contain a coat of arms or crest embossed without colour if the hosts are entitled to them, are usually about 4 in. × $5\frac{1}{2}$ in., but often about $5\frac{1}{2}$ in. × 7 in. and are placed unfolded in an envelope.

If there is more than one host and hostess, their names are placed in alphabetical order.

If the invitation is to a very large function such as one given by the President of a Society, the guest's name is omitted. The wording then reads 'request the pleasure of your company at a reception in honour of The Secretary General of . . .' ('Honour' is spelt in the English way).

It is usual to put 'The favour of a reply is requested', but R.S.V.P. and R.s.v.p. are more often employed.

Answering Formal Invitations

Mr. and Mrs. David Falconer
accept with pleasure
the kind invitation of
Mr. and Mrs. Battle
to a reception
Thursday, July fourth
six to nine o'clock
The Rocks, Easthampton

If they are unable to accept the invitation, they would reply

> Mr. and Mrs. David Falconer
> regret that they are unable to accept
> the kind invitation, etc.
> because of illness/absence.

Illness and absence from the locality are the two most usual and acceptable reasons.

Informal Invitations

A visiting card is often used for an informal invitation, but it is more usual today to have a larger card which would measure $5\frac{1}{2}$ in $\times 4\frac{1}{2}$ in.

> Mr. and Mrs. John Henry Form
> request the pleasure of the company of
> Mr. and Mrs. Brown
> at dinner
> on Thurs. July 4th
> at 8.00 p.m.
>
> *R.S.V.P.*   16 *Richmond Hill*

The name of the host or hostess may be written or engraved. Very often a card $4\frac{1}{2}$ in. $\times 3\frac{1}{4}$ in., with the details underlined in the above example, are engraved.

If invited to meet a special guest, a line 'in honour of Mr. and Mrs. Howard' may be added after the type of function. ('Honour' is spelt in the English way.)

Guests' names may be omitted on an invitation to an informal dance, when the wording is 'request the pleasure of your company at a small dance', etc.

This form is especially popular for drink parties. The word 'cocktails' and the date are written below the host's name.

Answering Informal Invitations

One may answer an informal invitation as for a formal invitation, but it has become the custom in recent years to answer an informal invitation with a short handwritten letter to the host or hostess. If the wording is to 'a small dance', the word 'small' is omitted in the reply, or the function not mentioned.

Verbal Invitations

These are always in the name of the hostess, and are often made by telephone. If no reply from a guest has been received, a reminder card is often sent. More often than not this is a visiting card. At the top left hand corner is written 'To remind'. Above .is added 'Dinner, Monday, June 4th' and below the name, 'at eight o'clock' and the address.

Reminder Cards

Formal engraved reminder cards are occasionally sent, when no answer has been received by the hostess. They are as follows:

> *To remind*
> *Mr. and Mrs. Dawson*
> *of dinner*
> *with Mr. and Mrs. John Eden*
> *on Wednesday, the tenth of May*
> *at . . . .*

Formal Invitations on 'At Home' Cards

They are not much used today, being restricted to a very formal evening reception, dance, or a debutante reception in a private house or club. The only function in the afternoon where an 'At Home' card may be used is for a debutante reception.

> *Mr. and Mrs. William Russell*
>
> *At Home*
> *Wednesday, the third of January*
>
> *at ten o'clock*
>
> *Four Albemarle Avenue*
>
> *The favour of a reply is requested*   *[Dancing]*

Wedding Invitations

All wedding invitations must be engraved, usually on a thick cream paper. If the host is entitled to a coat of arms, the full coat of arms, without colour, rather than only the crest, is sometimes embossed at the top of the invitation.

There is a general rule that all wedding invitations are sent out in two envelopes.

The outer envelope is addressed with the full name of the guests, e.g. 'Mr. and Mrs. John Stuart Godfrey'. The inner envelope is addressed 'Mr. and Mrs. Godfrey' with no address. The inside envelope must face the back of the outside envelope. It is usual to leave the tissue paper on the invitation when posting. The inner envelope is not sealed.

The invitations should be posted 20–30 days before the wedding. One addresses an envelope for a wedding to husband and wife, but each child in the family must receive a separate invitation.

The phrase 'honour of your presence' is always used for a religious ceremony, with 'honour' spelt in the English way. 'The pleasure of your company' is always used for a wedding reception.

Guests are often invited to a wedding ceremony, but not to the reception. Others are invited to the reception only. Consequently there are four types of invitation, worded as below.

1. A single invitation to both the church and the reception. This is also adopted if the wedding takes place at a house, when all the wedding guests automatically continue to the reception (see Invitations to a House Wedding, p. 365).

2. Two invitations, which are prepared when more guests are invited to the wedding than the reception. A full size wedding invitation, and with it a smaller card to the reception, usually a stiff card about 4 in. × 3 in., engraved like the wedding invitation.

3. An invitation to the reception only. A large card, which is engraved as for a wedding invitation, but with the words 'request the pleasure of your company', in place of 'the honour of your presence', and 'at the wedding reception of their daughter' in place of 'at the marriage of their daughter'.

4. Two invitations, when more are invited to the reception than the church. The large card is identical to Example 3, and a smaller enclosed card inviting the guests to the

church. This has the same appearance as the smaller card in Example 2 below.

Numbers are usually spelt out unless they are lengthy. R.s.v.p. is sometimes worded 'the favour of a reply is requested', or 'the favour of an answer is requested'. Smaller cards never contain a coat of arms or crest.

Example 1

Mr. and Mrs. John Washington Selden

request the honour of your presence
at the marriage of their daughter

Mary Louise
to
Mr. Henry Black Campbell

On Tuesday, the fifteenth of September
at half after four o'clock
at Saint Andrew's Church
and afterwards at
1200 East Nineteenth Street Baltimore

R.s.v.p.

Example 2

The large card as in Example 1, but with details of the reception omitted. The smaller card is as follows:

Mr. and Mrs. John Washington Selden
requests the pleasure of your company
on Tuesday, the fifteenth of September
at half after five o'clock
1200 East Nineteenth Street Baltimore

R.s.v.p.

Example 3

Mr. *and* Mrs. *John Washington Selden*
request the pleasure of your company
at the wedding reception of their daughter
Mary Louise
and
Mr. *Henry Black Campbell*
on Tuesday, the fifteenth of September
at half after four o'clock
Forty Lakeside Avenue Fort Worth

R.s.v.p.

Example 4

The large card is as Example 3. The smaller enclosed card about 4 in. × 3 in., inviting guests to the church, reads:

Mr. *and* Mrs. *John Washington Selden*
requests the honour of your presence
at the marriage ceremony
at half after four o'clock
Saint Andrew's Church
1200, *East nineteenth Street Baltimore*

INVITATIONS TO A HOUSE WEDDING

These invitations are similar to those to a church wedding, except that the address of the house takes the place of the church. If the wedding takes place at a house other than the hosts', the wording is 'at the house of Mr. and Mrs. Warren, Campville, Albany'. As guests automatically come to the reception, they receive an invitation as in Example 1, amended as above.

CARDS OF ADMITTANCE TO THE CHURCH AND PEW

If a wedding is a very large one, admittance cards to the church are occasionally enclosed with invitations. They are of the same colour and finish as the invitation, and are about $3\frac{1}{2}$ in. $\times$ $2\frac{1}{2}$ in. but never include a crest or coat of arms. The form adopted is:

Please present this card

at St. Andrew's Church

on Tuesday, the fifteenth of September

If guests are to be admitted to special pews, 'Pew No. . . .' is engraved in the lower left hand corner. The pew number is added by hand. For smaller weddings, 'Pew No. 6' is written in the top left hand corner of a visiting card. Guests should bring the card of admittance and pew card to the church.

TRAIN AND AIRPLANE CARDS

If a wedding takes place in the country, an extra card showing travel times and arrangements for guests is sometimes enclosed in the envelope with the invitation. This gives the times of departure from the city and arrival, and similar information for the return journey.

If a special train or airplane has been arranged, the wording should include the above information and other instructions, such as 'please present this card to the conductor/steward', or 'please show this card at the gate'. In this case, the guest does not need a ticket.

AT HOME CARDS

Sometimes a card showing the future address for the bride and bridegroom is enclosed with the invitation. This may be either the same size as the visiting card or slightly larger, and is engraved as follows:

Mr. and Mrs. John Henry Adams

After December 15th

5000 Lakeside Avenue

Palm Springs

WEDDINGS OF OFFICERS IN THE ARMED FORCES

When a serving Officer, or an Officer on active duty in the Reserve, appears on a wedding invitation, the line following his name is

engraved in a smaller type than that of the rest of the invitation.
E.g., if he is in the Regular Army he is shown as:

John Henry Smith
Lieutenant, United States Army
or
Lieutenant John Henry Smith
United States Army

The respective arms, such as Signal Corps, may be added, but
in the Infantry, the Regiment is not specified, merely 'Infantry'.

If a Reserve Officer on active duty, the phrase 'Army of the
United States' takes the place of 'United States Army'. Similarly
in the Navy, 'United States Naval Reserve' is substituted for
'United States Navy'.

Officers of the United States Air Force follow the Army rules.
The Marine Corps follows rules for the Navy, i.e. United States
Marine Corps or United States Marine Corps Reserve.

No abbreviations for rank or Service are used. If the bride's
father is an Army or Naval Officer *the form is* Colonel and Mrs.
John D. Herbert *or* Lieutenant Commander and Mrs. John D.
Herbert.

REPLIES TO WEDDING INVITATIONS

An engraved invitation to a church only does not require an
answer. Otherwise the wording of a reply follows the invitation.
An alternative reply is as follows:—

Mr. and Mrs. Henry Wilson Stone
accept with pleasure
the kind invitation
of Mr. and Mrs. Kingdom
for
Monday the fifteenth of June
at half after four o'clock

For non-acceptance it is unnecessary to include the time of the
ceremony and the address of the church.

Place Cards

At a public banquet names on the place cards are written in full, e.g. for the President of the United States 'The President', 'HE the French Ambassador', 'The Speaker', 'Mrs. Jones'. At a semi-formal dinner, place cards, which may have an embossed crest, are hand-written, either in first names, nicknames, or surnames. The cards are laid on the top of the napkin.

Part VII

USAGE IN OTHER FOREIGN
COUNTRIES

USAGE IN OTHER FOREIGN COUNTRIES

Foreign Sovereigns Still Regnant

European.—Belgium (Kingdom), Denmark (Kingdom), The Holy See or Vatican (The Pope), Liechtenstein (Principality), Luxembourg (Grand Duchy), Monaco (Principality), Netherlands (Kingdom), Norway (Kingdom), Spain (Kingdom), Sweden (Kingdom).

It is important to use the correct official designation, e.g. The King of the Belgians (*not* of Belgium), and The Queen of the Netherlands (*not* of Holland).

Others.—Iran and Japan (Empires), Afghanistan, Bhutan, Jordan, Morocco, Nepal, Saudi Arabia and Thailand (Kingdoms). There are also other rulers bearing various designations. The Sultan of Oman is styled His Majesty, and the Amirs of Bahrain, Kuwait, and Qatar, His Highness.

The United Arab Emirates, which was formed by the union of Abu Dhabi, Ajman, Dubai, Fujairah, Ras al Khaimah, Sharjah, Umm al Qaiwain, all have Shaikhs, with the prefix of His Highness. They are addressed as follows: His Highness Shaikh, followed by the name, Ruler of (Abu Dhabi), etc.

Foreign Reigning Sovereigns and their Wives

BEGINNING OF LETTER

Emperor or Empress	Your Imperial Majesty *or* Sir/Madam
King or Queen	Your Majesty *or* Sir/Madam
Reigning Prince or	Your Royal Highness/Your Highness/
Princess	Your Serene Highness *or* Sir/Madam

ENDING OF LETTER

Formal	I have the honour to remain (*or* to be), Sir/Madam, Your Majesty's (or appropriate title) (most) obedient servant
Social	I have the honour to remain (*or* to be) Your Majesty's (or appropriate title) loyal (*or* devoted) friend

Envelope

His Royal Highness
The Grand Duke of Luxembourg
Her Serene Highness
The Princess of Monaco

VERBAL ADDRESS

Emperor or Empress	Your Imperial Majesty (for the first time), otherwise as for a King or Queen
King or Queen	Your Majesty (for the first time), subsequently Sir *or* Ma'am (to rhyme with Pam).
Reigning Prince or Princess	Your Royal Highness/Highness/Serene Highness (for the first time), subsequently Sir *or* Ma'am

DESCRIPTION IN CONVERSATION

Formal	His/Her Imperial Majesty *or* The Emperor/Empress.
	His/Her Majesty The King/Queen
	His Royal Highness/Highness/Serene Highness.
	The country may be mentioned for purposes of differentiation
Social	The Emperor/Empress
	The King/Queen
	The Prince/Princess[1]
	The country may be mentioned for purposes of differentiation

Widow of a Sovereign

She is addressed as Her Majesty The Dowager Queen of . . ., or the appropriate title with its proper prefix.

The widow of a previous Sovereign is known by her christian name, e.g. 'Her Majesty Queen Ingrid of Denmark.'

[1] Prince and Princess are also non-Royal Titles, see p. 377.

If she is the mother of the reigning Sovereign, she is sometimes styled 'Her Majesty The Queen Mother of . . .'.

If the style is not known, the appropriate Embassy should be approached.

In other respects as for the wife of a Sovereign.

The Husband of a Reigning Sovereign

Should the Sovereign of a Kingdom be a woman, her consort is usually accorded the style of 'His Royal Highness' and created a Prince, e.g., the husband of The Queen of Denmark is H.R.H. Prince Henrik of Denmark.

The Eldest Son of a Reigning Sovereign

He is known as His Royal Highness The Crown Prince of . . ., unless there is a special title for the heir apparent, such as The Prince of The Asturias.

The eldest son of the Grand Duke of Luxembourg is styled 'The Hereditary Grand Duke of Luxembourg', and the eldest sons of the Prince of Liechtenstein and the Prince of Monaco are styled 'Hereditary Prince' of these countries. The word 'Hereditary' in this context is a mistranslation of the French 'Héritier', i.e. Heir-Prince (Erbprinz).

BEGINNING OF LETTER

'Your Royal Highness', or 'Sir'.

ENDING OF LETTER

As for a Sovereign, with the substitution of 'Your Royal Highness's' for 'Your Majesty's'.

ENVELOPE

His Royal Highness
The Crown Prince (or appropriate title).

VERBAL ADDRESS

'Your Royal Highness' for the first time, and subsequently 'Sir' (as for the British Royal Family).

DESCRIPTION IN CONVERSATION

Formal   His Royal Highness

Social

The Crown Prince,
or The Duke of . . ., as appropriate.
The country may be mentioned for purposes of differentiation or on introduction outside his own country.

Wife of the Eldest Son, or a Crown Princess in Her Own Right

She is known as 'Her Royal Highness the Crown Princess of . . .' or by her husband's title, e.g. 'Her Royal Highness the Duchess of . . .'.

Forms of address are as for her husband, with the substitution of 'Madam' for 'Sir' in the written form, and 'Ma'am' (to rhyme with Pam) in the spoken form.

Younger Sons, and Princes of Younger Branches

Younger sons of a Sovereign are usually known as, e.g. 'His Royal Highness Prince Richard of . . .' unless a Dukedom has been created for him, when he is known as 'His Royal Highness the Duke of . . .'. Other forms of address are as for the eldest son, with the substitution of his christian name or title. The social form is 'Prince Richard', or by his title if appropriate. His wife is known as 'Her Royal Highness Princess Richard' or by his title. The social form is 'Princess Richard' or, 'The Duchess of . . .'. Other forms of address are as for the wife of the eldest son, with the substitution of her husband's christian name or title.

Younger branches of a Royal Family may be styled 'His Highness', which is senior to 'His Serene Highness'.

Daughters, and Princesses of Younger Branches

Daughters of a Sovereign are usually known as, e.g. 'Her Royal Highness Princess Louise of . . .', or sometimes 'Her Highness Princess Louise of . . .'. Other forms of address are as for the wife of the eldest son, with the substitution of her christian name. The social form is 'Princess Louise'. Married princesses take their style from their husband unless they marry commoners, when they usually retain their own style in conjunction with their married name, e.g.:

Her Highness Princess Ragnhild, Mrs. (*or* Fru) Lorentzen

Otherwise a princess may give up her Royal Style and become Mrs. John Smith.

Former Foreign Sovereigns and their Wives

Should a Sovereign no longer reign he is addressed as for a reigning sovereign, except that on the envelope his christian name is added, e.g. His Majesty King Leopold III of the Belgians. The form 'ex-King', 'ex-Emperor', or appropriate title, is never used.

The exception is when a former sovereign receives a lesser title, e.g. after abdication His late Majesty King Edward VIII became His Royal Highness The Duke of Windsor, and Her late Majesty the Queen of The Netherlands became Her Royal Highness Princess Wilhelmina of The Netherlands.

Members of Former Reigning Families

Members of families who reigned in the past (including those within the German Empire with Royal prefixes[1]), continue to inherit the same ranks and titles, e.g. Prince, Archduke, Duke and Margrave, unless a family council has authorised any changes. There is one exception: the head of a family who himself has never reigned does not succeed to the title of King or Grand Duke.

The title of Archduke is confined to members of the Habsburg family. That of Grand Duke has become extinct in Germany, and almost so in the Romanov family. Before 1917 nearly all members of the Russian Imperial Family were either Grand Dukes or Grand Duchesses. This title is now confined to the Head of the family (The Grand Duke Vladimir), his wife and children.[2] Many of those who would have succeeded as Grand Dukes in Germany have revived the old title of Margrave, such as Baden (with the style 'H.R.H.'). Members of the Russian Imperial Family are known as 'His Highness Prince or Princess Constantine of Russia', or 'His (Her) Highness Prince or Princess Constantine Romanov'.

Forms of address are as for members of a Royal Family, but some prefer a simpler form.

The head of the former ruling House of France is the Comte de Paris, addressed as 'Monseigneur'. His title is never translated as 'Count of Paris'.

His Highness (Hoheit) is senior to His Serene Highness (Durchlaucht), which is based on a French mistranslation.

[1] Including such prefixes as 'His (or Her) Highness' (HH), 'His (or Her) Serene Highness' (H.S.H.), etc.
[2] Austrian Archdukes and Archduchesses have the style 'His (Her) Imperial and Royal Highness' (H.I. & R.H.), and The Grand Duke Vladimir of Russia, is 'His Imperial Highness' (H.I.H.).

Non-Royal Titles

Although foreign titles are often the same as those used in Britain, their structure and laws of succession are markedly different, notably in the use of adopting, purchase, recognition, etc. In Europe, a family once ennobled includes every member of it and their descendants in perpetuity, whether titled (which they usually are) or untitled. Unlike the British peerage, no one, however junior in line, is a commoner, though they do not as a rule resort to courtesy titles as we know them. There is no such institution as our peerage.

The devolution of titles is different and often much wider than our peerage. Those of the Holy Roman Empire descend to all male descendants in the male line and all their issue, and those of certain of the old Italian states can be given, or left by will, by the holder. In the main, all sons and daughters are known by the family title before their christian name and surname, but in some countries (e.g. Spain and occasionally in France), certain titles may pass to their children, including a daughter if there is no son.

The titles of Earl, Lord, Lady, and Sir, are exclusively British, and cannot be used by foreign nobles.

It is always advisable to refer to a well-known authority, such as an Embassy, or the publications of *Genealogisches Handbuch des Adels* (published by C. A. Starke & Co., Limburg a.d. Lahn, Germany), notably *Genealogisches Handbuch der Fürstlichen Häuser*, which has virtually replaced the defunct *Almanach de Gotha*.

Status of Foreign Titles Borne by British Subjects

Only those held in accordance with a Royal Warrant are officially recognized. Royal Warrants are no longer granted for this purpose.

Status of Foreign Titles

The position is complicated in that many countries have formally abolished the use of titles (e.g. Austria and Japan). Some States, such as those in Eastern Europe, ignore their existence, whereas others, like the Federal Republic of Germany, continue to recognize them (see Germany, below). The only European countries where titles are still conferred are Belgium, the Netherlands, Spain, the Holy See, and (rarely) Sweden, Liechtenstein, Luxembourg, and Monaco. Titles formerly recognized by former rulers or heads of states are generally accorded.

The following titles are usually written in English.

Prince and Princess—(N.B., this is not exclusively a Royal title)[1]

Duke and Duchess
Count and Countess
Baron and Baroness

Other foreign titles are written in the language of the country concerned, including that of Viscount which is confined to France, Belgium, Spain and Portugal. See table below for the principal titles.

France/Belgium	*Italy*	*Spain*	*Portugal*
(The feminine form is placed in brackets)			
Prince de	Principe di	Principe de	Principe de
(Princesse de)	(Principessa di)	(Princesa de)	(Princeza de)[2]
Duc de	Duca di	Duque de	Duque de
(Duchesse de)	(Duchessa di)	(Duquesa de)	(Duqueza de)
Marquis de	Marchese di	Marqués de	Marquez de
(Marquise de)	(Marchesa di)	(Marquesa de)	(Marquêza de)
Comte de	Conte di	Conde de	Conde de
(Comtesse de)	(Contessa di)	(Condesa de)	(Condessa de)
Vicomte de	—	Vizconde de	Visconde de
(Vicomtesse de)		(Vizcondesa de)	(Viscondessa de)
Baron de	Barone	Barón de	Barão de
(Baronne de)	(Baronessa)	(Baronesa de)	(Baronesa de)

Germany and Austria

Prince	Fürst[3]	Duke	Herzog
Princess	Fürstin	Duchess	Herzogin
Count	Graf	Baron	Freiherr[4]
Countess	Gräfin	Baroness	Freifrau[4]

German and Austrian titles may be written in English, but Graf and Gräfin are usually written in German. Graf is sometimes abbreviated to Gf. and Freiherr to Frh.

[1] By a ruling dating from the time of Queen Victoria a British lady married to a Russian Prince is not styled Princess at the Court of St. James, although she is otherwise accorded this title.
[2] This is only borne by members of the former Royal House of Braganza.
[3] The head of the family is Fürst (Fürstin), but Prinz (Prinzessin) is used for other members of the family. All royal princes are Prinz, and princesses are Prinzessin as being cadets. All are translated into English as Prince (Princess).
[4] Some families are known as Baron (Baroness), see p. 383. In English usage no distinction is made, and they are all termed Baron (Baroness).

The nobility of the Holy Roman Empire (dissolved in 1806) consists of Reichsfürst (Prince), Reichsgraf (Count) and Reichsfreiherr (Baron).

Other titles

Other titles include that of knight, viz. Chevalier, Ritter, Cavaliere, etc., which is sometimes hereditary, such as in Belgium, Austria and Italy.

Titles and Styles in Foreign Countries

See also *Foreign equivalents of 'Mr.'* (see p. 384). It is customary in certain circles for unmarried women of senior age to use the form of address of a married woman.

France

'Monsieur', 'Madame', and 'Mademoiselle', followed by the christian name and surname, are used in place of the title, both in writing and speech, except verbally by employees,[1] but a Duke or Duchess is addressed as 'Monsieur le Duc' or 'Madame la Duchesse'.

Titles may be used socially on the envelope, or on an invitation card.

'Monsieur' is appended before all appointments and names, e.g. Monsieur le Président de la République, Monsieur le Docteur.

Ambassadors are addressed as 'Excellence'.

When writing or speaking to an officer of the Armed Forces, he is referred to by men as 'Mon Colonel', 'Mon Général' and by women as 'Colonel' or 'Général', but Monsieur le Maréchal.

The wife of those with high office is often colloquially referred to by her husband's rank, e.g. Madame la Générale. The widow of a Marshal of France is referred to for all purposes as 'Madame la Maréchale'.

Monsieur is better *not* abbreviated to M., nor Madame to Mme., nor Mademoiselle to Mlle. in correspondence. Mons. is never used.

'Monsieur', 'Madame', and 'Mademoiselle' are universally used in speech to everyone, whatever their status.

Belgium

The envelope is normally addressed 'Comte de . . .' or 'Comtesse de . . .'. It is not usual to add 'Monsieur', 'Madame', or 'Mademoiselle' before the title, with the following exception.

[1] Who use the form 'Madame la Marquise', etc.

In Belgium, members of the Royal Family and their Households, whether or not they are titled, are *officially* addressed on the envelope:

> A Monsieur
>> Monsieur le Comte de Bruges, *or*
>
> A Madame
>> Madame la Comtesse de Bruges

This form was once adopted on the envelope for all those with titles, but is now considered old fashioned.

Monsieur is appended before appointments and names, as in France.

Monsieur, Madame, and Mademoiselle are *not* abbreviated in correspondence.

The Netherlands

There are four hereditary titles, Graaf, Baron, Ridder and Jonkheer. Graaf and Gravin are usually translated as Count and Countess, and Baronesse as Baroness. Ridder is confined to one or two families only. The word 'Jonkheer' is placed before the initials or christian name. His wife has 'Mevrouw', and unmarried daughters 'Jonkvrouwe', before the name.

Dutch titles are not used in speech. All are referred to as Mijnheer (Mr.), Mevrouw (Mrs.), and Freule (Miss) van Dam. For acceptable translations of Mr. see p. 384.

Italy

Titles were abolished by the 1947 Constitution and no longer have official status or legal protection, the only trace of them remaining being a territorial designation which may continue to be recognized as an adjunct to the surname. Titles are, however, used socially, and are complicated in that they were conferred in a variety of states, and cannot be treated as an entity. Rules governing the use of a title by other members of the family accordingly vary. If the title has a Frankish origin in remote feudal times, it is based upon the German custom of equal sharing between males. Titles of the Holy Roman Empire are borne both by males and females. Generally Italian titles are restricted to the head of the family, and all recent letters patent embody this system.

Some great families have several territorial titles (from fiefs held). Some are known by their title and surname (e.g. Il Principe Colonna); others are styled formally by their title and fief (e.g.

Il Principe di Montesole), or less formally by their title, fief and surname (e.g. Il Principe di Montesole Castagnaro), which is useful for purposes of identification.

Members of certain families of the nobility bear the styles of Don and Donna, which form four main groups, viz. in Lombardy, Rome, Naples and Sardinia. In *Lombardy* (where titles were reviewed by the Empress Maria Theresa, also Duchess of Milan) they are borne by children and other collaterals of certain families, which may belong to any of the ranks of the nobility. In *Rome* they are borne by the children and collaterals of Princes and Dukes. In some families, Donna is used by all females, and in others the style is somewhat restricted. In *Naples* the styles are used by the children and collaterals of Princes and Dukes, both by males and females. In *Sardinia* a grade of the nobility is styled Nobile, Cavaliere, Don, but they are addressed in speech as Don and Donna.

Children of a noble without the styles of Don and Donna, and without a territorial title are styled, e.g. 'Nobile Antonio dei Conti Selvatichelli', and with a territorial title 'Nobile Antonio Selvatichelli dei Conti di Acquatorta' (dei = of the family).

There are also municipal titles conferred by cities up to the time of the French Revolution, which saw the end of the residual forms of medieval urban self-government. Up to that time they were replenished as families became extinct. These titles are Patrician (Patrizio) and Noble (Nobile), and are now highly prized for their rarity. The Nobili, apart from being the style of members of the 'feudal' nobility, may thus denote membership of the body of nobles of a city. In large cities there were two tiers, governing families with the title of Patrizio in addition to the Nobili. Both are used by males and females, but only in writing, e.g. a noble of a city is addressed on the envelope 'Giovanni Argentari, Nobile di Vigevano' and not 'Giovanni Argentari di Vigevano', which has the appearance of a feudal territorial title. A patrician likewise is addressed 'Andrea Pagliardi, Patrizio di Perugia'. The spoken form is Signor (Giovanni) Argentari or Signor (Andrea) Pagliardi.

Personal styles may be listed as under, (1) Cavaliere ereditario (hereditary knights, which are usual in Sardinia, Lombardy and Venice), (2) Nobile, Cavaliere, Don (Sardinia), (3) Nobile, as a title, and (4) Nobile, as a member of a noble family. Wives of those in group 1 are addressed, both in writing and speech, as Signora . . .

Papacy

The Holy See confers titles of Prince, Marchese, and Count, but not Baron, on Roman Catholics, in countries all over the world, e.g. Count John MacCormack.

Spain

The eldest son and heir of the Sovereign is Prince of the Asturias. Younger sons receive the title of Infante, and daughters that of Infanta. These titles were also granted by the Sovereign to other members of the Royal Family.

All Dukes, some Marqueses and Condes, and a few Vizcondes are Grandees of Spain. All Grandees and their consorts are Excellencies. The form of address of Excellency is also given to holders of Grand Crosses of various Orders, Ambassadors, Generals, Bishops, and eldest sons of Grandees of Spain, and their wives.

An envelope to a person with the style of Excellency is addressed Excelentisimo Señor, usually abbreviated to Excmo. Sr., followed by his title, e.g. 'Excmo. Sr. Duque de . . .'. If he has no title, this is followed by Don, e.g. Excmo. Sr. General Don, followed by his christian name and surname. Married ladies are addressed similarly as Excelentisima Señora, usually abbreviated to Excma. Sra.

Nobles who are not Grandees are addressed on the envelope 'El Visconde de . . .' or the appropriate title.

Grades of various Orders below Excellency rank are addressed Illustrious, viz. Ilustrisimo (feminine Ilustrisima), of which the abbreviations are Ilmo. and Ilma.

Don is a customary form of respect, rather equivalent to our Esquire. It is used in polite speech when referring to a person by his christian name, e.g. Don Juan. An envelope is addressed Señor Don Juan before his surname. Doña, the feminine form, is used in the same way, both in speech and on the envelope.

Señor (Sr.), Señora (Sra.) and Señorita (Srta.) are the usual forms of address for those without titles. 'Señora' is followed by the addition of 'de' before the surname on the envelope. A married lady may also be addressed by her maiden surname, with her husband's appended, e.g. Sra. Doña Maria Luisa (then her maiden name) de (followed by her husband's surname). If a husband and wife are addressed jointly, his full name is given, before his wife's, e.g. Señor Don Juan Lopez and Señora de Lopez. An unmarried lady is called and addressed 'Señorita Doña Maria Luisa' (followed by her surname). A man's surname is often followed by his mother's maiden name, e.g. Señor Don Francisco Moreno y Garcia, both in correspondence and on visiting cards.

Portugal

Those with titles are addressed formally as:

> Excelentíssimo Senhor
> Conde de ... (or appropriate title)

but envelopes are now often addressed:

> Dom Manuel de Bragança

'Dom' is restricted to a few families, but the feminine equivalent 'Doña' is customarily used for all ladies, whether married or single. The abbreviation D. is frequently used for both Dom and Doña.

Excelentíssimo (or the feminine form Excelentíssima) is written in full for a distinguished person, such as a Minister, Ambassador, etc. For others, including wives of ministers, etc., the abbreviations Exmo. and Exma. are used.

It is customary for those with appointments to be addressed 'Senhor Professor ...' ('Prof.' is abbreviated for ordinary schoolmasters), 'Senhor Doutor (Doctor) ...', etc., with their degrees and university appended after the name. Those with degrees of Licenciado (Master) or Bacharel (Bachelor) are styled 'Dr.' 'Doutor' is only written in full for one with a Doctor's degree.

Portuguese men may add their mother's name *before* the surname. A married lady may retain her maiden surname before her married surname.

Latin America

Though the language of all countries is Spanish, except for Brazil, which is Portuguese-speaking, forms of address vary according to the country. In some countries accents have been abolished. Mr., Mrs. and Miss are translated in Spanish-speaking countries as Señor, Señora and Señorita, and in Brazil, Senhor, Senhora and Senhorita. Here, unmarried ladies who are senior in age are addressed as Senhora.

The prefixes of Excelentísimo and Excelentísima (ladies) (Excelentissimo and Excelentissima in Brazil) are given in some countries, often abbreviated to Exmo. and Exma. or Excmo. and Excma. In Brazil, Ilustríssimo and Ilustríssima are used, often abbreviated to Ilmo. and Ilma.

The use of Don (Dom in Brazil) and Dona varies according to the country. In Brazil, Dom is not used as a form of address, apart from special instances, such as to priests. Dona is placed after Senhora, when writing formally. It is also used in speech to slight acquaintances, e.g. Dona Maria . . . In Mexico, Don and Doña are less used than in Colombia but often formally in the provinces. In Peru, don (note small 'd') is used on envelopes, e.g. Señor don Pablo Sanchez, but doña is only used in special instances. In Chile, Don and Doña are not generally used.

It is a general rule to include Doctor, Professor, etc. between Senor and Don, or between Senor and the name.

Germany

The Republican Constitution of 1920 did not abolish titles of nobility but stipulated that they were to be an integral part of the name. This was confirmed by the Federal Republic 1949. Thus the christian name is used before the title on the envelope.

Graf is often left untranslated, but sometimes Count is used. It is sometimes followed by the family name (e.g. Wolff-Metternich), but more often by von, or very occasionally 'von' and 'zu' (e.g. 'von und zu Bodman'). 'Zu' means that the family still owns their name place. 'Von and zu' is a 19th century bit of nonsense which nevertheless exists. Schwarzenberg and Hohenlohe are 'zu' alone. It is suggested that a handbook on the nobility be consulted for the exact wording.

Baron, in place of the older German title of Freiherr, is used extensively in South Germany, and also in the Baltic states from where some families had migrated. Both are normally translated in English to Baron.

The prefix 'zu' is only used in writing. A Baron with both designations, would be announced either as 'Baron von . . .', or 'Herr von . . .', but would not introduce himself with either prefix.

For those with an appointment such as Professor, Doctor, etc. it is customary to refer to them as Herr Professor or Frau Doktor.

BEGINNING OF SOCIAL LETTER

Dear Graf (von) Blank (feminine form, Gräfin)

Dear Baron (von) Blank (Baronin is translated Baroness)

Titles (see p. 384) are also borne by sons and unmarried daughters before their christian names. They are not retained by daughters who have married outside the nobility.

ENVELOPE

German	English
Moritz, Graf/Freiherr/Baron (von) . . .	Graf (von) . . . (or appropriate title)
Anna, Gräfin/Freifrau/Baron-in (von) . . .	Gräfin (von) . . . (or appropriate title)

Sons and daughters are addressed, both in German and English, by their titles before their christian names, e.g. Graf Luitpold von Blank and Gräfin Anna von Blank though they sometimes are addressed Moritz, Graf von . . . , on the grounds that Graf von . . . is the surname. An unmarried daughter of a Freiherr is Freiin, of a Baron is Baronesse, and of a Graf is identical with his wife, viz Gräfin.

Austria

Titles are not recognized under the Constitution but are used socially.

Russian, Polish, and Hungarian Families

They share the ranks of Prince, Count and Baron, which all precede the family name, e.g. Prince Orlov, Count Potocki, and Baron Orczy. In Magyar, 'Graf' comes *after* the surname, but not in translation of Hungarian names.

In Russia, unless a name has a foreign origin when it is indeclinable, the feminine form of -ski (meaning 'of') becomes -skaya, similarly with -skoy, e.g. Trubetskoy, Trubetskaya. Names from the Ukraine which end with 'o' are also indeclinable. It is usual to add the father's name before the patronymic, viz. Count Ivan Ivanovich Tolstoy, Countess Anna Alexandrovna Tolstaya. Many families who have settled outside Russia do not use the feminine ending.

In Poland, the usual ending is 'ski', with the feminine form 'ska'. If the ending of the name is -cki the feminine form is -cka, e.g. Count Potocki, Countess Potocka. Certain names, such as Dubis, have the feminine form 'owa' (pronounced 'ova'), i.e. Dubisowa. Others are indeclinable, e.g. Debiec for both sexes.

Foreign Equivalents of 'Mr.', 'Mrs.', etc.

It is permissible to address citizens of other countries as under, these being the forms used by the Foreign and Commonwealth Office, though certain pitfalls are avoided by always using 'Mr.',

'Mrs.' and 'Miss', since the forms of address in certain countries include certain administrative titles and offices held, such as Engineer. These are sometimes extended to include their wives.

English

Mr. (Mrs., Miss)	Commonwealth countries, except in India, where Shri is the equivalent of 'Mr.', Shrimati of Mrs. and Kumari of Miss.
	Asian countries, including Turkey, but excluding Indonesia, the Philippines, and those which were formerly part of the French Empire
	United Arab Republic (Egypt)
	Algeria
	Morocco
	Other African countries, except those which were formerly part of the French Empire, and those which are French-speaking.

French

Monsieur (Madame, Mademoiselle)	All European countries[1] (including Switzerland[2]) *except* for Germany, Austria, Italy, San Marino, Spain, Portugal
	Ethiopia
	Indonesia
	Countries which were formerly part of the French Empire (e.g. Tunis, Laos, Lebanon, Gabon, but *not* Algeria or Morocco)

German

Herr (Frau, Fräulein)	Germany
	Austria

Italian

Signor (Signora, Signorina)	Italy
	San Marino

[1] This is adopted officially for the Soviet Union, though sometimes 'Mr.' is used.
[2] In Switzerland, some prefer to be addressed in German.

Spanish

Señor (Señora, Señorita)	Spain
	Other Spanish-speaking countries (e.g. Central and South American republics (except Brazil), Cuba, Dominican Republic, Philippines)

Portuguese

Senhor (Senhora, Senhorita)[1]	Portugal
	Brazil

Other styles

Sayed is used in Sudan, and U in Burma (except for military ranks).

Civic Heads Abroad, see p. 250.

---

[1] Unmarried ladies in Portugal are known as 'Senhora', but 'Senhorita' is used in Brazil.

APPENDICES

1. Rules for Hoisting Flags on Government and other Public Buildings.
2. Pronunciation of Titles and Surnames.

1. Rules for Hoisting Flags on Government and other Public Buildings

The following paragraphs accord with the regulations circulated by the Department of the Environment by Command of The Queen.

DATES ON WHICH FLAGS ARE TO BE FLOWN

The dates named in the Schedule below, plus such additions as are notified by the Department of the Environment.

The principal flag to be flown on the majority of buildings is the Union Jack (as it is usually, but erroneously called: its proper name is the Union *Flag*).[1]

PROVINCIAL BUILDINGS

This Schedule applies to Provincial as well as to London Buildings (but see notes 1 and 3), but not to Customs Houses and to Armed Forces Establishments which are authorised to fly their appropriate flags daily.

OCCASIONS ON WHICH FLAGS ARE TO BE FLOWN AT HALF MAST

(a) From the announcement of the death up to the funeral of the Sovereign, except on Proclamation Day, when they are hoisted right up from 11 a.m. to sunset.

(b) The funerals of members of the Royal Family, subject to special commands from Her Majesty in each case.

[1] The White Ensign and the Royal Air Force Ensign shall only be flown where specifically authorized by the Ministry of Defence.

(c) The funerals of Foreign Rulers, subject to special commands from Her Majesty in each case.

(d) The funerals of Prime Ministers and ex-Prime Ministers of the United Kingdom.

(e) Other occasions by special command of Her Majesty, which will be communicated by the Department of the Environment to other Departments.

RULES WHEN DAYS FOR FLYING FLAGS COINCIDE WITH DAYS FOR FLYING FLAGS AT HALF MAST

To be flown right up—

(a) although a member of the Royal Family, or a near relative of the Royal Family, may be lying dead, unless special commands be received from Her Majesty to the contrary.[1]

(b) although it may be the day of the funeral of a Foreign Ruler.

If the body of a very distinguished subject is lying at a Government Office the flag may fly at half-mast on that office until the body has left (provided it is a day on which the flag would fly) after which the flag is to be hoisted right up. On all other Public Buildings the flag will fly as usual.

DAYS FOR HOISTING FLAGS ON GOVERNMENT AND OTHER PUBLIC BUILDINGS

From 8 a.m. till sunset

6th February—Her Majesty's Accession
19th February—Birthday of The Prince Andrew
1st March—St. David's Day (See Note 1(a))
10th March—Birthday of The Prince Edward
21st April—Birthday of Her Majesty The Queen
23rd April—St. George's Day (See Note 1(b))
2nd June—Coronation Day
. . . June (as appointed)—Official Celebration of Her Majesty's Birthday; Commonwealth Day[2]

[1] Flags were flown at half-mast between the death of The Duke of Windsor (formerly King Edward VIII) on 29 May 1972 and his funeral on 5 June 1972. This period included Coronation Day and The Queen's Official Birthday: by The Queen's Command flags remained at half-mast on both these days.
[2] Her Majesty's Official Birthday is now celebrated on the second Saturday in June. At a recent Commonwealth Conference a proposal was made that Commonwealth Day should be celebrated throughout the Commonwealth on the second Monday in March, but at the time of going to press no decision has been announced.

10th June—Birthday of The Duke of Edinburgh
4th August—Birthday of Her Majesty Queen Elizabeth The
         Queen Mother
15th August—Birthday of The Princess Anne
21st August—Birthday of The Princess Margaret
November—Remembrance Day (See Note 2)
14th November—Birthday of The Prince of Wales
20th November—Her Majesty's Wedding Day
30th November—St. Andrew's Day (See Note 1(c))

Also : The day of the opening of a Session of the Houses of
Parliament by Her Majesty. (See Note 3)
   The day of the prorogation of a Session of the Houses of Parliament by Her Majesty. (See Note 3)
   During the whole of a State Visit by a Head of State in such city
or borough as he may be the guest of Her Majesty The Queen
(London, Windsor, Edinburgh). Also on the relevant day in any
other place which he may visit during his State Visit. The national
flag of the Head of State may only be flown where specifically
authorized by the Department of the Environment. The Head of
State's personal standard or flag is not flown.

Note 1.—(a) Flags should be flown on this day in Wales only.
        (b) Flags should be flown on this day in England only.
        (c) Flags should be flown on this day in Scotland only.

   Where a building has two or more flagstaffs the appropriate
National flag may be flown in addition to the Union Flag, but not
in a superior position.[1]

Note 2.—Remembrance Day is the second Sunday in November.
Flags should be flown right up all day.

Note 3.—Flags should be flown on this day irrespective of whether
or not Her Majesty performs the ceremony in person, but only
from buildings in the Greater London area.

Note 4.—The Royal Standard is never hoisted when Her Majesty
is passing in procession; nor likewise are the personal standards of
other members of the Royal Family. If The Queen, or another
member of the Royal Family, is to visit a building, instructions
should be sought from the Private Secretary (from whom the
appropriate standard may be borrowed for the occasion).

[1] When two or more flagstaffs are available, the superior position is the flagstaff furthest to the
left, as seen by an observer looking at the front of the building from outside it.

Note 5.—The United Nations flag may be flown from 8.0 am until sunset throughout United Nations Week. If a second flagstaff is available, the Union Flag should also be flown.

Note 6.—County, Borough and District Councils, and other Local Government bodies may arrange for their civic flags to be flown on buildings within their respective areas on such days as they consider appropriate, subject always to the above rules which take precedence.

Note 7.—Flags other than those mentioned above may be flown locally in special circumstances (e.g. the National Savings flag during a Savings Week).

Note 8.—A flag to be flown at half-mast shall always be first hoisted close up and then lowered to half-mast. Likewise before a flag flying at half-mast is lowered at sunset, it shall first be hoisted close up.

2. Pronunciation of Titles and Surnames

'Ch' in Scottish, Welsh and Irish names is pronounced as in 'loch'. Mac is not normally stressed so the 'a' is hardly pronounced at all. In Scots the letter 'z' stood for a guttural 'y', which explains why Menzies was originally Meyners; also Elizabeth (English) is spelt Elisabeth in Scotland.

The Scots 'l' in such prefixes as Col, Fal, Bal, and Dal was usually not pronounced, and 'quh' was the Scots way of writing 'wh' (e.g. 'what' was spelt 'quhat'). This explains the pronunciation of Colquhoun.

With names ending in intrusive forms for s (e.g. ys, yss and is), the vowel should not be pronounced, such as in Wemyss, Inglis and Spottiswoode.

Abercrombie	Aber-crum-by (but sometimes as spelt)
Abergavenny	Aber-*genny* (title) (hard 'g'); town as spelt
Abinger	Abin-jer
Acheson	Atchesson
Adye	Aydi
Aldous	*All*-dus
Alleyne	Alleen (but sometimes as spelt)

Alnwick	Annick
Althorp	*All*-trup
Altrincham	Altringham
Alvingham	All-ving-am
Aman	Amman
Ampthill	Ampt-hill
Annesley	*Anns*-li
Apethorpe	App-thorp
Arbuthnot(t)	A-*buth*-not
Ardee	A-*dee*
Arundel	*Arun*-del
Ashburnham	Ash-*burn*-am
Assheton	*Ash*-ton
Atholl	*Uh*-thol *or*
	Ah-thol
Auchinleck	Affleck *or Ock*-inleck
Audley	*Awd*-li
Ava	Ah-va
Ayscough	Askew
Babington	*Babb*-ington
Baden-Powell	Bayden-Poell
Bagot	*Bag*-ot
Balcarres	Bal-*carris*
Balogh	Balog (Bal as in Hal)
Bampfylde	*Bam*-field
Baring	*Bear*-ing
Barnardiston	*Bar*-nar-*dis*-ton
Barttelot	Bartlot
Basing	Bayzing
Bathurst	*Bath*-urst (a as in cat)
Bazalgette	Bazl-jet
Beauchamp	Beecham
Beauclerk	Bo-clare
Beaudesert	Bodezair
Beaufort	*Bo*-foot
Beaulieu	*Bew*-ly
Beaumont	Bo-mont
Becher	Beacher
Bechervaise	*Besh*-er-vayse
Bedingfeld	Beddingfield
Behrens	Barens
Belfast	Bel*fast*

Bellew	*Bell*-ew
Bellingham	Bellingjam *or* Bellingum
Belvoir	Beevor
Bengough	Ben-*goff*
Beresford	*Berris*-fud
Berkeley	Barkli
Bertie	Barti
Betham	*Bee*-tham
Bethune	Beaton
Bicester	Bister
Blakiston	Blackiston
Bledisloe	Bledslow
Blenheim	*Blen*-im
Bligh	Bly
Blithfield	Bliffield
Blois	Bloyss
Blomefield	Bloomfield
Blount	Blunt
Blyth	Bly
Boevey	Boovey *or* Buvey (short u)
Boleyn	*Bull*-in
Bolingbroke	*Bulling*-brook
Boord	Board
Boreel	Borale
Borrowes	Burrows
Borwick	Borrick
Bosham	*Bos*-am
Bosanquet	*Bozen*-ket
Boscawen	Bos-*cowen*
Botetourt	Botti-tort
Boughey	Boey
Boughton	Bought-on (family)
	Bough-ton (N'hamptonshire)
Bourchier	*Bough*-cher
Bourke	Burke
Bourne	Boorn
Bowden (Aylestone)	Bowden (as in now)
Bowden (Baron)	Bowden (as in no)
Bowes	Bose (to rhyme with rose)
Bowman	Boman
Bowyer	Bo-yer (as in no)
Brabazon	*Brab*-azon

Brabourne	*Bray*-burn
Breadalbane	Bread-*au*burn
Breitmeyer	Bright-mire
Brereton	Breer-ton
Brise	Brize
Brocas	Brockas
Broke	Brook (but H.M.S. *Broke* as spelt)
Bromhead	Brumhead
Brougham	Broom or Brooham
Broughton	Brawton
Broun	Brune
Bruntisfield	Bruntsfield
Brynkir	Brinkeer
Buccleuch	Bu-*cloo*
Bulkeley	Buckley
Burgh	Borough
Burghersh	Burg-ish
Burghley	Ber-li
Bury	Berry (England) Bure-y (Ireland)
Caccia	Catch-a
Cadogan	Ka-*dugan*
Caius	Keys (College)
Caldecote	Call-di-cot
Calderon	*Call*-dron
Callaghan	*Calla*-han
Calver	Carver
Calverley	*Car*-verly or *Calf*-ley
Camoys	Cam-oyz
Capell	*Cay*ple
Carew	As spelt—Cary has become archaic
Calthorpe	*Call*-thorpe—Cal-trop has become archaic
Carnegie	Car-*neggie*
Carteret	*Carter*-et
Cassilis	Cassels
Castlereagh	*Castle*-ray
Carthcart	Cath-*cart*
Cathie	*Cay*-thie
Cato	*Kate*-o

393

Cator	*Cay*-tor
Caulfield	*Caw*-field
Cavan	*Cav*-en (a as in cat)
Cavanagh	*Cava*-na
Cecil	Cicil
Chandos	Shandos
Charlemont	Shar-le-mont
Charteris	As spelt—Charters is archaic[1]
Chattan	Hattan
Chenevix	*Sheen*ivix
Chernocke	Char-nock
Chetwode	Chetwood
Chetwynd	Chetwind
Cheylesmore	*Chyles*-more
Cheyne	Chain, Chainy *or* Cheen
Chichele	*Chich*-ley
Chisholm	*Chis*-um
Cholmeley ⎫ Cholmondeley ⎭	*Chum*-li
Cilcennin	Kil-*kennin*
Cirencester	As spelt—Sisiter is becoming archaic
Claverhouse	Clayvers
Clerk	Clark
Cloete	Clootie
Clough	Cluff
Clowes	Clues
Clwyd	*Cloo*-id
Cochrane	*Coch*-ran
Cockburn	*Co*-bun
Coghlan	*Co*-lan
Coke	Cook (Earl of Leicester) and others, but sometimes as spelt
Coleraine	Cole-*rain*
Colquhoun	Ca-hoon
Colvile ⎫ Colville ⎭	*Col*-ville
Combe	Coom
Combermere	*Cumber*-mere
Compton	Cumpton (usually)
Conesford	*Connis*-ford

[1] The old pronunciation of Charters is derived from the French place name of Chartres.

Conolly	*Con*-olly
Constable	*Cun*stable
Conyngham(e)	Cunningham
Cosham	As spelt
Cottenham	*Cot*-nam
Cottesloe	*Cots*-low
Couchman	Cowchman
Courthope	Cort-hope
Cowper	Cooper
Cozens	Cuzzens
Cracroft	*Cray*-croft
Craigavon	Craig-*avv*-on
Craster	Crarster
Creagh	Cray
Creighton	Cryton
Crespigny	See De Crespigny
Crichton	Cryton
Cromartie	*Crum*-aty
Crombie	Crumbie
Culme	Cullum (sometimes as spelt)
Cuming	Cumming
Cunynghame	Cunningham
D'Abrell	*Dab*-roo
Dacre	Dayker
Dalbiac	*Dawl*-biac
Dalhousie	Dal-*howsi*
Dalmeny	Dul-*menny*
Dalyell	
Dalzell	Dee-el (sometimes Dayli-el)
Darcy de Knaith	Darcy de Nayth
Daresbury	Darsbury
Daubeney	*Daub*-ny
Daventry	As spelt—Daintry is archaic
Davies	Davis
De Blacquiere	De *Black*-yer
De Burgh	De *Burg*
Decies	Deeshies
De Courcy	De Koursey
De Crespigny	De *Crepp*-ni
De Eresby	see Willoughby
De Freyne	De *Frain*
De Hoghton	De Hawton

De la Warr	Della-ware
Delamere	Della-mare
De la Poer	De la *Poor*
De la Rue	Della-rue
De L'Isle	De Lyle
De Lotbinière	De Lobin-yare
De Moleyns	*Demo*-lins
Dering	*Deer*-ing
De Ros	De *Roos*
Derwent	Darwent
De Salis	De Saals
	De Sal-is (according to branch of family)
De Saumarez ⎫	De *Summer*-ez *or*
De Sausmarez ⎭	De *Saumer*-ez
Devereux	Dev-rooks (Viscount Hereford) *or* Dever-oo
De Vesci	De Vessy
De Villiers	De Villers
Diomede	Di-o-meed
Dilhorne	*Dill*'n
Dominguez	Dum-*ing*-ez
Doneraile	Dunnaral
Donoughmore	Duno-more
Doune	Doun
Douro	*Dur*-o
Drogheda	*Droyi*-da
Drumalbyn	Drum-*albin*
Duchesnes	Du *Karn*(s), but sometimes with French pronunciation Du-shayn
Ducie	*Dew*-si
Du Cros	Du *Crow*
Dukinfield	*Duckin*-field
Dumaresq	Du-*merrick*
Dunally	Dun-*alley*
Dundas	Dun-*das*
Dungarvan	Dun-*gar*-van
Dunglass	Dun-*glass*
Dunsany	Dun-*saney*
Duntze	Dunts
Du Plat	Du-Pla

Dupplin	*Dupp*-lin
Durand	*Du*-rand *or* Dur-*rand*
Dymoke	Dimmock
Dynevor	*Dinny*-ver
Dysart	*Dy*-z't
Ebury	*Ee*-bri
Echlin	Eck-lin
Edwardes	Edwards
Egan	*Ee*-gan
Egerton	*Edger*-ton
Elcho	Elco
Elgin	El-gin (hard g)
Elibank	Elli-bank
Elphinstone	*Elfin*-ston
Elveden	*Elve*-den (place Elden)
Elwes	*El*-wes
Erle	Earl
Ernle	Earnley
Erskine	*Ers*-kin
Eveleigh	*Eve*-ley
Eyre	Air
Every	As spelt
Eyton	*I*-tun
Falconer	Fawkner
Falkiner	Fawkner
Faringdon	Farringdon
Farquhar	Farkwar
Farquharson	Farkwerson
Fayrer	*Fair*-er
Featherstonhaugh	Fetherston-haugh or occasionally Fetherston[1]
Feilding	*Field*-ing
Fenwick	*Fenn*-ick
Fergusson	Ferguson
Fermor	Farmer
Feversham	Fevver-sham (place Favversham)
ffolliott	*Foll*-y-ot
ffolkes	Foaks
Fiennes	Fines
Fingall	Fin-*gawl*

[1] I can find no record that this name was ever pronounced Fanshaw or Feeston as is popularly believed.

Fitzhardinge	Fitzharding
Foljambe	Full-jum
Forestier	Forest-tier
Fortuin	Fortayne
Foulis	Fowls
Fowke	Foke
Fremantle	*Free*-mantle
Freyberg	*Fry*-burg
Froude	Frood
Furneaux	*Fur*-no
Gairdner	Gardner
Galston	*Gaul*-ston
Galway	Gaulway
Garioch	Ghorric
Garvagh	*Gar*-va
Gathorne	Gaythorn
Geoghegan	*Gay*-gan
Gerrard	Jerrard
Gervis	Jervis
Giffard	Jiffard
Gifford	Jifford
Gill	As spelt (hard g)
Gillespie	Gill-*es*-py (hard g)
Gilmour	Gillmoor (hard g)
Glamis	Glahms
Glasgow	*Glass*-go
Glenavy	Glen-*avy* (as in day)
Glerawly	Gler-*awly*
Gorges	Gorjes
Gormanstown	*Gor*-mans-ton
Goschen	*Go*-shen
Gough	Goff
Goulding	Goolding
Gower	Gore
	(Gower Peninsula and Gower St., London, as spelt)
Graeme	Grame (to rhyme with Frame)
Grantham	*Gran*-tham
Greaves	Graves
Greig	Gregg
Grosvenor	*Grove*-nor
Guise	Gyze

Gwynedd	*Gwinn*-eth
Haden-Guest	Hayden-Gest (hard g)
Haldane	*Hall*-dane
Halsey	*Hall*-sey
Halsbury	*Halls*-bry
Hamond	Hammond
Harcourt	*Har*-cut
Hardinge	Harding
Harewood	*Har-wood* (title)
	Hare-wood (village)
Harington	Harrington
Harwich	Harrich
Hawarden	*Hay*-warden
Haworth	*Hay*-worth
	Harden for the title has become archaic
Heathcoat ⎫	
Heathcote ⎭	Heth-cut
Heneage	Hennidge
Hepburn	*Heb*-b'n
Herschell	*Her*-shell
Hertford	*Har*-ford
Hervey	Harvey
Hever	Heaver
Heytesbury	*Hetts*-b'ry
Heywood	Haywood
Hindlip	*Hynd*-lip
Hippesley	*Hips*-ley
Hobart	Hubbard (but as spelt for the city)
Hogan	*Ho*-gan
Holbech	*Hole*-beech
Home	Hume
Honywood	Honeywood
Hopetoun	Hopeton
Horsbrugh	Horsbro'
Hotham	*Huth*-am
Housman	House-man
Howick	Hoyck
Hugessen	*Hu*-ges-*son* (hard 'g')
Huth	Hooth
Hylton	Hilton

Iddesleigh	*Idd*-sli
Ikerrin	I-kerrin
Iliffe	I-liffe
Inchiquin	Inch-quin
Inchrye	Inch-rye
Inchyra	Inch-*eye-ra*
Inge	Ing
Ingestre	Ingustry (like industry)
Inglis	Ingles, *or* as spelt
Inigo	*Inni*-go
Innes	Inniss
Inveraray	Inver-*air*-a
Ionides	Ion-*ee*-diz
Isham	I-sham
Iveagh	I-va
Jervis	as spelt *or* Jarvis
Jervoise	Jervis
Jocelyn	Josslin
Jolliffe	*Joll*-if
Kaberry	*Kay*-berry
Kavenagh	*Kavan*-a
Kekewich	*Keck*-which
Keighley	*Keith*-li
Kemeys	Kemmis
Kennard	Ken-*ard*
Kenyon	*Ken*-yon
Ker } Kerr }	Car *or* Cur (hard c)
Keynes	Kaynes
Killanin	Kil-*lah*-nin
Kilmorey	Kil-*murray*
Kingsale	King-*sale*
Kinnoull	Kin-*ool*
Kirkcudbright	Cuck-*coo*-bri
Knollys	Nowles
Kylsant	Kill-*sant*
Knyvett	Nivett
Lacon	*Lay*-kon
Laffan	Laf-*fan*
Lamplugh	*Lamp*-loo
Lascelles	*Lass*-ells
Lathom	*Lay*-thom

LaTouche	La *Toosh*
Latymer	Latimer
Laurie	Lorry
Layard	Laird
Leacock	Laycock *or* Leecock
Lechmere	Letchmere
Le Fanu	*Leff*-new
Lefevre	Le-*fever*
Legard	Le-jard
Legh	Lee
Leighton	Layton
Leinster	Linster
Leitrim	Leetrim
Le Mesurier	Le *Mezz*-erer
Leominster	Lemster
Leven	*Lee*-ven
Leverhulme	*Leaver*-hume
Leveson-Gower	Loosun-Gore
Levinge	As spelt (hard g)
Levy	Levvy or Leevi
Ley	Lay or Lee
Leycester	Lester
Liardet	Lee-ardet
Liddell	*Lid*-el
Lisle	Lyle
Listowel	Lis-*toe*-ell
Lombe	Loam (sometimes Lumb)
Londesborough	Londs-bro'
Londonderry	*London*d'ry (title)
	London-*Derry* (city)
Loudon	*Loud*-on
Loughborough	*Luff*-bro
Louth	(England) *th* as in mouth
	(Ireland) *th* as in breathe
Lovat	Luv-at
Lowson	*Lo*-son (lo as in go)
Lowther	*Low*-thėr (low as in now)
Lycett	Lisset
Lygon	Liggon
Lyon	Lion
Lysaght	Ly-set
Lyveden	*Live*-den (as in give)

Macara	Mac-*ara*
Macbean	Mac-*bain*
McCorquodale	M'*cork*-o-dale
McCulloch	M'*cull*-och
McDonagh	Mac-*Donna*
McEvoy	*Mac*-evoy
McEwan ⎫ 　Ewen ⎭	Mac-*ewen*
McFadzean	Mac *fadd*-yen
McGillycuddy	*Mac*-li-*cuddy*
Machell	*May*-chel
McIvor	Mac-*Ivor*
McKay	M'*Kye* (as in eye)
McKie	*Mack*-ie (though some branches pronounce their name M'*Kye*)
Maclean	Mac-*layne*
Macleay	Mac-*lay*
Macleod	Mac-*loud*
McLachlan	Mac-*loch*lan
Macnaghten	Mac-*nawton*
Macmahon	Mac-*mahn*
Maelor	Myla
Magdala	Mag-*dahla*
Magdalen ⎫ Magdalene ⎭	Maudlin
Magrath	Ma-*grah*
Mahon	Mahn *or* Ma-*han*
Mahony	*Mah*-ni
Mainwaring	*Manner*-ing
Mais	Mayz
Majendie	Ma-*jendy*
Makgill	Mc-*gill* (hard g)
Malpas	*Mawl*-pas
Malet	Mallet
Malmsbury	*Marms*-bri
Mandeville	Mande-ville (first 'e' slightly inflected)
Mander	Mahnder
Mansergh	Manser
Margesson	*Mar*-jesson
Marjoribanks	Marchbanks
Marlborough	*Maul*-bro

Marquand	Mark-wand
Martineau	Martinowe
Masham	*Mass*-hàm
Masserene	Mazereen
Mathias	Math-*ias*
Maugham	Mawm
Mauchline	*Mauch* (as in loch)-lynn
Maunsell	*Man*-sel
Meath	Meeth (th as in breathe)
Meiklejohn	*Mickel*-john
Melhuish	*Mell*-ish
Menteth	Men-*teeth*
Menzies	Ming-iz (Scotland)
Merioneth	Merry-*on*-eth
Mereworth	*Merry*-worth
Metcalfe	Met-calf
Methuen	Meth-wen
Meux	Mews
Meynell	*Men*-el
Meyrick	Merr-ick
Michelham	*Mitch*-lam
Michie	Micky
Midleton	*Middle*-ton
Millais	*Mill*-ay
Mocatta	Mow-*catta*
Molyneux	*Mully*-neux (senior branches) or Mully-nu
Monaco	*Mon*-aco
Monck	Munk
Monckton	Munkton
Moncreiffe ⎫ Moncrieff ⎭	Mun-*creef*
Monro	Mun-*roe*
Monson	*Mun*-sun
Montagu	*Mon*-tagu
Montgomery ⎫ Montgomerie ⎭	Mun-*gum*-eri
Monzie	M'*nee*
Moran	Moor-*an*
Moray	Murray
Mordaunt	*Mor*-dant
Mosley	Mozeley

Mostyn	*Moss*-tin
Mottistone	Mottiston
Moulton	*Mole*-ton
Mountmorres	Mount-morris
Mowbray	*Mo*-bray
Mowll	Mole
Moynihan	*Moy*-ni-han
Munro	Mun-*roe*
Myddelton	Middle-ton
Mytton	Mitton
Naas	Nace
Naesmyth	*Nay*-smith
Nall	Nawl
Napier	*Nay*-pier
Nathan	Naythan
Nepean	Ne-*peen*
Newburgh	*New*-bro'
Niven	Nivven
Northcote	*North*-cut
Nunburnholme	Nun-burnham
Ochterlony	Ochter-*lony*
Offaly	*Off*-aly
Ogilvie ⎫	
Ogilvy ⎭	*Ogle*-vi
O'Hagan	O'*Hay*-gan
Olivier	⎧O-livier
	⎩Lord O-liviay
O'Loghlen	O'*Loch*-len
Ormonde	*Or*-mund
O'Rourke	O'Rork
O'Shaughnessy	O'*shaw*-nessy
Outram	*Oot*-ram
Pakington	Packington
Paget	*Paj*-it
Pakenham	*Pack*-en'um
Pasley	*Pais*-li
Paton	Payton
Paulet	*Paul*-et
Paunceforte	*Pawns*-fort
Pauncefote	*Pawns*-foot
Pechell	*Peach*-ell
Pennefather	*Penn*-ifither *or* Penny-feather

Pennycuick	*Penny*-cook
Pepys	Peppis (Peeps has become archaic, except for the Diarist, and the Pepys Cockerell family)
Perceval	Percival
Pery	Pairy
Peto	*Peet*-o
Petre	Peter
Petrie	*Peet*-rie
Peyton	Payton
Phayre	Fair
Pierpoint	Pierpont
Pleydell	Pleddel
Plowden	Ploughden
Plumtre	*Plum*-tri
Pole	Pole *or* Pool (see also Carew)
Poltimore	Pole-ti-more
Polwarth	*Pol*-worth
Pomeroy	*Pom*-roy
Pomfret	*Pum*-fret
Ponsonby	Punsunby
Poulett	*Paul*-et
Powell	Powell (as in now) usually, *or* Poell
Powerscourt	*Poers*-caut
Powis	*Po*-iss (Earl)
Powlett	*Paul*-et
Powys	Po-iss (name)
	Powiss (place) (as in now)
Praed	Praid
Prevost	*Prev*-o
Prideaux	Priddo
Puleston	*Pill*-ston
Purefuy	Pure-foy
Pytchley	*Pietch*-li
Quibell	Quy-*bel* (as in high)
Raleigh	*Raw*-li
Ranfurly	*Ran*-fully
Rankeillour	Rank-illour
Ratendone	Ratten-dun
Rathdonnell	Rath-*donnell*

Rea	Ree
Rearsby	*Rears*-bi
Reay	Ray
Redesdale	*Reads*-dale
Renwick	*Renn*-ick
Reresby	*Rears*-bi[1]
Reuter	*Roy*-ter
Rhyl	Rill
Rhys	Rees (usually), *or* Rice
Riddell	*Ri*ddle
Rideau	*Reed*-owe
Roborough	*Roe*-bra'
Roche	Roach, *or* sometimes Rosh
Roden	Roe-den
Rolfe	Roaf (as in loaf)
Rolleston	*Roll*-ston
Romilly	*Rum*-illy
Romney	Rumney
Ronaldshay	*Ron*-ald-shay
Rotherwick	as spelt
Rothes	*Roth*-is
Rous ⎤ Rouse ⎦	Rowse (as in grouse)
Rowley	*Roe*-li
Roxburghe	Rox-bro'
Ruabon	Ru-*a*-bon
Ruthin	Ruth-in (as the girl's name)
Ruthven	Rivven
Sacheverall	Sash-*ever*-al
Sacheverell	Sash-*ev*-rell
St. Aubyn	S'nt. *Aw*-bin
St. Clair	Correctly Sinclair, but sometimes as spelt
St. Cyres	S'nt Sires (to rhyme with fires)
St. John	Sin-jun
St. Leger	Correctly *Sill*-inger but often St. Leger
St. Levan	S'nt Leaven (as in leaven for bread)
St. Maur	S'nt *More*
Salisbury	*Sawls*-bri

[1] Roars-by has become archaic.

Salkeld	Saul-keld
Saltoun	*Salt*-on
Salusbury	*Sawls*-bri
Sandbach	Sandbatch
Sandeman	*Sandy*-man
Sandys	Sands
Sanquhar	Sanker (Sanwer is historically correct)
Saumarez } Sausmarez }	Summer-ez *or Saumer*-ez
Savernake	Savver-nack
Savile	Saville
Saye and Sele	Say and Seal
Schilizzi	Skil-it-zy
Schreiker	Shryber
Schuster	*Shoo*-ster
Sclater	Slater
Scone	Scoon
Scudamore	*Scooda*-more
Scrymgeour	*Scrim*-jer
Segal	Seagal
Segrave	Sea-grave
Sele	Seal
Sempill	Semple
Seton	Seaton
Seymour	Seamer but sometimes as spelt
Shakerley	As spelt
Shaughnessy	Shawnessy
Sherborne	Shirb'n
Shrewsbury	*Shrows*-b'ry (town has alternative pronunciation of *Shrews*-b'ry)
Shuckburgh	*Shuck*-bro'
Sieff	Seef
Simey	Symey
Skene	Skeen
Skrine	Screen
Smijth	Smyth
Smyth	Smith or Smythe[1]
Smythe	Smythe
Sneyd	Sneed
Somers	Summers

[1] The family of Smyth of Methven, Scotland, is pronounced 'Smith of Meffane'.

Somerset	Summerset
Sotheby	*Sutha*-by
Soulbury	*Sool*-bri
Southwark	*Suth*-erk
Southwell	*Suth*-ell (surname and city)
Sowerby	Sour-by
Spottiswoode	Spotswood
Stanhope	Stannup
Stavordale	*Stav*-erdale
Stonor	Stone-er
Stourton	Sturton
Strabane	Stra-*bann*
Strabolgi	Stra-*bogie* (hard g)
Strachan ⎫	
Straghan ⎬	Strawn
Strahan ⎭	
Strachie	*Stray*-chie
Stratheden	Strath-*eden*
Strathspey	Strath-*spay*
Streatfield	Stret-field
Stucley	*Stewk*-li
Suirdale	Sure-dale
Sysonby	*Size*-on-by
Synge	Sing
Talbot	*Tall*-bot
Tangye	Tang-y
Taverne	Tav-*erne*
Taylour	Taylor
Teignmouth	*Tin*-muth
Terregles	Terry-*glaze*
Teynham	*Ten*-'am
Thame	Tame
Thellusson	*Tellus*-son
Theobald	Tibbald some families, *or* as spelt
Thesiger	*Thesi*-jer
Thorold	Thurrald
Thynne	Thin
Tichbourne	*Titch*-bourne
Tighe	Tie
Tollemache	*Tol*-mash (Tall-mash has become archaic)

Torphichen	Tor-*fikken*
Touchet	*Touch*-et
Tovey	Tuvvy
Trafalgar	Traffle-*gar* (title only)
Traquair	Tra-*quare*
Tredegar	Tre-*deegar*
Trefusis	Tre-*fusis*
Trevelyan	Tre-*villian*
Trimlestown	*Trimmels*-ton
Trowbridge	Troobridge
Tuchet	*Touch*-et
Tuite	Tute
Tullibardine	Tulli-*bard*-in
Turnour	Turner
Tuvey	Tuvvy
Twohy	*Too*-y
Twysden	Twis-den
Tynte	Tint
Tyrrell	Tirrell
Tyrwhitt	Tirrit
Tyzack	*Tie*-sack
Urquhart	*Urk*-ut
Uvedale	*Youv*-dale
Vachell	*Vay*-chell
Valentia	Val-*en*-shia
Valletort	Valley-tort
Van Straubenzee	Van Straw-*ben*-zie
Vaughan	Vawn
Vaux	Vokes
Vavasour	*Vav*-assur
Verschoyle	Ver-*skoil*
Vesey	Veezy
Vigor	Vygor
Villiers	Villers
Vyvyan	Vivian
Waechter	Vechter (guttural ch)
Wagner	As spelt (English families)
Waldegrave	Wall-grave
Waleran	*Wall*-ran
Walmer	*Wall*-mer
Walrond	*Wall*-rond

Walsingham	*Wall*-sing'm
Walwyn	Wall-wyn
Wathen	Wothen
Wauchope	*Walk*-up (ch as in loch)
Waugh	As spelt, to rhyme with flaw
Wavell	*Way*-vell
Weighall	*Wy*-gall
Weighill	*Wey*-hill
Wellesley	*Wells*-li
Wemyss	Weems
Wernher	Werner
Westenra	*Westen*-ra
Westmeath	West-*meath* (th as in breathe)
Westmorland	*West*-morland
Wharton	*Whor*-ton
Wigoder	*Wigg*-oder
Wigram	*Wigg*-ram
Wilbraham	*Will*-bram
Willoughby de Eresby	*Willow*-bi *deersby*
Willoughby de Broke	*Willow*-bi de *Brook*
Winder	*Winn*-der
Woburn	*Woo*-burn
Wodehouse	*Wood*-house
Wollaston	*Wool*-aston
Wolley	Wooly
Wolmer	*Wool*-mer
Wolrige	*Wool*-ridge
Wolseley	*Wool*-sli
Wombwell	*Woom*-well
Wontner	Wantner
Worsley	*Wers*-li *or* Werz-li
Wortley	*Wert*-li
Wriothesley	Rottisli[1]
Wrottesley	*Rotts*-li
Wykeham	*Wick*-am
Wyllie	*Wy*-lie
Wyndham	*Wind*-'am
Wynford	*Win*-fud
Wynyard	Win-yard
Wythenshaw	*With*-in-shaw

[1] The pronunciation Risely is archaic.

Yeatman	Yaytman
Yerburgh	*Yar*-bra'
Yonge	Young
Zouche	Zooch

SPELLING OF PEERAGE TITLES

Note, the following spellings differ from those now adopted for place names.

England :   Ailesbury, Guilford, Scarbrough, Winchilsea.
Wales :   Carnarvon, Powis
Ireland :   Donegall, Downe, Kingsale, Rosse.

INDEX

413